"Constitutions are forward-looking attempts to structure future politics, but also have to confront legacies of the past. This volume brings together a group of star scholars to consider the intersections of constitutions and transitional justice in a range of important and varied settings. Highly recommended!"

Tom Ginsburg, *Leo Spitz Professor of International Law, The University of Chicago Law School*

"This book wonderfully illuminates the problems that arise when societies attempt to respond to their past record of injustice during the difficult period of transition. Its careful case studies alert us to the complexities of this process, including the problem that transitions may be retrogressive as well as progressive."

David Dyzenhaus, *University Professor of Law and Philosophy, University of Toronto*

"Insightful and topical array of essays addressing the constitutionalism of transitional justice worldwide: this volume will be of profound interest to scholars and practitioners alike."

Ruti Teitel, *Ernst C. Stiefel Professor of Comparative Law, New York Law School*

Constitutionalizing Transitional Justice

This book explores the complicated relationship between constitutions and transitional justice. It brings together scholars and practitioners from different countries to analyze the indispensable role of constitutions and constitutional courts in the process of overcoming political injustice of the past. Issues raised in the book include the role of a new constitution for the successful practice of transitional justice after democratization, revolution or civil war, and the difficulties faced by the court while dealing with mass human rights infringements with limited legal tools. The work also examines whether constitutionalizing transitional justice is a better strategy for new democracies in response to political injustice from the past. It further addresses the complex issue of backslides of democracy and consequences of constitutionalizing transitional justice. The group of international authors address the interplay of the constitution/court and transitional justice in their native countries, along with theoretical underpinnings of the success or unfulfilled promises of transitional justice from a comparative perspective.

The book will be a valuable resource for academics, researchers, and policymakers working in the areas of transitional justice, comparative constitutional law, human rights studies, international criminal law, genocide studies, law and politics, and legal history.

Cheng-Yi Huang is Research Professor at the Institutum Iurisprudentiae, Academia Sinica, and Professor at the Institute of Law for Science and Technology, National Tsing Hua University, Taiwan.

Routledge Socio-Legal Frontiers of Transitional Justice
Edited by:
Chrisje Brants Langeraar
Susanne Karstedt
Nandor Knust

This series addresses the future potential, developments and success of transitional justice and its multi-faceted approaches. To this end, it focuses on the socio-legal aspects of transitional justice in the widest sense.

Available titles in this series include:

Futures of International Criminal Justice
Edited by Emma Palmer, Susan Harris Rimmer, Edwin Bikundo, and Martin Clark

Constitutionalizing Transitional Justice
How Constitutions and Constitutional Courts Deal with Past Atrocity
Edited by Cheng-Yi Huang

For more information about this series, please visit: www.routledge.com/law/series/FTJ

Constitutionalizing Transitional Justice

How Constitutions and Constitutional Courts Deal with Past Atrocity

Edited by Cheng-Yi Huang

Routledge
Taylor & Francis Group
LONDON AND NEW YORK

First published 2023
by Routledge
4 Park Square, Milton Park, Abingdon, Oxon OX14 4RN

and by Routledge
605 Third Avenue, New York, NY 10158

Routledge is an imprint of the Taylor & Francis Group, an informa business

British Library Cataloguing-in-Publication Data
A catalogue record for this book is available from the British Library

ISBN: 978-1-138-58575-1 (hbk)
ISBN: 978-1-032-36944-0 (pbk)
ISBN: 978-0-429-50508-9 (ebk)

DOI: 10.4324/9780429505089

Typeset in Galliard
by Apex CoVantage, LLC

ACADEMIA
SINICA

This book is dedicated to people who suffered or are suffering political injustice around the world.

Ad astra per aspera.

Contents

List of Tables xi
List of Contributors xii
Acknowledgments xiii

Contexts of Constitutionalizing Transitional Justice: An Introduction 1
CHENG-YI HUANG

PART 1
Constitutional Origins of Transitional Justice 19

1 **The Dilemmas of Transitional Justice and the South African Experience** 21
RICHARD J. GOLDSTONE

2 **Facing the Shadows of the Past during Transitions: The Role of the Constitutions in the Case of Hungary** 38
KRISZTA KOVÁCS

3 **Constitutional Divergence and Transitional Justice in South Korea and Taiwan** 57
CHENG-YI HUANG AND YI-LI LEE

PART 2
Constitutional Process of Transitional Justice 95

4 **Constitutional Justice and Negotiated Peace in Colombia** 97
NELSON CAMILO SÁNCHEZ LEÓN

5 **Constitutions, Courts, and the Quest for Transitional Justice: The Case of Chile** 115
JAVIER COUSO

6 **Coordinated Transition in East-Central Europe and the Role of Constitutional Courts in Transitional Justice: Experiences from Hungary and Moldova** 131
GÁBOR ATTILA TÓTH

7 **The Determinants of the Polish Transformation at the Turn of the 21st Century: In View of the Judgments of the Constitutional Tribunal of Poland** 153
MAREK ZUBIK

PART 3
Constitutional Consequences of Transitional Justice 171

8 **Transitional Justice in a 19th-Century Constitution: Cautionary Observations from the United States** 173
VICKI C. JACKSON AND HARRY LARSON

9 **"Cadres" in Post-communist Transition: Shifting the Loyalty Standards in Public Service after Regime Change** 198
ANNA ŚLEDZIŃSKA-SIMON

10 **Between Blaming and Naming: Constitutional Review of Bans on Communist Parties in Post-Soviet States** 222
ALEXEI TROCHEV

Index 249

Tables

1.1 Types of Constitutionalizing Transitional Justice 6
10.1 Fates of the Communist Parties in the Post-Soviet States 226
10.2 Constitutional Court Decisions Regarding Bans on Communist Parties and Communist Symbols in Moldova, Ukraine, and Russia, 1992–2019 244

Contributors

Javier Couso, Professor of Public Law, Universidad Diego Portales, Chile; Chair in Global Trends in Constitutionalism, Utrecht University, the Netherlands

Richard J. Goldstone, Former Justice of the Constitutional Court, South Africa

Cheng-Yi Huang, Research Professor, Institutum Iurisprudentiae, Academia Sinica; Joint-Appointment Professor, Institute of Law for Science and Technology, National Tsing Hua University, Taiwan

Vicki C. Jackson, Laurence H. Tribe Professor of Constitutional Law, Harvard Law School, USA

Kriszta Kovács, Senior Research Fellow, WZB Berlin Social Sciences Center, Germany; Associate Professor, ELTE Faculty of Social Sciences, Hungary

Harry Larson, Law Fellow, American Law Institute, USA

Yi-Li Lee, Assistant Professor, Institute of Law for Science and Technology, National Tsing Hua University, Taiwan

Nelson Camilo Sánchez León, Assistant Professor of Law, General Faculty; Director, Center for International & Comparative Law, University of Virginia School of Law, USA

Anna Śledzińska-Simon, Associate Professor of Constitutional Law, Department of Law, Administration, and Economy, University of Wrocław, Poland

Gábor Attila Tóth, Associate Professor of Constitutional Law and Human Rights, University of Debreen; Associate Professor of Bioethics, Semmelweis University, Budapest, Hungary

Alexei Trochev, Associate Professor, Department of Political Science and International Relations, Nazarbayev University, Kazakhstan

Marek Zubik, Professor of Law, Faculty of Law and Administration, University of Warsaw; Judge of the Polish Constitutional Tribunal in retirement, Poland

Acknowledgments

The origins of this book can be traced back to a 2016 conference at Academia Sinica in Taiwan. At the time of the conference, which aimed at comparing constitutional justifications of transitional justice, the Transitional Justice Commission of Taiwan was still about a year and a half shy of being established. Time flies so fast. Founded in May of 2018 and to be dissolved in May of 2022, the commission has rendered the first national report on the structure of the party state and alleged crimes committed during the post-1945 authoritarian period of Taiwanese history. Accompanying the conference was a Constitutional Court Simulation sponsored by both the Taiwan Association for Truth and Reconciliation (TATR) and the Taipei Bar Association. I was especially delighted that Justice Richard J. Goldstone, Judge Marek Zubik, Professor Javier Couso, and Professor Susanne Karstedt not only participated in the conference but also served as expert witnesses during the Constitutional Court Simulation. As introduced in Chapter 3 of this book, the Taiwanese Constitutional Court finally acknowledged the constitutional principles of transitional justice in Interpretation No. 793 of 2020, some thirty-three years after Taiwan had become a democracy.

Transitional justice is a combination of social movement, political action, and judicial endeavors to answer why past atrocity happened and how reconciliation among all members of society is possible. The chapters in this book present important constitutional deliberation on transitional justice in East Asia, South Africa, the United States, Latin America, Central and Eastern Europe, and the former Soviet Republics. I am immensely grateful to all the authors for their contributions to this book and for their extraordinary patience during the prolonged editing process.

Without the unwavering support from my home institute, Institutum Iurisprudentia of Academia Sinica, over the last several years, this book would not have been possible. Two directors, Professor Tzu-yi Lin and Professor Chien-liang Lee, endowed this project with critical administrative and financial support, and I thank them for their generosity and leadership. Professor Yu-hsiu Hsu, the founder of Constitutional Court Simulation and a former justice of the Taiwanese Constitutional Court, has been a major driving force behind the concurring project of moot court, bringing constitutional debate over transitional justice to life. It is worth noting that the simulations have received financial support from the Taiwan Foundation for Democracy and Taipei Bar Association. Between 2016 and 2018, I served as the chairperson of the TATR, the leading NGO in Taiwan to promote transitional justice. It is my TATR colleagues who enrich my understanding to transitional justice and exemplify the spirit of social activism. Among them, Professors Nai-teh Wu, Chang-ling Huang, and Tsui-lien Chen deserve special mention.

The editing process of this book has been very time-consuming and much more difficult than I initially expected. With the encouragement of the series editors, I can now say that, after four years, the job is finally accomplished. I would like to thank Chrisje Brants, Susanne Karstedt, and Nandor Knust for their patience and substantive advice throughout the entire process. Peter Seelig has provided extraordinary proofreading, editing, and reference-formatting services. I am thankful for his always-timely and high-quality services. Over these years, my assistants Yi-chen Huang, Shi-an Wang, Tsung-yuan Lee, and Chun-kai Chang have helped lessen the burdens of this book project in many useful ways. Before publication, David Dyzenhaus, Tom Ginsburg, and Ruti Teitel generously agreed to read the manuscript and kindly offered me invaluable comments and recommendations, for which I am very thankful.

This book is dedicated to people who suffered or are suffering political injustice around the world. These words are exactly the same words printed on the dedication page of my doctoral dissertation thirteen years ago. The pursuit of transitional justice is a long journey, and this book is simply one step along the way. I look forward to more constitutional thinking on transitional justice, and may the history of oppression not repeat itself in the future.

Contexts of Constitutionalizing Transitional Justice

An Introduction

Cheng-Yi Huang

Political transition does not always come with vindications of justice. The rules and procedures of democratization are usually defined and controlled by authoritarian rulers (O'Donnell and Schmitter 1986, 6). The transition starts with a political moment necessitated by social discontent and mass social movements. Sometimes the transition leads to an abrupt revolution, while in most cases, it produces an uncharted process of negotiation. In either situation, transitional societies must not only "rebuild the ship on the sea" but also address the continuing legacy of the ancien régime. In the case of a negotiated transition, the opposition camps bargain with the authoritarian rulers and, sometimes, offer or accept a political compromise permitting most stakeholders to reach a consensus. Under this circumstance, it is difficult, if not impossible, to include in any political agreement a mechanism designed to punish wrongdoers who operated during the authoritarian period. The outgoing regime wants to secure its safety by way of a credible commitment and does so by means of a constitution, which serves as a political pact in which each party contributes to an abiding consensus. The outgoing authoritarian government and the incoming democratic leadership may confer on a third party the responsibility of safeguarding these political compromises. This third party is oftentimes a constitutional court, as is typically the case in third-wave democracies (Ginsburg 2003).

Transitional justice aims at redressing past atrocities yet paradoxically creates disincentives for the perpetrators to join the political agreement. Whether or not the values and rules characterizing a particular mechanism of transitional justice are inscribed in a constitution depends on the political context in which a given society is undergoing transition. However, as Ruti Teitel cogently argues, "Transitional constitutions not only operate as codifications of prevailing consensus but also transform that consensus" (2000: 210). According to her, constitutionalism can facilitate "the move to a more liberal regime." Transitional justice, enabled by constitution making, has symbolic power that legitimizes the rule of successive regimes. Indeed, with its normative dimension, transitional justice can be likened to the rule of law and human rights protection (Murphy 2017: 50). The ultimate goal of transitional justice is consistent with the core values of modern constitutionalism, which embraces the substantive idea of freedom and equality. But its measures and mechanisms are, in practice, essentially retroactive and may conflict

DOI: 10.4324/9780429505089-1

with such core rule-of-law principles as *nulla poena sine lege*, the prohibition of bills of attainder, and nonretroactive application of law. Jon Elster argues, "When many violations accumulate or where core criteria are violated, there comes a point, however, when legal justice is replaced by political justice" (2004: 88). Therefore, the issue of whether to include transitional justice in new constitutions becomes a thorny one for transitional democracies.

A transitional democracy's new constitution represents "a chance to define affirmatively the principles that will mark off the 'new era' from the 'old regime'" (Ackerman 1992: 69). As Václav Havel once declared, "We are not like them." How to integrate transitional justice into a new constitutional order is commonly an urgent challenge for new democracies.[1] In general, transitional justice can be implemented by extraordinary mechanisms, like an international criminal trial (e.g., the Nuremburg trials and the International Criminal Tribunal for the former Yugoslavia), a truth-and-reconciliation commission, a special prosecutor, or a temporarily appointed investigative unit. Ordinary courts may also take appeals of political cases after the lifting of martial law or emergency decrees. However, the legality of authoritarian law is usually beyond the reach of ordinary courts and reserved to constitutional courts. Meanwhile, measures of transitional justice, such as lustration, prosecution, restitution, open access to political archives, dissolution of authoritarian parties, and confiscation of party assets, are all likely to involve intense political antagonism and to result in fierce courtroom fights challenging the constitutionality of the laws or decrees.

This book analyzes the origins, processes, and consequences of constitutionalizing transitional justice. By the term "constitutionalizing transitional justice," we mean that the values of and mechanisms for transitional justice are either written into constitutional documents or justified by constitutional courts through constitutional doctrines. Nevertheless, we are aware of the fact that not all transitional societies have the chance to pass a new constitution or, if such a constitution exists, to insert in it any language regarding transitional justice. Based on their empirical survey, Elkins, Ginsburg, and Melton point out that "new democrats who inherit an authoritarian constitution were not especially likely to replace the constitution" (2009: 137). This outcome might reflect the absence of a "collective agency" balancing the needs of social transformation and power

1 Jon Elster elaborated on the idea behind this slogan: "When [incoming democratic leaders] set out to deal with the lawless practices of the past, they do not want to do it in a lawless manner" (2004: 83). It should be noted that Bruce Ackerman was skeptical of the compatibility of corrective justice and constitutional creation. According to him, "Constitutional creation unites; corrective justice divides" (1992: 71). However, drawing from Hobbes' political theory, David Dyzenhaus argues there is a mediating way to reconcile the two conflicting needs of constitutional creation and transitional justice. According to Dyzenhaus, "The actors who take the initiative and those who respond have to have the relish of justice, and that requires an understanding of and a commitment to the laws of nature. Should they follow through on that commitment, a civic order will begin to emerge that will make, as we have seen Hobbes say, trust and even reconciliation possible, though these goods will come about as by-products of the actors' focus on the logic of reciprocity" (2012: 209).

reconfiguration (Ackerman 2019: 40). In most countries, political transition is a continuing process that, especially in the cultural dimension, never fully says goodbye to the past.

Three Models of Constitutionalizing Transitional Justice

In this book, the case studies addressing the divergent paths to constitutionalizing transitional justice can be clustered into three models: written-in constitutions, court-enforced constitutionalism, and unilateral executive decisions. In each of the three models, constitutional courts are critical not only to the processes of transitional justice but also to both the positive and the negative consequences of transitional justice. The first model (written-in constitutions) refers to cases in which transitional-justice values and mechanisms are codified in a constitution. The model covers two main types of written-in constitutions. The first is an explicit text, as exemplified by South Africa's Interim Constitution of 1994. The Interim Constitution explicitly includes an epilogue in the name of National Unity and Reconciliation, making reconciliation a constitutional commitment. On the basis of this clear mandate, the South African Constitutional Court has justified the amnesty power of the Truth and Reconciliation Commission. Two further examples are the 14th Amendment of the Constitution of the United States, passed after the Civil War, and Article 66 of the Colombian Constitution (2012), commonly known as the Legal Framework for Peace. The second type of written-in constitution is exemplified by the Polish Constitution of 1997. Though it does not write down the values of transitional justice in the emphatic language typical, for example, of the South African Interim Constitution, the preamble of the 1997 Polish Constitution provides that the nation should be "mindful of the bitter experiences of the times when fundamental freedoms and human rights were violated in our Homeland." Since the passage of the 1997 Constitution, this constitutional mandate has crystalized in the civic ethos the mantra of transitional justice: "Never again." Moreover, as Marek Zubik points out in his chapter in this book, Articles 13 and 44 of the Polish Constitution prohibit political parties from embracing totalitarianism and grant extensions of statutory limitations for past atrocities. These two clauses, though not expressly mentioning transitional justice, express the values of transitional justice, and this expression has lent support to Poland's Constitutional Tribunal in relevant cases.

Some new democracies adopt a new constitution or thoroughly amend an old one without any explicit or implicit reference to transitional justice. However, the act of constitution making per se represents the founding of a new constitutional order with a clear departure from the past. The 1987 Constitution of South Korea has this symbolic function[2] and endowed the country with a new

2 The Constitution of the Republic of Korea (South Korea) was not repudiated after democratization. It had been promulgated in 1948 and then fully revised five times: in 1960, 1962,

Constitutional Court, which started to apply the principles of modern constitutionalism to various rights-infringement cases, including several that addressed the political oppression of May 18, 1980. Meanwhile, even though Taiwan did not abandon the constitution inherited from the Republic of China, the country's constitutional court acted as a guardian of individual rights throughout the 1990s. Based on constitutional amendments after democratization, the Taiwanese Constitutional Court developed a jurisprudence based on a "constitutional order of liberal democracy," which had been transplanted from the German Basic Law. Almost two decades later, the national legislature of Taiwan enacted transitional-justice legislation based on the court's jurisprudence. Both the case of South Korea and that of Taiwan demonstrate how court-enforced constitutionalism can promote transitional-justice legislation. By contrast, Hungary tells a very different story. In 1989, the country underwent a coordinated transition from authoritarian communism to liberal democracy. The product of a series of roundtable negotiation was the 1989 Constitution of Hungary, which was a revision of the 1949 Constitution. Even though the 1989 Hungarian Constitution has no provision directly relevant to transitional justice, the preamble states that the constitution was enacted "with a view to promoting a peaceful political transition to a rule of law state implementing a multi-party system, parliamentary democracy, and a social market economy." However, unlike its counterpart in Poland, the Hungarian Constitutional Court never used these words as the constitutional basis for transitional-justice legislation. According to Kriszta Kovács, legal formalism has permeated the post-1989 constitutional interpretations of the Hungarian Constitutional Court. The court struck down at least three key pieces of transitional-justice legislation in the 1990s, holding that legal certainty and other rule-of-law requirements are more important than "necessarily partial and subjective justice" (Decision No. 11/1992; Kovács, 5). Among other things, frustration over Hungary's transitional justice created a major political opportunity for populist leaders. Viktor Orban mobilized supporters and rose to his second prime ministership in 2010 and – in the name of transitional justice – oversaw the passage of controversial legislation like Article U of the Fourth Amendment to the Fundamental Law.

The model of court-enforced constitutionalism focuses mostly on legislation that is passed by national legislatures and may be sustained or overruled by constitutional courts. Therefore, courts sometimes come under criticism for overstepping the political will of the people in new democracies. The third model of constitutionalizing transitional justice is unilateral executive decisions. In this model, transitional-justice mechanisms are dictated by the chief executive unilaterally, without participation of the legislature. For example, in 1990, right after stepping into power, President Patricio Aylwin decreed the establishment of the National Commission of Truth and Reconciliation. With neither

1972, 1980, and 1987. The 1987 revision has generally been considered a "new" constitution (Ginsburg 2003, 213–216).

legislative support nor a constitutional mandate, the commission's Rettig Report confronted severe criticism from the Supreme Court of Chile. Not until after the Supreme Court's composition changed did the court change its stance on the 1978 Amnesty Law and lift the statute of limitations so that criminal investigations into Pinochet-era rights violations could proceed. Likewise, decommunization in Russia, Ukraine, and Moldova has been carried out by the chief executive. These unilateral decisions have had different fates in courts. Some decisions remained unresolved for months, like President Yeltsin's decision regarding the Russian Constitutional Court; other decisions were delayed for years, like the suit against the Ukrainian executive's ban of the communist party; and yet other decisions were decided swiftly, like Moldovan President Mihai Ghimpu's decree regarding the Soviet occupation. The courts that rendered decisions in these cases had to navigate sometimes-treacherous political and social waters. It is not a surprise that all three post-Soviet constitutional courts refused to rule on the legal challenges pertaining to the legacy of the Communist Party.

Because the third model's transitional-justice measures hinge exclusively on the unilateral decisions of the executive, the measures have the weakest legitimacy of all three models – an issue with which a court seeking to constitutionalize such a measure must contend. The third model's transitional-justice measures also give courts a great deal of leeway in making decisions based on the courts' own political considerations rather than on a principled interpretation of constitutional law. In the second model, the constitutional courts review transitional-justice legislation by relying heavily on principles of liberal constitutionalism. However, without a clear statement by the constitution about transitional justice, the construction of transitional-justice values is left to courts, which inevitably take center stage in a nation's political turmoil. Often, the courts must weather criticism from the past rulers and their pro-authoritarian supporters. Sometimes, however, as in the Hungarian case, the criticism comes from supporters for democracy. Hence, judges need to perform a balancing test when they weigh constitutional values, like the principle of legal certainty, against rights protection of political victims. If it adheres to formalist understandings of the rule of law, a court may frustrate the project of transitional justice and infuriate rights groups and pro-democracy activists. When constitutions have explicit language regarding transitional justice, constitutional courts are operating in the first model: They enjoy the most support in rendering judgments on the basis of coherent, substantive reasoning. Though the courts obviously also have to deal with political and social pressures, constitutional provisions honoring transitional justice provide an anchoring point for deliberation and adjudication. However, as mentioned, when a country is in a transitional period, shifting away from authoritarianism and toward democracy, the political establishment cannot easily integrate clearly articulated, thoughtfully crafted transitional-justice clauses into a constitution, as such clauses would likely deter the authoritarian ruler from surrendering power. In fact, an explicit inclusion of transitional-justice values in a constitution happens only when democratic supporters in a country have recently enjoyed an overwhelming electoral victory. Even so, the US experience with abolition, Reconstruction, and then segregation

Table 1.1 Types of Constitutionalizing Transitional Justice

	Embedded Mandate of Transitional Justice	*Inferred Mandate of Transitional Justice*
Constitutions (including amendments, preambles, and epilogues)	*Written-In Constitution* (1) explicit: South Africa, USA, Colombia (2) implicit: Poland	*Court-Enforced Constitutionalism* (1) positive: South Korea, Taiwan (2) negative: Hungary
Decrees of the Chief Executive	*Unilateral Decision of the Executive* Chile, Ukraine, Russia, Moldova	(none)

demonstrates that the meaning and importance of constitutional provisions regarding transitional justice can change significantly over time.

The three models of constitutionalizing transitional justice can be illustrated in a two-by-two table (Table 1.1.) with two major variables: (1) whether the mandate of transitional justice comes from constitution or executive decrees and (2) whether the mandate of transitional justice is embedded or inferred. If the mandate is embedded in the newly minted constitution, it is the first model: written-in constitution, including two types, the South African type and the Polish type. If the mandate is inferred from the constitution by constitutional courts, it is the second model: court-enforced constitutionalism. However, in terms of the consequence of constitutional judgments, the second model may bring out two outcomes: legitimizing transitional justice measures like what the constitutional courts in Taiwan and South Korea have done (positive) or invalidating transitional justice measures like what happened in Hungary (negative). The third model refers to transitional justice policy mandated directly by the chief executive without any constitutional provision or interpretation, mostly witnessed in former Soviet countries. Since the chief executive has the power to regulate with clear policy statement and to amend it handily, there is no case representing inferred mandate by the chief executive. The chapters discuss not only which model chosen by the case study countries but also how transitional politics lead to those choices. Overall, the task of determining which model of constitutionalizing transitional justice best suits the needs of a transitional democracy depends largely on political context. We will elaborate on this theme in each chapter of the book.

Origin of Constitutionalizing Transitional Justice

This book is divided into three parts. The first part consists of three chapters, which analyze the constitutional origins of transitional justice. The second part consists of four chapters, which explore the processes that underlie constitutionalizing transitional justice, with a focus on the roles of constitutional courts therein. The third part consists of three chapters, which analyze the constitutional consequences of transitional justice. Throughout these the chapters, two major questions are addressed: (1) Does the inclusion of a transitional-justice clause in a constitution foster a political culture of trust and reconciliation in a new democracy? (2) Do constitutional courts play a more critical role than a constitution in the success of transitional justice? There are no boilerplate answers to these questions, just as there is no standard route to successful transitional justice.

The first chapter, written by Richard J. Goldstone, points out the significance of the constitutional entrenchment of transitional-justice clauses in the historical context of post-Apartheid South Africa. Many family members of the political victims of Apartheid-era crimes were demanding the full prosecution of perpetrators, though the Promotion of National Unity and Reconciliation Act of 1995 authorized the Truth and Reconciliation Commission (TRC) to grant amnesty to qualified applicants. The TRC received more than 7,000 amnesty applications, of which 900 received amnesty. Objecting to these cases of amnesty, the aforementioned family members appealed to the Constitutional Court, arguing that the amnesty clause was unconstitutional. In *Azanian Peoples Organization (AZAPO) and Others v. President of the Republic of South Africa and Others* ([1996] ZACC 16), the Constitutional Court held that the TRC's power to grant amnesty was constitutional. The main reasoning, argued by Goldstone, who was also one of the justices on the bench, was predicated on the mandates written into the epilogue of South Africa's 1993 Interim Constitution, in the name of "national Unity" and "reconciliation." The epilogue states, "The pursuit of national unity, the well-being of all South African citizens and peace require reconciliation between the people of South Africa and the reconstruction of society." The court justified the amnesty clause on the grounds that reconciliation was a constitutional mandate and that the interim constitution's epilogue rested on South Africa's past experiences.

In the early days of South African democratization, riots and other forms of violence erupted on the streets. The ensuing chaos interrupted the peaceful negotiations of multiparty members. Therefore, in 1991, President F. W. de Klerk set up the Standing Commission of Inquiry Regarding the Prevention of Public Violence and Intimidation, which was chaired by Richard J. Goldstone. According to Goldstone's chapter, the Commission of Inquiry conducted forty inquiries and reached the conclusion that much of the violence marring the transition period had been carried out by a "third force" – that is, by senior white military and police officials who had hoped to derail the power transition. The conclusion of the commission lead to the dismissal of senior members of the South African Army. Unlike the TRC, the Commission of Inquiry did not have the power to grant immunity to the "third force." Rather, the commission had to follow the nation's procedural requirements for criminal justice, all while exercising its powers of searches, seizures, and summons. The work done by the commission demonstrated the difficulty of conducting criminal investigations into the perpetration of human rights abuses: Such investigations consume large amounts of time and resources. If South Africa were to investigate serious political crimes that took place roughly between 1960 and 1994, the entire nation would be consumed by a years-long political and social conflagration. This concern was also strongly felt and expressed by Goldstone in his unfulfilled work as the chief prosecutor of the United Nations International Criminal Tribunal for the former Yugoslavia (ICTY). According to Goldstone, the goal of transitional justice should be not the enactment of revenge but the unification of society, which is understandably an enormously difficult undertaking after decades of political oppression and violence. Nevertheless, constitutions should establish and protect the right to truth finding and the means of reconciliation. Otherwise, any work regarding transitional justice would be highly contested and, in the end, unsettled.

While South Africa's story exemplifies the significance of a new constitution containing a transitional-justice clause, Hungary presents the other side of the same coin. In Hungary after 1989, the country's political transition from communism to democracy took place in roundtable negotiations, which upheld the continuity of the country's legal system (Kovács [p. 3]). Simultaneously, the opposition insisted on acting lawfully to deal with Hungary's communist past. Kriszta Kovács argues in the second chapter that the traditions of formalistic legalism cast a huge and probably negative shadow over the transitional-justice jurisprudence of the country's newly established Constitutional Court. Unlike its counterpart in South Africa, the 1989 constitution made no mention of the past atrocities and restricted itself to outlining the principles of liberal democracy and the importance of commitment to the rule of law. With no constitutional foundation for transitional justice, the Hungarian Constitutional Court twice struck down legislation regarding the criminal prosecution of individuals accused of perpetrating crimes against humanity during and after the 1956 Revolution (Decision No. 53/1993 and Decision No. 11/1992). The court stressed the importance of legal certainty, *nullum crimen sine lege*, prohibitions of retroactive applications of law, and ex post extensions of statutes of limitation. The Hungarian Constitutional Court also rejected legislation that would have institutionalized lustration – that is, the disclosure of the personal information of perpetrators – because the court regarded the privacy of perpetrators as constitutionally protected. On the one hand, the Constitutional Court – although it upheld the values of the new constitution – could find no constitutional justification for the measures in the lustration legislation. On the other hand, as Kovács argues, the unresolved issues of transitional justice reflected stark disagreements among Hungarian political elites. Hungarian society's frustration with transitional justice fueled the successes of right-wing political actors, who claimed the 1989 revolution unfinished. A consequence of this political shift was the 2013 Amendment to the Fundamental Law – that is, the previously mentioned Article U – which declared transitional justice a measure necessary in the country's efforts to overcome its communist past. From Kovács' perspective, the conservative government's appropriation of history through a measured use of constitutional language has exacerbated the problems that Hungary faces regarding transitional justice.

Controversies surrounding transitional justice have arisen in East Asia. The experiences of South Korea and Taiwan offer mixed messages on this topic. The two countries began to democratize in the same year, 1987. That year, South Korea revised its constitution after political negotiations between the military dictators and the opposition camp. By contrast, Taiwan preserved its 1947 constitution, which the Kuomintang (KMT) had brought to the island from mainland China. Only minor amendments, in the 1990s, were made to the document. The two countries have also differed from each other regarding their handling of transitional justice. In the 1990s, activists in South Korea attempted to bring to justice the perpetrators of human rights violations committed during the 518 Movement in 1980; however, prosecutors and the Constitutional Court refused to pursue the perpetrators owing to the statute of limitations. After the National Assembly passed the 518 Special Act in 1995, the Constitutional Court shifted gears and declared the Special Act constitutional.

As for Taiwan, its Constitutional Court in 1991 upheld the constitutionality of the National Security Act (1987), which prohibited any political prisoners from appealing their cases to ordinary courts after the lifting of martial law. When, in 2016, the opposition party took control of both the executive and the legislative branches from the former authoritarian party (the KMT), special legislation was passed, authorizing the government's confiscation of KMT property. The Taiwanese Constitutional Court declared the special legislation a legitimate and constitutional response to the KMT's appropriation of government funds during the authoritarian period from 1949 to 1991. In both the case of South Korea and that of Taiwan, their respective constitutions have provided no anchor for transitional-justice legislation. However, the constitutional courts of the two countries seized the momentum of popular support for transitional justice in the wake of electoral victories for anti-authoritarian parties. In other words, the courts could not single-handedly establish the legitimacy of transitional justice; they had to wait until a degree of socio-political support for transitional justice emerged, which is what happened following democratic elections. In essence, the elections bestowed legitimacy on such legislation. Therefore, the stories of South Korea and Taiwan show that, in general, a constitutional court can defend transitional-justice measures even if the corresponding constitution makes no explicit reference to the matter.

Process of Constitutionalizing Transitional Justice

The second part of this book further explores the interventions of constitutional courts in the advancement of transitional justice, with a special focus on two geographic regions: Central Eastern Europe (Poland, Hungary, and Moldova) and Latin America (Colombia and Chile). The third wave of democratization brought with it a bourgeoning of constitutional courts in post-authoritarian states. One exception is the Polish Constitutional Tribunal, which was established in the early 1980s by the communist government. In 1989, when the communist regime collapsed, about half of the court's communist-era judges continued to occupy their seats in this adjudicating body. In fact, the new constitution of Poland came into effect only after October 1997, and as Marek Zubik points out in his chapter, the main focus during the early days of the transition concerned economic restructuring and state building. Addressing past atrocities was not high on the to-do list. Against this backdrop, the Constitutional Tribunal reviewed – and in 1992 upheld as constitutional – legislation that nationalized the Communist Party's property. However, regarding lustration, the tribunal in 1992 declared unconstitutional a parliamentary resolution requesting that the government hand over a list of current government workers who, during the communist era, had secretly collaborated with the authoritarian government. Later, the tribunal similarly ruled unconstitutional the Law of December 17, 1997, which stripped special pensions from – and sacked – judges and prosecutors who had worked with the communist-era security apparatus. Another piece of legislation, which invalidated judicial decisions between 1944 and 1989, was considered by the Constitutional Tribunal several times. As we can see, the tribunal never fully endorsed the idea of transitional justice, especially in the realm of judicial personnel. In fact, transitional justice in Poland was a tug-of-war between the parliament and the Constitutional Tribunal. In recent years, the government led by the conservative Law and Justice party (PiS) has expressed a keenness to pass or amend laws strengthening Poland's lustration, pension deprivation, and reprivatization. These legislative efforts had met with considerable challenges from not only the Constitutional Tribunal but the European Court of Human Rights as well. The tribunal's judgments sometimes invited fierce public debates about such topics as the restitution of property in Warsaw, and consequently, social pressure and populist legislation gained strength.

If the Polish Constitutional Tribunal's jurisprudence of transitional justice is interpreted as pragmatic conservative, the Hungarian Constitutional Court's approach has been more bewildering. Drawing from a bigger picture of the evolution of constitutional courts in East-Central European countries, Gábor Attila Tóth explains how the Hungarian Constitutional Court's most progressive judgment – the abolition of capital punishment – is reconcilable with the court's very restrained view of transitional justice. As one of the third-generation constitutional courts, the Hungarian Constitutional Court embraced international human rights standards and constitutionalism. Therefore, when abolishing the death penalty, then chief justice Sólyom connected the judgment with Hungary's oppressive past and declared the judgment to be a sign of the court exercising its responsibility to protect human dignity and life from the potential and real abuses of state power. However, despite its firm support for the abolition of the death penalty, the Constitutional Court rejected retroactive punishment for perpetrators. According to Tóth, the court was dissociating itself from natural law and was sticking to a formalistic conception of the rule of law. Indeed, the Hungarian Constitutional Court declared that "the basic guarantees of the rule of law cannot be set aside by reference to historical situations and the state governed by the rule of law is a requirement of justice." More intriguingly, the court upheld the doctrine of the separation of church and state but recognized "historical churches" (Catholic, Calvinist, Lutheran, and Jewish institutions) as entitled to property restitution. The court, which exempted religious leaders from lustration, has seemingly lost itself in the conflict between democratic constitutionalism and cultural traditionalism. Tóth also examines the Moldovan Constitutional Court's intervention in the official status of the Moldovan language to show that transitional justice, even if it revolves around language issues, is deeply embedded in the national identities of post-transitional countries. Nonetheless, identity is the thorniest issue in almost every society that has undergone a political transition from authoritarianism to democracy. Courts' constitutional interpretations of legislation may not be the most convenient way to resolve debates about identity.

Legal formalism not only haunts liberal courts but also lends support to reactionary courts. In the case of Chile, the country's Supreme Court repudiated criticisms leveled against its deferential jurisprudence during the junta's rule (1973–90). The Supreme Court argued that it could obey the existing laws only, even if they were egregious. However, with changes in both the composition of the judiciary and the mentality of society, the Supreme Court reversed its interpretation of the 1978 Amnesty Law, which had created a safety net protecting junta-affiliated perpetrators of rights violations for the period between 1973 and 1978. The Supreme Court also held that the statute of limitations should not impede investigations into past atrocities. According to Javier Couso, the changing positions of the Supreme Court, rather than reflecting some post-democratization independence, constituted the court's "strategic adjustment to a new democratic context." Couso also argues that the arrest of General Pinochet in the United Kingdom reshaped public perceptions of the dictator, eventually leading to a retraction of his lifetime immunity. From Couso's perspective, the growing public consciousness of – and support for investigations into – Chile's past were key to the achievement of transitional justice in the country. Even the military came to recognize as legitimate the Rettig Report, which was issued by Chile's Truth and Reconciliation Commission in 1991.

The cases of Poland, Hungary, and Chile exemplify the ambiguous roles of constitutional courts in the pursuit of transitional justice. A slightly more positive example is the Colombian Constitutional Court. Having waged a decades-long civil war, the Colombian government and guerilla groups, including the Revolutionary Armed Forces of Colombia (FARC), finally reached a consensus for a cease-fire and entered a peacemaking process. The Colombian Constitution of 1991 was deemed a peace pact, though neither FARC nor the National Liberation Army (ELN) participated in the drafting process. Against the backdrop of these peacemaking efforts, the legislature passed Law 975 (2005). Also known as the Justice and Peace Law, it granted amnesty to perpetrators of all but the most heinous rights violations. The Justice and Peace Law prioritized peace over justice for sentencing but not for judgments of culpability. The law was challenged in the Constitutional Court of Colombia. According to Nelson Camilo Sànchez, the Constitutional Court played a "standard-setting role" while interpreting both the victims' right to truth and the notion of transitional justice, the latter of which receives no mention in the Colombian Constitution. The court appealed to human rights soft law and to judgments of the United Nations and the Inter-American Court of Human Rights to justify the assertion that victims have the right to know the truth and to seek justice. The Constitutional Court also held that the granting of amnesties and pardons for the purpose of transitional justice is constitutional.

In 2012, the Congress of Colombia passed a constitutional amendment (known as the Legal Framework for Peace). Included in the amendment was Article 66, which integrated the idea of transitional justice into the language of the Constitution, providing a clear constitutional basis for the path forward. Eventually, a peacemaking mechanism was put in place, and it made room for the political participation of ex-combatants. Sànchez argues that both the government and the guerillas "sought a legally viable arrangement that would ensure compliance. . . . The negotiating parties shared the view that the final agreement should have democratic legitimacy." Thus, the Constitutional Court's opinions were crucial to the various negotiating parties because the opinions lent the peacemaking process a degree of public, legal, and normative legitimacy.

In 2015 and 2016, legislators proposed two constitutional amendments to fast-track the peacemaking process, and both proposals fell in the hands of the Constitutional Court, which was tasked with determining their fate. The court upheld the proposals as constitutional but invalidated one aspect of the fast-track amendment. Sànchez points out that the court has tried to strike a balance between "correcting Congress' misinterpretation of the peace agreement and conveying that the peace agreement had not given the government a blank check to transform the existing political system." Even though the court later limited the jurisdiction of the special investigative court to voluntary third parties (Judgment C-674 [2017]), both the government and FARC honored the court's judgment. According to Sànchez, each side's compliance with the judgment is attributable to Colombia's "deeply rooted legalist culture, emphasizing the use of legal instruments and judicial processes to regulate most aspects of social, political, and institutional life." By leveraging its interpretations of the Constitution, the Colombian Constitutional Court has successfully mediated between the adversarial political camps.

Consequences of Constitutionalizing Transitional Justice

The last part of the book consists of three chapters, each addressing the consequences and possible pitfalls of constitutionalizing transitional justice. Vicki C. Jackson and Harry Larson discuss the uncertainty of transitional-justice provisions in the light of the 14th Amendment to the US Constitution. The authors argue that the 13th, 14th, and 15th Amendments, which aimed at eradicating slavery and securing the citizenship of the freed slaves, were transitional-justice provisions. According to Jackson and Larson, the oft-cited Section 1 of the 14th Amendment, which guaranteed the citizenship of black Americans, was less important at the time of enactment than were Sections 2 and 3, which served "to incentivize states to extend voting rights to freed slaves" and to purge Confederate leaders from public offices. However, within four years of the 14th Amendment's ratification, Congress reversed most of the disqualifications that Section 3 had imposed on former Confederates seeking office. The enactment of the 15th Amendment, which prohibited categorically the denial or abridgment of the right to vote based on race, diminished the function of Section 2 of the 14th Amendment to almost zero. Finally, Section 4 of the 14th Amendment, though rarely applied, has been mentioned in regard to the debt ceiling.

Jackson and Larson argue that transitional-justice provisions are usually passed during times of regime change, which lack precise timelines and can wear down the patience of participants seeking to craft workable provisions. Moreover, transitional-justice provisions that have no sunset date can be appropriated for unrelated purposes at some future point in time, and this risk is particularly apparent for provisions susceptible to varied readings and unexpected interpretations. Therefore, the authors argue, once a transitional-justice provision has been written into a constitution, they may have "unforeseeable or even, at times, perverse consequences" (25). Moreover, these provisions at the time of their enactment may fail to do full justice to the victims of the prior regime. Take Section 3 as an example: It is tantamount to lustration in the present day, but political compromises by Congress eliminated the efficacy of Section 3 and essentially provided Confederate leaders with amnesty. The failure of the US government to contain the threat from former secessionists and Confederate sympathizers led to the end of Reconstruction.

Anna Śledzińska-Simon elaborates on the complicated issues of lustration, arguing that democratizing governments in Central and Eastern Europe have experienced considerable difficulty in their effort to purge current governments of past communists. In fact, lustration (or failure to lustration) can take a toll on the democratic culture of post-transitional societies and, in some instances, can backfire on electoral systems, courts, news media, and other democratic institutions. As Śledzińska-Simon points out, the legitimate goal of lustration is not to retaliate but to uphold the neutrality and professionalism of public service to the extent "necessary in a democratic society" (pp. 5–6, 15). Of course, in practice, retaliation can be an outcome of lustration, whether intended or not. In the aftermath of democratization, countries in Central and Eastern Europe adopted a variety of lustration strategies. The most severe one was the Czech lustration law of 1991, which required civil servants, whether elected or appointed, to submit not only documentation regarding any relationship they may have had with the communist-era secret police but also an affidavit that they were not members of political groups specified in the act. Civil servants verified as a member of those groups or as a collaborator with the secret police were to be dismissed from their current position (David 2003: 409). The screening applied even to the presidency and the legislature and extended to state radio and television stations, state-owned companies, and universities, though candidates running for office were exempt (p. 9).

The Polish lustration law of 1997 adopted a more lenient approach. The law required only that certain individuals disclose their past involvement with the

Communist Party. People who sought public office and were truthful in their statement about party affiliation could not be purged. Only false statements could result in removal from office or other public position. The Polish Act of 2006 provided an extended catalogue of public offices subject to lustration, though, as Marek Zubik notes, some provisions were subsequently declared unconstitutional. In both Poland and the Czech Republic, lustration applied only to senior positions in government. In this way, the lustration laws could follow the standards adopted by the International Labour Organization's Committee of Experts on the Application of Conventions and Recommendations.

The Unification Treaty Between East Germany and West Germany allowed former East German civil servants to retain their job if they could pass the eligibility criteria of West Germany. People's past collaboration with the East German secret service would be deemed a mark against one's professional qualification but would not, in itself, be disqualifying (p. 15). The European Court of Human Rights gave broad margin of appreciation to member states on lustration. Śledzińska-Simon cogently argues that lustration carries with it two opposing risks: On the one hand, new governments can misuse lustration to attack their political rivals; on the other hand, "democratization can fail in the long run if the purging of a public sector is insufficient" (p. 23). According to her, the populist governments in Poland and Hungary have been using lustration as a weapon against the civil service, the courts, the media, and academics. She worries that, in these countries, the partisan "politicization of public administration" may have become normalized in ways that tarnish democratic standards of political loyalty.

The final chapter brings us to a rarely discussed topic in the literature on transitional justice: the former Soviet republics, where the legacy of the Communist Party has been a major issue since 1991. Drawing from abundant examples of transitional justice in Kazakhstan, Georgia, and other former republics, Alexei Trochev argues that transitional-justice policies in former republics are tightly controlled by the ruling elites, who "allowed policies thought to enhance the legitimacy of elites, and ended policies thought to threaten it," especially in the absence of strong social demand for transitional justice (p. 12). The ruling elite adopted a particular transitional-justice policy approach because they wanted to "maximize domestic and international benefits" such as funding from the World Bank. These inauthentic transitional-justice projects are particularly prominent in Uzbekistan, Kazakhstan, and Georgia. Meanwhile, most post-Soviet states have constitutions that protect rights, but constitution making in the former Soviet republics has been manipulated by former rulers turned presidents. For this reason alone, there should be little surprise at the fact that constitutional courts in former republics have been reluctant to deal with transitional-justice cases, which can run counter to the political interests of the ruling class (pp. 11–12).

After reviewing the decommunization in former republics, Trochev discusses, with in-depth analyses, three legal cases in which individuals challenged the constitutionality of a state ban on the Communist Party and its symbols. The cases, which arose in Russia, Moldova, and Ukraine, were offshoots of the political turmoil that followed bans placed on the communist parties. Critics of the bans referred to them as an abusive exercise of executive power and an infringement on freedom of association. These bans were accompanied by government confiscation of former Communist Party property, a fact that compelled constitutional courts in these former republics to separate the two issues and treat them independently. For example, the Russian Constitutional Court declined to make a judgment on the constitutional status of the Communist Party but upheld one of the most important parts of President Boris Yeltsin's ban: the ban of the top Communist Party bodies. Accordingly, the court reasoned that because no one had the standing to request a return of Communist Party assets, Yeltsin's expropriation of the property remained intact. However, because the Russian Constitutional Court did not declare the Communist Party a criminal organization, none of its leaders were deemed to be legally responsible for the widespread political oppression of the Soviet era. This move on the court's part left Yeltsin and his affiliates unsatisfied with the decision, and in response, they suspended the operations of the Constitutional Court in the fall of 1993. In fact, both the court and Yeltsin admitted later that they had been too weak to adopt a comprehensive strategy for decommunization. Nevertheless, the survival of the Communist Party in various forms gave Yeltsin's successor, Vladimir Putin, more leverage in securing the support of former Communist Party functionaries.

Ukraine and Moldova offer further examples of the political compromises that former Soviet republics made in the realm of transitional justice. In 1991, the two countries banned the Communist Party and confiscated its property. However, within three years of the ban in Ukraine, a new party with the same name, the Communist Party of Ukraine, took shape. It campaigned for a formal retraction of the ban and a return of the party's property. The Ukraine Constitutional Court, having taken four years to render its judgment on the matter, held the ban unconstitutional on the grounds of freedom of association and separation of powers.

As in Ukraine, the Communist Party in Moldova underwent a reincarnation, now referred to as the Party of Communists of the Republic of Moldova (PCRM) after 1993, when the presidium of the Moldovan parliament lifted its previous ban on the party. Since then, the new PCRM has played a vibrant role in Moldovan politics. In 2010, President Mihai Ghimpu set up a commission to investigate political oppression during the communist era. The commission later produced a final report condemning the communist regime's crimes against humanity and recommending that parliament pass legislation prohibiting the use of communist symbols and terms. Acting President Ghimpu then decreed that June 28 would henceforth be known as the Day of Soviet Occupation, commemorating the fights against the communist regime. Members of the PCRM challenged the decree in the Moldovan Constitutional Court, which agreed with the petitioners and held the decree unconstitutional. However, the Moldovan Constitutional Court, similar to its counterpart in Russia, declined to comment on the legality of the over five decades of communist rule. Nevertheless, Ghimpu convinced parliament to pass a resolution condemning the totalitarian communist regime and to enact a law banning communist symbols. Soon enough, the Moldovan

Constitutional Court found itself reviewing the constitutionality of the law. This time, the court consulted the opinions of the Venice Commission and the Office for Democratic Institutions and Human Rights (the central institution belonging to the Organization for Security and Co-operation in Europe). In 2013, the two bodies issued a joint opinion on the ban, claiming that it could be legitimate if the government could demonstrate that its adoption of the measure satisfied a "pressing social need." In the absence of such proof, the ban was likely illegal as it violated the freedom of expression. Consequently, the Moldovan Constitutional Court declared the ban unconstitutional and based its decision on the European Court of Human Right's "pressing social need" formula and proportionality test. Nevertheless, the chief justice wrote a dissenting opinion criticizing the majority for neglecting the historical context of Moldova's suffering under the Soviet regime.

Like the Moldovan Constitutional Court, the Ukrainian Constitutional Court had to deal with challenges to the Ukrainian legislature's ban on the use of communist symbols, but unlike the Moldovan Constitutional Court, the Ukrainian Constitutional Court issued a 2019 decision upholding the ban. The Ukrainian Court justified its decision by arguing that the communist symbols had been used to "delegitimate" Ukrainian statehood during the communist era and that, between 1917 and 1991, they represented "negative and destructive ideas" depriving Ukrainians of an independent nation-state (p. 23). However, as was the case in the Moldovan Constitutional Court, the Ukrainian chief justice wrote a dissenting opinion that characterized the majority's reasoning as political, not legal. According to Trochev, the transitional-justice cases in these two former republics have "split the bench even further, making it easier for the rulers to manipulate the Court" (p. 24).

Unpacking Politics of Constitutionalizing Transitional Justice

The ten chapters in this book address transitional-justice measures in former authoritarian states around the world. For transitional justice to flourish in a democracy, there must be a reasonably solid consensus, yet the profoundly antagonistic nature of transitional justice erects barriers to the realization of such a consensus. In a country's quest for transitional justice, compromises are typically necessary. These compromises, constituting a modus vivendi, must emerge within the four corners of a transitional democracy's constitution. All sides in the transitioning society can turn to constitutional reasoning and constitutional courts in order to establish a new culture for public deliberation. Constitutional courts, though they sometimes exacerbate polarizing issues, can play a vital role in crystalizing the values of transitional justice. When performed fairly and when justice is the central objective, the role of constitutional courts can send a warning to future power holders that liberal constitutionalism is an abiding and growing force. Of course, the task of constitutionalizing transitional justice varies from one decade to the next and from one country to the other. And of course, no single constitutional judgment will end, once and for all, the struggle for power. Oftentimes the very act of constitutionalizing transitional justice triggers a backlash, whether from supporters of the former authoritarian regime or from democratic activists. As Ruti Teitel points out, "Transitional phenomenology is not simply the product of its abiding political circumstances but is, instead, a function of contemporary political circumstances and historical legacies of injustice" (2000: 223). Each constitutional democracy that finds itself emerging from the dark shadows of an authoritarian past reconstitutes its own identity through the unfolding story of its struggles with the historical legacies of injustice. In the politics of constitutionalizing transitional justice, the story of these struggles goes on and on as a nation's quest for self-understanding never ends.

References

Ackerman, Bruce. 1992. *The Future of Liberal Revolution*. Yale University Press.

Ackerman, Bruce. 2019. *Revolutionary Constitutions: Charismatic Leadership and the Rule of Law*. The Belknap Press of Harvard University Press.

David, Roman. 2003. "Lustration Laws in Action: The Motives and Evaluation of Lustration Policy in the Czech Republic and Poland (1989–2001)." *Law & Social Inquiry* 28(2) 387–493.

Dyzenhaus, David. 2012. "*Leviathan* as a Theory of Transitional Justice," in Melissa S. Williams, Rosemary Nagy, and Jon Elster eds., *Transitional Justice: Nomos Li*, pp. 180–217, New York University Press.

Elkins, Zachary, Tom Ginsburg, and James Melton. 2009. *The Endurance of National Constitutions*. Cambridge University Press.

Elster, Jon. 2004. *Closing the Books: Transitional Justice in Historical Perspective*. Cambridge University Press.

Ginsburg, Tom. 2003. *Judicial Review in New Democracies: Constitutional Courts in Asian Cases*. Cambridge University Press.

Murphy, Colleen. 2017. *The Conceptual Foundations of Transitional Justice*. Cambridge University Press.

O'Donnell, Guillermo, and Philippe C. Schmitter. 1986. *Transitions from Authoritarian Rule: Tentative Conclusions about Uncertain Democracies*. Johns Hopkins University Press.

Teitel, Ruti G. 2000. *Transitional Justice*. Oxford University Press.

Part 1

Constitutional Origins of Transitional Justice

1 The Dilemmas of Transitional Justice and the South African Experience

Richard J. Goldstone

Introduction

Societies that emerge from oppression and egregious human rights violations frequently adopt measures to redress the legacies of the previous regime. These measures may be judicial or nonjudicial. On the one extreme, there may be criminal prosecutions of the former leaders. On the other, there may be blanket amnesties. The dilemma facing most nations recovering from massive human rights violations can be summarized thus: Should the violations be forgiven, if not forgotten, in an effort to move forward into democracy and freedom, or should governments adopt measures that recognize and acknowledge the victims of a former regime (Teitel 2000)?

Broadly, there are three options in response to this dilemma:

(1) Nuremberg-style trials for the perpetrators of the violations;
(2) explicit or implicit amnesty for the perpetrators;[1] and
(3) truth-and-reconciliation commissions in which the victims are given a public platform to speak about their experiences and, in that way, to receive acknowledgment of what they experienced (Van Zyl 1999).

The first option, criminal prosecution, is calculated to bring substantial justice to victims. Where the crimes are particularly egregious, and especially where genocide has been committed, this path might be the only moral and strategic one to follow. Following World War II, a debate surfaced as to whether Nazi and Japanese leaders linked to crimes against humanity should be tried before a court or summarily executed. Documents declassified in October 2012 confirm that Britain opposed putting the Nazi leaders on trial. The preference of British premier Winston Churchill was to summarily execute some of them and to imprison others without trial. President Franklin Roosevelt strongly opposed such a policy

1 An example is Chile's Amnesty Decree Law. Passed in 1978, the law exempts all individuals who committed human rights violations between September 11, 1973, and March 10, 1978, from criminal responsibility (Decree Law, No. 2191, 1978).

DOI: 10.4324/9780429505089-3

and claimed that the American public would insist on proper trails. Joseph Stalin favored "show trials" that for years had been staged in the Soviet Union (Cobain 2012). The trials that followed at Nuremberg and Tokyo unquestionably brought some measure of solace and acknowledgement to victims. The trials also brought home to many millions of Germans and Japanese the enormity of the crimes committed by their leaders and in their name. While Holocaust denial is hardly unknown, the Nuremberg trials make it difficult to sustain, let alone justify it. However, the problem with the option of Nuremberg-style trials is that they usually carry with them a substantial political cost. They might result in further violence and deny the nation a peaceful transition to democracy. In the case of post–World War II trials, both Germany and Japan unconditionally surrendered, thus removing any political opposition to the prosecution of their leaders. In other cases, there might be high political risk in adopting this approach.

The second option, a general amnesty, is the most tempting of the three and is usually embraced as an acceptably easy way out. Its major attraction is avoidance of political fallout that often accompanies investigations into the purported crimes of a previous administration. However, this option denies the victims the opportunity to receive justice, which specifically includes appropriate acknowledgment of what they suffered. General amnesty creates resentment in many victims and the demographic groups from which they come. The larger the class of victims, the greater the pool of resentment. That was the experience in both the former Yugoslavia and Rwanda, where, over many decades, a widespread tendency to ignore former human rights violations led to cycles of violence.[2] Indeed, international law requires that persons who commit international crimes be prosecuted and, if found guilty, suitably punished.[3]

The third option, truth-and-reconciliation commissions, requires political and moral compromises. The victims are given a platform on which to make public whatever human rights violation was perpetrated against them. This option

2 For theorizing violence as behavior that breeds cycles, *see* Brown (1994, 19). To understand participation in cycles of violence from a perspective of political psychology, *see* Littman and Paluck (2015). There is also empirical evidence suggesting that exposure to war-related trauma positively correlates with aggression and community and family violence. See Hecker et al. (2015).

3 International legal norms and theories address two types of crimes: international crimes and crimes of international concern. The former refers to genocide, torture, and war crimes, and the latter usually includes international drug trafficking, terrorism, hijacking, and enslavement. For the former, prosecution and punishment have generally been incorporated into international treaties. In the context of transitional justice, domestic human rights infringement requires further and complex consideration, hence the importance of constitutional-law doctrine in domestic law. *See* generally *Convention on the Prevention and Punishment of the Crime of Genocide* (1948); *Geneva Conventions* (1949); and *Convention Against Torture and Other Cruel, Inhuman or Degrading Treatment or Punishment* (1984). It should be noted that the Nuremberg trials and the International Military Tribunal for the Far East (also known as the Tokyo War Crimes Tribunal) were also referred to in arguments relying on moral grounds for legal prosecution even in the absence of positive laws.

provides the victims with important public acknowledgment that lies at the heart of justice. However, the option simultaneously deprives them of full justice – there are no prosecutions or appropriate punishments of those individuals most responsible for victims' victimhood.

These approaches are not necessarily mutually inconsistent. For example, one can have criminal prosecutions as well as a truth-and-reconciliation commission. Such a dual approach was indeed the position adopted in both South Africa and Sierra Leone.[4]

Which of these three choices a nation adopts in the aftermath of serious human rights violations depends upon many factors that are often peculiar to that nation. The factors include the political reality on the ground, the nature of the violations, and the available economic and human resources. Above all, the options require the political will to implement whatever form of transitional justice is at their heart.

Both prosecutions and truth-and-reconciliation commissions inevitably invite fierce resistance from the leaders of the outgoing regime, who prefer their nefarious conduct to be hidden rather than publicized. In order to avoid any unpleasant consequence of an investigative effort, they might well resort to violent means as a way to abort the transition. For this reason, a nation emerging from oppression to democracy is well advised to make provision for the mechanisms of transitional justice in fundamental legislation and preferably in a new constitution. In this way, it becomes more difficult for former leaders and those complicit in their crimes to question or undermine the legality of the prosecutorial or commission-based mechanisms.

The Violence Accompanying South Africa's Transition to Democracy

After he served twenty-seven years of a life sentence, in February 1990, Nelson Mandela was released from prison. So, too, were many of his comrades. The liberation organizations, including the African National Congress, the Pan-Africanist Congress, and the South African Communist Party were unbanned. Many black leaders who were in exile were able to return home. The issue of transitional justice became central to South Africa's way forward. Multi-party negotiations got underway, and South Africa's leaders became involved with the design of a roadmap for South Africa's transition to democracy (Klug 2000). There was every expectation that the negotiations would be conducted in an atmosphere of peace. However, unexpectedly, the last years of Apartheid witnessed a high level of political violence. That transition has often been referred to as a "peaceful transition."

4 *See* Stovel (2010), which examines (1) how former civil war combatants and civilian survivors struggled to reconcile and build trust in communities and (2) how the Sierra Leone Truth and Reconciliation Commission contributed to reconciliation and justice.

This characterization is inaccurate. During that period, many thousands of South Africans lost their lives in political violence (Waldmeir 1997).

In the middle of 1991, the South African government persuaded the parties to the multiparty negotiations to agree on the appointment of a judicial commission of inquiry to investigate the causes of the political violence. It had been claimed by Nelson Mandela that much of the violence was the consequence of what he called "third force" activities on the part of the South African Defence Force and the South African Police. Those activities were allegedly driven by senior white military and police officials and were designed to subvert the transition of South Africa from Apartheid to democracy. Those covert activities had been consistently denied by President de Klerk. The negotiating parties and, in particular, the African National Congress agreed to the appointment of the commission, but only on condition that all the parties agreed unanimously on the identity of the chairman and four members of the commission.

As fate would have it, I played a significant role in the commission. By the early 1990s, I had completed a nine-year stint as a judge of the Transvaal Supreme Court and in 1990 had been elevated to the then highest court, the Supreme Court of Appeal. Against this backdrop, in the middle of October 1991, I was informed by the Minister of Justice that it had been agreed that I should chair the commission. Its official title was the Standing Commission of Inquiry Regarding the Prevention of Public Violence and Intimidation.

For almost three years, I chaired the commission.[5] In order to conduct our inquiries, we established five investigation units. They were made up of carefully chosen and vetted members of the South African Police, senior police officers seconded by five member countries of the European Union, and a former commissioner of the Royal Canadian Mounted Police. The commission, under its founding statute, was given wide powers of search and seizure and the power to summon any persons to provide testimony under oath and to produce documents. More than forty discrete inquiries were conducted, and we succeeded in establishing that the main cause of the political violence was indeed the consequence of the so-called "third force." When confronted with the evidence, President de Klerk took decisive steps against some of the officials responsible for the nefarious activities. It led to the dismissal of twenty-three senior members of the South African Army, including a number of generals and brigadiers.

Agreement on a New Constitution[6]

A dilemma that faced South Africa during the negotiating period between 1990 and 1994 was the manner in which a new constitution should be drafted and agreed upon. On the one side, the Apartheid leaders were not prepared to give a blank check to the black majority. They feared that property that they had

5 For an account of the work of the commission, *see* Goldstone (2000, 25–28).

6 For more discussion on constitution making in South Africa, *see also* Ebrahim (1998).

acquired would be confiscated and that a socialist, if not communist, state would be established. On the other side, the black leaders were not prepared to allow the white minority to have a right to veto any of the provisions of the new constitution. The solution was unusual. It was agreed that there would be a two-part process. There would be an Interim Constitution that would provide for the first democratic elections, and it would contain the fundamental provisions that would have to be contained in the "final Constitution" (the Constitutional Principles). That final Constitution would be drafted by a Constitutional Assembly that would consist of all of the democratically elected members of both Houses of the new parliament.[7] They would be bound by the Constitutional Principles. Who would determine whether there was such compliance? It was agreed that the newly established Constitutional Court of South Africa would have to make that determination.

It was at the insistence of the African National Congress that a new apex court was to be established as the final arbiter of any constitutional issues that might arise under the new constitution. At the end of the Apartheid era, the judges were almost entirely white men and the judiciary was thus quite unrepresentative of the majority of the people. With great reluctance, the Apartheid leaders agreed. In this regard, South Africa followed the example of Germany under its 1949 constitution. The German judges then in office had been appointed during the Nazi era, and it was thought inappropriate and unacceptable that the provisions of the new constitution should be interpreted and applied by those judges. Hence, the Constitutional Court of Germany (the *Bundesverfassungsgericht*) was established and its members were elected by both Houses of the German Parliament (Bundesverfassungsgericht n.d.). The South African Constitutional Court was inaugurated by President Mandela on February 15, 1995.[8]

In 1996 the Constitutional Court of South Africa, after receiving oral submissions over a period of two weeks, determined unanimously that in some twelve respects, the draft constitution had failed to comply with the Constitutional Principles (*Certification of the Constitution of the Republic of South Africa* [1996] ZACC 26). Under the terms of the Interim Constitution, the Constitutional Assembly had regard to the full reasons furnished by the court and sent an amended draft back to the Constitutional Court. This time the Constitutional Court, again unanimously, held that the draft did comply with the Constitutional

7 The Interim Constitution of 1993 was in force from the commencement of the first democratic election on April 27, 1994, and was superseded by the final constitution on February 4, 1997.

8 Both the German and South African Constitutional Courts became the apex courts in constitutional matters. They were each placed above the previously existing supreme courts. The first time that the eleven original members of the South African Constitutional Court (including me) met together was in Karlsruhe, the seat of the court's German counterpart. The then president of the German Constitutional Court took cognizance of the similar rationales for the founding of each court and invited the eleven of us to attend a week of seminars on issues that might be helpful to the new court.

Principles and certified it accordingly (*Certification of the Amended Text of the Constitution of the Republic of South Africa* [1996] ZACC 24). The South African final Constitution came into operation on February 4, 1997.

The stark change brought about by the Interim Constitution was eloquently described as follows by Mahomed J in *S v. Makwanyane and Another* [1995] ZACC 3: "In some countries the Constitution only formalises, in a legal instrument, a historical consensus of values and aspirations evolved incrementally from a stable and unbroken past to accommodate the needs of the future. The South African Constitution is different: It retains from the past only what is defensible and represents a decisive break from, and a ringing rejection of, that part of the past which is disgracefully racist, authoritarian, insular, and repressive, and a vigorous identification of and commitment to a democratic, universalistic, caring, and aspirationally egalitarian ethos expressly articulated in the Constitution. The contrast between the past which it repudiates and the future to which it seeks to commit the nation is stark and dramatic" (*S v. Makwanyane and Another* [1995] ZACC 3, para. 262).

The founding values of the South African Constitution are contained in Section 1 of the 1996 Constitution. There, the following is stated:

> The Republic of South Africa is one sovereign, democratic state founded on the following values:
>
> (a) Human dignity, the achievement of equality and the advancement of human rights and freedoms;
> (b) Non-racialism and non-sexism;
> (c) Supremacy of the constitution and the rule of law;
> (d) Universal adult suffrage, a national common voters role, regular elections and a multi-party system of democratic government, to ensure accountability, responsiveness and openness.

While the other provisions of the Constitution may be amended by a two-thirds majority in the lower house and six of the nine provinces in the upper house of Parliament, Section 1 may be amended only by a three-quarters majority in the lower house and six of the nine provinces in the upper house (The Constitution of the Republic of South Africa 1996, sec. 74).

In *Pharmaceutical Manufacturers Association of South Africa and Another: In re Ex Parte President of the Republic of South Africa and Others* (2000 ZACC 1), Chaskalson P. stated, "The exercise of all public power must comply with the Constitution which is the supreme law, and the doctrine of legality which is part of that law" (para. 20). This judgment gave full effect to the notion that the substance of our constitutional order is founded upon democracy and the rule of law.

The Truth-and-Reconciliation Commission

At the time of the constitutional negotiations, the question of whether a truth-and-reconciliation commission should be established was a controversial one. For obvious reasons, the outgoing Apartheid government was strongly opposed to it while the ANC and other freedom parties were equally strongly in favor of it. Only at the end of the negotiation process was a compromise reached, and that included a provision for the grant of amnesties. This compromise was added to the Interim Constitution as an addendum, or a "postamble," as it was called. It reads as follows:

> *National Unity and Reconciliation*
>
> This Constitution provides a historic bridge between the past of a deeply divided society characterised by strife, conflict, untold suffering and injustice, and a future founded on the recognition of human rights, democracy and peaceful co-existence and development opportunities for all South Africans, irrespective of colour, race, class, belief or sex. The pursuit of national unity, the well-being of all South African citizens and peace require reconciliation between the people of South Africa and the reconstruction of society.
>
> The adoption of this Constitution lays the secure foundation for the people of South Africa to transcend the divisions and strife of the past, which generated gross violations of human rights, the transgression of humanitarian principles in violent conflicts and a legacy of hatred, fear, guilt and revenge. These can now be addressed on the basis that there is a need for understanding but not for vengeance, a need for reparation but not for retaliation, a need for ubuntu but not for victimisation. In order to advance such reconciliation and reconstruction, amnesty shall be granted in respect of acts, omissions and offences associated with political objectives and committed in the course of the conflicts of the past. To this end, Parliament under this Constitution shall adopt a law determining a firm cut-off date, which shall be a date after 8 October 1990 and before 6 December 1993, and providing for the mechanisms, criteria and procedures, including tribunals, if any, through which such amnesty shall be dealt with at any time after the law has been passed.
>
> With this Constitution and these commitments, we, the people of South Africa, open a new chapter in the history of our country.

This provision was held by the Constitutional Court to be as binding as other provisions in the Interim Constitution and authorized Parliament to set up a truth-and-reconciliation commission.

In considering whether to establish a truth-and-reconciliation commission, Nelson Mandela and his African National Congress faced the three options, to which I have referred previously. The strong preference voiced by the former white Apartheid leaders, represented by the last Apartheid president, F.W. de Klerk, was for a blanket amnesty. Why rake up past violations? Instead, South Africans should link hands and walk together into a bright future of reconciliation. After all, such a commission would risk a coup d'état orchestrated by the previous military and police officials who, it had been agreed, would remain in their positions. Those were the questions and assertions emphasized by De Klerk and his colleagues. The strong preference of the majority of South Africans, especially black South Africans, was for their victimhood to find redress in Nuremberg-style trials of those individuals most responsible for this victimhood – that is, trials of those individuals complicit in murder, torture, and the daily indignities suffered under the oppressive and racist Apartheid laws.

I know from personal discussions with Nelson Mandela during the time of the transition that he was tempted to let bygones be bygones and allow the people of South Africa to devote their attention and resources to building a new democracy and redressing the egregious disparities between black and white people.

There were two considerations that led Mandela to favor a truth-and-reconciliation commission. The first arose from reports that surfaced in 1992 to the effect that, in their camps in Angola, Zambia, and Tanzania, ANC members had tortured people who were suspected of being South African government agents (Amnesty International 1992). In that same year, the ANC set up its own commission of inquiry in which it was found that "staggering brutality" had been used in those camps. It was recommended that compensation be paid to the victims. That was not a popular recommendation and was not implemented. Instead, a second inquiry was set up by the ANC under the chairmanship of a leading businessman, Mr. S.M. Motsuenyane. This commission also found that the ANC had tortured people under its control and that specific individuals were responsible for those acts. The ANC accepted "collective guilt" for those human rights violations (South African History Online 2011). The fact that the ANC investigated itself regarding allegations of human rights violations committed by the ANC outside South Africa made it a compelling demand that the incomparably more serious human rights violations committed inside South Africa by the Apartheid government should also be investigated.

The second catalyst for Mandela's support of a truth-and-reconciliation commission was a visit to South Africa by the former president of Chile, Patricio Aylwin, together with a leading Chilean human rights lawyer, José Zalaquett. It was President Aylwin who, in 1990, was responsible for setting up the Chilean National Commission for Truth and Reconciliation (known as the Rettig Commission, named after its chair, Raúl Rettig). Zalaquett was one of its six members. The commission investigated the deaths and disappearances that had occurred in Chile between 1973 and 1990, during the military dictatorship of Augusto Pinochet. The commission reported on over 2,000 people who had been "disappeared" for political reasons. Aylwin and Zalaquett explained that the Chilean Commission was substantially limited by the demands made by Pinochet, who was unprepared to allow democratic elections to take place unless his demands were accepted by Aylwin. Pinochet insisted that (1) the commission investigate only disappearances, thereby ensuring that there would be no identification of the perpetrators; (2) there be no publication of the names of any of the perpetrators; and (3) there be no public hearings. Aylwin had little choice but to accept these conditions.

The Rettig Commission completed its work in 1991. It found that the Pinochet regime had killed 2,279 people for political reasons. Where the victims could be identified, they were named in the report of the commission. In presenting the report to the public on national television, Aylwin apologized to the victims and the people of Chile. He sent copies of the report to the families of each of the victims named in the report (United States Institute of Peace 1990). The publication of the report undoubtedly helped bring about a measure of reconciliation in Chile. It should be mentioned that before he handed power to a civilian government, Pinochet appointed himself a senator for life and, in that way, benefited from an effective amnesty in respect of all the crimes he might have perpetrated. When that amnesty was removed in the aftermath of Pinochet's arrest in London in 1999,[9] the people of Chile demanded additional justice. Pinochet was stripped of his amnesty and faced charges from the prosecuting authority. He died at the end of 2006, before he was to appear in court to face those charges.[10] The new cries for justice so many years after the crimes had been perpetrated illustrates that the restrictions placed upon the truth-and-reconciliation commission satisfied some, but certainly not all, the demands of victims for justice.

Meriting a full investigation, the evidence collected by my Commission of Inquiry relating to the "third force" prevented the Apartheid leaders from easily denying allegations of serious human rights violations. That evidence, there was no doubt, represented the tip of the iceberg.

Support for the establishment of such a commission continued to grow, and after his election as president, Mandela and his government decided that they would indeed establish the Truth and Reconciliation Commission (TRC) by an Act of Parliament. However, Mandela did not rush the legislation. He waited until he had replaced the Apartheid-appointed senior officers in the military and police. He was not prepared to risk (even if a remote possibility) a coup d'état designed to thwart the complete abolition of Apartheid. During that period, a host of nongovernmental organizations, government leaders, lawyers, and religious leaders engaged in public dialogue on the advantages and disadvantages of a truth-and-reconciliation commission. Not unexpectedly, there was strong support for it and especially from many of the victims of Apartheid (Boraine 2000).

The result was the TRC established by the Promotion of National Unity and Reconciliation Act, No. 34 of 1995. It consisted of 17 commissioners who were appointed by President Mandela after wide public consultation and public interviews.

The legislation made provision for the TRC to consist of three committees. The first was the Human Rights Violations Committee. It was to investigate gross human rights violations that had taken place between 1960 and 1994. This was to be achieved by inviting the victims of those abuses to provide evidence to the commission – both oral and written. Once identified, victims were to be referred to the second committee, the Reparation and Rehabilitation Committee.

9 At the instance of Pinochet-era torture victims, a Spanish investigating judge ordered the arrest of Pinochet. *See* Connett et al. (1998).

10 For a useful brief history of the rule of General Pinochet, *see* Kandell (2006).

That committee was to provide support for victims and formulate policy proposals and recommendations on the rehabilitation of survivors, their families, and the affected communities at large. The third committee was the Amnesty Committee. Its function was to ensure that applications for amnesty were made in accordance with the provisions of the legislation and to hear and rule on those applications. The TRC was required to produce a final report containing a detailed account of the body's work and recommendations on ways to prevent future violations of human rights.

The Human Rights Violations Committee received over 22,000 statements from victims. It held public hearings in which over 5,000 of those victims testified on the egregious crimes committed during the Apartheid era. These included murder, disappearances, and torture. There were also people who testified on the human rights violations committed by the liberation organizations. The commission received over 7,000 amnesty applications. More than 2,500 amnesty hearings were held by the Amnesty Committee. Approximately 900 amnesty applications were granted. To qualify for amnesty, applicants had to present supporting evidence that contained comprehensive details on the alleged crimes committed. In addition, the given crime for which amnesty was sought had to have been committed for a political motive. The evidence heard by the Human Rights Violations and Amnesty Committees consisted of an outpouring of statements about many thousands of serious violations committed during the years under investigation. The TRC established an efficient investigation department. It built up an impressive database and verified the evidence of witnesses, to the extent possible, before applicants for amnesty and witnesses appeared before the TRC.

There were daily live radio broadcasts of the hearings of the Human Rights Violations Committee, and television coverage was frequent as well. During the period of the TRC hearings, the weekly Sunday prime-time television summaries of the highlights of the week's proceedings ranked as South Africa's most widely watched television programming.

The constitutionality of the TRC's amnesty provisions was contested by some family members representing relatives who, as anti-Apartheid activists, were alleged to have been murdered or tortured by members of the Apartheid security forces. The effect of amnesty under the relevant legislation was to protect perpetrators from both criminal and civil liability. In a seminal decision in 1996, *Azanian Peoples Organization (AZAPO) and Others v. President of the Republic of South Africa and Others* ([1996] ZACC 16), the Constitutional Court held that those provisions would have been open to serious doubt if there had been no constitutional provision to justify them and, in particular, to deprive the victims of the right to a civil remedy in an open court. The Constitutional Court held that the epilogue, contained in the Constitution, was an integral part of it. On the strength of the wording of the epilogue, the amnesty provisions were upheld by the court. It is unlikely that the TRC would have survived the court challenge if the Interim Constitution had not provided for the body's establishment.

The Successes and Failures of the TRC

In my opinion, the TRC was substantially successful. It provided all South Africans with a single and full history of the serious human rights violations that had been suffered by a majority of South Africans. Without that accounting, broadly speaking, there would have been two histories of the violations committed during the Apartheid era. The black majority knew what they had suffered, and their history would have approximated the truth. The majority of white South Africans tended to believe the fabricated denials and justifications that had been put out by the Apartheid government. These South Africans would have found it more comfortable to accept the inaccuracies than to admit to the unethical conduct that had been committed in their name and for their benefit. In the absence of the TRC, this inaccurate historical narrative would have survived the end of Apartheid. In the words of Archbishop Desmond Tutu, "Unless we look the beast in the eye we will find that it returns to hold us hostage" (Tutu 1999, 31). The TRC undercut the moral justifications advocated by some South Africans who opposed substantial programs that would provide water, electricity, and upgraded schools and housing to impoverished black areas and that thus would undo some of the Apartheid-era deprivations.

Many people resented the TRC and refused to cooperate with it. On the one side, the leaders of the Apartheid-era military and police opposed the whole idea, and most of them did not apply for amnesties. On the other side, many leaders of the armed wings of the liberation movements were adamant that they had fought a just war and that they should not be called upon to confess to any "crimes."

As mentioned earlier, the TRC was concerned only with gross human rights violations. This meant that the TRC did not hear evidence or report on the daily human rights violations that all black South Africans suffered every day of their lives during the Apartheid era. The oppressive and racist laws dictated how these people lived life from the day they were born in a segregated hospital to the day they died in a segregated hospital and were buried in a segregated cemetery. These profound daily indignities were known euphemistically as "petty Apartheid." They did not fall under the category of "serious violations," over which the TRC exercised jurisdiction. In my opinion, this lack of attention is a matter for regret. It would have been appropriate for white South Africans – who were not innocent bystanders but the major beneficiaries of a wholly unjust system – to be confronted with evidence pertaining to all human rights violations.

The Reparation and Rehabilitation Committee made a number of recommendations. One was a reparation program under which each victim named by the TRC would receive reparations in the form of a payment of approximately US$3,500 a year for six years. It also recommended that in cases where there was sufficient evidence available, prosecutions should be pursued not only against those who had refrained from seeking amnesty but also in respect of those whose amnesty applications had been rejected.

The follow-up to the TRC report was disappointing. The amount of compensation paid to approximately 21,000 victims was considerably less than that recommended by the TRC. The few prosecutions that were launched proved to be less than successful. The most important, that against the Apartheid Minister of Defense, Magnus Malan, after months of evidence, failed to achieve a conviction. Prosecutions were labor-intensive, and the appetite to prosecute was generally lacking in the national prosecuting authority. With regard to reparations, post-Apartheid South Africa had grossly insufficient resources to launch programs capable of bringing meaningful relief to the majority of South Africans who had been deprived by Apartheid of so many rights and privileges. In addition, the human rights violations had been committed not by the new democratically elected government but by its predecessors. Nonetheless, Nelson Mandela, following the example of Patricio Aylwin, apologized to the people – particularly the nonwhites – of South Africa for what they had suffered during the Apartheid era.

When Nelson Mandela became South Africa's first democratically elected president, a state of euphoria gripped the country. Archbishop Tutu coined the expression "rainbow nation" to describe South Africa with its many races and languages at peace with itself. The euphoria did not take long to dissipate. The negative legacy of over three centuries of racial oppression has required more than goodwill to overcome. Stark economic imbalances among large segments of South Africa's population remain in place today and will take generations to end. There are too many people in South Africa who have not yet benefited from freedom and democracy. Why should those deprived citizens put their faith and confidence in a democratic dispensation? There are many calls for substantive equality and the removal of the imbalances in economic advancement and educational opportunities that remain the legacy of Apartheid. Government leaders who claim that there are insufficient funds for free tertiary education have too frequently been accused, and some found guilty, of corruption, gross mismanagement, and acts of inexcusable greed. While the TRC achieved the successes to which I have referred, there remain systemic fault lines that, neglected by our current leaders, will have to be addressed if we are to succeed in our democracy and make freedom a reality.

I remain optimistic that a growing number of South Africans will benefit from their country's hard-won democracy. I also have no doubt that, if this optimism is justified, the TRC will have made a major contribution to the successful outcome.

International Consequences of the South African Truth and Reconciliation Commission

Internationally, much attention and acclaim accompanied not only South Africa's transition from Apartheid to democracy but also, more specifically, the successes of the TRC. Our country's experience encouraged other countries to follow our example. However, it soon became clear that the South African experience, including the TRC, could not easily be transplanted. When contemplating a form of transitional justice, each country should carefully and fully analyze its proper circumstances. In particular, it should account for its prevailing political, economic, cultural, and security structures. South Africa was fortunate in having the political freedom to have a transparent truth-and-reconciliation commission, the economic resources to fund the commission's significant expenses. and the charismatic leadership of Archbishop Desmond Tutu. Most important of all, it was fortunate in having Nelson Mandela, who represented the wishes of the majority of his people and who did not seek revenge for what they had endured during more than three centuries of oppression. They sought what Justice Albie Sachs has called "soft vengeance" (Sachs 2014), represented by the TRC. Too many white South Africans tend to take this magnanimous spirit for granted.

I was disappointed that no truth-and-reconciliation commission was established in Bosnia and Herzegovina in the aftermath of the Balkan wars of the first half of the 1990s. At a meeting I attended in Sarajevo in 1997, a majority of civil-society organizations clearly and fully supported such a commission (Jelacic and Ahmetasevic 2007). However, it was opposed by Louise Arbour, the chief prosecutor of the United Nations International Criminal Tribunal for the former Yugoslavia (ICTY). It was her view that a truth-and-reconciliation commission would interfere with the criminal investigations that were being conducted by her office. I did not agree – those investigations could have been given primacy, and the Office of the Prosecutor could have directed that no commission investigations or proceedings could proceed in situations that were being investigated by the Office of the Prosecutor. In any event, the ICTY investigations did no more than scratch the surface of the totality of war crimes and human rights violations that had been perpetrated in the region. The opposition of Louise Arbour proved to be fatal to the endeavor. The United Nations would not go against the views of their Chief Prosecutor. I would suggest that such a truth and reconciliation commission could materially have assisted in bringing a measure of reconciliation that has thus far eluded the people of Bosnia and Herzegovina.

The problems facing nations in the process of transition are manifold. The most serious is the sheer number and extent of the violations that have been committed and the inability to investigate more than a small number of them. It is in this context that a truth-and-reconciliation commission is attractive. In its busiest period, the ICTY had three courtrooms available to it, and its human resources were limited. During a period of over three decades, the ICTY prosecuted 161 individuals for war crimes committed in the former Yugoslavia (The International Criminal Tribunal for the former Yugoslavia n.d.). By contrast, the South African TRC, during a period of about two years, was able to consider thousands of cases of serious human rights violations and to report on them. It heard not only the evidence of the victims but, in the amnesty applications, that of the perpetrators, as well. Prosecutions are neither designed nor able to record the history of an event; they only canvass the facts relevant to the charges brought against the individuals accused of criminal conduct. A truth-and-reconciliation commission, because of its wider mandate, is better designed to capture the history and context of the preceding era.

I have already referred to some of the dilemmas faced by nations transitioning from repressive regimes to democracy. The most difficult is the decision of whether to criminally prosecute leaders of the old regime or whether to deprive the victims of the full justice to which they are morally entitled. There is frequently the reality that full justice will retard and even derail the transition. Should the leaders of the previous regime be allowed to hold public office, or should there be a form of lustration (purging) that appealed to some central European states after the fall of the Berlin Wall?

At the very heart of all systems of and mechanisms for justice for victims of prior human rights violations is the acknowledgment that it brings to the victims. This is true of criminal prosecutions as well as of truth-and-reconciliation commissions. And such acknowledgement is not infrequently explicit in the apologies that have been made by leaders for the crimes committed by their predecessors.

In recent years, leaders who have publicly apologized for previous human rights violations did so, in part, to explicitly acknowledge the victims of those violations. In 2008, the prime minister of Australia, Kevin Rudd, apologized to the aboriginal populations of his country for government-sanctioned actions that had entailed the often-forcible separation of aboriginal children from their families and the conversion of these children into "white" Australians (Australia Government 2008). In the same year, the prime minister of Canada, Stephen Harper, apologized for the Indian Residential Schools, which had housed aboriginal children forcibly removed from the care of their families (Government of Canada 2008). And more recently, in August 2016, President Tsai Ing-wen of Taiwan publicly acknowledged her country's mistreatment of the island's aboriginal peoples (Office of the President, Taiwan, Republic of China 2016). I understand that the last-mentioned apology did not address issues of transitional justice faced by Taiwan with regard to its more recent political history and, in particular, the serious violations of human rights that had occurred during the country's prolonged state of emergency. However, these are all important and meaningful acknowledgements, which undoubtedly bring solace to many of the victims and facilitate reconciliation.

Whatever form it takes, the mechanism of transitional justice chosen by a nation can be implemented only if the strong will of political leaders is present. The absence of such political will is demonstrated by the truth-and-reconciliation commission established by Kenya. In the aftermath of the violence that accompanied the elections of 2007 and 2008, the Truth and Reconciliation Act of 2009 established the Truth, Justice, and Reconciliation Commission (TJRC). It was mandated to inquire into gross violations of human rights including disappearances, torture, sexual violations, murder, and extrajudicial killings. After four years, in 2013, the TJRC submitted its report to President Kenyatta. The report implicated senior officials in the present and preceding governments in the perpetration of serious human rights violations. It recommended that the prosecuting authorities should investigate charges against those most culpable (Ndungú 2014). Today, some years after the TJRC report was submitted, government officials have yet to activate a mechanism that, proposed by the commission, would assist in implementing its recommendations. Indeed, there is little hope that any of the recommendations will ever be implemented. The political will to do so is absent, as evidenced by the fact that the Kenyan parliament has yet to even table and discuss the report.

It is important to consider the role of constitutionalism in transitional justice. The rule of law lies at the very heart of democracy. If the processes of transitional justice are antithetical to the rule of law, they will not and cannot succeed in bridging the gap between past illegalities and present or future legalities. In any transitional society, a natural opposition arises between the interests of the leaders of the ancien régime and the interests of the leaders' victims. The methods adopted by any nation facing such a transition have to be thoughtfully considered, carefully designed, and transparently implemented. If they are not part of the constitution, they are likely to be fragile, subject to attack, and forced into a state of impotence.

As I have sought to demonstrate, the amnesty provisions of the South African TRC would most likely have failed to pass constitutional muster if they had not been anticipated and protected in the constitution that provided for the transition. From this historical legacy, we can reasonably infer that the countries seeking to successfully implement transitional justice should give appropriate consideration to the all-important variable of constitutional processes. Only by doing so can these countries have institutions whose legislative foundations successfully promote transition. The decision by the South African Constitutional Court to uphold the constitutionality of the truth-and-reconciliation commission came during the first year of the court's existence. The empathetic words in which the court articulated its decision resonated with the people and thus achieved wide acceptance.

I hold firm to the conclusion that institutions of transition cannot necessarily or easily be transplanted from one country to another. This contention notwithstanding, the experiences of countries that have gone through transition will provide useful lessons for other countries that are designing their own transition process. It is in this context that I have described, although very briefly, the experiences of my own country, South Africa.

References

Amnesty International. 1992. *South Africa: Torture, Ill-treatment, and Executions in African National Congress Camps.* Accessed November 2, 2016. www.amnesty.org/en/documents/afr53/027/1992/en/.

Australia Government. 2008. *Apology to Australia's Indigenous Peoples.* Accessed November 2, 2016. www.australia.gov.au/about-australia/our-country/our-people/apology-to-australias-indigenous-peoples.

Azanian Peoples Organization (AZAPO) and Others v. President of the Republic of South Africa and Others (CCT17/96) [1996] ZACC 16; 1996 (8) BCLR 1015; 1996 (4) SA 672.

Boraine, A. 2000. *A Country Unmasked: Inside South Africa's Truth and Reconciliation Commission.* Oxford: Oxford University Press.

Brown, S. 1994. *The Causes and Prevention of War.* Houndmills: Palgrave Macmillan.

Bundesverfassungsgericht. n.d. *Milestones in the History of the Federal Constitutional Court.* Accessed November 2, 2016. www.bundesverfassungsgericht.de/EN/Das Gericht/Zeitstrahl/zeitstrahl_node.html

Certification of the Amended Text of the Constitution of The Republic of South Africa (CCT37/96) [1996] ZACC 24; 1997 (1) BCLR 1; 1997 (2) SA 97.

Certification of the Constitution of the Republic of South Africa (CCT 23/96) [1996] ZACC 26; 1996 (4) SA 744 (CC); 1996 (10) BCLR 1253 (CC).

Cobain, I. 2012. "Britain Favoured Execution over Nuremberg Trials for Nazi Leaders." *The Guardian*, October 26. Accessed November 2, 2016. www.theguardian.com/world/2012/oct/26/britain-execution-nuremberg-nazi-leaders

Connett, D., J. Hooper., and P. Beaumont. 1998. "Pinochet Arrested in London." *The Guardian*, November 18. Accessed November 2, 2016. www.theguardian.com/world/1998/oct/18/pinochet.chile

Convention Against Torture and Other Cruel, Inhuman or Degrading Treatment or Punishment (1984). 1465 U.N.T.S. 85, opened for signature 10 December 1984, entered into force 26 June 1987.

Convention on the Prevention and Punishment of the Crime of Genocide (1948). 78 U.N.T.S. 277, opened for signature 9 September 1948, entered into force 12 January 1951.

Decree Law No. 2191 1978, (Chile).

Ebrahim, H. 1998. *The Soul of a Nation: Constitution-Making in South Africa.* Cape Town: Oxford University Press.

Geneva Convention relative to the protection of civilian persons in time of war. 1949. 75 U.N.T.S. 287, adopted 12 August 1949.

Goldstone, R.J. 2000. *For Humanity: Reflections of a War Crimes Investigator.* New Haven: Yale University Press.

Government of Canada. 2008. *Statement of Apology to Former Students of Indian Residential Schools.* Accessed November 2, 2016. www.aadnc-aandc.gc.ca/eng/1100100015644/1100100015649

Hecker, T., S. Fetz, H. Ainamani, and T. Elbert. 2015. "The Cycle of Violence: Associations between Exposure to Violence, Trauma-Related Symptoms, and Aggression – Findings from Congolese Refugees in Uganda." *Journal of Traumatic Stress* 28, no. 5: 448–55.

Jelacic, N., and N. Ahmetasevic. 2007. "Truth Commission Divides Bosnia." *Balkan Insight*, September 18. Accessed November 2, 2016. www.balkaninsight.com/en/article/truth-commission-divides-bosnia

Kandell, J. 2006. "Augusto Pinochet, Dictator Who Ruled by Terror in Chile, Dies." *NY Times*, December 11. Accessed November 2, 2016. www.nytimes.com/2006/12/11/world/americas/11pinochet.html?_r=0.

Klug, H. 2000. *Constituting Democracy: Law, Globalism and South Africa's Political Reconstruction.* Cambridge: Cambridge University Press.

Littman, R., and E.L. Paluck. 2015. "The Cycle of Violence: Understanding Individual Participation in Collective Violence." *Political Psychology* 36: 79–99.

Ndungú, C.G. 2014. *Lessons to Be Learned: An Analysis of the Final Report of Kenya's Truth, Justice, and Reconciliation Commission.* International Center for Transitional Justice (ICTJ), Briefing. Accessed November 2, 2016. www.ictj.org/publication/kenya-TJRC-lessons-learned

Office of the President, Taiwan, Republic of China. 2016. *President Tsai Apologizes to Indigenous Peoples on Behalf of Government.* November 2. http://english.president.gov.tw/Default.aspx?tabid=491&itemid=37801&rmid=2355

Pharmaceutical Manufacturers Association of South Africa and Another: In re Ex Parte President of the Republic of South Africa and Others (CCT31/99) [2000] ZACC 1; 2000 (2) SA 674; 2000 (3) BCLR 241.
Sachs, A. 2014. *The Soft Vengeance of a Freedom Fighter*. Berkeley: University of California Press.
South African History Online. 2011. *The Motsuenyane Commission Finds the African National Congress Guilty of Abuse in Its Camps*. Accessed November 2, 2016. www.sahistory.org.za/dated-event/motsuenyane-commission-finds-african-national-congress-anc-guilty-abuse-its-camps
Stovel, L. 2010. *Long Road Home: Building Reconciliation and Trust in Post-War Sierra Leone*. Antwerp: Intersentia.
S v. Makwanyane and Another (CCT3/94) [1995] ZACC 3; 1995 (6) BCLR 665; 1995 (3) SA 391; [1996] 2 CHRLD 164; 1995 (2) SACR 1.
Teitel, R.G. 2000. *Transitional Justice*. New York: Oxford University Press.
The Constitution of the Republic of South Africa 1996, (South Africa).
The International Criminal Tribunal for the former Yugoslavia. n.d. *Achievements*. Accessed November 2, 2016. www.icty.org/en/about/tribunal/achievements
Tutu, D. 1999. *No Future Without Forgiveness*. London: Rider.
United States Institute of Peace. 1990. *Truth Commission: Chile 90*. Accessed November 2, 2016. www.usip.org/publications/truth-commission-chile-90
Van Zyl, P. 1999. "Dilemmas of Transitional Justice: The Case of South Africa's Truth and Reconciliation Commission." *Journal of International Affairs* 52, no. 2: 647–67.
Waldmeir, P. 1997. *Anatomy of a Miracle: The End of Apartheid and the Birth of the New South Africa*. New York: W.W. Norton & Co.

2 Facing the Shadows of the Past during Transitions

The Role of the Constitutions in the Case of Hungary

Kriszta Kovács[1]

During a transition from an authoritarian or totalitarian regime to a democratic system, a political community has to reinvent itself in ways that will allow it to live with its own past. In this process, the community faces difficult choices. Some of the hardest questions to answer are the following: How to identify the perpetrators, facilitators, beneficiaries, and victims of the past regime? How to convict those who collaborated with the previous nondemocratic regime without appropriating its nondemocratic methods? How to compensate those who were the victims of human rights violations in the past regime? How to provide victims with property restitution or compensation in the face of substantial obstacles?

The law has a limited capacity to cope with the complex issues surrounding a nondemocratic regime's legacy, but in this chapter, I focus only on the legal – and, more specifically, on the constitutional – aspects of this matter. The current chapter does not deal with issues of apology, forgiveness, or reconciliation, although they are part of the transitional-justice vocabulary (Kritz 1995). Nor does the chapter focus on the strategies developed by the successor state's political elites (Huyse 1995). Here, the focus is on legal solutions to a previous regime's mass violation of human rights. Rather than approach these solutions as they concern the treatment and compensation of victims, the chapter discusses state-sponsored crimes in terms of the accountability of the perpetrators: retroactive justice as a response to the security measures of a past authoritarian state. The emphasis is on the roles that constitutions and constitutional courts play in the process of transitional justice. There is a popular argument that a constitution is just a piece of paper. A constitution is one thing; reality is another. In what follows, I will give examples of how constitutional texts and their judicial interpretations have consequences in the transitional-justice process, and the target of this inquiry will be Hungary.

1 For reading and commenting on earlier drafts of this article, the author wishes to thank the participants in the POMP Seminar on Dealing with a Difficult Past (University of Oxford – May, 2016) and the Workshop Constitutionalizing Transitional Justice (Academia Sinica Taipei – November, 2016). I am grateful for the constructive suggestions from the editor and the proofreader of this volume.

DOI: 10.4324/9780429505089-4

Every nation has to face up to the dark side of its history, and Hungary is no exception to this rule. One of the greatest challenges for Hungary is to cope with the grievances over its authoritarian and totalitarian regimes of the twentieth century. The question of how to settle the pro-Nazi and communist pasts of the country was raised during the democratic transition in 1989. Beginning in this year, Hungarians could come to terms with the past by creating laws and institutions pertaining to the remarkable difficulties of the previous decades.

The first part of this chapter discusses how the first democratic constitution of Hungary, and related judicial interpretations handed down by the Constitutional Court, dealt with the problem of transitional justice, and how this approach influenced reconciliation and democratic consolidation. The 1989 Constitution did not dictate a certain form of transitional justice. The constitution drafters realized that rival political conceptions of transitional justice provide different answers to the question of the scope of reparation and redistribution and to the question of what kind of institutional settings are required. The constitution only entrenched the principles that should govern the processes of transitional justice concerning democracy, rule of law, equality, fair trial, and the like. Oriented toward transitional justice, these principles served as decision-making guides for public-policy choices. The national legislature in Hungary adopted several laws on retroactive punishment and lustration, but the Constitutional Court rejected all these attempts to indict perpetrators and even to disclose their identity. It did not seize the momentum by responding to public calls for political justice. The dark past remained unresolved, and it still occasionally tugs at the present.

Recently, the question of settling the past has again been raised as part of the country's turn toward authoritarian rule. Therefore, the second part of the chapter discusses the 2011 Constitution in relation to the country's dynamic history in the twentieth century. The new constitution, renamed the Fundamental Law (The Fundamental Law of Hungary 2011), was intended to be a definitive break, "at least in a legislative and symbolic manner," with Hungary's totalitarian past (Varga 2015, 5) but, first and foremost, with the country's communist past. The Fundamental Law labels the whole Hungarian pre-1989 authoritarian regime "communist" and the post-1989 regime "post-communist." The result is a kind of negation of the two eras' respective complexities: While condemning the country's communist past and addressing specifically the "de-communization" of politics and society, the Fundamental Law denies the historic role of the late eighties' opposition movements. The constitutional text, by directly regulating the country's transitional-justice measures (retroactive prosecution, data disclosure, etc.), leaves no room for ordinary democratic decision-making on this issue. Furthermore, the constitutionalization of transitional-justice measures excludes the possibility of the effective constitutional review of the applied measures.

I. The Paradox of the Rule of Law: Transitional Justice and the Constitutional Court after 1989

In 1989, Hungary gained its independence from "milder authoritarian" (Linz and Stepan 1996, 255) Soviet rule and became an independent republic without adopting an entirely new constitution. The 1989 constitutional revision was formally only an amendment to the 1949 Constitution, but on October 23, 1989, "in fact, a new Constitution came into force" (Decision No. 11/1992). The legal relationship between the state and society, as well as the form of government, changed substantially. Liberal democracy replaced single-party authoritarianism, the country held competitive elections to launch a multiparty parliamentary system, and democratic institutions emerged (representative government, an independent judiciary, a Constitutional Court, and an ombuds system). The 1989 constitutional structure reflected two guiding principles: separation of powers and rule of law.

Roundtable negotiations were critical to the establishment of Hungary's democratic regime. The coordinated transition was accompanied by unbroken legal continuity since all the actors adhered to the letter of law (Arato and Miklósi 2010, 353). This model was possible thanks to Hungary's formal written Constitution of 1949 and to at least the appearance of some parliamentary sovereignty (Arato and Cohen 1999, 344). As the authority of the law had already begun to strengthen in the eighties (Havel 1986, 95), formal legalism played a crucial role in the process of transition after 1989. Indeed, formal legalism was such a highly relevant feature of the transition from authoritarianism to democracy that the opposition embraced a type of disobedience characterized not by violations of the law but by "sticking to it, practicing it publicly, challenging the powerholders to come to terms with the rules of a legal State in which citizens have rights" (Kis 1998, 336).

This legalism turned into the principle of the rule of law after 1989. The 1989 Constitution was adopted, as declared in its preamble, "with a view to promoting a peaceful political transition to a rule of law State implementing a multi-party system, parliamentary democracy, and a social market economy." The constitution further asserted that Hungary is a republic and an independent, democratic state governed by the rule of law (Article 2). This commitment to the rule of law was constitutive of the regime, and the specific content of this foundational principle was determined over time by the constitutional organs (first and foremost by the newly established Constitutional Court) through practice and interpretation.

It is possible to describe the rule of law simply in formal terms, but it is also possible to argue that the rule of law is a substantive requirement (Krygier 2012, 233). The Constitutional Court opted for a formalistic understanding of the rule of law. The court insisted that political intentions could only be implemented lawfully and within the framework of the Constitution – in contrast to the period before 1989, when the law was conceived as a merely political tool. In the court's phrase, a "revolution under the rule of law" took place in 1989. The revolutionary changes took root through a rather strict allegiance to all constitutional guarantees. By respecting constitutional limitations, Hungary's revolutionary changes would avoid crimes and other injustices normally wrought by revolutions on the premise that the actions are justified and permissible (Sólyom and Brunner 2000, 38–9). As Czarnota and Krygier put it, "The revolutionary part was that existing law would be taken seriously . . . . Those tensions between the formal demands of law and material justice allowed those revolutions to avoid the flaw at the heart of most previous revolutions, where the logic of righteous virtue and morality justified everything" (Czarnota and Krygier 2006, 328).

In Hungary, however, the court's concept of the rule of law went further than mere legalism. Case law confirmed that the rule of law had a fundamental value. The court identified "legal certainty" as a core element of the rule of law (Decision No. 9/1992), which required not only that the state's legal norms be unambiguous but also that legal institutions' operations be predictable. For this reason, procedural guarantees emerged as important features of the rule of law and included protection against retroactive laws and insistence on the passage of "reasonable time" before an adopted law's entry into force. In the court's interpretation, the rule of law also required that public authorities act in accordance with the law (Decision No. 56/1991). This rule-of-law concept led the court to conclude in questions concerning ex post facto criminal legislation that the formal rule of law has priority over the pursuit of substantive justice.

Retroactive Punishment: Rule of Law over Substantive Justice

In its landmark Decision No. 11/1992, the Constitutional Court annulled the law adopted on November 4, 1991, concerning the right to prosecute serious crimes committed between December 21, 1944, and May 2, 1990, that had not been prosecuted for political reasons. The law would have retroactively extended the statute of limitations and would have allowed for the prosecution of perpetrators of murder and torture in the aftermath of the 1956 Revolution against Soviet rule. The president of the republic did not promulgate the law; he petitioned for the preliminary review of its constitutionality. According to the president, the retroactive criminal law violated the principle of legal certainty by reason of vagueness and ambiguity in definition as well as the legal doctrine of *nullum crimen sine lege*. The president also criticized the law for recommencing the already expired statute of limitations (Kim 2013).

The case illustrated the relationship between the law of the preceding nondemocratic political systems and the rule of law ensured by the 1989 Constitution. The question the court had to answer was whether in judging the constitutionality of new laws intended to remedy the unconstitutional measures of the previous systems, one should consider the unique historical circumstances of the transition. The court argued that historical context, questions of justice, and related considerations are of extraneous significance in this matter. As the court famously put it, "Legal certainty based on formal and objective principles is more important than necessarily partial and subjective justice." (Decision No. 11/1992, III/4) Exemptions from the guarantees of criminal law (legal certainty, the prohibition of ex post facto law, *nullum crimen sine lege*, and the constitutional requirements of necessity and proportionality for the imposition of a criminal punishment) would be possible only if the legislature overtly disregarded these criminal law guarantees, which is against the principle of the rule of law. Thus, the court held that the law overstepped the limits of the state's criminal powers by providing for the reimposition of criminal punishability for offenses whose statutes of limitation had already expired. A statute of limitations would guarantee lawful accountability for criminal liability by imposing a temporal restriction on the exercise of the state's punitive powers. Failure to apprehend a criminal and dereliction of duties should be risks borne by the state. If a statute of limitations expired, a person would have a right to immunity from criminal punishment. In the court's view, the legislature's only constitutionally permitted discretion to interfere with a statute of limitations would be to enact a more lenient standard. However, legislation seeking the opposite goal would be unconstitutional (see also the chapter by Gábor Attila Tóth in this book).

The year 1993 was meant to be a turning point in the court's jurisprudence. In Decision No. 53/1993, the court examined a law adopted on February 16, 1993, pertaining to crimes committed during the 1956 Revolution. The president of the republic did not promulgate this law; in fact, he petitioned for a preliminary review of its constitutionality. The central question at hand was whether or not the crimes committed immediately after the 1956 Revolution were war crimes and crimes against humanity. The court, claiming that perpetrators were protected under Hungary's absolute prohibition on the retroactivity of domestic law, considered it possible to invoke generally accepted principles of international law – for instance, Common Article 3 of the Geneva Conventions – in order to prosecute people suspected of having committed serious crimes during the 1956 Revolution. The law was amended accordingly and promulgated as Law XC of 1993 on the Procedure Related to Crimes Committed during the 1956 Revolution and Struggle for Freedom. Shortly afterward, a handful of trials were held in Hungary. One of these involved a retired military officer, Captain János Korbely, who was charged with having shot and having ordered his 15-man squad to shoot at civilians while attempting to regain control of an insurgent-held police station two days after the government's introduction of martial law on October 26, 1956. The Budapest military public prosecutor indicted Korbely, and after a long procedure, the Military Bench of the Budapest Regional Court convicted him of having committed a crime against humanity consisting of the murder of more than one person. Korbely complained before the European Court of Human Rights that he had been prosecuted for an act that, when committed, had not been a crime. The European Court of Human Rights agreed, stating that whether or not the captain was guilty had to be assessed on the basis of the laws and their interpretation prevailing at the time of the acts (*Korbely v. Hungary*, No. 9174/02, Grand Chamber Judgment of September 19, 2008). And in light of the general international law applicable at the time, the victims were insurgents who had taken an active part in anti-state hostilities; therefore, they could not be regarded as noncombatants.

The trials of Korbely and other alleged actors involved in putting down the 1956 Revolution provided little or no sense of political justice for those who demanded substantive transitional-justice steps. More broadly, owing to the "complexity and in-comprehensibility of the legal disputes for the general public, the judgments drew little attention. The accused persons were mostly ill and old men" (Hack 2007, 270).

Lustration and Its Major Obstacle: The Former Agents' Right to Privacy

Instead of criminal prosecution, amnesty, or truth commissions (Méndez 2012, 1273), Hungary chose the truth-revelation procedure called lustration to deal with the sordid past of the state's former security apparatus.

A study on lustration identified three versions of this procedure: dismissal, exposure, and confession lustration (Choi and David 2012, 1172). The Hungarian version was exposure without dismissal (Hack 2007, 274). According to the Law XXIII of 1994 on Controlling Certain Persons in Important Positions (the Lustration Law), public officials who previously had worked as former personnel for the communist state's secret police as professional employees or operative contact persons and those who had passed on information to them as collaborators (agents) were confronted with evidence about their acts and could either be forced to step down or face public exposure of their misconduct (David 2011, 35). Just before its term ended, Hungary's first freely elected parliament adopted this law, which would thus be valid only for the subsequently elected parliaments. In addition, the scope of the law was limited because it covered only the past activities of the domestic political-repression organs of the Interior Ministry, not the foreign-intelligence and counterintelligence organs. Hungary's lustration law differed from neighboring countries' corresponding laws insofar as it neither declared past personnel ineligible for current office nor unveiled the defunct communist state's information-gathering system. Laws of greater severity were passed in the Czech Republic (Kosař 2008, 470) and Germany (Williams et al. 2007, 37).

Nevertheless, the Hungarian law required the screening of certain public officials and others occupying key positions in public life. The screening was aimed at determining whether or not these individuals had carried out activities on behalf of the communist state-security organs, had obtained data from these organs to facilitate pro-state decision-making, or had been members of the pro-Nazi Arrow Cross Party. If, in the course of the screening, an individual was found to fall under one of the previously mentioned categories, the results were to be publicized in the official gazette unless the given individual first resigned from his post. The person could resign before completion of the process, which would lead to the immediate termination of the screening process. A special committee, whose members were judges, carried out the screening. The individual under scrutiny could file a counterclaim with the court, but the proceedings would be conducted behind closed doors.

Very soon the Constitutional Court had an opportunity to determine the constitutionality of this law. In Decision No. 60/1994, the court emphasized that the constitutionality of the lustration law should not rest on the special circumstances of Hungary's transition to democracy, implying that the transition had been successful despite the absence of lustration-based personnel changes (Sadurski 1999, 18). The decision upheld most parts of the law but announced a balancing test for determining whether or not the data handling of the Lustration Law was consistent with the 1989 Constitution: the privacy rights of both the "victim," that is to say, the person kept under secret state surveillance, and the "perpetrator," that is, the professional employee or the agent of the state secret service (Apor and Horváth 2017, 105), had to be weighed against the public interest pertaining to the accessibility of information. Thus, the main clarification made by the court in this decision concerned the task of distinguishing personal information that would stay private from personal information that would become public. Already in Decisions Nos. 20/1990 and 15/1991, the court had interpreted the protection of personal data as a matter of individuals' right to self-determination, that is, as individuals' right to determine – or at least to receive clarification about – disclosure of their own personal data. After examining whether or not the law met these standards, the court held that opening various state records to the public did not entail that anyone could access any data contained in the records. The termination of secrecy surrounding some state records was acceptable only insofar as all persons concerned might get to know and dispose over their own personal data. Some of those data were of public interest, and the variable that made a screened person's data a matter of public interest was the public function that the person had fulfilled. Nevertheless, the court made it clear that public interest alone does not justify the state's restriction of people's right to informational self-determination, regardless of whether those people are under surveillance or are agents.

Later, Parliament tried to find a solution that would enable a lustration law to meet these standards. The Law LXVII of 1996 on Amending the Lustration Law secured for Hungarians the right to informational self-determination by giving them access to their past secret service files. For that purpose, the government set up a new institution called the Historical Archive Office, which would serve as a depository for documents of the former secret services not relevant to contemporary national-security services. Researchers could obtain documents on people kept under surveillance by Hungary's former security services, but in contrast to Germany for instance, the measure provided that the names of agents in each file should be blackened to protect their identities (Tomiuc 2002). The constitutionality of this amendment was tested before the Constitutional Court, which upheld the main provisions in Decision No. 23/1999, with the exception of the rule according to which the personal data of operative contact persons at the state secret service and agents enjoyed the highest level of protection and were thus subject to the most stringent restrictions on public access.

Lustration after 2000

Lustration became a topic of heated debate again when, in 2002, a conservative daily revealed that the then Socialist prime minister, Péter Medgyessy, had been a counterintelligence secret agent from 1977 until 1982. The prime minister argued that the legal regulations in force did not allow the naming of those formerly involved in counterintelligence activities. The government proposed changes to the laws on lustration and on secret-police files so that the public could better access all former secret-police archives and the files of all public personalities. Ultimately, the Law III of 2003 on the Disclosure of the Secret Service Activities of the Communist Regime and on the Establishment of the Historical Archive of the Hungarian State Security made accessible most but not all of the past secret-police files, and a civil committee ensured that files from these agencies would be transferred to an archive. The law aimed at achieving "informational compensation" of victims by ensuring a graduated system of access, which, depending on the status of the person seeking access (from the person under surveillance to the public at large), allowed for access to uncensored data or anonymized data (Láncos 2019, 393).

Two years later, on May 30, 2005, Parliament passed an amendment allowing anyone to access the personal and operative data of those professional employees, operative contact persons, and agents whose personal files were on deposit at the Historical Archive, regardless of whether or not those persons had been public figures. Following the East German model, the amendment would have allowed people to identify anyone who had informed on them. The president of the republic did not promulgate the amendment; instead, he petitioned for a preliminary review of the amendment's constitutionality. The court, in Decision No. 37/2005, found the amendment unconstitutional in that it "granted one-sided, unconditional and unrestricted priority" to the enforcement of the freedom of information. People who had been under surveillance may have access to the data necessary for identifying the perpetrators. Hence, full disclosure of the perpetrators' personal data was not necessary for the victims' adequate "informational compensation." According to the court, the data related to the activity of professional employees, operative contact persons, and agents are personal data, and such data might only be disclosed when the persons were participating in public service. In all other cases, the personal data of the perpetrators were under constitutional protection.

As in the case of retroactive punishments, interactions between Parliament and the Constitutional Court shaped how lustration in Hungary would deal with its recent dark past (Tóth 2007, 283). Although Parliament tried to broaden the scope of lustration gradually, the court rejected many of these initiatives. One of the main reasons for these rejections was the court's viewpoint on former perpetrators' privacy. According to the court, not only the personal data of former victims were worthy of strong constitutional protection, but so, too, were those of former perpetrators. The court did not acknowledge the assertion that data protection extends chiefly to people's private life, not to their public activities, particularly when these activities took place in support of an authoritarian state's domestic secret service apparatus (Tóth 2007, 285). Hence, in contrast to Germany and the Czech Republic (Kosař 2008; Letki 2002; Williams et al. 2007), Hungary has not systematically opened its secret service files. One explanation for this pattern is that no consensus exists among Hungary's political elite as regards the proper handling of lustration (Nalepa 2010, 78ff). There were intense political discussions on the scope of the targets of lustration. The political elite agreed that lustration should include public officials, but disagreements arose about the asserted need to vet a vast range of professions, from journalists to judges, from attorneys to clerics. Meanwhile, lists of doubtful origins have appeared from nowhere, claiming to identify former agents and other persons complicit in support for the former communist regime's secret police. Perhaps not surprisingly, politicians have used lustration to discredit their opponents (David 2011, 147–9). These incidents revealed deep flaws in Hungary's lustration procedure and were further indications that the post-authoritarian state was keeping important truths from the public, whether rightly or not.

II. Fracture of Democracy, Reappropriation of the Past: Transitional-Justice Measures in the 2011 Fundamental Law

Where is Hungary in the process of transitional justice? Is it over? Hungarian society is deeply divided in its opinions regarding this question. When was the transition concluded, if at all? Many Hungarians, mostly left-leaning liberals, think that the transition period, which began with the roundtable "resolution of 1989" (Ash 1989), with a reform from above in response to pressures for revolutions from below, ended in 2004, when the country joined the European Union. Others, mostly on the conservative end of the political spectrum, think that the transition has not yet concluded despite Hungary's accession to the EU. In general, those on the right have argued that two key players – the Hungarian Socialist Workers' Party, which was the then ruling party, and the liberal-democratic forces – entered into a political compromise that resulted in a thoroughly corrupt foundation for the 1989 republic. Thus, for the conservatives, the "revolution of 1989 was unfinished" (Elek 2009, 9–14). The right-wing Fidesz party, which came to power first in 1998 and later in 2010, claimed to be able to complete this "unfinished revolution." It has kept the issue of transitional justice on the agenda both to remedy the "original sin" (Czarnota 2007, 228) – that is, the negotiated transition – and to ensure justice. The narrative of the 1989 democratic regime's original sin is now engraved in the 2011 Fundamental Law. According to its narrative, 2010 was just as much of a revolutionary year as 1989 because of the landslide victory of the Fidesz party in 2010. However, this second transition shifted not from an authoritarian to a democratic order but vice versa. What happened?

By the middle of the first decade of the 21st century, with accession to the EU safely behind Hungary, the country's then governing socialist-liberal coalition faced several crises that shook its legitimacy. Prime Minister Ferenc Gyurcsány campaigned on the assertion that the Socialists had advocated democratic development in Hungary since 1945, when they had supported the Red Army's "liberation" of Hungary from the preceding "reactionary," conservative political system (Mark 2010, 21). He also identified his party's aspirations with Imre

Nagy, who, as prime minister and chairman of the Council of Ministers from October 24, 1956, to November 12, 1956, had fought in the 1956 Revolution for independence and democratic socialism (Mink 2008, 172–3). But a "tape scandal," in which Gyurcsány was recorded admitting that the wining socialist party had lied about the financial state of the country during its 2006 election campaign, led to violent street protests in September, 2016 (Tomiuc 2006). His enraged opponents occupied public spaces, demonstrated violently with a Soviet tank stolen from an open-air museum in Budapest, and organized protests weeks before the fiftieth anniversary of the 1956 Revolution. Fidesz, being the central opposition party, called for mass protests "in the spirit of 1956" (Mark 2010, 10) and used them as a means of invoking the past on behalf of the right. All these acts of resistance were attempts to identify the Gyurcsány government as the direct successor of those who had suppressed the revolutionaries in 1956. Shortly after the Fidesz-led protests, financial problems caused in part by Gyurcsány's leaked confession and in part by a burst housing bubble alongside the 2008 global economic crisis turned public opinion sharply against the Gyurcsány government. A combination of political crisis, collapsing state finances, and a global economic crisis that pushed Hungary into an IMF bailout made the electorate ready for a change in 2010 (for a more detailed explanation of these events, see Kis 2012, 11–20).

That year, Fidesz, with its satellite Christian Democratic Party, gained a supermajority in Parliament, opening the way for a profound shift in direction, even though the parties did not campaign on a platform of constitutional reform. In 2010 and 2011, a wholesale constitutional review of the 1989 Constitution occurred, and in 2011, Fidesz adopted the Fundamental Law. Those in power argued that the period of post-communist transformation should draw to a close, and for this reason, Hungary needed a new constitution that could provide a "foundation for the spiritual and intellectual renewal of Hungary" (Navracsics 2011, 1). Accordingly, the Fundamental Law has changed the characteristics of Hungarian constitutionalism. It breaks with the principles that guided the 1989 Constitution: republican government, democracy, the rule of law, and equal human rights (Tóth 2012). In their place are historical and religious considerations. The Fundamental Law, and especially its preamble titled National Avowal, expresses that the present Hungarian constitutionalism is based upon traditional Christian faith and that the sacred values of the Hungarian people are "God, homeland, family" (Kovács and Tóth 2011, 198). I address the Fundamental Law's appropriation of historical narratives since the historical references used by the Fundamental Law are particularly focusing on how Hungary has been dealing with its authoritarian past.

The Fundamental Law: Reappropriation of the Past

István Rév argued that "if memory constitutes identity, then it is history – that is, the writing of history – that establishes and reestablishes identity" (Rév 1995, 9). History cannot be described and explained in the way in which natural scientists describe the laws of nature. History is not a natural science; hence, as Isaiah Berlin reminds us, one cannot exclude moral categories and judgments from history (Berlin 1959, 267). But this does not mean that the writing of history is inevitably biased. The construction and reconstruction of history can be self-reflective as much as it can be false and misleading. When is it false or misleading? Rewriting history is so when it, in practice, creates an "apologetic relationship to one's own national past" and when "historical narratives are replaced by an ideological agenda and a sense of victimization" (Michnik 2009, 446).

The self-understanding of the Hungarian nation as a "victim of great powers" in the Fundamental Law is particularly telling. It depicts Hungarians as victims, stripped of two-thirds of their lands after World War I by the Treaty of Trianon and then occupied by Nazi Germany. The constitutional text asserts that Hungary had been a victim and not an ally of Hitler and portrays the Holocaust as an exclusively German crime. Moreover, the text claims that after World War II, Soviet troops invaded the country. Thus, according to the prevailing ideology of the Fundamental Law, the country was a victim of occupying foreign forces. Nevertheless, the constitutional text does not condemn the violence of both right and left equally; it demonizes the communist regime while curiously whitewashing the pro-Nazi regime. Although the National Avowal contains a sentence condemning "the inhuman crimes committed against the Hungarian nation and its citizens under the national socialist and the communist dictatorship," the rest of the constitution deals only with the "communist crimes." For instance, the Fundamental Law declares the "Communist constitution" of 1949 "invalid" because it was the basis for "tyrannical rule," and Article U deals only with the communist past. The National Avowal declares that the country lost its autonomy on March 19, 1944, when Nazi troops set foot upon Hungarian soil. This autonomy was restored on May 2, 1990, with the opening session of the first freely elected National Assembly. Thus, for example, the Fundamental Law denies that the Hungarian state played a decisive role in the tragedy of the Hungarian Jews during World War II. In the Fundamental Law's narrative, Hungary lost its sovereignty because foreign troops, whether German or Soviet, had occupied the country from 1944 until 1990.

In order to put history at the service of politics, the Orbán government set up museums such as the House of Terror, established under the first Orbán government (1998–2002) and characterized by Prime Minister Viktor Orbán himself as "the only honest part of facing up to our past" (HungarianTV2, February 24, 2003). The museum is in a building that served as political prison until 1956 and was designed by a film-set designer rather than authentically reconstructed by a museologist (Mark 2010, 247). It sees itself as a narrative museum that wishes to establish an exact interpretation of history. However, from this interpretation, the liberation narrative of the Red Army is absolutely absent, and Nazism and the Holocaust receive a milder treatment than does communism. Although the name of the museum, the House of Terror, would suggest that the memorial is dedicated to the victims of both totalitarian eras, "Fascism is employed only in so far as it has the capacity to demonize Communism by association" (Mark 2010,

76). Two rooms are devoted to the pro-Nazi Arrow Cross Party rule, but there is nothing about the Hungarian Jewish experience of terror, which centered on the deportation of approximately 600,000 Hungarian Jews for extermination long before this party came to power in Hungary.

Similarly, exhibits and memorials show the events that took place after the Nazi occupation of Hungary but not the path to the Holocaust. The third Orbán government (2014–8), in 2015, erected a controversial memorial dedicated to "all the victims" of the "German" occupation of Hungary. The memorial is composed of a tympanum with a bronze eagle, representing Nazi Germany, and below the eagle, a bronze statue of Archangel Gabriel, representing "innocent" Hungary. One of the eagle's talons is tagged 1944, the year of the invasion. Because of heavy protests by Hungarians against the statute plan, the government erected the memorial under the cover of darkness. Since then, the protests have evolved into a "living memorial," which is "not made of bronze and stone, but of the presence, thoughts and conversations of the citizens who now gather on Szabadság square every evening" (Zöldi 2014, 2).

The Fundamental Law's moral break with the communist regime involves rehabilitating the pre–World War II authoritarian one. The constitutional text connects the post-1989 Constitution era to the pre–World War II era, the Horthy period, in order to establish the "continuity of the nation." Miklós Horthy led a "national conservative" regime between World Wars I and II, introduced racial Jewish Laws in 1920, and later became a faithful ally to Hitler. The basis of his regime was mainly a self-professed "Christian middle class," a social group with traditionalist, anti-Bolshevist, and anti-Semitic sentiments, which strengthened their sympathies for Nazi Germany (Kis 2012, 17). Between 2011 and 2014, Hungary's most famous city square, called Kossuth Square, located in front of Parliament, underwent reconstruction aiming at restoring the urban space to its pre-1944 appearance. Today the square is a metaphor for how Hungary's current conservative government has reshaped historical memory. The organizers of the restoration removed three of the square's most celebrated statues: those of Attila József, "the proletarian poet"; Mihály Károlyi, a social democrat leader of the 1918 Republic; and Imre Nagy, prime minister during the 1956 Revolution. Today, marking the ideological preferences of Hungary's conservative government, the square boasts statues István Tisza, a prime minister before World War I; Gyula Andrássy, a conservative prime minister in the second half of the 19th century; and Ferenc Rákóczi, a leader of the uprising against the Hapsburgs. A monument commemorating the victims of a short-lived Hungarian Soviet Republic in 1919 replaces the Nagy statute. In addition, a 100-meter-long granite ramp, the Memorial of National Unity, was erected in 2020 to signify the hundred years that have gone by since the 1920 Treaty of Trianon, the World War I peace deal. On the ramp, the names of the almost 13,000 towns and villages of historical Hungary are engraved as they were used in the registry of 1913. The aim is to symbolize "national cohesion" that was divided by the Treaty of Trianon (Woods 2019, 1).

The chosen historical narrative is a potent mixture of elements from Hungary's history, including Hungary's "freedom fights" against the Ottoman empire, the

Hapsburgs and later the USSR (Magyar 2019, 4), and Hungary's role as a victim of the Allied powers. The regime finds its roots in Horthy's authoritarian regime by considering itself to be the heir of Horthy, which proves that, after 1989, the political right reemerged on the political scene without significantly distancing itself from its ideological and political heritage (Kis 2012, 18).

Article U: Transitional-Justice Measures in the Constitution

In 2013, the Fourth Amendment to the Fundamental Law included a new article, known as Article U. It addresses Hungary's "Communist past" by transforming the duty of memory into a constitutional demand that Hungarians, through the mechanism of transitional justice, confront the inhumane crimes of the country's communist dictatorship. Article U (1) condemns the communist past of Hungary; (2) calls for a truthful revelation of the operations of the communist dictatorship; (3) establishes the Committee of National Memory; (4) obliges former high-ranking members of the communist dictatorship to tolerate factual criticism of their actions; (5) allows for the reduction of their statutory pensions; (6–8) prolongs the statute of limitations for unprosecuted crimes perpetrated during the communist dictatorship; (9) rules out further compensation for the communist dictatorship's victims; and (10) provides for the transfer of documents to public archives. Whilst a full and detailed depiction of Article U would be beyond this chapter's scope, an overview of the article's significant elements is both useful and feasible here.

Article U(1) of the Fundamental Law reads that political organizations, having gained legal recognition during the democratic transition as legal successors of the Hungarian Socialist Workers' Party, continue to share the responsibility of their predecessors as beneficiaries of their unlawfully accumulated assets. This means that one of the left-wing political parties, the Hungarian Socialist Party, remains responsible for the wrongdoings of its legal predecessor, the Hungarian Socialist Workers' Party. The Socialist Party had been established in 1989, when the reform wing of the Socialist Workers' Party had split with the hard-line communist faction opposed to systemic change. According to the Fundamental Law, the Socialist Workers' Party is criminal in nature, and for political reasons, its "leaders" not only committed crimes but escaped prosecution as well. Article U(1) promotes the idea of "collective responsibility" and, in so doing, weakens any normal procedural effort to hold individual former perpetrators responsible for their concrete actions. The Venice Commission rightly notes that this provision, rather than establish any procedure permitting the examination of individual cases, uses vague criteria and terms ("holders of power," "leaders") to inculpate groups, not individuals, for past offenses (Venice Commission 2013, 8).

Article U(3) calls for Hungarians to confront their country's communist past and for a national committee tasked with documenting national memory in this regard. Accordingly, Law CCXVI of 2013 established the Committee of National Memory, which would investigate communist-era crimes and would allow victims of communist surveillance to identify and publicly reveal people who, acting as secret agents or informants, had spied on or reported on fellow citizens. This law does not entail the complete opening of all files, since the archives are accessible, in strictly limited ways, only to archive staff at the request of possible communist-era victims and to historians who have official backing for their research. In addition, democratic control over the committee is nonexistent; its members are appointed by ruling parties. Article U(10) provides that documents issued by the Hungarian Socialist Workers' Party, by its affiliated civil-society organizations, and by trade unions created during the communist dictatorship shall be state property and shall be deposited in public archives as are most current government files.

Article U(4) provides that the former communist leaders are public persons in respect to their past political actions and, as such, must tolerate public scrutiny and criticism except for falsehoods. The former communist leaders must also tolerate disclosure of personal information linked to their functions and actions. The problem with this provision is that it constitutes an irrefutable allegation of truth, which cannot be subject to evidence to the contrary. Furthermore, the public disclosure of the aforementioned personal information might contravene the presumption of innocence (Delpérée et al. 2016, 161).

Article U(5) provides grounds for reducing the pensions and other benefits of specific leaders of the communist dictatorship. Accordingly, Law CXII of 2012 allows the scrapping of "communist" pension allowances in the cases of people who "contributed to dismantling democracy between 1945 and 1949, or worked as secret agents, or played a role in crushing the 1956 Revolution, or held leading positions in the Communist Party or its youth arm." The provision likely contravenes property rights (Delpérée et al. 2016, 162) since it retroactively deprives the affected persons of their possession.

Article U: Intuitive Justice as a Political Tool

As mentioned in the first part of this chapter, one of the underlying values of Hungary's first two decades of liberal democracy was the country's commitment to the rule of law. Conversely, Article U elevates "society's sense of justice" above the rule of law. And contrary to the Constitutional Court's previous rule-of-law interpretation, Article U asserts that the Hungarian government shall ensure society's sense of justice by making possible the retroactive prosecution of politically motivated crimes committed and not prosecuted during the communist regime. Articles U(6) through U(8) relate to the tolling and interruption of the statute of limitations for specific serious crimes that Article U(1) implies are not time barred. This provision should be read together with the constitutional provision under which it is not against the principle of *nullum crimen sine lege* to prosecute or convict a person for an act that, when it was committed, was criminal according to the generally recognized rules of international law. Correspondingly, the Hungarian government has embraced retroactive prosecutions by adopting Law CCX of 2011 on the Punishability and the Exclusion of the Statute of Limitations of Crimes against Humanity and the Prosecution of Certain Crimes Committed During the

Communist Dictatorship. The law has been nicknamed "Lex Biszku" since the 94-year-old Béla Biszku, the interior minister of the early totalitarian period, was charged with multiple homicides and high treason under this law; his trial began in 2014, but he died during the proceedings. Article U contains further rules on the statute of limitations. Article U(7) provides that the statute of limitations would go back into effect on January 1, 2012 (when the Fundamental Law went into effect) if the statute of limitations had been in effect at the time of the criminal act but had expired before May 2, 1990 (when the first freely elected Parliament was formed). Article U(8) provides that, if the statute of limitations had tolled after May 2, 1990, the statute-of-limitations clock, which would start again on January 1, 2012, would cover only the period of time during which, prior to May 2, 1990, the statute of limitations had been in effect. As the reasoning explains, the extension of time for prosecutable cases covers only Hungary's communist era.

The Venice Commission examined Article U regarding how it treats the responsibility assignable to communist-era political organizations and their leaders as well as to successor organizations. Recalling Resolution 1481 (2006) of the Parliamentary Assembly of the Council of Europe on the Need for International Condemnation of Crimes of Totalitarian Communist Regimes, the Venice Commission acknowledged that Hungary was trying to come to terms with its communist past. However, the Venice Commission discussed whether or not Hungary should introduce the provisions on individual and collective responsibility even though more than twenty years had already passed since Hungary's transition to democracy and whether or not the country risked raising doubts about the actual goals of the constitutional provisions on transitional justice measures. As the Venice Commission put it, "Revenge should not prevail over protecting democracy" (Venice Commission 2013, 7).

One might imagine that the purpose of the unusually long Article U is to compensate the victims of the communist regime and to preserve their memory. That view would be in harmony with the European Union's commitment to transitional justice. The EU document titled "EU Policy Framework on Support to Transitional Justice" calls for the design and implementation of transitional justice to be based on a "victim-focused approach" (Foreign Affairs Council of the European Union 2015, 7). But Article U(9) specifically rules out any new laws that might provide compensation to individuals who suffered harm during the very period reexamined through these cases (Halmai 2015, 18). Article U(9) stipulates that law should not establish new legal grounds for compensation to individuals who were unlawfully deprived of their lives or freedom for political reasons and who suffered undue property damage by the state before May 2, 1990. Thus, while ostensibly rendering substantial justice to people who suffered under Hungary's communist regime was the aim, in reality Article U puts history at the service of politics. The constitutional text prescribes "required" interpretations of historical events for legislation, and the motivation behind this requirement is political revenge. In Hungary, conservative political groups are using the new politics of memory policy to settle scores with political rivals, first and foremost with socialist politicians.

Conclusion

Constitutions make a difference when a country addresses the consequences of its dark past. That is a lesson we can learn from the Hungarian experience. The 1989 Constitution's underlying principles served as guidelines for politicians' policy choices in the field of transitional justice: Ordinary law regulated questions of individual responsibility and limitation periods and was subject to constitutional review by the Constitutional Court. Therefore, under the 1989 Constitution, settling the past by assuming responsibility for current grievances was possible though limited. The Constitutional Court was trying to consolidate democracy through a series of judgments based upon the formal rule of law, which was incompatible with attempts by the parliament to introduce transitional-justice measures: retroactive punishment and lustration. Neither the prosecutions at the end of the very few criminal trials that took place nor the lustration law that, narrow in scope, was introduced late in the transition process could deliver justice. Unlike other countries in the region, such as Germany and the Czech Republic (Letki 2002, 550), Hungary has not revealed the names of secret-police collaborators from the totalitarian and authoritarian eras.

The 2011 Fundamental Law has failed to correct the errors or fill the significant long-standing voids that remained under the 1989 Constitution. In fact, the Fundamental Law has exacerbated these problems. It delegitimizes the Constitutional Court's heritage of transitional justice and directly regulates collective responsibility in general and the limitation period in particular, excluding effective constitutional review of given measures. Moreover, the Fundamental Law uses the task of "dealing with the past" as an excuse to appropriate history and imposes a specific historical narrative on Hungary by mythologizing historical facts. It is the realization of the official state policy that makes Hungarian involvement in the Nazi regime taboo and demonizes the communist regime. The constitutional text of the Fundamental Law follows the formula that after the Nazi occupation came the Soviet occupation – a formula that conveniently stigmatizes one of the main political rivals of Hungary's current governing majority. Therefore, the specific historical narrative found in the Fundamental Law functions more as a political "witch-hunt" (Michnik 2007) than as a sincere effort to acknowledge Hungary's painful past.

Although a significant part of the totalitarian past remains obscured in many countries, Hungary is the sole country in the East-Central European region where the constitution itself imposes on society a certain historical narrative that renders impossible any meaningful reconciliation with the past. This means that Hungary still has to wait to come to terms with the past in a way that makes sincere public historical self-examination possible.

References

Apor, Péter and Sándor Horváth. 2017. "Closing the Past – Opening the Future: Victims and Perpetrators of the Communist Regime in Hungary." In *Secret Agents and the Memory of Everyday Collaboration in Communist Eastern Europe*, 105–28. London-New York: Anthem Press.

Arato, Andrew and Jean Cohen. 1999. "Civil Society and the Public Sphere." In *Civil társadalom, forradalom és alkotmány/ Civil Society, Revolution, and Constitutions*, 118–48. Budapest: Új Mandátum.

Arato, Andrew and Zoltán Miklósi. 2010. "Constitution Making in Hungary 1989–1996." In *Framing the State in Times of Transition: Case Studies in Constitution Making*, edited by Miller, Laurel E. and Louis Aucoin, 350–90. Washington, DC: United States Institute for Peace.

Ash, Timothy Garton. 1989. "Revolution: The Springtime of Two Nations." *New York Review of Books.* June 15.

Berlin, Isaiah. 1959. "Historical Inevitability." In *The Philosophy of History in Our Time*, edited by Meyerhoff, H., 24–271. New York: Doubleday Anchor.

Choi, Susanne Yuk Ping and Roman David. 2012. "Lustration Systems and Trust: Evidence from Survey Experiments in the Czech Republic, Hungary, and Poland." *American Journal of Sociology* 117 (4): 1172–201.

Czarnota, Adam. 2007. *The Politics of the Lustration Law in Poland, 1989–2006.* https://is.muni.cz

Czarnota, Adam and Martin Krygier. 2006. "After Postcommunism: The Next Phase." *Annual Review of Law and Social Sciences* 2: 299–340.

David, R. 2011. *Lustration and Transitional Justice: Personnel Systems in the Czech Republic, Hungary, and Poland.* Philadelphia, PA: University of Pennsylvania Press.

Delpérée, Francis, Delvolvé, Pierre, and Eivind Smith. 2016. "Opinion on the Fourth Amendment to the Fundamental Law of Hungary." In *The Dilemmas of Drafting the Hungarian Fundamental Law*, edited by László Trócsányi, 154–62. Passau: Schenk.

Elek, István. 2009. *Rendszerváltoztatók húsz év után* (*System Changers after Twenty Years*). Budapest: HVG.

Foreign Affairs Council of the European Union. 2015. *The EU's Policy Framework on Support to Transitional Justice.* http://eeas.europa.eu/archives/docs/top_stories/pdf/the_eus_policy_framework_on_support_to_transitional_justice.pdf

The Fundamental Law of Hungary. 2011. The official English-language translation of the Fundamental Law is available at https://www.parlament.hu/documents/125505/138409/Fundamental+law/73811993-c377-428d-9808-ee03d6fb8178

Hack, Péter. 2007. "Transitional Justice." In *The Transformation of the Hungarian Legal Order 1985–2005*, edited by Jakab, András, Takács, Péter, and Alan Tatham, 266–80. Alphen an de Rijn: Kluwer Law International.

Halmai, Gábor. 2015. *The Role of Constitutionalism in Transitional Justice Processes in Central Europe.* www.eui.eu/Documents/DepartmentsCentres/Law/Professors/Halmai/Constitutions-and-TJ.pdf

Havel, Václav. 1986. "The Power of the Powerless." In *Living in Truth*, edited by Vladislav, J. London: Faber and Faber.

Huyse, Luc. 1995. "Justice after Transition: On the Choices Successor Elites Make in Dealing with the Past." *Law & Social Inquiry* 20 (winter): 51–78.

Kim, Dae Soon. 2013. *The Transition to Democracy in Hungary: Árpád Göncz and the Post-Communist Hungarian Presidency.* London: Routledge.

Kis, János. 1998. "Between Reform and Revolution." *East European Politics and Society* 12 (2): 300–89.

Kis, János. 2012. "From the 1989 Constitution to the 2011 Fundamental Law." In *Constitution for a Disunited Nation: On Hungary's 2011 Fundamental Law*, edited by Tóth, Gábor Attila, 1–24. New York-Budapest: CEU Press.

Kosař, David. 2008. "Lustration and Lapse of Time: 'Dealing with the Past' in the Czech Republic." *European Constitutional Law Review* 4: 460–87.

Kovács, Kriszta and Gábor Attila Tóth. 2011. "Hungary's Constitutional Transformation." *European Constitutional Law Review* 7: 183–203.

Kritz, Neil J., ed. 1995. *Transitional Justice: How Emerging Democracies Reckon with Former Regimes, Vol. I.* Washington, DC: United States Institute of Peace Press.

Krygier, Martin. 2012. "Rule of Law." In *The Oxford Handbook of Comparative Constitutional Law*, edited by Rosenfeld, Michel and András Sajó, 233–50. Oxford: Oxford University Press.

Láncos, Petra Lea. 2019. "Freedom of Information in Hungary: A Shifting Landscape." In *The Laws of Transparency in Action: A European Perspective*, edited by Dragos, Dacian C., Kovač Polonca, and Albert T. Marseille, 389–424. Cham, Switzerland: Palgrave Macmillan.

Letki, Natalia. 2002. "Lustration and Democratisation in East-Central Europe." *Europe-Asia Studies* 54 (4): 529–52.

Linz, J. Juan and Alfred Stepan. 1996. *Problems of Democratic Transition and Consolidation: Southern Europe, South-America and Post-Communist Europe.* Baltimore-London: The Johns Hopkins University Press.

Magyar, Beda. 2019. "Hungary Is Lost." *Zeit Online* 2019.04.09.

Mark, James. 2010. *The Unfinished Revolution. Making Sense of the Communist Past in Central-Eastern Europe.* New Haven-London: Yale University Press.

Méndez, Juan E. 2012. "Constitutionalism and Transitional Justice." In *The Oxford Handbook of Comparative Constitutional Law*, edited by Rosenfeld, Michel and András Sajó, 1270–86. Oxford: Oxford University Press.

Michnik, Adam. 2007. "The Polish Witch-Hunt." *New York Review of Books.* June 28.

Michnik, Adam. 2009. "The Trouble with History: Tradition – Imprisonment or Liberation?" *International Journal of Politics, Culture, and Society* 22 (4): 445–52.

Mink, András. 2008. "The Revisions of the 1956 Hungarian Revolution." In *Past in the Making: Historical Revisions in Central Europe after 1989*, edited by Kopeček Michal. Budapest: CEU Press.

Nalepa, Monika. 2010. *Skeletons in the Closet: Transitional Justice in Post-Communist Europe.* New York: Cambridge University Press.

Navracsics, Tibor. 2011. "A New Constitution for Hungary: Locking in the Values of 1989–1990 – 'Transition, at Last'." *The Wall Street Journal.* April 19.

Rév, István. 1995. "Introduction: Identity by History." *Representations* 49: 1–14.

Sadurski, Wojciech. 1999. *Postcommunist Constitutional Courts in Search of Political Legitimacy.* https://pdfs.semanticscholar.org

Sólyom, László and Georg Brunner. 2000. *Constitutional Judiciary in a New Democracy: The Hungarian Constitutional Court.* Ann Arbor: University of Michigan Press.

Tomiuc, Eugen. 2002. "Hungary: Government Proposes Further Opening of Communist-Era Files." *RadioFreeEurope, RadioLiberty.* rferl.org.

Tomiuc, Eugen. 2006. "Gyurcsany's Controversial Comments True to Form." *RadioFreeEurope, RadioLiberty*, rferl.org.

Tóth, Gábor Attila. 2007. "The Bitter Pills of Political Transition." In *The Transformation of the Hungarian Legal Order 1985–2005*, edited by Jakab, A., Takács, P., and Tatham, A., 281–86. Alphen an de Rijn: Kluwer Law International.

Tóth, Gábor Attila. 2012. *Constitution for a Disunited Nation: On Hungary's 2011 Fundamental Law*. Budapest: CEU Press.

Varga, András Zs. 2015. "Lustration: The Experience of Hungary." Venice Commission Report CDL-PI(2015)026.

Venice Commission. 2013. "On the Fourth Amendment of the Fundamental Law of Hungary." Venice Commission Report CDL-AD(2013)012, 720/213, Strasbourg.

Williams, Kieran, Brigid Fowler, and Aleks Szczerbiak. 2007. "Explaining Lustration in Central Europe: A 'Post-communist Politics' Approach." *Democratization* 12 (1): 22–43.

Woods, John. 2019. "Hungary to Erect Memorial of Trianon Peace Treaty for the 100th Anniversary in 2020." *DailyNewsHungary*. April 13.

Zöldi, Blanka. 2014. "In Budapest a Living Memorial Arises in the Shadow of a Dead One." *The Budapest Beacon*. August 19.

3 Constitutional Divergence and Transitional Justice in South Korea and Taiwan

Cheng-Yi Huang and Yi-Li Lee

1. Introduction

Both South Korea and Taiwan are among the countries in the third wave of democratization. Their journeys of transformation started in 1987: In that year, mass popular protests in the aptly named June Democratic Struggle prompted South Korean President Chun Doo-hwan (전두환) and his designated successor, Roh Tae-woo (노태우), to concede to demands for direct presidential elections and constitutional reform; and also in that year, Taiwan's longtime authoritarian party, the Kuomintang (KMT, i.e., the Chinese Nationalist Party), lifted the country's decades-old martial law. Both South Korea and Taiwan embraced peaceful revolution almost simultaneously, but they diverged significantly from each other regarding how they dealt with the political oppression of the past. During its first ten years after democratization, the National Assembly of South Korea passed special legislation to investigate the Gwangju Incident (or the May 18th Movement) and other political atrocities during the Cold War (Hanley 2014). In 1996, South Korean prosecutors brought charges against two generals turned president and other high-ranking officials. President Chun was sentenced to life and President Roh to seventeen years, though both were pardoned by President Kim Young-sam (김영삼) later in 1997. In Taiwan, by contrast, the KMT continued to rule for another thirteen years and only awarded monetary compensation to political victims, foregoing retrials and official investigations (Huang 2019). In 2016, almost thirty years after its foray into democracy, Taiwan's Legislative Yuan passed special legislation establishing two commissions to deal with transitional-justice policies. The commissions – made possible by the fact that the Democratic Progressive Party (DPP, the longtime opposition party) controlled both the legislature and the presidency for the first time – collected governmental archives, investigated political oppression, annulled unfair judgments, and demanded the return of unduly obtained KMT party assets (Huang 2021). Nevertheless, no major figures were held accountable for the atrocities that the state had committed during the KMT's authoritarian rule. The status of transitional justice in Taiwan has thus been described as "ten thousand victims without a single perpetrator" (Wu 2005, 91).

Although these two countries share some common characteristics of democratization, their historical and institutional backgrounds are idiosyncratic. As Tom

DOI: 10.4324/9780429505089-5

Ginsburg precisely pointed out, South Korea was a military dictatorship while Taiwan was a party-dominant state (Ginsburg 2003, 206). Likewise, the successor of the authoritarian regime in Taiwan, President Lee, enjoyed a longer presidential term than his South Korean counterpart, President Roh. It was not until Roh's departure from the presidency that the pro-democracy President Kim Young-sam seized the chance to pass special legislation addressing South Korea's recent authoritarian past. A third difference between the two countries concerns how their constitutional courts addressed the legacy of authoritarianism. The Taiwanese Constitutional Court in the early 1990s rejected any retrials of or criminal investigations into certain political cases. By contrast, the South Korean Constitutional Court, though reluctant at first, eventually offered its full-fledged support to President Kim's special legislation in 1996. These are only a few of the differences between South Korea and Taiwan regarding the timing and scale of their transitional justice. In the chapter that follows, we first briefly introduce transitional justice in South Korea and Taiwan. We then focus on the transitional-justice roles of the constitutional courts in both countries from three perspectives: legal stability, the legality of authoritarian law, and the legitimacy of authoritarian rule. By comparing the two courts from these three perspectives, we elaborate on both the structural origins of the two courts' differences and their implications for transitional justice. We argue that the decisions of each constitutional court have reflected the relationship between the judiciary and the newly established democracy, be it South Korea or Taiwan. In other words, each court was embedded in a battleground of political change after democratization. As Ruti Teitel cogently unfolds the issue, law not only reflects "political circumstances . . . but itself structures the transition" from authoritarianism to democracy: Courts' decisions regarding transitional justice represent "a way both to delegitimate the past political regime and to legitimate its successor by structuring the political opposition within the democratizing order" (Teitel 2000, 6).

2. Correcting Historical Wrongs and Engineering Transitional Justice: The Role of South Korea's Constitutional Court

South Korea evolved from an authoritarian regime into a democratic state in the late 1980s, following a series of public protests and political negotiations. At that time, unresolved disputes concerning authoritarian-era human rights violations gained widespread attention in South Korea. Consecutive democratic governments undertook various transitional-justice measures to identify perpetrators for prosecution and to compensate victims. The new democratic atmosphere therefore required that the courts manage transitional-justice lawsuits.

2.1. Background of Past Human Rights Violations in South Korea

Like other nations in the third wave of democratization, South Korea experienced massive human rights violations under its authoritarian regimes until democratic elections were held in 1987. Torture, enforced disappearances, extrajudicial killings, and mass executions happened under the country's nearly forty years of authoritarian rule, but so, too, did oppressive emergency decrees and legislation. This legislation violated the civil and political rights secured in the Korean Constitution, which dated back to 1987. The history of human rights violations in South Korea can be divided into three phases: the Jeju 4.3 Incident under the US occupation, the Korean War, and the authoritarian regimes, many of which were military and were presided over by a series of authoritarian rulers, including Park Chung-hee (박정희, 1961–79) and Chun Doo-hwan (1979–88).

2.1.1. Under the US Occupation: The Jeju 4.3 Incident

Toward the end of the Pacific War (the Second World War), in August 1945, Japan offered to surrender upon the condition that the emperor would be exempt from war trials and that he would remain the ceremonial head of state (Kim 2009). Immediately after the surrender of Japan, US armed forces arrived on the Korean Peninsula and set up a military government amid escalating tensions between the United States and the Soviet Union. The US Army Military Government in Korea (hereinafter USAMGIK) occupied and essentially governed the southern portion of the peninsula until the establishment of the South Korean government in 1948 (Kim 2014). The Soviet Union expanded its authority in the northern portion of the peninsula and backed North Korean authorities led by Kim Il Sung in their efforts to establish a communist regime. Political conflicts between leftists and rightists triggered the division between the North and South (Baik 2013).

Following these events, the USAMGIK implemented several drastic measures to repress any actions that appeared to favor socialism, communism, or progressive movements for an independent Korean nation. Political tension between the left and right wings on the Korean Peninsula was an especially strong factor affecting the political climate on Jeju Island, the largest island belonging to the Korean Peninsula, which a group of organized leftists, backed by the Soviet Union, sought to unify before the arrival of the US military (Merril 1980). Constantly hindered by the USAMGIK and rightists (Chang 2009), Korean leftists plotted against their oppressors. On April 3, 1948, members of the Workers' Party of South Korea assembled 350 armed guerillas to assault police stations on Jeju Island. The aim of the guerillas was to protest the escalating oppression by the USAMGIK. The guerillas' efforts, though ultimately unsuccessful, convinced the USAMGIK to consider negotiations with the leftists (Baik 2005).

Nevertheless, government oppression grew more severe when Syngman Rhee (이승만) was elected president of South Korea's newly formed government on August 15, 1948 (Kim 2009). The central government dispatched troops to stop leftist disturbances (Chun and Han 2017), and martial law was proclaimed on November 17, 1948 (Baik 2005). The armed conflict between domestic communists and right-wing South Korean police and paramilitary forces, backed by US military forces, lasted for several years after the Korean War, ending only with a formal termination of hostilities on September 21, 1954 (Baik 2012). The South Korean government's violent military response to communist resistance was effective yet devastating: The overall number of individuals murdered, arrested, tortured, or abducted during and after the Jeju 4.3 Incident is estimated to be between 25,000 and 30,000 (Jeju 4.3 Peace Foundation 2014).

2.1.2. The Korean War

On June 25, 1950, North Korean forces, known formally as the Korean People's Army, with support from China and the Soviet Union, crossed the 38th parallel to invade noncommunist South Korea, which was backed by the US military (Kim 2010). According to the final report of the Truth and Reconciliation Commission of South Korea (2010), the nationwide systematic killing of civilians committed by all parties in the war can be divided into four categories:

i. The first category is the execution of civilians or political dissidents by Syngman Rhee's government under the banner of "anti-communism." The case of the National Guidance Alliance serves as an example of this oppression. When Syngman Rhee came to power in 1948, his administration passed several laws targeting communist activities. For example, the National Security Law (국가보안법) was passed by the South Korean National Assembly in 1949 (Cho 1997). This law had permitted authoritarian regimes to impose draconian sanctions on political dissenters. Later, the Rhee government created the National Guidance Alliance, which acted as a "re-education" program for suspected communist sympathizers. The Alliance's central purpose was to eradicate leftist political activity in the country, and under the supervision of the Ministry of Justice, around 350,000 political dissidents were forced to join it (Kim 2005). When communist forces in the north attacked the south, the Rhee administration feared that political dissidents would collaborate with the invading forces and thus permitted the mass execution of detained persons without due process (Kim 2005). Military and police across the country executed the "members" of the Alliance (Presidential Truth Commission on Suspicious Deaths 2004). According to a report published by the Truth and Reconciliation Commission (2010), an estimated 1,800 members of the National Guidance Alliance were executed in different prisons without due process.
ii. The second category of the nationwide systematic killing of civilians covers the arrest and execution of suspicious individuals who, without any concrete evidence, were accused of having cooperated with North Korea. During the course of the Korean War, military forces on both sides resorted to executing civilians as a deterrence measure. As in most situations, when the Korean People's Army retreated from its occupied areas, the South Korean military took them over and killed some civilians who were accused of having cooperated with the communist occupiers (Kim 2010). For instance, in the province of Gyeonggi (경기), South Korean police executed around 240 civilians without due process because they were accused of collaboration with the enemy (Truth and Reconciliation Commission of South Korea 2010).

iii. The third category of civilian killings involves the military operations launched by the South Korean government against guerrilla forces sympathetic to the North Korean government. The operation resulted in massive civilian casualties. The Geochang Incident (거창사건) exemplifies these violent government actions. In February 1951, the 11th Army of South Korea was searching for guerrillas hiding in mountainous regions. To prevent local residents from aiding the guerillas, South Korean army leaders ordered the killing, burning, and looting of nearby civilians. Thousands of civilians died as a result of these operations (Kim 2002).
iv. The fourth category was the US Air Force's indiscriminate bombing of civilians during the Korean War. Such was the case in the No Gun Ri Massacre (노근리사건), when, on July 26, 1950, the US military, including military aircraft, attacked and killed numerous South Korean refugees from the village of No Gun Ri (Truth and Reconciliation Commission of South Korea 2010).

2.1.3. The Authoritarian Regimes of South Korea

After the Korean War, President Syngman Rhee remained in power for several years. However, in 1960, college students and labor groups protesting his government's prolonged corruption and election fraud staged the April Revolution, which forced him to resign on April 19 (Stone 1974; Kim 1996). Shortly thereafter, on August 13, 1960, Yun Bo-seon (윤보선) was elected president (Yoon 1988). At the same time, Chang Myon (장면) was appointed prime minister on the promise that he would enforce parliamentary democracy. However, the fledgling democracy was soon replaced by a group of military elites headed by Park Chung-hee in May 1961, with economic decline, social disorder, and political instability being the main reasons for the military takeover (Oh 1999).

Park Chung-hee's successful coup led to the imposition of martial law throughout the country (Lee 1974). The Supreme Council for National Reconstruction consolidated Park's power by dissolving all political parties and civic organizations under the Law Concerning Registration of Social Organizations (사회단체등록에관한법률) (Roehrig 2002). The Law on the National Movement for National Reconstruction (재건국민운동에관한법률) permitted the Park administration to carry out wide-scale arrests of suspected anti-government agitators, including of progressives and proponents of peninsular unification (Goedde 2008). With the passage of the Anti-Communist Act (반공법) of 1961, suppression of communist activities escalated. The act prohibited any and all criticism of the Park administration, declaring such behavior to be pro-communist. The government further cemented its hold on power by fully exploiting a series of repressive laws, such as the Law on Punishment of Specified Crimes (폭력행위 등 처벌에 관한 법률), and did so on the pretexts of fighting communism and of supporting national security and economic development (Goedde 2008). The Social Safety Law (사회안전법) empowered the government's oppression of suspected dissidents (Presidential Truth Commission on Suspicious Deaths 2004). The

Supreme Council for National Reconstruction established the Korean Central Intelligence Agency to monitor anti-government activities and arrest, imprison, or torture persons without due process (Presidential Truth Commission on Suspicious Deaths 2004). The oppressive tactics of the Park government targeted not just communist activities but democratic movements as well. For example, from 1964 to 1965, domestic disquiet surrounding peace talks between South Korea and Japan led the South Korean military, on Park's orders, to shut down Yonsei and Korea Universities and to arrest students and professors (Lee 1974).

Park's influence grew after the enactment of the Yushin Constitution (유신 헌법) in 1972, at which point the government's suppression of democratic movements intensified (Lee 1973; Kim 2013c). From 1974 to 1975, Park issued a number of emergency orders prohibiting the establishment of political organizations and criminalizing all activities deemed to be anti-government (Han 1975). For example, Emergency Decree No. 1 prohibited all actions that denied, opposed, or defamed the Constitution and prohibited any proposed amendments to the Constitution. Emergency Decree No. 2 established an emergency military court and an appeals court under the Ministry of National Defense, both of which had the power to hear cases purported to involve violations of the emergency orders. Emergency Decree No. 9 punished all individuals linked to antigovernment activities in universities (Kim 1978). About 1,100 people are said to have been convicted by the court for violations of the emergency orders (Kim 2013c).

On December 12, 1979, Park was assassinated by Kim Jae-gyu (김재규), one of his close associates and chief of the Korean Central Intelligence Agency (West 1997). Park's death spelled the end of his regime. Immediately following the assassination, Chun Doo-hwan seized power in a coup d'état. On May 31, 1980, Chun oversaw the establishment of the Special Committee for National Security Measures, which was to monitor all national plans implemented by the government (Lee 1974). Like the Park government, the Chun government quashed internal democratic movements by any means necessary: Numerous political leaders, human rights activists, scholars, and journalists were arrested, tortured, or even made to disappear through various repressive measures, including such legislations as the Political Climate Renovation Law (정치풍토쇄신법) and the Social Protection Act (사회보호법) (Kim 2001). Under the military dictatorship of Chun Doo-hwan, state-sponsored and systematic violence, torture, and other human rights violations were widespread. Among those violations, the Gwangju Incident drew nationwide attention. The controversial actions took place between May 18 and May 27, 1980, when demonstrators in Gwangju City (광주광역시) protested against dictator Chun Doo-hwan and government violence despite the imposition of martial law on the entire nation. The troops were finally dispatched to the city, leading to a situation in which soldiers killed or seriously injured 600 people. The Chun Doo-hwan government not only severely violated the basic civil and political rights of the people but also intensively silenced the media. For example, the National Assembly of South Korea in 1980 passed the Basic Press Act (언론기본법), which severely restricted journalistic freedoms (Sa 2009). To control public opinion, the Chun government implemented a "purification campaign," the central aim of which was to force a reorganization of the media on terms that glorified the government (Truth and Reconciliation Commission of South Korea 2010).

2.2. *Diverse Transitional-Justice Measures*

In the late 1980s, South Korea underwent large-scale political, social, and economic reforms. Democratization gave the country a more liberal outlook and created an extensively revised constitution in 1987 (Yeh and Chang 2011). During South Korea's dynamic transition to democracy, the abuses of state power and the violations of human rights that had occurred under the oppressive regimes drew widespread national attention. To address the violations, the South Korean government implemented various transitional-justice mechanisms, including criminal trials, truth commissions, compensation plans, retrials, and rehabilitation of victims' legacies. For example, two ex-presidents, Chun Doo-hwan and Roh Tae-woo, were sent to jail in 1997 after a two-year trial in South Korean courts. Additionally, several truth commissions, such as the Truth and Reconciliation Commission of South Korea, were formed to investigate human rights violations (Truth and Reconciliation Commission of South Korea 2010). Citing the results of their investigation, the commission recommended that those who had been falsely convicted should have an opportunity for retrial. In addition, the National Assembly passed several laws compensating victims and restoring their honor.

2.2.1. *Addressing Abuses under the US Occupation: The Jeju 4.3 Incident*

The South Korean government has sought to compensate the victims of the Jeju 4.3 Incident and their families. One special committee that was set up to investigate the incident was established by order of President Kim Young-sam in March 1993 (Kim 2009). By March 1998, when Kim Dae-jung (김대중) was elected president, efforts to compensate the victims of the Jeju 4.3 Incident had gained wide support among the South Korean public. The National Commission for the Investigation of the Truth about the Jeju 4.3 Incident was created in 2000, after the Korean National Assembly in 1999 had passed the Special Law for the Investigation of the Jeju 4.3 Incident and Recovering the Honor of Victims (제주4 · 3사건 진상규명 및 희생자 명예회복에 관한 특별법). Article 2(1) of the Special Law defined the incident as "the armed conflicts against residents on Jeju Island from March 1, 1947 to April 3, 1948." Authorized by this special law, the new commission was empowered to investigate and reveal the truth, to identify victims, and to restore their honor (Jeju 4.3 Peace Foundation 2014).

The special law mandated the commission to conclude the investigation within two years and to release its final report at some point during the subsequent six months. The final report was issued in October 1993 and confirmed that the government of Syngman Rhee bore ultimate responsibility for the incident's gross human rights violations, which included the killing of civilians by government troops (Jeju 4.3 Peace Foundation 2014). The report estimated the number of victims of the Jeju 4.3 Incident to be between 24,000 and 30,000 (Jeju 4.3 Peace Foundation 2014). Children, the elderly, and women accounted for 33% of the victims. The report further recommended that the government should apologize to the victims and their families and should make additional compensation available to victims and their families (Jeju 4.3 Peace Foundation 2014). In accordance with the report's recommendations, President Roh Moo-hyun (노무현) made an official apology to the victims and their families on behalf of the government on October 31, 2003 (Kim 2009; Baik 2005).

2.2.2. Addressing Massacres during the Korean War

Before democratization, early attempts to address civilian massacres in South Korea met with various hurdles. A breakthrough emerged when President Kim Young-sam took power in 1993. Because much of his support came from Gyeongsang Province (경상도) (Kim 2013a), President Kim promised to investigate the Geochang Incident, which had occurred there. At the same time, similar events that had taken place during the Korean War came under investigation. On January 5, 1996, the Review Committee for Restoring Honor for Victims of Geochang and Other Massacres was established under the Act for Restoring Honor for Victims of Geochang and Other Massacres (거창사건등 관련자의 명예회복에 관한 특별조치법) (Kim 2013a). After the investigation, the committee announced that the Geochang Incident had claimed over 700 victims (Kim 2013a). The committee further pointed out that all the victims were innocents caught up in wartime violence. Therefore, according to the committee, the government should rewrite the previously whitewashed history of the incident, restore the reputations of the victims, preserve the cemetery where the victims are now buried, hold a national memorial ceremony, and build a memorial for the incident. However, the committee did not have the power to accept claims for compensation, and the victims' compensation lawsuit against the state was unsuccessful (Wolman 2013; Baik 2013).

An even more comprehensive set of investigations and compensatory plans was undertaken when the Truth and Reconciliation Commission of Korea was established in 2005 (Kim 2013a). Authorized by the Framework Act on Clearing Up Past Incidents for Truth and Reconciliation (진실・화해를 위한 과거사정리 기본법), the Truth and Reconciliation Commission of Korea was mandated to investigate domestic and overseas independence movements during Japanese rule, civilian massacres during the Korean War, and human rights violations by the governments under South Korea's military dictatorships (Kim 2013a). The commission's final report, published in 2010, recommended the enactment of special laws to compensate the victims of the Korean War, excavate and bury victims, and establish a foundation to study past events. The report also declared that the acts carried out by the parties in the Korean War constituted acts of torture, as laid out in Article 2 of the Convention on the Prevention and Punishment of the Crime of Genocide. Moreover, in accordance with the relevant provisions of the 1968 Convention on the Non-Applicability of Statutory Limitation to War Crimes and Crimes against Humanity and the 1998 Rome Statute of the International Criminal Court, no statute of limitations applies to the criminal acts under investigation (Nathan and Park 2013).

2.2.3. Addressing Human Rights Violations under South Korea's Authoritarian Regimes

After South Korea embarked on democratization, vibrant civil movements sought truth and justice for the victims of the Gwangju Incident (Cho 2013). On December 21, 1995, the National Assembly, supported by President Kim Young-sam, passed the Special Act on the May 18th Democratic Movement Etc. (5・18 민주화운동 관련자 보상 등에 관한 법률): The act, which suspended the statute of limitations, was upheld by the Constitutional Court of South Korea. Later, the Korean Supreme Court held that the Special Act could legally suspend the statute of limitations for crimes against the constitutional order (Han 2005; Cho 2013). Hence, the government sought to prosecute perpetrators of crimes linked to the Gwangju Incident. One year later, the Supreme Court upheld the convictions of Presidents Chun and Roh for treason and for ordering murders for the purpose of treason, as discussed in the following detail (Cho 2007; Hwang 1997).

In addition to imposing criminal sanctions on perpetrators of human rights abuses, post-democratization South Korean governments have made frequent use of truth commissions that address systematic abuses in authoritarian contexts (Kim 2021). For example, the Review Committee for Restoring the Honor of Participants in the Democratization Movement and for Providing Compensation to Them was created on January 15, 2000, after the passage of the Act for Restoring the Honor of Participants in the Democratization Movement and for Providing Compensation to Them (민주화운동 관련자 명예회복 및 보상 등에 관한 법률) (Cho 2013; Wolman 2013). This act mandated that the commission identify victims and offer them compensation. Another well-known commission is the Presidential Truth Commission on Suspicious Deaths, which was established, in 2000, by the Special Act to Find the Truth on Suspicious Deaths (의문사진상규명에 관한특별법) (Hayner 2010). This commission was mandated to investigate the suspicious deaths of South Korean citizens, purportedly carried out by government agents, directly or indirectly, between 1975 and 1987 (Hong 2002; Kim 2013b). The final report of the commission recommended that the government further investigate suspicious deaths, officially apologize to victims and the general public, prosecute perpetrators, restore victims' honor, undertake commemorative projects, prohibit the destruction of government records, document the suffering of bereaved family members in detail, and initiate criminal and military reforms to prevent future abuse of government power (Presidential Truth Commission on Suspicious Deaths 2004).

Following the achievements of the previous commissions, the Truth and Reconciliation Commission of South Korea was established in 2005 with widespread support from South Koreans generally (Kim 2012). Stemming from the 2005

Framework Act on Clearing Up Past Incidents for Truth and Reconciliation, the commission screened individual applications for further investigation, recommended policies to relevant government branches, and helped establish further research institutes addressing past history (Kim 2013a; Baik 2013). The commission made 16 recommendations in its final report. Those recommendations can be divided into four categories: the punishment of perpetrators, the compensation of victims, the opening of archives, and the promotion of reconciliation and the prevention of future human rights violations (Nathan and Park 2013). In May 2020, the Korean National Assembly passed the Transitional Justice Law for Truth and Reconciliation (진실 · 화해를 위한 과거사정리 기본법 시행령). This law reopened the work of the Truth and Reconciliation Commission, offering two more years for victims and their families to submit their petitions and creating more time for the commission to investigate the cases (Ko 2021).

2.3. Leading Decisions of the Constitutional Court of South Korea

South Korea experienced authoritarian rule under dictatorial regimes for decades. During this time, the courts functioned as pawns of the authoritarian regimes (Kim 2019). The constitutional adjudication system had a notorious reputation at the time, and many South Koreans expressed distrust for the Supreme Court. Eventually, in 1988, all political parties agreed to establish an independent constitutional court to adjudicate on all constitutional matters (Chon 2015; Park 2008). Since its establishment, the South Korean Constitutional Court has played an active role in building a new constitutional order and in protecting the fundamental human rights of the people (Ginsburg 2014; Hahm 2018; Chang and Lee 2018). The Constitutional Court was required to focus specifically on three main transitional-justice issues: the criminal prosecution of former authoritarian leaders who were involved in human rights abuses, the invalidation of authoritarian laws through the elimination of the vestiges of authoritarian legacies, and the adjudication of the former repressive regimes' emergency orders regarding their constitutionality and legitimacy.

2.3.1. Challenging the Stability of Authoritarian Regimes

During the period of transition, most emerging democracies experience difficulty in maintaining political stability, as they are usually fragile and politically and socially vulnerable (Kritz 1995; Teitel 1997). Any official effort to prosecute former political leaders or delegitimize previous regimes presents the likelihood of political conflict and may undermine the country's pursuit of liberal democracy (Ackerman 1992; Huntington 1993; Chang and Lee 2016). These efforts often produce many legal disputes that require judicial solutions. Courts are usually tasked with mediating deeply opposing interests between political stability and justice. For developing democracies, this challenge is daunting.

The Constitutional Court of South Korea faced this challenge when the justices of the court were asked to adjudicate on the criminal responsibility of various individuals for their alleged involvement in the infamous 1980 Gwangju Incident, which concerned not only military officers but also former presidents Chun and Roh, who had been military generals prior to seizing the presidency (Cho 2007). On July 29, 1993, surviving victims of the Gwangju Incident demanded that public prosecutors initiate criminal proceedings against the suspects (Oh 1997; Hwang 1997). However, the Seoul District Prosecutor's Office decided not to indict the accused leaders on the charges of treason and mutiny. Disappointed with this decision, activists lodged a complaint before the Constitutional Court on November 24, 1994. After evaluating the relevant facts, the court held that the decision not to prosecute had not been arbitrary. The court decided that the charge of treason lacked legal interests because the period of limitations for instituting the charge had expired. However, the court emphasized that it had power to review the charge of mutiny since its period of limitations was suspended. Following the review, the court reasoned that the pivotal roles of the defendants in establishing the national order and constitutional foundation justified their exemption from prosecution on the charge of mutiny.

Subsequently, the Seoul District Public Prosecutor's Office rejected a second petition to prosecute those who were involved in the Gwangju massacre. The main legal ground for not prosecuting Chun Doo-hwan and other military leaders was that they had executed a successful coup and had formed a new constitutional order – one that was not subject to judicial review (Oh 1997; Hwang 1997). This decision upset the public and victims' rights groups; hence, surviving victims petitioned the Constitutional Court for a review of the prosecutorial decision. By December 15, 1995, the court had not issued a decision because the complaint had been withdrawn. However, before the court terminated the proceedings, a dissenting opinion offered a double-edged solution on the dilemma (May 18 Incident Non-institution of Prosecution Decision case, 7–2 KCCR 697, 95Hun-Ma221, etc.):

> Even if a successful coup makes it practically impossible to punish the perpetrators during their incumbency, they can always be punished whenever the constitutional institutions recover their proper function and thereby regain de facto power to punish them. However, if treasonous activities were the means to create a democratic civil state and to restore the people's sovereignty previously suppressed and excluded under a feudal monarchy or despotism, they can be justified before or after the fact by the will of all the people. Therefore, a successful [act of] treason becomes not punishable under the exceptional circumstances that the people have ratified it through free expressions of their sovereign wills.
>
> In this case, the treasonous acts of the two former Presidents were neither justified by the circumstances nor were ratified by free expressions of the people (denying legitimacy of the treasonous government does not mean denying the legal effects of all of its acts). The prosecutor's non-institution of prosecution decision for reason of immunity of a successful coup engenders misunderstanding of the ideals of the Constitution and the criminal jurisprudence of treason.

The opinion made an important statement that a successful coup d'état is subject to judicial review. Later, on December 21, 1995, the National Assembly passed the previously mentioned Special Act on the May 18th Democratic Movement Etc. The Special Act suspended the statute of limitations for the crimes against constitutional order, particularly crimes that had been committed on or around December 12, 1979, and May 18, 1980. The act stipulated that limitation period ceased to run during the presidencies of Chun and Roh, in which "there existed obstacles for the State to institute prosecution." The act also allowed the Constitutional Court to review the prosecutorial disposition of cases where a prosecutor had declined to prosecute. However, the act's constitutionality was challenged before the Constitutional Court because the suspension of the statute of limitations violated Article 13(1) of the Constitution of South Korea, which prohibits retroactive legislation. The act was also alleged to constitute a case-specific law that violated the principle of equality in Article 11 of the Constitution of South Korea. However, the Constitutional Court held that the case-specific legislation did not violate Article 11 of the Constitution. The court reasoned that case-specific legislation is not inherently unconstitutional if its discriminatory provisions can be justified with reasons. In the view of the court, any discrimination leveled at accused individuals on the basis of the May 18th Democratic Movement Act can be justified considering the illegalities they committed when they came to power. Acknowledging the mandate both to rectify the past and to pave a constitutionally and historically sound path forward, the court held that this case-specific legislation is constitutional. The court also held that Article 2(1) of the act, which suspended the application of the statute of limitations for the crimes that took place on or around December 12, 1979, and May 18, 1980, did not violate Article 13(1) of the Constitution.

After the Constitutional Court rendered its decision based on the provisions of the Special Act in 1996, the Korean Supreme Court affirmed the defendants' convictions for treason and killing on April 17, 1997. The Supreme Court held that the Special Act lawfully suspended the statute of limitations for crimes against the constitutional order, and the prosecution was instituted before the period expired. Finally, Chun was sentenced to life imprisonment, and Roh was imprisoned for seventeen years. Other military leaders received prison sentences ranging from three and a half to eight years. In addition, acting in accordance with Article 7 of the Special Act, the government retracted decorations given to the military leaders. The intertwined series of judicial decisions to punish the perpetrators of the coup and the massacre demonstrate that the judiciary was prepared to strip the previous authoritarian regimes of any legitimacy.

2.3.2. Invalidating Authoritarian Laws

One of the major legal tools used by authoritarian regimes to control society and consolidate power is the enactment of repressive legislation. Before democratization came to South Korea in the late 1980s, the country's authoritarian regimes had enacted many restrictive laws either suspending fundamental constitutional rights or destroying democratic values. South Korea initiated its democratization through political negotiations between the old ruling party (the Democratic Justice Party), led by Roh Tae-woo, and the newly created opposition party (the Reunification Democratic Party). Following the negotiated agreement, the government created an extensively revised constitution (the 1988 Constitution of the Sixth Republic) and proceeded to launch numerous legal and political reforms. The establishment of a democratic regime, including the Constitutional Court of South Korea, enabled South Korea to challenge the decidedly non-democratic laws and legacies that had prevailed under the countries' authoritarian regimes (Ginsburg 2014). For example, the Constitutional Court, in the *Preventive Detention Case* (1989), reviewed the constitutionality of Article 5 of the former Social Protection Act, which the National Security Emergency Legislative Council had enacted during the Fifth Republic, led by Chun Doo-hwan. Specifically, Article 5, which imposed mandatory preventive confinement on defendants found guilty of crimes, was challenged for violating the principle of *nulla poena sine lege*, prescribed in Article 12 of the Constitution. The court decided that the principle was violated specifically by Article 5(1) of the act because it set out the legal requirements for preventive confinement but did not cover recidivism. The court also noted that Article 20(1) of the act, which required judges to make preventive confinement decisions in cases involving recidivism, violated the right to a fair trial and was thus unconstitutional.

Subsequently, the court considered the constitutionality of the Act on the Special Measures for the Punishment of Persons Involved in Anti-State Activities (hereinafter the SPAA) (반국가행위자(反國家行爲者)의처벌(處罰)에관한특별조치법), which had been enacted under the authoritarian regime of President Park Chung-hee in 1977. Article 7(5) of the SPAA provided that a case could proceed to trial in the absence of a defendant where a satisfactory reason for the defendant's absence is not adduced. Subsections (6) and (7) of the same article prohibited an attorney or agent acting on behalf of a suspect from appearing at a default trial and further demanded that courts make their final judgment on the basis not of evidence but of prosecutors' submission. In addition, Article 8 of the same act provided that if suspects twice failed to comply with prosecutors' summons, the government could confiscate the suspects' property. The Constitutional Court decided that Article 7(5) of the SPAA violated a defendant's right to trial since it required courts to hold a default trial upon a prosecutor's request and did not allow postponement of trials, thus entirely preventing defendants from defending themselves against charges of a serious nature.

The Constitutional Court was also actively involved in considering disputes related to the legacy of the National Security Law. In 1990, a constitutional petition that challenged Article 7(1) of the National Security Act was filed at the Constitutional Court. This article permitted the government to punish individuals who supported antigovernment organizations. The court, in its 1990 decision, held that this article was vague, too broad, and a threat to the constitutional guarantees of freedom of the press, freedom of speech, freedom of academic research, and freedom of conscience. Later, a similar petition was filed against Article 19 of the National Security Act. Article 19 extended the period of pretrial detention to 50 days, which exceeded the normal period of 48 hours under the Criminal Procedure Code. In a 1992 decision, the Constitutional Court struck down this provision since it violated the right to a speedy trial as guaranteed by the Constitution of South Korea. Again, in 1994, the court decided Article 58–2(1) of the Private School Act (사립학교법) unconstitutional, which mandated the termination of employment of all private school teachers undergoing criminal prosecution. In this case, a teacher who was fired was prosecuted under the National Security Act. The court found that this rule violated the presumption of innocence in Article 27(4) of the Constitution. It further held that Article 58–2(1) breached the freedom of occupation, as captured in Article 15 of the Constitution, by excessively restricting the freedom without regard to the principle of proportionality, as contained in Article 37(2) of the Constitution.

In addition, the Constitutional Court, in the early stages of its establishment, was mandated to review the constitutionality of an administrative decision to dissolve the Kukje Group, which had been formed by the Ministry of Finance in the Fifth Republic, led by Chun Doo-hwan. The court, in a 1993 decision, held that the administrative decision was unconstitutional. The court noted that the intervention of the Chun administration in the management of a private business violated constitutionally protected economic freedoms, including the creativity of enterprises. Thus, the government's decision to dissolve the Kukje Group constituted a de facto exercise of governmental power resulting in an abuse of power and a violation of both the principle of equality and entrepreneurial freedom.

2.3.3. Denying the Legitimacy of Authoritarian Rule

As previously mentioned, Park's administration used various emergency decrees under the authorization of the 1972 Yushin Constitution. The decrees, which prohibited the establishment of political organizations and criminalized all activities deemed to be antigovernment, resulted in thousands of killings and disappearances. The 1972 Yushin Constitution not only concentrated extensive powers in Park's presidency but also precluded judicial review of the emergency decrees. The use of emergency decrees operated as a supraconstitutional norm during Park's dictatorship. In the 2000s, however, South Korea's judiciary retried cases relating to alleged violations of emergency decrees. The aim was to have the Constitutional Court, in the context of a democratic South Korea governed by the rule of law, hear various challenges to the constitutionality of the emergency decrees. Before doing so, the court decided (1) whether or not the Yushin Constitution provided those emergency decrees not subject to judicial review and (2) was still applicable to the disputes in question. In a 2013 decision, the court declared that the normative standard for reviewing the constitutionality of the emergency decrees was not the previous Yushin Constitution but the current constitution, which has no provisions excluding judicial review of emergency decrees. Unencumbered by any obstacle to a constitutional review of the emergency decrees, the Constitutional Court, in 2013, made a landmark decision declaring unconstitutional many emergency decrees issued by former President Park Chung-hee.

In this decision, the court ruled that Emergency Decree No. 1 and Emergency Decree No. 2 violated the principle of national sovereignty and the basic free and democratic order at the heart of the current Constitution. Emergency Decree No. 1 prohibited criticizing the Yushin Constitution and imposed punishment, without due process, on individuals found to have fabricated groundless rumors. The court found that this decree violated the principle of clarity and the definiteness of law since the decree infringed on the constitutional right to free speech. Likewise, regarding Emergency Decree No. 2, which established an emergency military court to arrest suspected violators of emergency orders and to adjudicate the cases, the court concluded that the decree infringed on people's right to a fair trial. Further, the court ruled that Emergency Decree No. 9, punishing all individuals linked to antigovernment activities in universities, failed to satisfy the requirements of legitimate purpose and appropriate means. The court decided that Emergency Decree No. 9 infringed on freedom of assembly and demonstration and violated the principle of academic freedom, campus autonomy, and personal responsibility, all protected under the current constitution.

As the previous discussion demonstrates, the Korean Constitutional Court has been extensively involved in cases relating to transitional justice since its establishment in 1988. The court's legal dealings with transitional justice issues not only establish and solidify its judicial power but also help construct a new constitutional order and protect the fundamental human rights of citizens for the Korean society.

3. A Game Changer or a Collaborator? The Role of the Constitutional Court in Taiwan's Pursuit of Transitional Justice

3.1. A Brief History of Political Oppression in Taiwan after World War II

As mentioned in the introduction, the path to transitional justice in Taiwan differed significantly from that in South Korea largely because Taiwan had a dominant party, the KMT, before and after democratization. Beginning in 1895, Taiwan ceased to be a territory of China and became a colony of the Japanese Empire – a situation that continued until the end of World War II. During much of this fifty-year stretch, Korea, too, was a colony of the Japanese Empire. However, unlike Korea, Taiwan did not have a chance to exercise its right to self-determination. Instead, on October 25, 1945, the KMT government, which lay claim to all of China, seized control of Taiwan. China under the control of the KMT was a party state. The Constitution of the Republic of China went into effect on December 25, 1947, only one and a half years before the KMT's relocation to Taiwan, following the KMT military's total defeat by the armed forces under the Chinese

Communist Party.[1] Therefore, between late 1945 and 1948, the KMT exercised single-party rule over Taiwan as well as over mainland Chinese provinces. The KMT-appointed governor of Taiwan relentlessly pushed through oppressive policies, which resulted in considerable discontent among wide swaths of the island's local population, leading to the notorious February 28 Incident (or the "228 Incident") in 1947. The incident began when, in response to local rioting, the government dispatched troops from mainland China to Taiwan and declared two months of martial law. Upon arriving to the island, the military reinforcements arrested, tortured, and executed thousands of local Taiwanese. Later, the KMT government implemented a cleansing policy for Taiwanese governmental personnel, including the judiciary. Reeling from its military defeats at the hands of Chinese communist forces, the KMT government in May 1949 declared another decree of martial law. This decree lasted for 38 years in Taiwan, not ending until July 15, 1987. During this decades-long period of martial law, civilians were subjected to military trials on charges of treason, espionage, and rebellion. However, the intelligence agencies and secret police often expanded the scope of those political crimes to include personal opinions and criticism of the government. Furthermore, the procedures for military trials were rudimentary and often abusive, usually depending on forced or induced personal confessions by defendants. More than 10,000 civilians lost their lives, liberty, or property without due process of law during this era, known as the White Terror (Huang 2019).

The state apparatus of the KMT in the 1950s targeted the underground members of Taiwan's Chinese Communist Party. Moreover, the outbreak of the Korean War in 1950 solidified the US government's commitment to a foreign policy of containment, and the KMT regime was seen as an ally in this effort. Over time, the threat of underground Chinese communist activities dimmed, so the KMT government started to focus on noncommunist threats to the KMT's rule. Of particular concern to the KMT government were political dissenters and cultural elites who, having recently arrived in Taiwan from mainland China, might harbor pro-democracy sentiments. Individuals who fit this profile and worked in the media or in higher education were singled out for special attention. The KMT's aim was to maintain the autocracy of Generalissimo Chiang Kai-shek (蔣介石) for as long as possible. Legislation served this aim for decades, as was the case in 1966, when the National Assembly struck presidential term limits from the Constitution. Despite these domestic successes, the KMT government suffered a profound weakening on the international stage when, in 1971, the United Nations declared that Beijing (essentially the Chinese Communist Party), not Taipei (essentially the KMT), would henceforth be the official representative of China.

1 The Constitution of the Republic of China was approved by the Constituent National Assembly on December 25, 1946, and publicized on January 1, 1947. It went into effect on December 25, 1947. The first National Assembly was instituted on March 29, 1948, and it passed the Temporary Provision on April 18, 1948, which bestowed on the president unlimited power to exercise emergency powers.

The KMT, under the leadership of Chiang's son, Chiang Ching-kuo (蔣經國), launched political reforms that, among other aims, increased recruitment of local Taiwanese for government positions. Though the KMT attempted to sugarcoat its growing deficit of legitimacy by preserving seats for mainland representatives in Taiwan's three parliaments (i.e., the National Assembly, the Legislative Yuan, and the Control Yuan), times were changing, and new generations were preparing to exercise power. Many aged representatives became too old to participate in parliamentary proceedings and passed away. The KMT therefore opened a very limited number of parliamentary seats for election in the early 1970s. Though the number was disproportionately small, it encouraged younger generations of local Taiwanese to participate in politics.

Fearful of losing its power in the long run, the KMT government had forbidden anyone from organizing opposition parties and had exercised strict prior scrutiny of publications, including daily newspapers and magazines. Throughout the 1970s and early 1980s, the government's intelligence agencies also kept a close eye on mild political activists (*Tangwai*, literally "outside the party"). In the aftermath of the US diplomatic recognition of the People's Republic of China (i.e., China, ruled by the communists) as the only legitimate government of China in December 1978, the KMT government declared an emergency decree, which halted an ongoing national election. One year later, the government arrested various political activists after a protest appealing for freedom of expression on International Human Rights Day in Kaohsiung. This event, known as the Formosa Incident (or Kaohsiung Incident), involved a group of political activists who published monthly magazines in the name of "Formosa" ("Meilidao," literally "beautiful island Taiwan"). The publisher of Formosa had established branches throughout the island in order to unite its disparate *Tangwai* sects. The KMT government identified the political movement as a separatist one, the outcome of which would be not only an independent Taiwan but also a renunciation of any claim to mainland China. In response to this attempted usurpation of power by the threat of mass protests and popular elections, the government arrested more than 150 people; 8 of them, as prominent leaders, were tried in military courts, while the other defendants were tried in ordinary courts. During the military trials, the mother and twin daughters of Yi-hsiung Lin (林義雄), who was a leading democratic activist, were slain in the basement of their apartment in downtown Taipei on February 28, 1980. No charges were ever made, and this tragedy remains one of the most chilling political murders of the 1980s.[2]

The Formosa Incident happened almost at the same time as the previously mentioned Gwangju Incident in South Korea and had a long-lasting impact on

2 Among others, Chen Wen-chen (陳文成), a statistics professor at Carnegie Mellon University, was found dead on the campus of National Taiwan University, after having been detained by the Taiwan Garrison Command in the summer of 1981. Henry Liu (劉宜良), a writer who published an unauthorized biography of Chiang Ching-kuo, was shot to death in his home in Daly City, California, in 1984. Later the US FBI found that the killers had close connections to Taiwan's military and secret service.

Taiwan. The most important message it sent to locals was that their country's authoritarian leadership would respond ruthlessly to any perceived threats to its power. Political liberalization, it seemed, would not come to Taiwan without a price. In the meantime, the international politics of the 1980s were changing drastically. While China had recently started its economic reforms and had opened itself up to the world, President Chiang Ching-kuo was under growing pressure from the United States to liberalize Taiwan. A despotic Taiwan, some people argued, was no better than a communist China. On the domestic side, political activism did not quiet down after the Formosa Incident. Rather, popular support for *Tangwai* flourished in election after election throughout the 1980s, challenging the legitimacy of not only the ruling party, the KMT, but also the state that they had brought to Taiwan, the Republic of China. In a 1986 interview with Katharine Graham of the *Washington Post*, Chiang Ching-kuo finally extended an olive branch of democratization to the many Taiwanese in favor of a more liberal society. Afterward, the government swiftly drafted the National Security Act during the Period of National Mobilization for Suppression of the Communist Rebellion (the National Security Act, 動員戡亂時期國家安全法), which the Legislative Yuan passed two weeks before the lifting of martial law. Article 9 of the act prohibited political prisoners from appealing their cases to ordinary courts, even though the right to appeal was guaranteed in both the Act of Martial Law (戒嚴法) and the Constitution. In fact, the lifting of martial law did not bring substantial change to the constitutional state of exception. The Temporary Provisions of the Republic of China Constitution remained intact until May 1991. True constitutional change came after the Wild Lily student movement of March 1990. At that time, Lee Teng-hui (李登輝), a native-born Taiwanese, was president. He had served as vice president under President Chiang Ching-kuo and had replaced Chiang upon his death in 1988. Under President Lee's leadership, the constitution went through six rounds of amendments, including the abolition of the "mainland" representatives and establishment of direct presidential elections.

3.2. Transitional-Justice Legislation and Policies after Democratization

The first official response to the outcry over past atrocities committed by the KMT party state came during Lee Teng-hui's presidency, a position that he successfully defended in May 1990, following a series of internal challenges to his rule in the post-Chiang KMT. In November 1990, the Executive Yuan (i.e., the premier and the cabinet) set up a committee to investigate the 228 Incident and, in January 1991, appointed a task force of experts to write a report. The experts delivered their final report in February 1992. Without holding any government or party official accountable for the atrocities, the report attributed the origins of the 228 Incident to several factors, including both the mishandling of the local politics and economy by Governor Chen Yi (陳儀) and widespread disillusionment among the Taiwanese population toward the KMT government. The report noted the government's reluctance to revisit the dark history of its past. On February 28, 1995, President Lee issued an official apology to the victims and their families. He also inaugurated a memorial monument in a Taipei park, which, in 1998, was renamed the 228 Peace Memorial Park. In March 1995, the Legislative Yuan passed the 228 Incident Disposition and Compensation Act (known also as the 228 Compensation Act, 二二八事件處理及補償條例). That same month, the Ministry of Interior Affairs created the 228 Memorial Foundation and tasked it with reviewing and deciding on applications for compensation. As of January 2021, the Foundation had awarded US$242 million to 10,175 persons, covering 2,324 cases, including 686 deaths and 181 disappearances.[3]

Prior to the passage of the 228 Compensation Act, the government passed in January 1995 the Act Governing the Recovery of Damage of Individual Rights During the Period of Martial Law (or the Restitution Act, 戒嚴時期人民受損權利回復條例), which restituted victims' entitlement to civil service jobs, pensions, professional licenses, and candidacy for elected office. However, the government did not provide a clear rationale as to why these entitlements, which had been stripped by military tribunals, deserved to be restituted. No explanation was given about whether or not the government had committed wrongdoings during the authoritarian era. Later, in 1998, the Legislative Yuan, with a majority of KMT representatives, passed a special law addressing the wrongs done to political prisoners during the authoritarian era. Modeled after the 228 Compensation Act, the Compensation Act for Improper Trials on Charges of Sedition and Espionage During the Martial Law Period (the White Terror Compensation Act, 戒嚴時期不當叛亂暨匪諜審判案件補償條例) established the Compensation Foundation, which awarded monetary compensation to qualified applicants. However, the law excluded those who had belonged to the Communist Party. According to the legislators, because the Chinese Communist Party was committed to overthrowing the KMT government, party membership was not only treasonous but also an act of espionage. In arriving at this conclusion, the legislators cited authoritarian-era legislation, including criminal law and the 1949 Suppressing Rebellion Act (懲治叛亂條例). From this perspective, the aim of the White Terror Compensation Act was not to reevaluate the decisions of court martials from the perspective of the rule of law but to consolidate the legitimacy of the ROC in Taiwan. The act also excluded monetary compensation for political prisoners whose judgments were not related to espionage and treason. The important point here is that the authoritarian government sometimes did not use political crimes as grounds for political trials. In various cases, the government cited embezzlement or corruption as the grounds for these trials of political dissidents. Hence, the scope of compensation was limited to cases of espionage and treason. It is also worth noting that the government had already awarded US$660 million to 10,066 applicants (Chang-Liao and Chen 2019, 14).

3 See the statistical data on the foundation's website: www.228.org.tw/pages.php?sn=14 (last visited on July 12, 2021).

It has been argued that there were a "thousand victims but not a single perpetrator" in the monetary-compensation model, which excluded investigations into criminal and political wrongdoing during the authoritarian era (Wu 2005, 78). The model of monetary compensation was a compromise between the KMT regime and the opposition parties during the 1990s. In 2000, the KMT unprecedentedly lost the presidential election, and the DPP candidate, Mr. Chen Shui-bian (陳水扁), stepped into power. Chen had been a defense lawyer for the political prisoners of the Formosa Incident and, earlier in the 1980s, had been a political prisoner. His presidency witnessed several failed attempts to promote transitional justice. The most significant attempt was a 2008 referendum calling for the acquisition of unduly obtained KMT party assets. The referendum was defeated in a low-turnout vote and is today regarded as a factor in the DPP's dismal electoral prospects in 2008 presidential election (Caldwell 2018, 471). Probably the most successful achievement during Chen's presidency on transitional-justice policy was the 2007 decision to change the title of the 228 Compensation Act: The word "compensation" (*bu-chang*, 補償) was changed to "reparation" (*pei-chang*, 賠償). According to Taiwanese administrative law, the latter term implies government liability while the former term implies the good will of government. Interestingly, the change of title was made by the Legislative Yuan, a majority of whose members were still KMT representatives. Therefore, the change can be interpreted as a goodwill gesture by the KMT – a concession to the opposition. In fact, it was precisely because the DPP could not gain control of the Legislative Yuan that most of President Chen's proposed transitional-justice policies – including his push to rename the Chiang Kai-shek Memorial Hall – met with failure during his eight years in office.

President Chen Shui-bian's successor was Ma Ying-jeou (馬英九), who served in Taiwan's top post from 2008 to 2016. A celebrated KMT figure, Ma continued the party's policy of the 1990s: apologize to the 228 victims and offer monetary awards to the victims of 228 and the White Terror but refuse to return the party's unduly obtained assets and to conduct any investigation into human rights violations allegedly committed by past KMT regimes. The DPP returned to power in 2016, when Tsai Ing-wen (蔡英文) assumed the presidency. At the same time, her party controlled the Legislative Yuan for the first time. The whip of the DPP immediately started drafting two important bills, the Act Governing the Settlement of Ill-Gotten Properties by Political Parties and Their Affiliate Organizations (the Ill-Gotten Party Assets Act, 政黨及其附隨組織不當取得財產處理條例) and the Act on Promoting Transitional Justice (the Transitional Justice Act, 促進轉型正義條例). Pursuant to these two pieces of legislation, the government set up two independent agencies in charge of affairs regarding transitional justice: One agency, the Ill-Gotten Party Assets Settlement Committee, handled the KMT's properties, and the other agency, the Transitional Justice Commission, undertook a thorough investigation into the past authoritarian regimes. The Ill-Gotten Party Assets Act was passed within three months of the president's inauguration, while the Transitional Justice Act was shelved one and a half years after Tsai's inauguration. Apparently, from the perspective of the DPP leadership, the Ill-Gotten Party Assets Act was more attractive politically than the Transitional Justice Act. Surrounding the Transitional Justice Commission was a great deal of political turbulence, which seems to have weakened, in 2018, the DPP's prospects for securing sufficient votes both in mayoral campaigns and in important referenda (Huang 2021). Since the 2018 election, Taiwan's polarized politics have led to the DPP's ambivalent attitude toward transitional justice. The Transitional Justice Commission failed to submit its final report on the DPP elections within the statutory timeframe. Some political commentators have argued that a lack of leadership and political determination in the Tsai administration caused her transitional-justice policies to stagnate (Huang 2021).

In 2020, the Constitutional Court heard a case petitioned by a group of Taipei High Administrative Court judges regarding the constitutionality of the Ill-Gotten Party Assets Act. In its Interpretation No. 793, the Constitutional Court upheld the act's constitutionality. KMT supporters argued that DPP actors had politically manipulated the court and that its decision in no way helped Taiwanese society to uncover important truths or to reach the goal of reconciliation; instead, so the KMT argument went, the court's decision only fueled the confrontation between political and ideological camps. However, this decision marked the first time that the court had declared the KMT's authoritarian rule to be in conflict with liberal constitutional democracy, as the KMT had corruptly allocated much of its unduly obtained property through party-state channels during the authoritarian era. In this regard, the decision was a revolutionary moment for the court, whose previous conservative decision of 1992 had upheld the National Security Act's statutory restriction on civilians' appeal to ordinary courts after democratization. The court has thus been on a long journey to comprehensively delegitimate the KMT's authoritarian rule.

3.3. *A Responsive Taiwanese Constitutional Court in the Politics of Transitional Justice*

In the following section, we first analyze the transformation of the jurisprudence of Taiwan's Constitutional Court from three perspectives: legal stability, legality, and legitimacy. We argue that the Taiwanese Constitutional Court was reluctant to cope with the demands of revisiting the wrongdoings of the authoritarian-era KMT state because the KMT dominated political processes and, more specifically, controlled the Legislative Yuan throughout the 1990s. It was not until the first DPP president stepped into power in 2000 that the composition of the Constitutional Court began to undergo a gradual change in which the court became more and more willing to take on hard cases regarding the authoritarian-era state's targeting of political critics. After the DPP took control of the Legislative Yuan in 2016 and passed a series of transitional-justice laws, the court committed itself to addressing transitional-justice issues. The court reexamined the KMT's authoritarian legacy on the basis of liberal democratic standards. However, the court's reversal of focus raises an intriguing question about the court's role in politics. We argue that the court deliberately responded to political fluctuations after democratization and carefully calibrated its decisions in response to political changes. This pattern first emerged with the deluge of martial law cases that came before the court in the aftermath of democratization; later, the court addressed the legality of the martial law system, and finally, thirty years after democratization, the court reevaluated the legitimacy of the KMT's authoritarian rule. Interpretation No. 793, in which the court acknowledged that the KMT had maintained a party-state for over fifty years, could be regarded as a response to the Sunflower Movement, which, in 2014, had lashed out against a KMT trade agreement with China (Huang 2021). A responsive court is not necessarily an activist court, but in this instance, the Taiwanese Constitutional Court resonated with contemporary trends (Yeh and Chang 2011, 823–24). The context-dependent and politics-sensitive decisions of the court reflect quintessential characteristics of transitional-justice jurisprudence (Teitel 2000).

3.3.1. Stabilizing the Legacy of Taiwan's Authoritarian Rule

When, in the mid-1980s, the KMT government was planning to lift martial law, they first drafted the National Security Act: The aim was to restrict the freedom of expression and association after democratization so that the KMT could continue to dominate the country's political processes. Furthermore, Article 9 of the National Security Act prohibited civilians who had been tried by a court martial from appealing their cases before ordinary courts after the lifting of martial law. In fact, the Act of Martial Law expressly protected the right to appeal for those who had faced court martials during the martial law period (Article 10). Meanwhile, the Constitution of the Republic of China stated that "except those in active military service, no person shall be subject to trial by a military tribunal" (Article 9). Therefore, several former political prisoners brought their cases to the Constitutional Court in September 1987, shortly after the lifting of martial law, and asked the justices to declare Article 9 of the National Security Act unconstitutional. The court decided to hear such a case in January 1989 and then took two years to reach its decision: Interpretation No. 272 (1991).

In the decision, the court upheld Article 9 of the National Security Act as constitutional. The court stated that the purpose of Article 9 was to maintain the stability of legal decisions and of social order, which was deemed necessary by the court. In addition, if there was any cause for retrial or extraordinary appeal, defendants could still bring their cases before ordinary courts. In its reasoning, the court first described the gradual reform of the military-trial system, starting with the 1952 regulation on the jurisdictional distinction between ordinary courts and military tribunals. The Taiwanese Constitutional Court reasoned that this and other reforms, such as the 1956 Court-Martial Act (軍事審判法), had significantly narrowed the scope of military tribunals' jurisdiction. Meanwhile, the KMT authoritarian state's imposition of martial law in Taiwan lasted for more than thirty-seven years, and this lengthy span of time created difficulty in gathering and investigating evidence. In their holding, Interpretation No. 272 applied only to the decades-long martial law, not to other cases of martial law in the future.

Interpretation No. 272 was a compromise among the Constitutional Court's justices, as well as a compromise between the legal order and the political order. At least one justice vehemently opposed the decision. Justice Yang Jih-jan (楊日然) argued that the right to appeal was a fundamental right guaranteed by the Constitution, while Article 9 set a limitation on the right. According to the legal principle *lex retro non agit* (the law shall not be retroactive), such a stringent limitation should not be applied retroactively. Justice Yang insisted that the court should neither take its own workload into consideration nor overlook the significance of constitutional rights (Lin 2021, 124). Likewise, Justice Cheng Jian-tsai (鄭健才) mentioned that even though appeals to ordinary courts would create more work for the Supreme Court, the Constitutional Court should not deprive citizens of their constitutional right to petition the courts – democracy always comes with a price (Lin 2021, 126). However, the majority of the justices tended to recognize the constitutionality of Article 9. Justice Shi Xi-en (史錫恩) even said that military tribunals had promoted development in Taiwan. Justice Li Zhong-sheng (李鐘聲) expressed his loyalty to the Taiwanese government in general and pushed his colleagues to support the government's position and not to use the term "the region of Taiwan" because the Republic of China should, if only in principle, include what are commonly referred to as China and Mongolia (Lin 2021, 134). Justice Weng Yue-sheng (翁岳生) noted that when an issue at stake is not purely legal, the justices should fully rely on their own conscientious discretion. According to Justice Weng, the justices hearing the Article 9 case should have trusted each other and earnestly pursued common ground in support of the majority's opinion so that the authority of the court would not be jeopardized (Lin 2021, 139–40).

Interpretation No. 272 was a historic decision, which indefinitely delayed the process of criminal investigation into political oppression in Taiwan. The decision came after another landmark decision, Interpretation No. 261 (1990), which ruled that representative institutions should hold periodic elections and that all current mainland representatives not elected through periodic elections should retire from their position by the end of 1991. Interpretation No. 261 breathed new life into Taiwan's democratic politics. Its reasoning implicitly hinged on the constitutional principles of self-government and popular sovereignty.[4] Then-legislator Chen Shui-bian, who submitted the case to the Constitutional Court with another 25 legislators, revealed to the press that some justices had suggested that he refer the case to the Constitutional Court so that the court can ultimately

4 Although the court did not mention "popular sovereignty" in Interpretation No. 261, Justice Wu Geng (吳庚) wrote in his unpublished dissenting (in reasoning) opinion that the Court should clearly ground its arguments in democratic, republican, or popular-sovereignty principles (Chen 2021, 290).

and impartially resolve the issue of the legitimacy of the "million-year parliament" (the non-periodically elected parliament) (Chen 2021, 275).

The Constitutional Court rendered two judgments conveying very different approaches to the legacy of the authoritarian regime. On the one hand, the court actively responded in Interpretation No. 261 to social pressures from both civil society and the opposition party, which were demanding that the state should restore democratic elections, especially insofar as the government had lifted martial law over three years earlier. On the other hand, the justices denied in Interpretation No. 272 the request that the democratic government investigate the past activities of the authoritarian-era KMT government. This denial delayed the justice sought by former political prisoners. Together, the court seemed to have adopted a model of "democracy comes first, political justice later (or never)." The court emphasized the functioning of democratic institutions rather than the rehabilitation of individual rights: Democratic politics is forward-looking, while the politics of redress is backward-looking and may assign legal responsibility for past wrongdoing to the KMT as a party and to its leaders, including some who might still have been in power. The Constitutional Court carefully carved out its jurisprudence for the transitional politics in Taiwan.

In 1993, the court rendered Interpretation No. 328. It was a response to arguments made by parliamentarian members of the opposition party (the DPP) regarding the territory of the Republic of China. According to these opposition legislators, Article 2 of the Constitution provides that the sovereignty of the Republic of China belongs to the whole body of citizens. The Republic of China had never officially regarded nationals of the People's Republic of China as the citizens of the Republic of China, so Beijing had no claim to the Republic of China's sovereignty. The legislators further reasoned that the territory of the People's Republic of China should not be regarded as the territory of the Republic of China. The territory of the Republic of China should be limited to where its citizens reside – namely, Taiwan, Penghu, Kinmen, Matsu, Green Island, Orchid Island, and other annexed isles. However, according to Article 4 of the Constitution, the territory of the Republic of China is defined as "its existing national boundaries." But what exactly does "existing national boundaries" mean? The Constitutional Court ruled that this question is a political one beyond the reach of judicial review. A proper definition of the territory of the Republic of China was critical to the National Security Act since the act prohibited any organization, event, or person from upholding so-called separatism (i.e., Taiwan independence) or communism (recognizing the legitimacy of the People's Republic of China). The court denied a request to review this constitutional controversy and left the question to political actors. In May 1991, six months before the retirement of all "mainland representatives," they passed the Additional Articles (i.e., the amendments) to replace the Temporary Provisions. The foreword of the Additional Articles had championed the "One China" principle. The political symbolism in the Additional Articles consolidated the KMT's political heritage, and the Constitutional Court dared not challenge the symbolism of the Republic of China.

3.3.2. The Legality of Taiwan's Authoritarian-Era Laws

As mentioned previously, in the first decade of Taiwan's democratization, the Constitutional Court did not touch upon cases regarding the KMT's martial law rule, with one exception: Interpretation No. 272. However, the court announced in Interpretation No. 436 of 1997 that the power exercised by court martials is judicial power, so the procedures of military trials should meet the basic requirements of the due process of law, including the requirements of independent and impartial courts. Meanwhile, the Constitutional Court held that the 1956 Court-Martial Act had placed military trials under the supervision of the Ministry of Defense, an action that violated the Constitution: The Ministry of Defense could not exercise judicial power, and the commanders of armed forces should not intervene in the procedures and outcomes of military trials. Likewise, military commanders should not control military tribunals. The Constitutional Court went on to argue that, if military tribunals sentence members of Taiwan's armed forces to imprisonment or death, the defendants should have the right to appeal the sentence to ordinary courts. This opinion overthrew the legal regime of military trials, which had been in existence since the early authoritarian era; accordingly, the Constitutional Court held that the relevant provisions of the 1956 Court-Martial Act were unconstitutional. This landmark decision upheld the constitutional values of the due process of law, individual rights, and proportionality. By explicitly denouncing the old system of martial law and court martials, the Constitutional Court implicitly denounced the authoritarian regime as a whole.

In the second decade of Taiwan's democratization, the first transitional-justice case heard by the Constitutional Court concerned the Restitution Act of 1995. The Constitutional Court held in its Interpretation No. 477 of 1999 that the Restitution Act should be applied to two sets of people: (1) those who, after a period of detention, had been released by the police or intelligence agencies owing to a lack of evidence and (2) those who were still detained after a not-guilty judgment or after having completed a sentence associated with a guilty judgment (including rehabilitation sentences). As can be seen, the court was addressing people who either had not been formally prosecuted in military tribunals or should have been released immediately after completion of a military tribunal's sentence. All of these people had been detained without any legal reason but were not entitled to the restitution or the reimbursement outlined in the Restitution Act. The Constitutional Court recognized illegal detentions during the martial law era as an infringement upon people's rights and required that the Legislative Yuan amend the relevant law. By this interpretation, the court also upheld the constitutionality of the Restitution Act, which expressly admitted the wrongdoing of the KMT regime. In the same vein, the Constitutional Court ruled in Interpretation No. 624 of 2007 that people who had been wrongfully tried by a military tribunal should have the right to state compensation. The court combed through the legislative history of the Act of Compensation for Wrongful Detentions and Executions (冤獄賠償法), concluding that the act had unconstitutionally withheld from military-trial defendants the same right to state compensation as defendants in ordinary courts possess. The court further concluded that the political turmoil during the period of national mobilization and communist rebellion did not justify the withholding of this right; in other words, the court rejected political emergency as a justification of the unequal treatment. The court restated its position that the power exercised by court martials is the same as the power exercised by ordinary courts, so whoever has been wrongfully convicted should be equally entitled to state compensation.

The Constitutional Court's most significant discussion on the legality of authoritarian law occurred in Interpretation No. 567 (2003). The court dealt with Article 2 of the Disciplinary Measures Governing the Prevention of Recidivism by Communist Espionage Criminals during the Period of National Mobilization for the Suppression of Communist Rebellion (the Recidivism Prevention Measures, 戡亂時期預防匪諜再犯管教辦法), which delegated discretionary power to Taiwanese intelligence to decide whether political prisoners, after completion of their sentences, should be sent to labor reeducation camps or corrective education camps. The court ruled that, no matter what the name of the post-sentence measure, compulsory labor and other disciplinary steps following completion of a sentence are severe limitations on the personal freedoms guaranteed by Article 8 of the Constitution. The court added that this kind of decision should be decided by a court rather than by an intelligence agency, and that the legislature should carefully define who qualifies for compulsory labor and what constitutes necessary and proportionate post-sentence measures. In closing, the court ruled, "While the state may impose more restrictions on individual rights during extraordinary periods and due to necessity under extraordinary circumstances, such restrictions must nevertheless not violate the minimum core of rights protection" (Interpretation No. 567 2003, para. 3).

It was also the court's opinion that freedom of thought was among the most fundamental principles in the constitutional order of liberal democracy (Interpretation No. 567 2003, para. 4). Even in extraordinary periods, the government has no power to infringe upon people's indelible freedom of thought by compelling them to conform to state ideology. The disputed regulation, which had granted Taiwanese intelligence services the power to send political prisoners to a reeducation labor camp if they were regarded as ardent communist supporters, violated freedom of speech and intruded upon the minimum core of rights protection. Even though the Constitutional Court did not expressly hold the KMT government accountable for the wrongdoing of these camps, the opinion unrooted the alleged legality of the KMT's martial law regulations and legislation. The court anchored its judgment on the constitutional order of liberal democracy, an idea that had first surfaced in Interpretation No. 381 of 1995, regarding the procedural requirements of constitutional amendments. The court expanded on the idea in Interpretation No. 499 of 2000 regarding the unconstitutionality of constitutional amendments. According to Interpretation No. 499, the court listed at least four constitutional principles underpinning the constitutional order of liberal democracy: the principle of republican democracy, the principle of popular sovereignty, the principle of individual rights, and the principle of checks and balances. In this interpretation, the court subscribed to the unconstitutional constitutional-amendment doctrine (or the entrenchment clause of a constitution). If this doctrine had been applied to the Temporary Provisions enforced by the KMT government during its authoritarian reign, which cancelled presidential term limits, the constitutional foundation of KMT rule would have thoroughly imploded. However, the court did not go that far in either Interpretation No. 499 or Interpretation No. 567. The court focused only on rights protection *after* democratization (Interpretation No. 567) and the constitutional order of liberal democracy *after* democratization (Interpretation No. 499). Nevertheless, the court's jurisprudence in this period paved the way to an important reevaluation of the KMT's authoritarian party state in Interpretation No. 793 (2020).

3.3.3. The Legitimacy of Authoritarian Rule in Taiwan

The most distinctive difference between South Korea and Taiwan regarding their respective authoritarian regimes is that Taiwan was ruled by a party state for over forty years while South Korea was ruled by military generals and political strongmen without a powerful party machine. Since Taiwan's democratization in 1987, the Constitutional Court has not had a chance to address the legitimacy of the KMT's authoritarian-era rule. However, the court has addressed how Taiwan's red scare limited people's freedom of association on the island. Because the KMT's post-1949 raison d'être was to protect Taiwan from a Chinese communist invasion, the KMT sought to preserve its own existence by prohibiting any political organization or social gathering from discussing or even promoting communism. Thus, for example, Article 2 of the National Security Act of 1987 prohibited anyone from launching parades or establishing organizations in support of "unconstitutional" claims, communism, or separatism. Accordingly, both the Assembly and Parade Act of 1988 and the Civil Association Act of 1989 adopted these three restrictions. The Constitutional Court dealt with them separately in Interpretations No. 445 of 1998 (the Assembly and Parade Act) and No. 644 of 2008 (the Civil Association Act). The two interpretations stated that communism and Taiwanese independence are political issues that general populations should have the right to deliberate in a democratic society. The authoritarian KMT regime's prohibition on assemblies and parades infringed upon the general population's freedom of speech. The court in Interpretation No. 445 used the language of "clear and present danger," borrowed from jurisprudence of the US Supreme Court's First Amendment, to argue that the mere terms "communism" and "Taiwan independence" posed no threat to social order or public interest. The two interpretations reiterated the mechanism of unconstitutional party dissolution provided in Article 5 of the Additional Articles of the ROC Constitution in 1992. The court held that if a political party endangers the existence of Taiwan or the nation's constitutional order of liberal democracy, the Constitutional Court should dissolve the party. The court also held that neither the police nor the Ministry of Interior Affairs should have the power to base their approval of parades or organizations on political claims, which would constitute a content-based review. The two interpretations have upheld the liberal principle of freedom of speech, which treats communist claims as political advocacy rather than as acts of espionage or treason. These judgments substantiated the "constitutional order of liberal democracy."

After the Legislative Yuan passed the Ill-Gotten Party Assets Act in 2016, the Ill-Gotten Party Assets Settlement Committee confiscated properties of the KMT and its affiliated organizations. In response, the KMT brought several cases before the Taipei High Administrative Court, whose judges asked the Constitutional Court to decide on the constitutionality of the relevant articles of the Ill-Gotten Party Assets Act. The Constitutional Court upheld the disputed statutes and analyzed the nature of the authoritarian regime created by the KMT. The court argued that, although the Constitution of the Republic of China had gone into effect on December 25, 1947, the KMT had exercised almost total control over the state, with the party's chairman simultaneously acting as president of the Republic of China. The KMT continued the pre-1947 party-rule system after relocating to Taiwan, imposed martial law there, and – through the Temporary Provisions – expanded presidential power. The Constitutional Court ruled that the government had used national budgets to support the KMT, which should be deemed illegitimate benefits of the KMT. The legislative purpose of the Ill-Gotten Party Assets Act was to reestablish the constitutional order of liberal democracy and to create a sound system of party competition. To this end, the act expressly mentions transitional justice as a constitutional value (Interpretation No. 793 2020, paras. 10–12). In terms of retrospective applications, the Constitutional Court mentioned that generally speaking, the court should not retrospectively apply laws depriving or limiting people's rights. However, the KMT and its affiliates had received the aforementioned "illegitimate benefits," including significant swaths of property, through a party-state mechanism that was already in violation of the constitutional order of liberal democracy, so there are no "legitimate interests" to be protected. Meanwhile, the court added, the principle of nonretrospective application is not insurmountable: The Ill-Gotten Party Assets Act was meant to advance democratic politics and to vindicate transitional justice, which pursues substantial public interests. In this case, the court found that the Ill-Gotten Party Assets Act's retrospective application of confiscation of the KMT's property is constitutionally permissible. The court recognized the legislative purpose of the Ill-Gotten Party Assets Act, including the legislation's focus on fair competition in party politics and on the value of transitional justice. The court also confirmed that the party state created by the KMT was in violation of the constitutional order of liberal democracy. The function of transitional justice is to reflect on past wrongdoings, and to this extent, the court affirmed the need for retrospective application. Interpretation No. 793 is a landmark decision on transitional justice in post-democratization Taiwan and rests on jurisprudence that had developed since the mid-1990s regarding the constitutional order of liberal democracy. In the aftermath of democratization, the court had to contend with myriad authoritarian legal precedents and simultaneously lacked the political legitimacy to carry out transitional justice. But over the last thirty years of democratic politics in

Taiwan, the court has established a new constitutional jurisprudence on a case-by-case basis, the accumulation of which lends great support to the reasoning of Interpretation No. 793. This incremental process stands in stark contrast to the practices of the South Korean Constitutional Court. In the next section of this chapter, we focus on the roles that the constitutional courts have played in the countries' respective transitional-justice experiences.

4. The Embeddedness of Transitional Justice: Constitutional Courts and Democracy in South Korea and Taiwan

At the start of this chapter, we raised the issue of how constitutional courts in newly democratized South Korea and Taiwan have handled transitional justice. South Korea and Taiwan, though their timelines of constitutionalizing transitional justice differ greatly from each other, possess constitutional courts that have grown highly influential in their review of key transitional-justice legislation. However, this growing influence does not mean that constitutional courts are simply followers of their respective legislature or of mainstream public opinion on transitional justice. In fact, the courts' judgments have not only expedited the process of transitional justice but also consolidated the democratic states during and after the transition. Three critical factors – the path taken during democratic transition, civil society's engagement in the transition, and the timing of constitutional change – determined the major differences between South Korea and Taiwan regarding how each country's Constitutional Court handled transitional-justice cases.

South Korea's negotiated democratic transition and its subsequent political development have provided opportunities for the Korean Constitutional Court to deal with the issue of criminal responsibility. The two most difficult issues during the administrations of Roh Tae-woo and Kim Young-sam were (1) whether or not the government should bring former Presidents Chun Doo-hwan and Roh Tae-woo, and other military leaders, to justice and, if so, (2) how the Constitutional Court should deal with the legal dilemmas arising from statutes of limitation (Cho 2013). It is worth noting that vibrant street demonstrations, the corruption scandals of Roh and Chun, and the defeat of Kim Young-sam's party in the 1995 local elections forced the Kim administration to reconsider punishing Chun, Roh, and these other military leaders (West 1997). As previously mentioned, in December 1995, the Korean National Assembly passed the Special Act on the May 18th Democratic Movement. After the Constitutional Court upheld the constitutionality of this Special Act, the lower courts have an opportunity to reopen the cases and to prosecute two former presidents Chun and Roh. Before this transitional-justice legislation went into effect, the Constitutional Court had refused to substantively deal with the country's authoritarian past and had even anecdotally approved the justiciability of the coup d'état led by Chun and Roh. Therefore, the South Korean Constitutional Court took a detour on transitional justice in its 1996 judgment.

In reality, Korean society from the beginning of its democratic transition has been very supportive of efforts by the state, civil society, and other concerned groups to grapple with transitional justice (Lewis 2002). Opposition parties instituted a truth commission on the Gwangju Incident in 1988, right after the transition, and in the same year, victim families launched a 135-day protest asking the government to publish an investigative report on the tragedy. In November 1988, the National Assembly also held a public hearing on the Gwangju Incident (Ahn 2002; Chung 2009). This zealous quest for truth and justice pushed political parties to compete with one another on transitional-justice policies. This competition, coupled with public interest, is the mobilizing force behind the special legislation on the Gwangju Incident. For example, after the collapse of the authoritarian regime, civil rights groups actively requested that the new democratic government resolve the issue of extending the Statute of Limitations for crimes committed in the past (Lewis 2002). Religious groups also submitted a petition calling for the enactment of a special law and the appointment of a special prosecutor to punish Chun and others for their involvement in the Gwangju Incident (Lewis 2002). In addition, the legal community pressured the government to enact a special law. For instance, the Korean Council of Professors for Democratization requested that the government enact a special law permitting the prosecution of coup leaders; the council also submitted a petition that the Statute of Limitations not apply to those involved in the May 18th Movement (Kim 2001). Meanwhile, the Korean Bar Association called for all lawyers in the campaign to promote a special law that would lead to the punishment of those responsible for the Gwangju Incident. On a wider scale, large segments of the general populace demanded that the political parties, the political branches of government, and the judiciary support transitional justice. Feeling the pressure of these appeals, the Korean Constitutional Court had to respond to them.

In contrast to South Korea, Taiwan lingered indecisively over transitional-justice issues for a decade because, during that time, the conservative KMT controlled post-transitional politics in Taiwan. However, a younger generation of Taiwanese citizens, many of whom participated in the Sunflower Movement in 2014, recognized and opposed the brutality of state power exercised by the pre-democratic KMT government. The belated zealousness for historical truth among these Taiwanese prompted the DPP government to pass transitional-justice laws immediately after it took control of the Legislative Yuan and the presidency in 2016. At the same time, the New Power Party, which grew out of the Sunflower Movement, has competed with the DPP government on the issue of transitional justice. Therefore, the driving process for constitutionalizing transitional justice in Taiwan looks very similar to that in South Korea: pushing up from civil society and proceeding to political parties and then to the political branches of government and then to the judiciary (each country's Constitutional Court). In South Korea and Taiwan, many elements have interacted with one another in their efforts to reckon collectively with dark pasts. And constitutional courts, whether in South Korea or in Taiwan, have been mobilized by and have responded to the demands of vocal civil societies.

In South Korea and Taiwan, civil society in the two countries have been calling for truth and justice since the beginning of democratization. Why, throughout the 1990s, did the Taiwanese Constitutional Court show timidity in Interpretation No. 272 and only indirectly touch upon the legality of the authoritarian-era KMT legislation in Interpretations No. 436 and 477? Post-transitional politics and belated civic engagement in Taiwan may provide some clues in answering this question, but the country's legacy of both party-state ideology and constitutional conservatism explains why, in the early days of democratization, many Taiwanese people still viewed communist China as a state enemy and still viewed Taiwan as part of a Chinese mainland rightfully titled not the People's Republic of China but the Republic of China. Democratization in South Korea, by contrast, was initiated through peaceful negotiations between the old ruling party, led by Roh Tae-woo, and the newly created opposition party. Following the negotiated agreement, an extensively revised constitution (the 9th Amendment) was created in 1987, and numerous legal and political reforms were launched consecutively (Kim 2003). Soon, a new constitutional court was established in 1988. The nine justices of the Korean Constitutional Court are appointed equally and separately by the three constitutional institutions: the president, the National Assembly, and the president of the Supreme Court. This power-sharing design was set up to effectively secure the independence of the judicial system (Chang and Lee 2018). In addition, South Korea's new constitution provides the new Korean Constitutional Court a set of anchoring values for constitutional democracy in cases regarding transitional justice. The establishment of a democratic state in South Korea created an opportunity to overturn the decades-old dictatorial rules. For example, various actors in South Korea challenged the constitutionality of many past restrictive laws in front of the newly created Korean Constitutional Court during the early period of democratic transition. The new context of political transition offered genuine opportunities for the Korean Constitutional Court to declare most past authoritarian laws unconstitutional. As exemplified in the case concerning the constitutionality of the emergency decrees issued by former President Park Chung-hee, the Korean Constitutional Court drew on democratic values in delegitimizing the draconian emergency orders of the Park administration.

Whereas South Korea undertook constitutional change early in the post-transition period, the timing of constitutional change came late in Taiwan, which never had a particularly decisive, clear-cut separation with its past. The 1947 Constitution of the Republic of China remains the supreme law of the land, though there is no longer any pretense that it applies to China. The composition of Taiwan's Constitutional Court justices started to change only gradually and only after 1997, a full decade after democratization got underway on the island. In this circumstance, the Constitutional Court of Taiwan managed to create, almost from scratch, a jurisprudence of the "constitutional order of liberal democracy." The Taiwanese Constitutional Court established a certain momentum with Interpretation No. 499, in which the court struck down specific constitutional amendments on the grounds that they violated the core values of constitutional democracy. In short, the Taiwanese Constitutional Court forged many of its tools by itself and certainly had no new constitution on which to rely. This originality and creativity form a model of case-law and incrementalistic jurisprudence, the purpose of which is to aid a court system in tackling transitional-justice issues.

South Korea and Taiwan began their democratization at almost the same time but with different social and political settings, so the two countries understandably developed different tools and routes in handling transitional justice. However, the common feature of the two countries is their reverence for transitional-justice legislation. Civil societies' endorsement of legislative action is key to affirmative constitutional decisions, and the truth of this principle is borne out by the examples of South Korea and Taiwan. The importance of civil societies in this regard is due partially to the institutional weaknesses of courts, which have frequently been characterized in constitutional theory as countermajoritarian (Bickel 1962; Ely 1980). Cass Sunstein argues that judges sometimes act like functionaries in the service of "superiors, typically understood as the political branches of government" (2015, 6). This characterization might be especially evident in the context of transitional justice. According to Ruti Teitel, transitional law involves various measures that establish and validate political change, and courts' judicial review of these measures can lend the entire process a high degree of popular support, securing a "progressive role for a rule of law fully enmeshed in politics" (2000, 223). The cases of South Korea and Taiwan exactly demonstrate the distinctive role of constitutional courts in the highly political processes of transitional justice.

5. Conclusion

Transitional justice is not only about reflecting on past wrongdoings but also about forging a new democracy through constitutional reformation. While ordinary courts might deal with prosecution, sentencing, or access to political archives, constitutional courts lay down the foundation of a new democracy's constitutional values. However, transition does not occur overnight. South Korea commenced its democratization with a revamped constitution and a newly minted constitutional court. Bolstered by legislative mandates and popular demands, the Korean Constitutional Court confirmed the constitutionality of special transitional-justice legislation. The recent history of Taiwan tells a different story: early on in the country's democratization, the Taiwanese Constitutional Court endorsed the KMT's authoritarian party-state legacy by rejecting retrials for victims of political oppression. The court required more than three decades to develop a judicial toolbox capable of serving a "constitutional order of liberal democracy" and then to apply the tools to the difficult task of examining the KMT's party-state legacy. If the Korean Constitutional Court represents a "fairy tale" of judicial contributions to transitional justice, the Taiwanese Constitutional Court's struggles with transitional justice telling a tale of drawn-out perseverance punctuated by satisfying victories. South Korea was able to pursue transitional justice more vigorously than Taiwan because the latter faced persistent authoritarian apparatuses and ideologies, an unchallenged constitutional idolatry, ardent defenders of the recently deceased authoritarian government, and a constitutional court reluctant to inculpate its former masters.

Because transitional justice lies at the interface of law and politics, the task of constitutionalizing transitional justice requires a nuanced balancing act. Neither the Korean Constitutional Court nor the Taiwanese Constitutional Court has handled transitional justice with unerring skill. In South Korea's case, its Constitutional Court quite decisively severed ties with the authoritarian legacies of the country's coup d'états and military dictatorships, but the court had done so on the basis of popular will. In Taiwan's case, the initial waxing and waning of support for the new democracy meant that the Taiwanese Constitutional Court focused more on individual rights than on the unavoidably political construction of a transitional-justice system, and one outcome of this focus was the slow process of delegitimating the authoritarian rule. Interestingly, however, by emphasizing the freedoms of expression and association, the Taiwanese Constitutional Court proved to be responsive to popular sentiment and actually renovated, on a case-by-case approach, the entire legal regime inherited from the recent authoritarian past, replacing it with a constitutional order based on liberal democracy. In general, the purpose of constitutionalizing transitional justice is to establish a democracy capable of protecting people's rights. The South Korean and Taiwanese Constitutional Courts have helped realize this goal on the basis of constitutional values.

References

Ackerman, B. (1992) *The Future of Liberal Revolution*. New Haven, CT: Yale University Press.

Ahn, J. C. (2002) The significance of settling the past of the December 12 Coup and the May 18 Gwangju Uprising. *Korea Journal*, 142(3), pp. 112–38.

Baik, T. U. (2005) Justice incomplete. In: G. W. Shin, S. W. Park, and D. Yang eds. *Rethinking Historical Injustice and Reconciliation in Northeast Asia: The Korean Experience*. London: Routledge, pp. 94–113.

Baik, T. U. (2012) Social healing through justice: The Jeju 4.3 case. *World Environment and Island Studies*, 2(1), pp. 59–77.

Baik, T. U. (2013) Fairness in transitional justice initiatives: The case of South Korea. *Buffalo Human Rights Law Review*, 19, pp. 169–91.

Bickel, A. M. (1962) *The Least Dangerous Branch: The Supreme Court at the Bar of Politics*. New Haven, CT: Yale University Press.

Caldwell, E. (2018) Transitional justice legislation in Taiwan before and during the Tsai administration. *Washington International Law Journal*, 27(2), pp. 449–84.

Chang, J. (2009) National narrative, traumatic memory, and testimony: Reading traces of the Cheju April Third Incident, South Korea, 1948. PhD dissertation. New York University.

Chang, W. C. and Lee, Y. L. (2016) Transitional justice: Institutional mechanisms and contextual dynamics. In: *The Max Planck Encyclopedia of Public International Law*. Oxford University Law Online. [Viewed August 9, 2021]. Available from: https://opil.ouplaw.com/view/10.1093/law:epil/9780199231690/law-9780199231690-e2191

Chang, W. C. and Lee, Y. L. (2018) Competition or collaboration: Constitutional review by multiple final courts. In: R. Dixon and E. F. Delaney eds. *Comparative Judicial Review*. Cheltenham: Edward Elgar Publishing, pp. 164–83.
Chang-Liao, N. C. and Chen, Y. J. (2019) Transitional justice in Taiwan: Changes and challenges. *Washington International Law Journal*, 28(3), pp. 619–44.
Chen, H. W. (2021) Zai minzhu gaige de langchaoxia, zhung jie wannian guohui. (在民主改革浪潮下，終結萬年國會－釋字第二六一號解釋檔案, Ending the million-year parliaments under the wave of democratic reform: Archives of Interpretation No. 261.) In C. C. Lin et al. *Fengmin Shifa: Dafaguan yu zhuanxing Zhengyi* (*奉命釋法：大法官與轉型正義*, *Judicial Interpretation by Political Command: Grand Justice and Transitional Justice*). Taipei: Transitional Justice Commission, pp. 269–324.
Cho, K. (1997) Tension between the national security law and constitutionalism in South Korea: Security for what? *Boston University International Law Journal*, 14, pp. 125–74.
Cho, K. (2007) Transitional justice in Korea: Legally coping with past wrongs after democratization. *Pacific Rim Law and Policy Journal*, 16, pp. 579–611.
Cho, K. (2013) Transitional justice in Korea: Legally coping with past wrongs after democratization. In: H. Yang ed. *Law and Society in Korea*. Cheltenham: Edward Elgar Publishing, pp. 189–223.
Chon, J. I. (2015) The effect of constitutional adjudication on the judicial branch: The relationship between the constitutional court and the ordinary court. In: J. R. Yeh ed. *The Functional Transformation of Courts: Taiwan and Korea in Comparison*. Taipei: National Taiwan University Press, pp. 39–65.
Chun, J. H. and Han, J. S. (2017) Delayed reconciliation and transitional justice in Korea: Three levels of conditions for national reconciliation. *Asian Journal of Social Science*, 45(3), pp. 294–315.
Chung, I. J. (2009) Demilitarizing politics in South Korea: Toward a positive consolidation of civilian supremacy. In: G. Caforio ed. *Advances in Military Sociology: Essays in Honor of Charles C. Moskos*. Bingley: Emerald Publishing Limited, pp. 527–65.
Ely, J. H. (1980) *Democracy and Distrust: A Theory of Judicial Review*. Cambridge, MA: Harvard University Press.
Ginsburg, T. (2003) *Judicial Review in New Democracies: Constitutional Courts in Asian Cases*. Cambridge: Cambridge University Press.
Ginsburg, T. (2014) Constitutional courts in East Asia. In: R. Dixon and T. Ginsburg eds. *Comparative Constitutional Law in Asia*. Cheltenham: Edward Elgar Publishing, pp. 47–79.
Goedde, P. (2008) How activist lawyers mobilized the law for social and political change in South Korea, 1988–2007. PhD dissertation. University of Washington.
Hahm, C. (2018) Constitutional Court of Korea: Guardian of the constitution or mouthpiece of the government? In: A. H. Y. Chen and A. Harding eds. *Constitutional Courts in Asia: A Comparative Perspective*. Cambridge: Cambridge University Press, pp. 141–67.
Han, I. S. (2005) Kwangju and beyond: Coping with past state atrocities in South Korea. *Human Rights Quarterly*, 27(3), pp. 998–1045.
Han, S. (1975) South Korea in 1974: The "Korean Democracy" on trial. *Asian Survey*, 15(1), pp. 35–42.
Hanley, P. (2014) Transitional justice in South Korea: One country's restless search for truth and reconciliation. *East Asia Law Review*, 9(2), pp. 138–67.

Hayner, P. B. (2010) *Unspeakable Truths: Transitional Justice and the Challenge of Truth Commissions.* London: Routledge.

Hong, S. R. (2002) Finding the truths on the suspicious deaths under South Korea's military dictatorship. *Korea Journal*, 42, pp. 139–62.

Huang, C. Y. (2019) Frozen trials: Political victims and their quest for justice. In: J. A. Cohen, W. P. Alford, and C. F. Lo eds. *Taiwan and International Human Rights: A Story of Transformation.* Singapore: Springer, pp. 81–97.

Huang, C. Y. (2021) A noble dream undelivered: The quest for transitional justice during Tsai Ing-wen's first term. In: G. Schubert and C. Y. Lee eds. *Taiwan during the First Administration of Tsai Ing-wen: Navigating in Stormy Waters.* London: Routledge, pp. 209–33.

Huntington, S. (1993) *The Third Wave: Democratization in the Late 20th Century.* Norman, OK: University of Oklahoma Press.

Hwang, L. P. (1997) Trial of two former presidents of Korea: Comparative analysis of constitutional issues and justification. *The Korean Journal of International and Comparative Law*, 24, pp. 173–206.

Interpretation No. 567 [2003]. [Viewed August 9, 2021]. Available from: https://cons.judicial.gov.tw/jcc/zh-tw/jep03/show?expno=567

Interpretation No. 793 [2020]. [Viewed August 9, 2021]. Available from: https://cons.judicial.gov.tw/jcc/zh-tw/jep03/show?expno=793

Jeju 4.3 Peace Foundation. (2014) *The Jeju 4·3 Incident Investigation Report.* South Korea: Jeju 4.3 Peace Foundation.

Kim, C. I. E. (1978) Emergency, development, and human rights: South Korea. *Asian Survey*, 18(4), pp. 363–78.

Kim, D. C. (2002) Beneath the tip of the iceberg: Problems in historical clarification of the Korean War. *Korea Journal*, 42(3), pp. 60–86.

Kim, D. C. (2005) The war against the "enemy within": Hidden massacres in the early stages of the Korean War. In: G. W. Shin, S. W. Park, and D. Yang eds. *Rethinking Historical Injustice and Reconciliation in Northeast Asia: The Korean Experience.* London: Routledge, pp. 75–93.

Kim, D. C. (2010) The truth and reconciliation commission of Korea: Uncovering the hidden Korean War. [Viewed August 9, 2021]. Available from: http://japanfocus.org/-Kim-Dong_choon/3314

Kim, D. C. (2012) Korea's truth and reconciliation commission: An overview and assessment, *Buffalo Human Rights Law Review*, 19, pp. 97–124.

Kim, H. J. (2009) Seeking truth after fifty years: The national committee for investigation of the truth about the Jeju 4.3 events. *International Journal of Transitional Justice*, 3(3), pp. 409–26.

Kim, H. J. (2013a) Trial and error in transitional justice: Learning from South Korea's truth commissions. *Buffalo Human Rights Law Review*, 19, pp. 125–67.

Kim, H. J. (2013b) Presidential truth commission on suspicious deaths. In: L. Stan and N. Nedelsky eds. *Encyclopedia of Transitional Justice Vol. 3.* Cambridge: Cambridge University Press, pp. 380–84.

Kim, H. J. (2013c) South Korea. In: L. Stan and N. Nedelsky eds. *Encyclopedia of Transitional Justice Vol. 2.* Cambridge: Cambridge University Press, pp. 452–58.

Kim, H. J. (2014) *The Massacres at Mt. Halla: Sixty Years of Truth Seeking in South Korea.* Ithaca, NY: Cornell University Press.

Kim, H. J. (2021) A tale of two commissions: Explaining the different trajectories of human rights movements in Korea. *Peacebuilding*, 9(2), pp. 175–89.

Kim, M. S. H. (2013) Constitutional jurisprudence and the rule of law: Revisiting the courts in Yusin Korea. *The Hague Journal on the Rule of Law*, 5, pp. 178–203.
Kim, M. S. H. (2019) *Constitutional Transition and the Travail of Judges: The Courts of South Korea*. Cambridge: Cambridge University Press.
Kim, Q. Y. (1996) From protest to change of regime: The 4–19 Revolt and the fall of the Rhee regime in South Korea. *Social Forces*, 74(4), pp. 1179–208.
Kim, S. (2001) *Politics of Democratization in Korea: The Role of Civil Society*. Pittsburgh, PA: University of Pittsburgh Press.
Kim, Y.-C. (2003) The shadow of the Gwangju uprising in the democratization of Korean politics. *New Political Science*, 25(2), pp. 225–40.
Ko, N. C. (2021) *Truth, Justice, and Reparations in Peru, Uruguay, and South Korea: The Clash of Advocacy and Politics*. Singapore: Palgrave Macmillan.
Kritz, N. J. (1995) The dilemmas of transitional justice. In: *Transitional Justice: How Emerging Democracies Reckon with Former Regimes, Volume I: General Considerations*. Washington, DC: United States Institute of Peace, pp. xix–xxx.
Lee, C. J. (1973) South Korea: The politics of domestic-foreign linkage. *Asian Survey*, 13(1), pp. 94–101.
Lee, H. K. (1974) Constitutional development in South Korea. *Hong Kong Law Journal*, 4, pp. 41–51.
Lewis, S. L. (2002) Commemorating Kwangju: The 5.18 Movement and civil society at the millennium. In: C. K. Armstrong ed. *Korean Society: Civil Society, Democracy, and the State*. New York: Routledge, pp. 149–70.
Lin, C. C. (2021) Dadi Dangqian: Panluanfan zeishengsu pohui shehui zihsu? (大敵當前：叛亂犯再上訴破壞社會秩序？－釋字第二七二號解釋檔案, The enemy is coming: Would the appeal by political prisoners obstruct social order? Archives of Interpretation No. 272.) In: C. C. Lin et al. eds. *Fengmin Shifa: Dafaguan yu zhuanxing Zhengyi* (*奉命釋法：大法官與轉型正義, Judicial Interpretation by Political Command: Grand Justice and Transitional Justice*). Taipei: Transitional Justice Commission, pp. 120–49.
Merril, J. (1980) The Cheju-do Rebellion. *Journal of Korean Studies*, 2, pp. 139–97.
Nathan, M. A. and Park, E. J. (2013) Final recommendations of the truth and reconciliation commission, Republic of Korea. *Buffalo Human Rights Law Review*, 19, pp. 79–96.
Oh, G. (1997) Trial of two former presidents of Korea: A comparative criminal analysis. *The Korean Journal of International and Comparative Law*, 24, pp. 207–32.
Oh, J. K. C. (1999) *Korean Politics: The Quest for Democratization and Economic Development*. Ithaca, NY: Cornell University Press.
Park, J. (2008) The judicialization of politics in Korea. *The Asian-Pacific Law and Policy Journal*, 10(1), pp. 62–113.
Presidential Truth Commission on Suspicious Deaths. (2004) *A Hard Journey to Justice: First Term Report 10.2000–10.2002*. Seoul: Presidential Truth Commission on Suspicious Deaths.
Roehrig, T. (2002) *The Prosecution of Former Military Leaders in Newly Democratic Nations: The Cases of Argentina, Greece, and South Korea*. Jefferson, NC: McFarland Publishing.
Sa, E. S. (2009) Development of press freedom in South Korea since Japanese colonial rule. *Asian Culture & History*, 1(2), pp. 3–17.
Stone, A. (1974) The Korean student revolution: A political analysis. *Occasional Papers on Korea*, 2, pp. 132–43.

Sunstein, C. R. (2015) *Constitutional Personae: Heroes, Soldiers, Minimalists, and Mutes*. Oxford: Oxford University Press.
Teitel, R. (1997) Transitional jurisprudence: The role of law in political transformation. *The Yale Law Journal*, 106, pp. 2009–80.
Teitel, R. (2000) *Transitional Justice*. Oxford: Oxford University Press.
Truth and Reconciliation Commission of South Korea. (2010) *Comprehensive Report Vol. I*. South Korea: Truth and Reconciliation Commission of South Korea.
West, J. M. (1997) Martial lawlessness: The legal aftermath of Kwangju. *Pacific Rim Law and Policy Journal*, 6(1), pp. 85–168.
Wolman, A. (2013) Looking back while moving forward: The evolution of truth commissions in Korea. *The Asian-Pacific Law and Policy Journal*, 14(3), pp. 27–56.
Wu, N. T. (2005) Transition without justice, or justice without history: Transitional justice in Taiwan. *Taiwan Journal of Democracy*, 1(1), pp. 77–102.
Yeh, J. R. and Chang, W. C. (2011) The emergence of East Asian constitutionalism: Features in comparison. *The American Journal of Comparative Law*, 59(3), pp. 805–39.
Yoon, D. K. (1988) Constitutional amendment in Korea. *Korean Journal of Comparative Law*, 16, pp. 1–13.

Part 2

Constitutional Process of Transitional Justice

4 Constitutional Justice and Negotiated Peace in Colombia

Nelson Camilo Sánchez León

Colombia is living through a dilemmatic but hopeful stage in its history. Under the umbrella of "transitional justice," the Colombian government, since at least 2005, has implemented a series of strategies to put an end to a half-century-long conflict between the government and several guerrilla groups. The human impact of the conflict has been enormous, with at least 50,000 lives lost and one of the world's largest populations of internally displaced people. These transitional-justice strategies have tried to achieve two major goals: first, the voluntary demobilization of combatants, and second, guarantees for the rights of the victims of the conflict (Sánchez et al. 2016). The difficulty of achieving an acceptable balance between the two goals has given rise to sophisticated legal debates around constitutional justice, stirred by the Colombian Constitutional Court's central role in these matters.

Owing to its pursuit of the two goals, Colombia is internationally known today as a relatively successful peacebuilding case. The first round of negotiations among various factions in 2003 resulted in the demobilization of more than 30,000 right-wing paramilitary combatants (Laplante and Theidon 2006). More recently, the government reached a comprehensive peace agreement with the oldest and largest guerrilla factions in the Western Hemisphere (Colombian State and Farc 2016). All these achievements have depended on the country's use of innovative systems of truth-seeking, criminal accountability, and reparations, which today are the object of comparative studies.

However, as in any negotiation of this type, the domestic political stakes are high. Ideological differences between various sectors of society have obscured the progress made by the negotiating parties, thus significantly complicating efforts to implement any eventual agreements. Moreover, Colombians have been addressing whether or not the materializing agreements are compatible with international law as well as with Colombia's constitution, which has been in force since 1991.

In this chapter, I will present both the constitutional debates that Colombia's peace negotiations have triggered and the transitional justice mechanisms that the country has adopted. The timeframe of this study will extend roughly from 1991 to the present. My central argument will be that the Colombian Constitutional Court, by fulfilling various roles, has been able to position itself as a key

DOI: 10.4324/9780429505089-7

player within some very difficult political contexts and has thus created a space for political negotiations – all under constitutional controls that have prevented political interests from violating the rights of victims. Nevertheless, these constitutional controls have generated risks to both the court's legitimacy and the judicial system's consistency. If care isn't taken, the risks may turn into real problems that not only impede the adequate functioning of Colombia's transitional justice mechanisms but undercut the Constitutional Court's legitimacy as well.

This chapter proceeds as follows. In the first section, I briefly describe the creation of Colombia's 1991 constitution and why this document is referred to as a peace pact. In the second section, I present three recent phases in the relationship between Colombian constitutionalism and the country's transition from war to peace: The Constitutional Court establishes fundamental rights and transition options where the constitution itself is almost wholly silent (stage 1); the court seemingly defers to other powers so that they can negotiate effectively (stage 2); and the court becomes a legal referee bridging gaps in political consensus regarding peace and its meaning (stage 3). In the third and final section of this chapter, I offer my concluding thoughts on the various points theretofore raised.

The 1991 Constitution as a Peace Pact and the Constitutional Court as its Guardian

The armed conflict in Colombia dates back to 1964, when the country's first communist guerrilla groups emerged: the FARC-EP (Revolutionary Armed Forces of Colombia – People's Army), the ELN (National Liberation Army), and the EPL (Popular Liberation Army) (Offstein 2003). In the 1970s, these groups were joined by a second wave of guerrillas. Among them were M-19, *Movimiento Revolucionario Quintín Lame*, and *Corriente de Renovación Socialista*. During the 1980s, two Colombian governments advocated the realization of peace agreements with some of the guerrilla groups, one of whose key demands was sweeping reform targeting the then nearly century-old 1886 Constitution.

This negotiation process hinged quite significantly on the participation of citizens, led by progressive segments of the country's population, including university students who named themselves the Movement of the "Seventh Ballot" and who promoted constitutional and political reform (Uprimny 2001). As a result of these various activities, by the early 1990s, for the first time in the history of the country, a national constituent assembly in charge of drafting a new constitution was convened. Colombian scholars consider this outcome to be one of the greatest moments of democratization in the country (Gutiérrez Sanín 2011). To reintegrate former combatants who had agreed to lay down their arms, the government granted seats in the constituent assembly to guerrilla groups that had entered into the peace agreement with the state. One such group was M-19. (In fact, one of its members was co-president of the assembly.) Another such group was the *Movimiento Revolucionario Quintín Lame*, which had a strong indigenous base.

A fundamental purpose of creating a new constitution was to achieve peace with the guerrilla groups and to allow for a democratic handling of ideological and political differences. For this reason, the drafting and the ratification of the new constitution in 1991 have been characterized as elements of a peace pact. Whether from a domestic perspective or an international comparative one, many people including commentators, activists, and researchers have positively evaluated the fruits of the constitutional-drafting process. The Colombian Constitution of 1991 has been classified as cutting-edge in many respects, including its commitment to equality and protection of human rights as well as its creation of two fundamental elements to the protection of these rights: the Constitutional Court and the *Accion de tutela*.[1] The Constitutional Court's jurisprudence has earned considerable praise from Colombians who admire its rigorous yet creative constitutional activism (Cepeda and Landau 2017).

However, the constitutional convention's goal of ending the war was seriously weakened when the two largest and most powerful guerrilla groups (FARC and ELN) decided not to take part in the drafting of the 1991 Constitution. Therefore, in parallel with Colombia's democratization during the early 1990s, the country endured a resurgence of armed conflict attributable to the strengthening of the two aforementioned guerrilla groups and paramilitary groups.[2] The upshot of this resurgent conflict was that Colombia experienced a major humanitarian crisis between 1999 and 2012 (UNHCR 2008).

Transitional Justice and the Constitutional Court's Standard-Creation Role

Álvaro Uribe became president of Colombia in August 2002, pledging to throw the full might of the country's military against FARC guerrillas. His pledge followed the collapse, in the late 1990s, of a new round of negotiations between the government and FARC. In December 2002, the right-wing paramilitary groups declared a unilateral ceasefire, which had been a government precondition for talks with any of the armed groups. Negotiations were formalized on

1 The *Accion de tutela* ("protective writ") is a flexible jurisdictional injunction designed to protect fundamental rights when violated or threatened by any public authority's action or omission.

2 In response to the insurgent violence, businessmen and landowners sponsored the creation of right-wing self-defense groups. In the 1990s, the groups restructured themselves as modern paramilitary forces under the banner United Self-Defense Forces of Colombia (*Autodefensas Unidas de Colombia*, AUC). Over time, the paramilitary groups consolidated territorial control and started to displace the guerrillas in certain regions. This was followed by the paramilitary groups' shift from their original leadership composed of rural elites to a new leadership made up primarily of military commanders. The increased presence of professional soldiers in the upper echelons of the paramilitary groups was accompanied by these individuals' incursion into formal politics. At the time, the state considered them allies in the anti-guerrilla effort and thus made no objection to their growing military and political power (Duncan 2006; Abdala et al. 2008).

July 15, 2003, with the Santa Fe de Ralito Accord, in which AUC leaders agreed to demobilize fully by the end of 2005.[3]

It was then that the language of transitional justice entered with force into the country's political and legal debates. The government introduced to Congress a draft bill known as the "alternative-sentencing project," which advanced the idea that retributive justice should cede place to restorative justice applied specifically to ex-combatants. The government claimed this reform would support reconciliation (Sánchez et al. 2016). The proposal faced strong opposition from local victim organizations and by international human rights bodies. Their view was that the reform amounted to legislatively mandated impunity for human rights violators, a situation that would fly in the face of recent developments in international human rights law (e.g., the standards of the Inter-American Court of Human Rights) and in international criminal law (whose seminal instrument, the Statute of Rome, was ratified by Colombia in 2002) (Sánchez 2016).

The forceful criticism leveled at the proposed restorative-justice reform led to its collapse, forcing Congress to consider alternative justice-system reforms. Some of these alternatives advocated a no-holds-barred punishment of human rights violators, the very idea of which would hamper any kind of voluntary demobilization. Other alternatives leaned toward general pardons, which – much like the proposed reform – cast doubt on the reformers' commitment to holding human rights violators accountable for their actions (Saffon and Uprimny 2008).

The legislative process for this reform culminated in the passage of *Law 975 of 2005*, known as the Justice and Peace Law.[4] It served as a framework for two things: first, the demobilization of the AUC under a *sui generis* model, referred to as the justice and peace model; second, a proper handling of the country's gravest human rights violations. The law provided, first, that criminal trials as a transitional mechanism should be used to punish only the worst offenders, leaving open the possibility of amnesties or pardons for perpetrators of other crimes. Second, the law introduced a procedure for managing the cases overseen by the executive branch, which could initiate the procedure by presenting lists of demobilizing paramilitary to the Attorney General's Office (Fiscalía General de la Nación). In turn, the office would investigate serious crimes on the basis of statements made by these demobilizing individuals. Third, the Justice and Peace Law prioritized peace over justice only in the proportionality and duration of sentences, not in judgments or attributing responsibility. In other words, rather than offer total amnesty, the Justice and Peace Law resulted in generously reduced sentences while ensuring that all defendants convicted of a serious crime would indeed face a prison sentence, even if amnesty were subsequently granted.

3 According to official sources, a total of 31,671 members of paramilitary groups had demobilized by August 2006, mostly through collective demobilization (Alto Comisionado para la Paz 2006).

4 *Law 975 of 2005* sets forth "provisions for the reincorporation of members of illegal armed groups who effectively contribute to the attainment of national peace."

The law's emphasis on mandatory but reduced sentences generated strong political opposition and legal challenges. Victims' organizations pointed out that because the state had scarcely any information on events that had allegedly happened during Colombia's years of armed conflict, the law established a sort of hidden amnesty for those combatants who did not confess to their crimes. The law's critics contended that the state had a duty to investigate each case before granting any type of amnesty or reduced sentence (for an overview of the procedures, see IACHR 2004).

At this point, the Colombian Constitutional Court began to weigh in on – and arbitrate – the debate over sentencing, amnesty, peace, and transitional justice. Lawsuits began popping up, questioning the constitutionality of the Justice and Peace Law. The specific legal questions raised were of three main varieties: First, does the Constitution substantiate the theory of transitional justice? If so, what kind of transitional justice does the Constitution accept?

The answers to these questions are complicated because concepts like "transitional justice" and "the rights of the victims of serious human-rights violations" are nowhere to be found in at least a strict reading of the Constitution. However, in which I call its standard-setting role, the court construed a line of jurisprudence defending that both concepts could be inferred from both general constitutional principles and certain constitutional clauses.[5] First, the court found that the Constitution's reference to the granting of amnesties and pardons (Art. 150) was an indication that the Constitution drafters had foreseen the compatibility of some transitional justice mechanisms with the Constitution. Second, the court turned to international human rights law to give recognition and content to the "rights of the victims of the conflict." The Constitution establishes that the human rights norms recognized by Colombia are binding in the country, in a similar range to constitutional norms (Botero and Restrepo 2005). Based on that principle, the court used the standards contained in United Nations soft law documents and the jurisprudence of the Inter-American Court of Human Rights to hold that victims of gross human rights violations have a range of constitutional rights, including the right to know the truth about what happened to them, to seek justice for the acts taken against them, and to have the perpetrator or the state make reparations for those acts.

The Constitutional Court has ever since sustained that any peace effort must be considered in light of victims' rights. Thus, while maintaining a flexible stand consistent with a transitional justice approach, the court has insisted on limits on the kinds of concessions that the state can make in return for peace. Among those

5 *Judgment C-370* (2006), *Judgment C-1199* (2008) (both related to claims of the unconstitutionality of *Law 975 of 2005* or the Law of Justice and Peace); *Case C-771* (2011) (related to a claim of the unconstitutionality of *Law 1424 of 2010*, known as the "Law on Agreements on Historic Truth"); *Case C-052* (2012) (related to a claim alleging unconstitutionality of some articles of *Law 1448 of 2011*, known as the Law of Victims and Land Restitution.

limits are core protections for victims and prevention of regimes that would allow impunity for the most serious crimes.

A Move Toward a More Deferential Role

Victims received the court's central thesis well. However, some decisions worried peacebuilding experts. Initially, the Constitutional Court took a strict interpretation of punishments for serious human rights violators that reflected the court's view that only prison time complies with international justice standards. An obvious problem of this approach is that inflexible unwelcome sanctions (prison time) would be profoundly unattractive to guerilla members. It is very unlikely – if not impossible – that a militarily undefeated guerrilla group would accept demobilization if, in the aftermath, the majority of the group's members would receive significant prison sentences (Sandoval 2015).

Responding to this profound dilemma, in 2010, a senator from the government coalition submitted to Congress a draft proposing constitutional reforms that would allow for the start of peace talks with active guerrilla groups. In this proposal, the senator identified four things the reforms would need to achieve: (1) the reforms would need to clear up the legal uncertainty regarding the state's ability to grant legal benefits to ex-combatants who had committed heinous crimes; (2) the reforms would need to clarify whether or not the Attorney General has the power to make use of modern prosecutorial methodologies, including mapping, selection, and prioritization of cases; (3) the reforms would need to determine whether or not the state could reintegrate former members of demobilized groups into Colombia's political life, including elected political life; and (4) the reforms would need to remove the risk that a court decision could overturn an agreement reached during the peace-accord negotiations (Sánchez and Uprimny 2013).

In 2012, this proposal became an amendment to the Constitution. Popularly known as the Legal Framework for Peace, the amendment consisted of two new articles introduced on a temporary basis. In the first place, the new provisional Article 66 of the Constitution integrated the concept of transitional justice into the Colombian Constitution. Previously, transitional-justice models had been based on ordinary laws, not the basic law of the land – the Constitution. Additionally, the reform established a clear constitutional basis for asserting that armed conflict's victims have a right to truth, justice, and reparations. In short, through this constitutional reform, Congress endorsed the jurisprudence of the Constitutional Court by integrating it into the body of the Constitution. Congress wanted this to give the guerrillas' members security that a future judicial decision would not reverse the standards outlined in the Constitutional Court's caselaw (Sánchez and Ibáñez 2014).

Another feature of this constitutional amendment was the executive and legislative branches' authorization to design judicial and extrajudicial transitional mechanisms to balance the quest to end impunity for the perpetrators of mass atrocity with the constraints of justice and accountability mechanisms. In that vein, the amendment lessens the Constitutional Court's uncompromising approach regarding the need to investigate and prosecute every former combatant formally. However, the amendment did not outline specific criteria for case selection. In terms of selecting which cases should be investigated and prosecuted, the constitutional reforms of 2012 state that Congress, at the behest of the government, may create the selection criteria for categorizing crimes and for ranking their importance. The reforms establish that, in determining the selection criteria, Congress should consider the seriousness and representativeness of the cases. In addition, the current constitution allows Congress (1) to establish under which conditions the suspension of a sentence would proceed; (2) to establish under which cases extrajudicial sanctions, alternative sentencing, or special arrangements for the implementation and enforcement of a sentence would apply; and (3) to authorize courts to conditionally waive criminal prosecution of all cases that are not selected.

However, the legal battle over the Constitution's interpretation did not end with the reform's congressional approval. A group of representatives from social organizations and political parties filed suits targeting the constitutional reforms.[6] These suits made use of a theory created by the court itself for constitutional review of reforms to the Constitution.[7] Several prominent Colombian and international human rights organizations submitted amici brief to the court supporting the call to strike down the reforms. One such actor was the prosecutor of the International Criminal Court. The prosecutor sent two private letters (which were later leaked to the public) where she warned about the possible incompatibility of the newly instituted constitutional provisions with international law (Ambos 2014).

Local analysts disagreed with the prosecutor's position. In their opinion, a court decision absolutizing the principle of justice would make a negotiated peace impossible to achieve. The analysts then asked the Constitutional Court to act in ways that would strengthen the likelihood of a just peace agreement sensitive to victims' rights and a conception of justice and victims' rights supportive of successful peace negotiations (Uprimny et al. 2013).

In the end, in two subsequent decisions, the court upheld both aspects of the reform – that is, the inclusion of mechanisms to flexibilize (but not eliminate) the punitive content of accountability in peace processes and to allow for the political participation of ex-combatants in Colombian politics so long as these

6 Some of the lawsuits were filed by victims' organizations that opposed criminal benefits accruing to those who had committed serious violations of human rights, while other lawsuits were filed by right-wing interest groups opposed to the prospect of former guerrillas participating in politics (Sánchez and Ibáñez 2014).

7 According to this theory, the powers that be (such as Congress) can only amend the Constitution, not modify its structural base. This base can be modified only by citizen voters because modification is tantamount to implementing a new constitution. Thus, if a proposed amendment were to modify the structure of the Constitution, the Constitutional Court could declare the amendment unconstitutional.

individuals engage in peace negotiations (see *Judgment C-579* [2013]; *Judgment C-577* [2014]). There was a shift in the role of the Constitutional Court. In these decisions, the court acted less as a creator of the standards and gave more leeway to other political powers. These decisions were essential in providing social and international legitimacy to Colombia's constitutional reforms and building trust between the government and FARC, which had already sat at the negotiating table with the government.

Polarization, Political Arbitration, and Lack of Popular Support for the Peace Agreement

While these legal proceedings were taking place in Colombia, in Havana, Cuba, FARC and the government delegations were making concrete progress in their peace negotiations. To the extent that they progressed, the number of constitutional and legal questions grew, not only regarding the topics already addressed by the Constitutional Court (justice, victims' rights, and political participation) but also regarding the legal status of the peace agreement under international and constitutional law (Uprimny and Guiza 2019).

In their peace negotiations, both the Colombian government and especially the anti-government forces sought more than a political arrangement: They sought a legally viable arrangement that would ensure compliance. In addition, many parts of the emerging peace agreement required some kind of legal status, including a sound constitutional status. The negotiating parties shared the view that the final agreement should have democratic legitimacy, and in fact, President Juan Manuel Santos publicly promised that nothing agreed upon in Havana would be implemented without the approval of the Colombian people.

From the very beginning of the negotiations, FARC and the Government agreed that the peace agreement should seek three objectives: popular legitimacy, legal validity, and normative regulation. For the FARC, the natural mechanism for achieving these objectives was the convening of a national constituent assembly that, as in 1991, would pave the way for the drafting of a new constitution. This process would not only enable the parties to address the aforementioned three points but also align attractively with the political project that the guerrillas wanted to implement. The government, however, was adamantly opposed to a constituent assembly. On the one hand, the government always tried to keep negotiating within a defined agenda that resulted in the fewest changes possible to the social and legal status quo. In this sense, a constituent assembly would reopen negotiated issues or bring to light new issues. On the other hand, the government always pursued a mechanism that was easy to control logistically and politically.

With no agreement in sight, in September 2015, the government submitted a proposal for a new constitutional amendment to Congress without the backing of the guerrillas. The proposal would have dismissed the constituent assembly and created a dual mechanism for giving the intended final agreement political legitimacy and legal validity. One part of the mechanism called for a yes-or-no referendum in which voters would voice their support for or opposition to an agreement. The other part of the mechanism called for a way to gradually incorporate the given agreement into the Colombian legal system without compromising the agreement's integrity.

The proposed mechanism allowed the Colombian Congress to expedite the legislative process for those constitutional amendments considered necessary for the implementation of the accord. In order to honor the Havana agreement, the houses of Congress would not be able to make modifications to the drafts submitted by the government. Both the House and the Senate could only approve or reject the constitutional amendment or draft bill in its entirety. Additionally, the mechanism reduced the required number of debates on the floor for both regular and constitutional laws and granted the president special executive powers to expedite the laws necessary for implementation of the accord.

Although the powerful *Centro Democrático* party – a right-wing political party headed by the former president Uribe – opposed negotiations with the guerrillas, in late 2016, legislators from other political parties approved the constitutional reform that is popularly known as the fast-track amendment.

The guerrillas again opposed this reform as they considered it an attempt by the government to unilaterally impose its preferences on the guerrilla at the negotiating table. Meanwhile, the *Centro Democrático* party and other opponents of the peace talks attacked both the referendum and the fast-track amendment. The Constitutional Court considered both of these issues. Indeed, the Constitution requires that referendums undergo automatic judicial review by the court. And in court, the *Centro Democrático* party challenged the Legislative Act for Peace and its fast-track amendment on grounds that the act supplanted the Constitution.[8]

The litigation against this constitutional amendment took place at a critical moment in the peace-negotiation process. While the parties had reached essential agreements in Havana, they still had significant disagreements on critical issues. At the same time, Colombian society was showing signs of weariness with the peace negotiation. These factors made the Constitutional Court's decision extremely important to boost the legitimacy of the peace process. However, great uncertainty existed as to whether or not the court would endorse the referendum. Some influential government officials and legal experts argued that a popular referendum reliant on a majority vote could not constitutionally determine a fundamental right – in this instance, the right to peace. Other experts claimed that it was unconstitutional to subject a long and complex agreement

8 This power of control derives from the already-mentioned doctrine of substitution of the Constitution created by the Constitutional Court itself. "The substitution of the Constitution is a competence error committed by the modifier of the Charter when it [not only] acts as a secondary or derivative constitutional assembly instead of making amendments to the Constitution according to the needs created by political, economic, and social changes, etc., [but also] inserts in it elements that change its meaning, making it radically different from the one adopted by the National Constitutional Assembly in 1991, which can occur fully or partially and also in a permanent or a transitory manner." (*Judgment C-332* [2017]).

to a yes-or-no vote because such a vote, by forcing and all-or-nothing decision, violates the principle of voter freedom.

Pressed for time, the government and FARC decided to leave the process's fate in the Constitutional Court's hands. FARC gave in to their demand for the immediate convening of a constitutional assembly. Instead, the government and FARC communicated that if the court approved the referendum's amendment, the two parties would accept this mechanism to regulate the agreement. With their decision, the parties admitted that the peace agreement would not be automatically considered a constitutional norm – as FARC intended – but that gradually, through the fast-track procedure, some parts of the agreement would become norms of constitutional and legal status. The only exception would be those provisions concerning human rights and international humanitarian law, which would directly integrate human rights principles into the Constitution through the "block of constitutionality," which is a set of normative rules that, though not explicitly stated in the Constitution, helps courts determine the constitutionality of laws.

In July 2016, the court issued a ruling that upheld the constitutionality of the special rules that had been designed by Congress for holding the referendum (*Judgment C-379* [2016]). This ruling was of vital importance, helping the government and FARC finalize negotiations just weeks later. The government called for an October referendum in which Colombians would endorse or reject the proposed agreement.

At the polls, the Colombian people rejected the agreement by a very narrow margin (less than 0.5%). Political analysts have cited several explanations as to why such a large number of voters voted against the agreement. A common argument is that citizens rejected the agreement on the grounds that members of the FARC would face lenient punishment (most of them would face alternative penalties to imprisonment). For their part, some influential critics of the peace negotiations argued – without providing any evidence – that the electorate had voted that way to reject the use of the constitutionality block to give the Havana agreement constitutional status.

The defeat of the referendum generated widespread unrest in public opinion and in political leadership. Nobody knew how to confront the situation. Even though the agreement had been popularly rejected, there was little understanding of the exact sentiments underlying this rejection. Also, people were unsure whether a completely renegotiated agreement or a strategically modified one would stand the best chance of attracting the support of a majority of voters in a future referendum. Indeed, doubts arose as to the viability of any future agreement (Uprimny Yepes and Güiza Gómez 2019).

The government was able to rapidly convince FARC of the need to renegotiate the agreement and to take into account the points that had been raised by the opposition. In this context, the negotiation teams met once again in Havana in October 2016 and successfully addressed most of their previously unresolved issues. The result was a new agreement that, though substantially different from the first one in several regards, remained largely unchanged regarding two central points: First, ex-combatants would continue to benefit from soft sentencing (which, the opposition had argued, was equivalent to impunity), and second, ex-combatants would be able to participate in politics.

While the international community, a majority of political parties, and an important cross-section of public opinion celebrated this agreement, the opposing parties voiced their disagreement with the new text. In their opinion, the agreement was illegitimate because it did not present substantial modifications to the two aforementioned points that had probably contributed to the first agreement's failure. At the same time, the constitutionalists, who generally supported the agreement, asked themselves if it was necessary to carry out a new referendum or if another institutional route of endorsement was viable. A form of political endorsement of the new agreement was necessary for Congress to begin processing draft bills through the previously mentioned *fast-track* reform.

Given the urgency surrounding the task of implementing the peace agreement (in particular the task of providing legal security to the ex-combatants who were already demobilizing and disarming), the government acknowledged that the two chambers of Congress would be responsible for endorsing or rejecting the new agreement. On November 30, 2016, all the political parties (with the exception only of the party headed by the ex-president Uribe) endorsed the agreement through a congressional resolution. This endorsement, despite encouraging the promoters of the peace accords, escalated social polarization. The opposition skillfully intensified opposition to the peace process, arguing that the government and its allies had committed fraud against the popular will of Colombia and that, thus, any implemented peace accords would be illegitimate. Meanwhile, members of the *Centro Democratico* party filed two suits before the Constitutional Court, compelling it to review whether or not the *fast-track* reforms were constitutional. The court had to resolve two issues. The first was whether it was constitutional for Congress to grant special powers to the president to issue decrees implementing the peace agreement on matters that should ordinarily be regulated by Congress's act. The second issue under the court's decision was whether or not the expedited procedure created for the processing of laws in Congress violated the Constitution.

The political forces once again bet that the Constitutional Court would arbitrate the dispute between supporters and detractors of the peace accords, especially given how polarized yet expectant the country was. In fact, the court began to do just that: It sought to pacify the opposing sides by issuing rulings that partially justified the arguments of each political camp (Uprimny et al. 2018).

In effect, by mid-December 2016, the court had issued its decision on the *fast-track* mechanism (*Judgment C-699* [2016]). The court found that Congress could authorize the extraordinary powers to the president but warned of the high risks that the exercise of these powers could pose to the balance of powers. The court went on to declare that these extraordinary powers are, in general, constitutional so long as the resulting decrees comply with a series of strict conditions (Roa 2017).

Months later, in May 2017, the court issued a decision on the second suit, in which it declared that the expedited procedure created by the fast-track amendment did not violate the Constitution. Nevertheless, this decision's wording strongly suggested that the court was seeking to counter its widespread perceptions as a government ally. The court declared unconstitutional a central aspect of the fast-track amendment: the prohibition for Congress to partially modify the bills submitted by the executive and admit only one general vote – affirmative or negative – on the introduced draft bills (Judgment C-332 [2017]). Thus, by declaring the expedited procedure's constitutionality, the government emerged victoriously, but by restricting the mechanism's all-or-nothing approach, the opposition enjoyed a partial victory.

The approval of this mechanism for the expeditious approval of norms for the peace agreement's implementation opened the way for an intense period of norm building. At the same time, the issuance of these norms brought with it a period of intense work for the court itself. According to the procedure approved in the rulings mentioned previously, the government was to use its fast-track powers within six months – extendable for an equal period.[9] Each of the norms approved through this mechanism was to be subject to mandatory review by the Constitutional Court.[10]

Within a context of political polarization and hyper-judicialization of the peace process, the Constitutional Court has aimed to maintain itself in the middle of political discussions. Its decisions seem calculated to give each political camp an opportunity to claim victory.[11] In being activist, the court runs two main risks: The first is that the general public and political forces begin to view the court as a political actor, not as a legitimate apolitical institution. The second is that the court's weak legal arguments amount to political balancing acts that create institutional instability which might abusively inflate its powers.

Between 2007 and 2019, the court's decisions exhibited a balance between correcting Congress' misinterpretations of the peace agreement and conveying that the peace agreement had not given the government a blank check to

9 This extension took place, and thus, the fast-track mechanism was valid in Congress until November 30, 2017, while the president's ability to issue special decrees ended on May 29, 2017.

10 According to information released by the court, "In this role, our work increased exponentially, as we had to accomplish for the country, in a reasonable time, the difficult task of pointing out which rules were in line with the Constitution and which were not. We reviewed a total of 46 sets of regulations, as follows: 5 legislative acts, 6 laws and 35 decree-laws, for a total of 774 regulatory provisions" (Corte Constitucional 2019: 5).

11 In the words of the then president of the Constitutional Court, "I want to give an account of the need we had to seek delicate balances and consensus within the Court, in the framework of a highly polarized country, marked by profound discrepancies. The implementation of the Final Agreement coincided with the recent electoral process, in which the peace agreements and the positions regarding them marked the political contest. This situation led the Court to seek moderate and balanced decisions, acting as a catalyst to mitigate radical political positions, using the Constitution to act as a referee" (Corte Constitucional 2019: 5).

transform the existing political system. This balance shows that court's role did not undercut public perception of its legitimacy. Although each of the decisions generated political interest and attracted passionate critiques, none of the decisions was flatly rejected by the legal community or political groups. For example, the court approved the Special Jurisdiction for Peace, although with some limitations (*Judgment C-674* [2017]), a decision that the respected Colombian scholar Mauricio García Villegas defended as a pacifying decision, since, in his opinion, it is "before anything, a political decision (non-partisan) that must not be read with the scrutinizing eyes of the jurist (provision after provision) but with the conciliatory and broad look of the constitutional judge" (García Villegas 2017).

Apart from the normal controversy that typically accompanies a decision by the court, no direct attacks by political camps against the court have surfaced regarding its intervention on peace-agreement-related matters. The court would have been an easy target for such attacks because, in 2018–19, accusations of corruption leveled against one of the justices had stained almost two decades of Colombian society's trust in the transparency of the court. Therefore, given the divisiveness of the political moment in 2018, opponents of the court would have found it easier than ever to politically confront the institution and publicly erode its legitimacy. In actuality, the politically balanced decisions of the court have likely helped it reclaim its legitimacy, which the corruption scandal had eroded.

However, the arguments used by the court to justify certain decisions have been extremely deficient. An example of these failings is the previously mentioned decision in which the court limited the *fast-track* procedure (*Judgment C-332* [2017]). The court found that the procedure was unconstitutional because it had an abbreviated mechanism by which (1) the executive alone could initiate the Congressional approval of norms and (2) Congress could approve or reject government-originated draft bills only en bloc – not through article-by-article voting. According to the court, the procedure undermined congress members' constitutionally protected powers to deliberate and vote on legislative matters effectively (*Judgment C-332* [2017]). The problem with the court's argument is that the 1991 Constitution establishes several situations where both the executive alone can propose a particular governmental draft bill and Congress must vote on the project en bloc. For example, according to the 1991 Constitution, Congress can approve treaties only through en bloc votes (Uprimny Yepes and Güiza Gómez 2019; Ceballos 2017).

Moreover, by focusing on the political impact of its decisions, the court has ended up altering some of the intrinsic power balances of the peace accord. This problem was most evident when the court reviewed the constitutionality of the amendment that constitutionalized the court system created by the accord to judge the most serious atrocities committed during Colombia's years of armed conflict – known as the JEP (*Judgment C-674* [2017]). In Judgment C-674, the court found that the JEP was constitutional. This finding, as with the finding in Judgment C-332, received praise from both the defenders of the peace process and its opponents. As per the peace agreement, the JEP has jurisdiction to prosecute any person who had participated, either directly or indirectly, in the commission of grave human rights violations during Colombia's armed conflicts. Under the agreement, not only combatants – whether guerillas, right-wing paramilitary fighters, or government soldiers – were subject to the JEP, but so, too, were public officials, financiers, and others whose actions had resulted in such violations (Sánchez and Marín 2017).

Some of the most virulent opposition to the agreement came from business people had engaged in potentially prosecutable actions. These people vocally supported the "no" vote in the referendum and heavily lobbied Congress so that it would prevent JEP from having jurisdictional reach over third parties. Finally, the Constitutional Court ruled in favor of the business sector. In decision C-674, the court held that only third parties who individually and voluntarily submit to the JEP are subject to its imperatives. The court's arguments, however, were very poor and have elicited a stream of legal criticism (Michalowski et al. 2018). Essentially, the court argued that, by granting the JEP mandatory jurisdiction over civilians, the amendment violated the right to a natural judge because the novel court system created an ex post facto jurisdiction.[12] But if this were the case, the court should have declared the creation and the jurisdiction of the JEP unconstitutional in its entirety.

Additionally, the content of the decision undermines the central purpose of the JEP – that is, to create a jurisdiction in which a transitional court can hear cases related to all individuals accused of having participated in serious human rights violations during Colombia's conflicts. This purpose of the JEP played a key role in the peace negotiations because, for the guerrillas, the transitional court had to be the result of an agreement between the disputing parties. The court's intervention altered this fundamental agreement between the government and FARC and left outside the jurisdiction of the transitional court a group considered by FARC as one of the main culprits of the violence against them.

In any case, the Constitutional Court's distortions in these rulings have not been fatal to the functioning of the JEP. The fact that FARC continued with the process despite feeling that the modifications introduced by the court did not honor the original agreement is a sign of the court's legitimacy, even for a guerrilla group that for decades distrusted state institutions.

From 2018, with the completion of the first stage of normative implementation of the peace agreement, the Constitutional Court has had less public involvement in peace issues. As for the transitional justice component, the implementation of the agreement has been slow but stable. Although the president elected in August 2018 represents a coalition led by the *Centro Democratico* party – and that then candidate promised in the campaign to reverse the transitional justice system established by the peace agreement – the court has not been forced to make politically controversial decisions. Congress's political forces have not

12 Using this same argument, the Court found that the compulsory jurisdiction of the JEP over nonmilitary state agents was unconstitutional.

approved the government's proposals that have sought to modify the system created in the agreement and endorsed by the Constitutional Court.

Conclusion

Since the 1990s, the transitional-justice process in Colombia has been closely intertwined with the country's peace negotiations, its efforts to implement peace settlements, and its demobilization of nonmilitary armed groups. These complex processes have involved the presidency, Congress, the judiciary, leaders of guerilla and paramilitary organizations, international organizations, and a wide range of other actors, including civil-society groups. Throughout these processes, there has been a focus on transitional justice and the role of human rights in peacemaking (Sánchez et al. 2016).

More than in the cases of some other countries, the transitional-justice process in Colombia has been anchored in the legal system. Colombia has a deeply rooted legalist culture, emphasizing the use of legal instruments and judicial processes to regulate most aspects of social, political, and institutional life. The Colombian Constitutional Court has been a principal institutional actor in this legalist culture, applying its jurisprudence to issues ranging from governance and public policy to the protection of citizens' rights. In particular, the court has overseen transitional-justice measures that have helped establish the constitutionality and legitimacy of the country's transitional-justice peacemaking agenda. The Colombian Congress has integrated transitional-justice concepts into successive legal instruments, starting with the Justice and Peace Law in 2005 and extending more recently to the Legal Framework for Peace in 2012. These instruments – be they laws, proposals, agreements, or other such documents – have had a significant bearing on Colombia's search for a lasting peace.

The relationship between constitutional law and peace took on new significance when Colombia enacted the Constitution of 1991 as a mechanism for peace and transition. Although the drafting of the constitution in itself led to the demobilization of several insurgent groups and the content of the Constitution has helped democratize Colombian government and society, the drafting and enactment of the constitution failed to end armed conflict in the country. In fact, violence worsened.

In this context, Colombian society and its institutions have counted on the Constitutional Court as a fundamental tool to establish a relationship between transitional justice and constitutionalism. In the relationship, the court has played three distinguishable roles. First, the court helped create a consensus regarding both the rights of victims and the goals of a negotiated peace. These actions by the court advanced the transitional-justice process but had two drawbacks: The court promoted a highly punitive form of justice, which threatened to antagonize guerrilla organizations critical to the peace negotiations. Also, the court substantively modified rules governing the peace negotiations, thus undermining them. A second role played by the court in the relationship between transitional justice and constitutionalism was the Colombian government's embrace of constitutional reform as a way to secure a successful peace accord. There again the Constitutional Court intervened, this time deferring to the government for the purpose of promoting peace negotiations. A third role of the court took shape as the peace negotiations progressed: When political and social fractures threatened to undermine the hard-earned progress, the court began serving as a legal "referee" between opposing sides. One method by which the court tried to heal these fractures was to announce decisions that essentially constituted a victory for each political camp invested in the given case.

These three roles of the court reveal how flexible it was in negotiating and shaping the relationship between transitional justice and constitutionalism. However, this delicate intervention was not exempt from risks. In this chapter, I have analyzed some of them: the risk that the court would lose political legitimacy, the risk that the court's poor legal reasoning would create instability, and the risk that the court would excessively expand its power. Overall, the court has managed to protect the agreements without negatively affecting its political legitimacy. The cost of this success has been some legal inconsistencies that have caused some institutional problems but have not jeopardized the viability of the agreement's implementation.

References

Abdala, Y., D. González, and E. González. (2008). *Tierra, oro y conflictos.* Bogotá: INDEPAZ.

Alto Comisionado de Naciones Unidas para los Refugiados (ACNUR). (2008). *2007 Global Trends: Refugees, Asylum-seekers, Returnees, Internally Displaced and Stateless Persons.* Ginebra: ACNUR.

Alto Comisionado para la Paz. (2006). *Proceso de paz con las autodefensas: Informe ejecutivo.* Bogotá: Presidencia de Colombia.

Ambos, K. (Coord.). (2014). *Justicia de transición y constitución.* Bogotá: Editorial Temis.

Bergsmo, M. and M.P. Saffon. (2011). "Enfrentando una fila de atrocidades pasadas: ¿Cómo seleccionar y priorizar casos de crímenes internacionales nucleares?" In *Selección y priorización como estrategia de persecución en los casos de crímenes internacionales: Un estudio comparado*, edited by K. Ambos, 23–112. Bogotá: GIZ.

Botero, C. and E. Restrepo. (2005). "Estándares internacionales y procesos de transición en Colombia." In *¿Justicia transicional sin transición? Verdad, justicia y reparación para Colombia*, edited by R. Uprimny. Bogotá: Dejusticia.

Ceballos, J. (2017). "Una Curiosa especie de zoología fantástica constitucional." *miblogdeconstitucional.com* (May, 21, 2017).

Cepeda, E.M.J. and D.E. Landau. (2017). *Colombian Constitutional Law: Leading Cases.* New York: Oxford University Press.

Colombian State and FARC-EP. (2016). *Final Agreement for Ending the Conflict and Building a Stable and Lasting Peace* (November 24, 2016).

Constitutional Court, Judgment C-052 of 2012 [2012].

Constitutional Court, Judgment C-332 of 2017 [2017].

Constitutional Court, Judgment C-370 of 2006 [2006].

Constitutional Court, Judgment C-379 of 2016 [2016].

Constitutional Court, Judgment C-577 of 2014 [2014].
Constitutional Court, Judgment C-579 of 2013 [2013].
Constitutional Court, Judgment C-674 of 2017 [2017].
Constitutional Court, Judgment C-699 of 2016 [2016].
Constitutional Court, Judgment C-771 of 2011 [2011].
Constitutional Court, Judgment C-1199 of 2008 [2008].
Corte Constitucional. (2019). *Resumen de las Decisiones de la Corte Constitucional en la Implementación del Acuerdo Final de Paz.* Bogota: Consejo Superior de la Judicatura-CENDOJ.
Duncan, G. (2006). *Los señores de la guerra: De paramilitares, mafiosos y autodefensas en Colombia.* Bogotá: Planeta.
García Villegas, M. (2017). "La gramatica de la paz." *El Espectador* (November 18, 2017). https://www.elespectador.com/opinion/columnistas/mauricio-garcia-villegas/la-gramatica-de-la-paz-column-723691/
Gutiérrez-Sanín, F. (2011). "La Constitución de 1991 como pacto de paz: discutiendo las anomalías." *Estudios Socio-Jurídicos* 13, no. 1: 419–447.
Inter-American Commission on Human Rights (IACHR). (2004). *Informe sobre el proceso de desmovilización en Colombia.* OEA/Ser.L/V/II.120. Washington, DC: OAS.
Laplante, L. and K. Theidon. (2006). Transitional Justice in Times of Conflict: Colombia's Ley de Justicia y Paz, 28 MICH. J. INT'L L.
Michalowski, S. et al. (2018). *Entre coaccion y colaboración. Verdad judicial, actores económicos y conflicto armado en Colombia.* Bogotá: Colección Dejusticia.
Offstein, N. (2003). "A Historical Review and Analysis of Colombian Guerrilla Movements: FARC, ELN, and EPL." *Desarrollo y Sociedad* 52: 99–142.
Roa, J. (2017). "La sustitución constitucional, el 'Fast Track; y el Acuerdo Final de Paz: Análisis." *Ambito Juridico* (May 25, 2017).
Saffon, M.P. and R. Uprimny. (2005). "¿Al fin, ley de justicia y paz? La ley 975 de 2006 tras el fallo de la Corte Constitucional." In *¿Justicia transicional sin transición? Verdad, justicia y reparación para Colombia*, edited by R. Uprimny, et al. Bogotá: Dejusticia.
Saffon, M.P. and R. Uprimny. (2008). "Usos y abusos de la justicia transicional en Colombia." In *Justicia y Paz, ¿cuál es el precio que debemos pagar?*, edited by A. Rangel. Bogotá: Intermedio.
Sánchez, N.C. (2016). *Acceptance of International Criminal Justice. Case Study on Colombia.* Nuremberg: International Nuremberg Principles Academy.
Sánchez, N.C., J. García-Godos, and C. Vallejo. (2016). "Colombia: Transitional Justice before Transition." In *The Transitional Justice in Latin America: The Uneven Road from Impunity towards Accountability*, edited by E. Skaar, C. Collins, and J. García-Godos. London: Routledge.
Sánchez, N.C. and C. Ibáñez. (2014). "La justicia transicional como categoría constitucional." In *Justicia de transición y constitución*, coordinated by K. Ambos. Bogotá: Editorial Temis.
Sánchez, N.C. and D. Marín. (2017). "Corporate Accountability in Transitional Justice in Colombia." In *Peace, Everybody's Business! Corporate Accountability in Transitional Justice: Lessons for Colombia*, edited by J. van de Sandt and M. Moor. Utrecht, The Netherlands: PAX.
Sánchez, N.C. and R. Uprimny. (2013). "El Marco Legal para la paz: ¿Cheque en blanco o camisa de fuerza para las negociaciones de paz?" In *Justicia para la paz:*

Crímenes atroces, derecho a la justicia y paz negociada, edited by R. Uprimny, L.M. Sánchez, and N.C. Sánchez. Bogotá: Colección Dejusticia.

Sandoval, C. (2015). *Facing the Justice Dilemma in Colombia*. Accessed March 20, 2020. www.justiceinfo.net/en/research/524-facing-the-justice-dilemma.html

United Nations High Commissioner for Human Rights. (2008). *Report on the Situation of Human Rights in Colombia – Draft* (31 December, 2008) (A/HRC/10/032).

Uprimny, R. (2001). "Constitución de 1991, Estado social y derechos humanos: promesas incumplidas, diagnósticos y perspectivas." In *El debate a la Constitución*. Bogotá: Universidad Nacional de Colombia, Ilsa.

Uprimny, R., D. Güiza Gómez, and H. Martínez Carrillo. (2018) "Domando la incertidumbre: el control constitucional de actos legislativos en tiempos de transición de la guerra hacia la paz negociada." In *La justicia al encuentro de la paz en contexto de transición. Reflexiones actuales para desafíos colombianos*, edited by C.E. Umaña Hernández. Bogotá: Universidad Ex- ternado de Colombia.

Uprimny, R., L.M. Sánchez, and N.C. Sánchez. (2013). *Justicia para la paz: Crímenes atroces, derecho a la justicia y paz negociada*. Bogotá: Colección Dejusticia.

Uprimny, R. and N.C. Sánchez. (2015). *The ICC and Negotiated Peace: Reflections from Colombia*. Accessed March 20, 2020. www.opendemocracy.net/openglobalrights/rodrigo-uprimny-nelson-camilo-sánchez/icc-and-negotiated-peace-reflections-from-col

Uprimny Yepes, Rodrigo and Diana Isabel Güiza Gómez. (2019). "Pacigerancia: el valor jurídico de los acuerdos de paz en el derecho internacional." *Latin American Law Review* no. 03: 49–78

5 Constitutions, Courts, and the Quest for Transitional Justice

The Case of Chile

Javier Couso

Introduction

One of the important developments in law and political science in the aftermath of the so-called *third way of democratization* (Huntington 1991) was the emergence of the field of transitional justice, something that confirms the universal relevance achieved by human rights in recent decades. This enterprise has produced a large body of literature (Fletcher and Weinstein 2015, 177–98) both of a theoretical and empirical nature, as well as the emergence of nongovernmental organizations dedicated to the promotion of transitional justice.

Having said this, there are relevant issues that the transitional justice field has barely addressed. One of them is the relationship between transitional justice, constitutional law, and constitutional courts. In this essay, I deal with this issue by analyzing the experience of Chile, a country regarded as a successful case in terms of the degree of truth, justice, and reconciliation achieved (after a brutal military regime).

The Concept, Goals, and Elements of Transitional Justice

Although it is beyond the scope of this chapter to fully explore transitional justice as a political practice or as a new field of social inquiry, it seems relevant to at least review its basic features. A good summary of its main tenets can be found in the United Nations' "Guidance Note of the Secretary-General: United Nations Approach to Transitional Justice" (United Nations 2010).

In this document, the United Nations begins its definition of "transitional justice" by making the following statement:

> For the United Nations, transitional justice is the full range of processes and mechanisms associated with a society's attempt to come to terms with a legacy of large-scale past abuses, in order to ensure accountability, serve justice and achieve reconciliation. Transitional justice processes and mechanisms are a critical component of the United Nations framework for strengthening the rule of law. (United Nations 2010, 2)

DOI: 10.4324/9780429505089-8

Note that, according to the United Nations, transitional justice is not merely about coming to terms with the past but also about looking to the future, particularly with an eye toward strengthening the rule of law. In other words, the United Nations states that dealing with past atrocities in a proper way is crucial to laying down a future where the rule of law thrives.

At this point, it is worth asking why addressing in a meaningful way past human rights violations represents a critical element of a strategy to strengthen the rule of law. The rationale for this seems to be the following: If the rule of law is fundamentally about furthering the universal values of controlling state power and ensuring equal treatment to all, there is a great chance that leaving atrocities unpunished would send those in power the message that constitutions and laws are not real constraints but mere advice capable of being set aside if it becomes a hindrance to governmental action.

After establishing the goals and purposes of transitional justice, the United Nations' "Guidance Note" goes on to describe the main components of transitional justice:

> Transitional justice consists of both judicial and non-judicial processes and mechanisms, including prosecution initiatives, facilitating initiatives in respect of the right to truth, delivering reparations, institutional reform and national consultations. Whatever combination is chosen must be in conformity with international legal standards and obligations. (The United Nations 2010, 3)[1]

1 As the statement transcribed states, for the UN, transitional justice should include prosecution initiatives, facilitating initiatives in respect of the right to truth, delivering reparations, institutional reform, and national consultations. Prosecution initiatives aim to ensure that those responsible for committing crimes, including serious violations of international humanitarian law and gross violations of international human rights law, are tried in accordance with international standards of fair trial and, where appropriate, punished. The credibility and legitimacy of prosecution initiatives require that they are conducted in a nondiscriminatory and objective manner, regardless of who the alleged perpetrators may be. States have the primary responsibility to exercise jurisdiction over these crimes. Truth-seeking processes help post-conflict and transitional societies investigate past human rights violations and are undertaken by truth commissions, commissions of inquiry, or other fact-finding missions. The right of individuals to know the truth is supported by several treaty bodies, regional courts, and international tribunals. Reparations programs seek to redress systemic violations of human rights by providing a range of material and symbolic benefits to victims. Reparations can include monetary compensation, medical and psychological services, health care, educational support, and return of property or compensation for loss thereof, as well as official public apologies, building museums and memorials, and establishing days of commemoration. Public institutions that helped perpetuate conflict or repressive rule must be transformed into institutions that sustain peace, protect human rights, and foster a culture of respect for the rule of law. By reforming or building fair and efficient public institutions, institutional reform enables post-conflict and transitional governments to prevent the recurrence of future human rights violations. National consultations are a critical element of the human rights-based approach to transitional justice, founded on the principle that successful transitional-justice programs necessitate meaningful public participation, including the different voices of men and women. Public participation reveals the needs of communities affected by conflict or repressive rule,

As these core components of transitional justice makes clear, the overarching goals of it are to end impunity through prosecutions and truth initiatives, to compensate victims for the terrible deeds inflicted upon them and their relatives, to introduce institutional reforms aimed at preventing human rights violations, and finally, to introduce a consultative process promoting local ownership of transitional-justice programs.

Transitional Justice and Constitutions

The relationship between constitutional law and transitional justice has many faces, depending, among other things, on whether or not the path to democratization includes a new constitution, something of critical importance if the former authoritarian regime imposed its own constitutional charter.

If the departing authorities did not touch the preexisting constitutional order, the restoration of the authority of the constitution will be a first step toward democratization and transitional-justice purposes. To the contrary, in countries where the authoritarian regime imposed a new constitution, the substitution of it becomes crucial once the authoritarian regime leaves power, both for the sake of the new democratic regime and in order to better deal with past human rights violations. The problem, however, is that no matter how important for the transitional period a new constitution might be, its substitution may prove to be impossible. Indeed, except in cases in which dictatorships experience a total collapse, transitions to democracy are constrained by the institutional structures (including constitutional charters) left in place by the authoritarian regime. Indeed, except for cases of decolonization and revolution, countries embarking on a transition to democracy are not in a position to pick and choose the institutions deemed ideal for advancing the transition. To the contrary, the new democratic authorities have to work with the "political cards" they have been dealt, and this cold, brutal fact often precludes the possibility of introducing a new constitution.

I now turn to the following question: Is it necessary for a country to get a new constitution in order to overturn past wrongs?

The answer to this question inevitably requires an account of two things: what a successful transition to democracy actually looks like and what constitutional law and courts can do to support the former. Thus, for example, in cases where the previous authoritarian regime perpetrated human rights violations in open disregard of the constitution, the introduction of a new charter – as a way to address past atrocities – would be unnecessary. After all, there would have been nothing substantially authoritarian characterizing the constitution in place during the dictatorial regime's rule. This was the case in Uruguay (1973–83) and in

---

allowing states to craft an appropriate context-specific transitional-justice program. Moreover, the consultative process helps victims and other members of civil society to develop local ownership of the resulting program (UN 2010, 7–10).

Argentina (1976–83), countries where the military perpetrated a coup d'état and then, while leaving the old constitutions intact, proceeded to rule de facto.

Contrasting with the cases just mentioned, there are instances in which authoritarian leaders establish a new constitution as a way, first, to legitimate their rule and, second, to entrench some of their recently imposed policies. In these cases, the substitution of the authoritarian constitution for one introduced in democracy is crucial. Indeed, given that in all likelihood, the authoritarian charter will consecrate legal concepts and institutions contrary to democratic values, it will be important to get rid of it. In such cases, the new authorities will have to be persistent in trying to adopt a new constitution and, at the very least, will have to purge the authoritarian charter of its most antidemocratic clauses. Furthermore, even if the constitution imposed by the dictatorship is not completely inadequate from a liberal-democratic point of view, the fact that an authoritarian regime introduced the charter that will govern the nation's return to democracy will be symbolically troubling (particularly in light of Jürgen Habermas' claim that democratically elaborated laws, including constitutions, help create social cohesion in modern societies.)[2]

In sum, although a fresh democratic start typically requires the introduction of a democratically enacted constitution, the constraints that characterize many transitional processes often make it impossible. This, however, is not always as bad as it sounds since the atrocities perpetrated by authoritarian regimes often violate the very constitutional order they imposed, and such violations will allow the new democratic authorities to heal the wounds of the past by implementing the former.

Transitional Justice and Constitutional Courts

Considering that – as we have seen in the preceding section – the introduction of a new constitution in the midst of a transition to democracy might prove unfeasible, the role of a constitutional court (or a high court with powers of judicial review) becomes crucial. In fact, given that the final word regarding the meaning of a constitution lies with such courts, judicial interpretations of a constitution can change it. Thus, the change-through-interpretation path could accomplish goals similar to the ones accomplished by the introduction of a new charter.

Looked at from the standpoint of political science, constitutional courts and other high courts endowed with the power of striking down legislation represent a technique of governance that has experienced unprecedented global expansion, particularly in the last three to four decades (Tate and Vallinder 1995). The vast literature on constitutional courts has analyzed their features, attitudes, and actions in an attempt to explain how these institutions have shaped the political arena and advanced important constitutional values (Stone Sweet 2000; Epp

2 Habermas 1996.

1998; Jacob et al. 1996; Tate and Vallinder 1995; Shapiro and Stone Sweet 1994; Tate and Jackson 1992; Holland 1991).

In addition to the possibility that courts can change an authoritarian-era constitution, they can bolster transitional justice by bringing into the country's legal order the standards that International Human Rights Law has elaborated precisely for countries that are coming to terms with their past human rights violations. Indeed, even in states that have not ratified the relevant international treaties setting the standards of proper transitional-justice processes, constitutional courts often invoke the former to reinterpret the constitution in a way that helps foster the goals of transitional justice. Also, a constitutional court can promote liberal democratic values by ruling that the country ought to introduce new legislation in each of the five core components of transitional justice identified previously (prosecutions, truth initiatives, reparations, the introduction of institutional reforms, and national consultations).

The potential of constitutional (and high courts with the power of judicial review) to further transitional justice should, however, be handled with care since, as students of constitutional courts know well, the risk of being perceived as too "activists" can put them at risk, as it has been the case in transitional countries such as Hungary or Poland. This suggests that constitutional and high courts should leave to a national legislature the bulk of the work relating to transitional justice, limiting their roles to tasks that legislatures are ill-equipped to undertake: for example, reinterpreting the parts of an authoritarian-era constitution that are blocking legislation supportive of democracy and transitional justice.

In the case of Chile, as we shall see next, the protagonist of the – ultimately successful – process of transitional justice was the Supreme Court, not the Constitutional Court. The Supreme Court is the head of the ordinary judicial branch, while the Constitutional Court is a special institution entirely concerned with the control of the constitutionality of legislation. Thus, while the Supreme Court reviews on appeal criminal cases (including past human rights violations), the Constitutional Court does not deal with such cases on appeal. Having said this, the constitutional adjudication powers of the latter would have allowed it to play an important role in Chile's transitional justice process, but for reasons that will be described next, the Constitutional Court decided to largely marginalized itself from this domain.

Constitutions, Courts, and Transitional Justice in Chile

In what follows, I address the roles of constitutions and courts in transitional justice by analyzing the case of Chile, a Latin American country that faced important constraints at the start of its transition to democracy. Chile represents an interesting case given that, although its transition took place under the constitutional terms established by the departing authoritarian regime, it managed to exceed expectations regarding its handling of past human rights violations (Collins 2010).

The Military Coup of 1973 and the Pinochet Dictatorship

After almost a century and a half of republican government that began in the early nineteenth century and that was interrupted only by a short period of crisis (in the late 1920s), Chile experienced a brutal military dictatorship. This unprecedented authoritarian period began on September 11, 1973, when the military overthrew the democratically elected president, Salvador Allende, whose left-wing politics and economic policies became intolerable to conservative segments of Chilean society. Given that the coup was forbidden by the existing Constitution (of 1925), the coup's leaders – the military junta – declared that they had the power to elaborate a new charter (Decree Law No. 128, of 1973).[3] Accordingly, in the following months, the junta passed a series of "constitutional decrees" providing a legal basis for its actions (Decree Law No. 527, of 1974).[4] This move signaled a conservative revolution that started with the dismantling of the entire institutional architecture of the previous democratic regime. In late 1974, the leaders of the junta designated Augusto Pinochet, who had been the commander in chief of the Army at the time of the coup, the supreme leader of Chile. His rule lasted until 1990, when Chile peacefully regained a democratic form of government.

The coup's leaders defended their overthrow of Allende by arguing that his leadership had posed an existential threat to Chile and that no other recourse of action had been possible. The alleged justification given by the military for its violent overthrow of a constitutional government was that it was about to establish a communist dictatorship. The irony is that, in order to prevent what they regarded as the imminent fall into an authoritarian order, the junta imposed an actual dictatorship. The late Robert Barros addressed these arguments in his analysis of the coup:

> [It] marked a clear break with the preceding democratic, constitutional form of rule of law and opened a period of de facto rule in which the validity of the dictatorship's legal acts rested solely upon the force of the military's coercive imposition and the claim that the circumstances provided no alternative but exceptional rule, not some prior positive grant of authority. (Barros 2000, 12)

As Barros rightly put it, Chile's military regime represented an unprecedented one, in that it disregarded the country's traditional adherence to legal forms.

3 The Decree Law No. 128 of November 16, 1973, interpreting Article 1 of Decree Law No. 1, stated, "*Since September 11, 1973, the military junta has assumed the constituent, legislative, and executive powers (. . .).*"

4 The Decree Law No. 527, article 4, of June 26, 1974, stated: "*The military junta exercises, through decree laws, the Constituent Power and the Legislative Power, in accordance with the provisions contained in this Decree and in the legal precepts that complement it. Said decree-laws must bear the signature of all their members and, when they deem it appropriate, that of the respective Ministers.*"

Once in power, the regime implemented a neoliberal "revolution" that completely reshaped Chile's economy and society. In the midst of this, Pinochet and his advisers started planning a strategy to ensure their conservative policies would survive the eventual return of democratic rule to Chile. Their shared distrust of democracy helps explain their keen interest in constitutional matters.

Meanwhile, in order to consolidate its grip on power, the authoritarian regime perpetrated gross human rights violations. The junta killed journalists as well as leaders of opposition parties, unions, and student organizations and passed the "Amnesty Law" of 1978 (Decree Law No. 2,191 of April 19, 1978). This law granted agents of the state immunity from prosecution for almost any crime they might have committed during the five-year period between September 11, 1973, and March 10, 1978. Given that the bulk of the human rights violations had been perpetrated precisely during those first five years, over a thousand individuals participating in the coup and the Pinochet regime benefited from this self-amnesty.

The Authoritarian Constitution of 1980

Just days after the coup, on September 24, 1973, the military junta organized a small commission entrusted with drafting a new constitution: the *Comisión de Estudios de la Nueva Constitución Política del Estado*, which worked for five years (Huneeus 2006, 231).[5] After the constitutional project was finished, it was studied and slightly amended by the Council of State ("Consejo de Estado") and then finally revised by the junta. The project was ratified by means of a fraudulent plebiscite on September 11, 1980 (Fuentes 2013; Delgado 1980; Barros 2000, 17).[6]

The resulting Constitution of 1980 established a *nueva institucionalidad* (a new institutional order) meant to be the formal expression of the foundational project in which Pinochet's regime had been engaged since 1973. The new charter aimed at ensuring that Chile would not return in the future to a system of government rooted in political parties, a system that Pinochet dismissively called *partidocracia*, meaning the demagogic capture of the state by the political parties. "The Constitution of 1980," Carl Bauer has stated, "thus embodied the ideals of a-politicism, technocratic efficiency, anti-communism and laissez-faire economics that the military regime of Pinochet had already been implementing" (Bauer 1998, 9). The idea was to ensure the continuity of the authoritarian project while giving the regime a certain degree of legitimacy. Of course, it may seem rather absurd that a dictatorship owing its existence to a violent coup d'état would give so much attention to the constitution. A possible reason for this

5 The commission was set up through Decree No. 1064 of September of 1973: it stated that "there is a need for a new Constitution in order to reconstruct, renew, and improve the fundamental institutional order of the Republic."

6 The plebiscite took place without an electoral registry (i.e., a list of eligible voters); without political parties (which were banned); and without a campaign against the adoption of the new Constitution.

apparent paradox is that, by giving the military a formal constitutional role, that of protecting the 1980 charter, Pinochet expected to provide the latter with an invulnerability lacking in previous Chilean charters.

Dealing with Past Human Rights Violations in the Era of Democratic Transition

After eight years of ruling with the help of a tailored Constitution, in 1988, General Pinochet confronted a plebiscite that was contemplated by the former, in which the people would be asked if he would continue in power for eight additional years. This time, however, the plebiscite was not fraudulent, thanks to a Supreme Court's decision that mandated that electoral registers and courts were in place and, significantly, the possibility that the opposition could publicize the "no" option.[7] In this scenario, the latter option prevailed, opening the door for an eighteen-month long period of negotiations between the military regime and the opposition, which led to another plebiscite (in 1989) reforming the most outrageous clauses of the 1980 charter. A few months later, a presidential election was held, and on March 11, 1990, the first democratically elected leader in two decades was sworn in, thus ending the dictatorship.

Just weeks after taking control of government, President Patricio Aylwin decreed the establishment of a Truth and Reconciliation Commission (*Comisión Nacional de Verdad y Reconciliación*), charged with investigating the widespread human rights violations perpetrated under the military regime. The commission worked intensively for one year to document its findings, and the result was *The Rettig Report*, which accomplished two aims: It accounted for human rights violations committed by not only the dictatorship but also antigovernment paramilitary organizations, and it issued important recommendations for preventing similar tragedies in the future. In light of the Rettig Report, Aylwin's administration worked with Congress to pass legislation aimed at compensating the victims of human rights violations (and their relatives). Furthermore, it pushed legislation for either freeing imprisoned anti-Pinochet guerrilla members or commuting their sentences (Cavallo 1998, 38–47; Loveman and Lira 2000, 502–11). Another important presidential initiative was to publicly request that courts end their refusal to investigate cases involving alleged human rights abusers who, in 1978, had received blanket amnesty from Pinochet's government (Loveman and Lira 2000, 498).[8]

Thanks to these initiatives, toward the end of his four-year term, in March 1994, Aylwin's administration had quite a lot to show in terms of truth and reparations. However, the administration failed to secure prosecutions of alleged perpetrators

7 See Decision N° 33/1985 of Chile's Supreme Court.

8 In August of 1990, the Supreme Court, sitting *en banc*, confirmed the constitutionality of the Amnesty Law of 1978 by an 11-to-4 vote.

because it lacked a congressional majority (due to the fact that the Constitution of 1980 provided for nonelected senators that altered the democratic correlation of forces in the upper house), which could have repealed the deeply problematic self-amnesty legislation.

During those first years of transition to democracy, Chile's courts weathered intense public criticism for their passivity in the face of the dictatorship's widespread human rights violations. *The Rettig Report* thoroughly confirmed many Chileans' belief that Pinochet-era courts had exhibited indifference to human rights violations (Berryman 2004). Specifically, *The Rettig Report* made the following statement:

> The Judicial branch did not react with sufficient energy to the widespread human-rights violations of the time (. . .). Indeed, the attitude adopted by the judicial branch during the military regime resulted in a deepening of the process of systematic human-rights violations both in the short term, because the courts did not protect detained individuals, and in the long term, because the courts gave human-rights violators a growing sense of impunity for their criminal actions. (Correa 1999, 302)

Confronted with such strong criticism of its performance during the military regime, the Supreme Court issued a condemnation of the Rettig Report (Corte Suprema 1991, 237–50), stating that it was "passionate, reckless, and biased" (Matus 1999, 59),[9] and that the Truth and Reconciliation Commission had violated the separation-of-powers clause in the Constitution by inserting itself in adjudicative matters (Corte Suprema, 302). President Aylwin rebuffed the judicial response by going on national television to declare that, in his view, the Chilean courts "had shown a lack of moral courage in the face of the vast human rights violations perpetrated by the military regime" (Corte Suprema 1991, 303).

The Supreme Court reacted to Aylwin's assertion by accusing him of not only undermining the judiciary's status as a separate branch of government but endangering the rule of law as well (Matus 1999, 61). The court defended its actions during the military regime by declaring that the mission of all courts was to obey the existing law and not judge the justice or injustice of it. According to this logic, Chilean courts had rightly limited themselves to applying the very law that prevented them from defending human rights. Hiding under a supposedly strict adherence to legal positivism (understood as a mechanical application of existing law, without concern for the fairness of it), the Supreme Court repudiated what they regarded as an "attack on the independence and honor of the judiciary" (Matus 1999, 61).

9 The text of the Supreme Court's response to the "Rettig Commission Report," issued on May 17, 1991.

Criticism of the courts was fierce and arose across the spectrum of political parties. A sense of political fragility consequently took hold within the judiciary. In Jorge Correa's words,

> The decade of the 1990s thus started with a judicial branch that was in the worst of worlds. It did not have the democratic legitimacy that the new government authorities wanted for all state institutions, nor the (technocratic) aura of modernity of other state institutions. The right wing, although it considered the Supreme Court one of the core enclaves for the defense of the new institutionality, regarded it as an organ incapable of modernizing itself. Particularly within entrepreneurial circles, the judicial branch was perceived as an inadequate forum for the resolution of their disputes. The 'Concertación' (government coalition), for its part, regarded the judicial branch as an entity whose behavior before human rights violations had demonstrated its lack of adherence to the democratic system. (Correa 1999, 292)

The general sense that the Chilean courts had become more corrupt during the authoritarian years eventually led to a series of constitutional impeachment procedures filed by Congress against justices of the Supreme Court. The first was promoted by a coalition of senators from both the government and the opposition in December of 1992, and resulted in the removal of one justice (Lira and Loveman 1999, 530; Jorge Correa 1999, 304). This constituted one of the most important blows suffered by the Supreme Court in a century. Not since 1868 had Congress impeached a member of the court, and it had never actually succeeded in removing one.

In this scenario, President Aywin's appointments gradually started to change the makeup of the superior courts (Matus 1999, 183; Correa 1999, 281).[10] The presidential appointments were done – as prescribed by the Constitution of 1980 – from a pool of five candidates elaborated by the Supreme Court itself. The judge picked by the president had then then to be ratified by the Senate. The availability of new positions in the Supreme Court was due to a combination of some early retirements, as well as a couple of impeachment procedures against judges accused of corruption.

The appointments of new justices, as well as the new political and social context, eventually led the Supreme Court to reverse its interpretation of the 1978 Amnesty Law (covering human rights violations committed between September 11, 1973, and March 10, 1978) and to adopt the doctrine that the penal courts should investigate alleged crimes covered by the Amnesty Law before

10 By March of 1990, when the new democratic government took office, General Pinochet had managed to successfully nominate 12 of the Supreme Court's 17 justices. By 1998, however, the number of justices having been nominated during the military regime was only 4. If we take into account the fact that by then, the number of justices of the Supreme Court had risen to 21, we can grasp just how substantially the military-era justices' control of the court had weakened.

pardoning anybody thought to be responsible for the crimes. Furthermore, the court ruled that the investigation of past human rights violations was not precluded by the statute of limitations.

Although some scholars have regarded this change in the courts' jurisprudence as an expression of a more liberal ethos in the judicial system (Skaar 2000),[11] this interpretation is not warranted by the evidence. In fact, the shift exhibited by the Supreme Court seems to have been a strategic adjustment to a new democratic context in which Chileans were beginning to acknowledge the drama of the disappeared.

Owing to the changing jurisprudence of the Supreme Court as well as to the persistence and organization of human rights lawyers working to address past atrocities, by 2018 Chile had become one of the world's most successful transitional democracies with regard to the prosecuting and sentencing of perpetrators of crimes against humanity. Indeed, a report issued that year by the Transitional Justice Observatory (of Universidad Diego Portales) established that, by the middle of that year, over 400 final judgments had been issued in cases involving past atrocities (Collins 2018).[12]

The Effect That Pinochet's Arrest in London Had on Chile's Transitional Justice

In the previous section, I argued that the change in the jurisprudence of the Supreme Court concerning the Amnesty Law of 1978 was a sign not of independence and political liberalism but instead a pragmatic adjustment to a new political context. The same argument applies to the courts' handling of the country's most famous human rights case – the one centered on General Pinochet himself. This judicial process began in the most unexpected way when, on October 16, 1998, British authorities arrested the former dictator while he was visiting London. The arrest was in response to an extradition petition issued by a Spanish judge attempting to try Pinochet for crimes against humanity.

The decision by the United Kingdom to arrest a foreigner for crimes committed in a third country stunned the legal community throughout the world. But more to the point I want to advance here, the arrest triggered a profound shift in the status of General Pinochet in Chile. Indeed, up until his doomed trip to London, the former dictator had managed not only to avoid prosecution for past human rights violations but also to become a senator for life (something that was

11 One such scholar is Elin Skaar, who argued that the willingness of the Chilean courts to try people for past human rights violations was a sign of increased judicial independence by the Chilean courts.

12 The report had this to say: "Between 1995 and June 30, 2018, a total of 367 final judgments have been issued in cases of crimes against humanity committed during the dictatorship: 332 addressing criminal and/or civil matters, and 35 of civil lawsuits only. The 367 final sentences of all types (criminal and civil) issued between 1995 and June 2018 refer to a total of 713 victims absent (358 DD and 355 EP)."

authorized by the Constitution he had imposed on the country but that most thought would not happen). As for his immunity from prosecution for crimes not covered by the 1978 Amnesty Law, this was actually a merely a de facto immunity but nonetheless a very powerful one, given the support that he had among the ranks of the military in Chile. The notion that Pinochet was "untouchable" was so deeply entrenched in both political and judicial circles of late 1990s Chile that even a government who strongly opposed the legacy of Pinochet's rule felt compelled to stop an impeachment proceeding brought against him by a group of center-left congressmen who wanted to prevent the former dictator from joining the Senate (Moulián 1997; Cavallo 1998).

The political context just outlined explains why, by October of 1998, seven years into the new democratic regime, Pinochet had remained almost untouched by legal suits against him (Lira and Loveman 1999, 368).[13] This situation, however, significantly changed after British authorities arrested the man. In fact, the event so completely rearranged the social and political dynamics surrounding Pinochet – especially for the judiciary and the government – as to ultimately end his judicial immunity.

The eighteen months of international humiliation that Pinochet faced while under house arrest in London transformed the perception held by most Chileans of him as a formidable figure invulnerable to the rule of law (Roht Arriaza 2006).[14] Contributing to his diminished image was his increasingly fragile physical and mental state, which resulted from a litany of ailments and which served as grounds for his lawyers' request of mercy from the British courts. In this new scenario, the Chilean government took direct aim at the enfeebled former leader by issuing a steady stream of statements to the effect that the UK should allow Pinochet to return to Chile because its national courts could try him.[15] The government strategy to appeal to the jurisdictional rights of Chile as a sovereign state was the common ground that President Eduardo Frei thought could unite a society deeply divided over Pinochet (with part of the population considering him a brutal dictator and others a hero). This strategy would in time profoundly influence how the judiciary eventually handled the former dictator.

The critical moment came when the British government released Pinochet on the grounds that his frail health rendered him incapable of facing trial. Upon the arrival of the general in Santiago, in March 2000, human rights groups and relatives of the victims filed over a hundred criminal cases against him. Thus, four months after his return to Chile, a case concerning whether or not the criminal

13 The sole exception was a case filed by the Secretary General of the Chilean Communist Party and by the widow of a disappeared, Gladis Marín, in January of 1998. According to Lira and Loveman (1999), not until the second semester of 1998 were the first lawsuits on human rights violations filed against Pinochet.

14 For a detailed account of General Pinochet's arrest and extradition proceedings in London, see Kornbluh (1998) and Evans (2006).

15 This pledge was repeatedly made by President Eduardo Frei and his Minister of Foreign Affairs, José Miguel Insulza.

courts could deprive Pinochet of his senatorial immunity against prosecution appeared on the Supreme Court's docket. By that point, the government's position was that a court-ordered end to his immunity could not endanger the country's transition to democracy. Ultimately, the court not only deprived Pinochet of his senatorial immunity but actually confirmed a judicial decree that indicted him, obliging his defense team to resort to the humiliating argument that he was legally "insane," since that is the only reason allowing the suspension of a criminal procedure in Chile's penal law.

Much as when changes took place to the jurisprudence of the Supreme Court interpreting the Amnesty Law of 1978, the shift in Chilean courts' treatment of criminal charges against Pinochet constituted, according to some scholars, yet another example of an increasingly independent and democratic judicial branch. This conclusion is, from my perspective, again unwarranted. Indeed, the evidence strongly suggests that the judicial branch was attempting to accommodate itself to a constantly evolving political scenario.

The effects of Pinochet's arrest in London were not limited to the Chilean judiciary. Public opinion was changing, and so, too, were the views of the Chilean military, which up until that time had shown a strong loyalty to both the former military regime and the person of General Pinochet himself. The first sign of this change occurred when the commander in chief of the Army officially recognized the "legitimacy" of the "Rettig report." This profoundly consequential action was then followed by several initiatives that the Chilean military undertook in order to distance itself from the former authoritarian regime.

The changing attitudes toward human rights in Chile have led to a number of public initiatives aimed at raising awareness of the value of human rights. Perhaps most prominent among these initiatives was the introduction of a National Human Rights Institute, a cabinet-level position aimed at promoting human rights, and the establishment of memorials throughout the country.

Conclusion

As Justice Richard J. Goldstone noted in his contribution to this volume, societies emerging from an oppressive regime often painfully confront its harsh legacies. This confrontation is typically regarded as a multifaceted effort to uncover the human rights violations of the regime (and sometimes of its militant opponents), to bring violators to justice, and to take measures capable of preventing the repetition of human rights violations in the future (through education, legislation, and so on). The important goals mentioned by Goldstone are not, however, easy to achieve. And when transitional societies achieve them, the success is, in general, mostly a result not of careful planning but of messy interactions characterized by a bit more serendipity than misfortune.

Some societies that have endured oppressive regimes achieve the goals stated by Goldstone. Nevertheless, the legacies of the regimes can live on, weakening democracy and human rights. One such legacy is the legal architecture that some oppressive regimes have been able to leave in place during and after their country's transition to democracy. This type of legacy is particularly salient when the end of the authoritarian era has resulted from what experts on democratization label "pacted transitions." In these cases, the "price" of democratization is the continued presence of distinctly undemocratic rules imposed by the departing regime. Attempts to rid the fledgling democracy of those rules are often fraught with difficulty.

This type of situation beset Chile, a country that, in spite of the said constraints, experienced a successful process of transitional justice: Truths have been revealed, punishments have been imposed, and reparations have been made. These achievements were possible even though the military regime led by Augusto Pinochet left behind a constitution that still possesses highly problematic clauses despite three decades of reforms (which explains why the population voted overwhelmingly to introduce a new constitutional charter in October 2020).

The Chilean path toward truth, justice, and reconciliation reveals the powerful effects that the political context of a democratic transition can have on transitional justice. Chilean democratic authorities exhibited determination and skill in establishing the Truth and Reconciliation Commission (which launched a strong moral indictment against the judiciary for its passivity toward human rights violations during the authoritarian period) and in issuing a formal petition demanding changes to the Supreme Court's jurisprudence on the self-amnesty legislation left in place by the military regime. These two actions eventually led the Supreme Court to allow penal court investigations into relevant allegations and to identify the perpetrators of human rights violations. These steps towards a transitional justice were furthered by the (completely unexpected) arrest of General Pinochet in London, an event which put the need to punish perpetrators of past human rights violations at the center of the political agenda.

As we have seen in this essay, the active role that Chile's Supreme Court eventually took on the transitional justice domain stands in stark contrast with that of the Constitutional Court, which remains largely passive in the matter (in fact, when one looks at the history of transitional justice in this country it is astonishing how absent the latter was). One of the reasons for this seems to be that, during the first decade and a half of Chile's transition, the Constitutional Court had mostly conservative justices.

Transitional justice is often highly reflective of the political and constitutional constraints specific to each democratizing country. However, several patterns have emerged from the Chilean experience. One of the most important is that a new constitution can be convenient yet not indispensable for the task of establishing a well-functioning transitional-justice process when the deposed authoritarian regime disregarded human rights in ways that clearly violated the existing constitution. If, to the contrary, the authoritarian regime enacted a constitutional charter filled with illiberal values and obstacles to a just handling of past human rights violations, the quest for a new constitution should be relentless.

Another lesson that Chile's experience suggest is that through interpretation a high court can align even an illiberal constitution with the most basic standards set by International Human Rights Law. In order for such jurisprudence to be sustainable, however, justices must be aware that such moves should always be handled with care, since if a court is perceived as being too "activist," that might trigger interventions by other state actors seeking to apply the brakes to such jurisprudential developments. In other words, even the best intentioned of justices have to understand that they cannot appear to be single-handedly changing their Constitution since their legitimacy rests on the idea that they should interpret the latter, not remake it.

References

Barros, R. 2000. "Dictatorship and the Rule of Law: Rules and Military Power in Pinochet's Chile." Paper presented at *Conference on Democracy and the Rule of Law*, Madrid, Centro de Estudios Avanzados en Ciencias Sociales, Instituto Juan March, June 22–4.

Bauer, C. 1998. *Against the Current: Privatization, Water Markets, and the State in Chile*. Boston: Kluwer.

Berryman, P.E. 2004. Trans., 1993, *Report of the Chilean National Commission on Truth and Reconciliation*. Notre Dame, IN: Notre Dame University Press.

Cavallo, A. 1998. *La historia oculta de la transición: Chile 1990–1998*. Chile: Grijalbo.

Collins, C. 2010. *Post-transitional Justice. Human Rights Trials in Chile and El Salvador*. University Park, PA: Penn State University Press.

Collins, C. 2018. "Negacionismo en la era de la postverdad: Verdad, justicia, y memoria en Chile, a dos decadas del 'Caso Pinochet'." In *Informe Anual de Derechos Humanos UDP 2018*, edited by T. Vial. Chile: Ediciones Universidad Diego Portales.

Correa, J. 1999. "Cenicienta se queda en la fiesta: El poder judicial chileno en la década de los 90." In *El modelo chileno: Democracia y desarrollo en los noventa*, edited by P. Drake and I Jaksic. Santiago, Chile: LOM Ediciones.

The Decree Law No. 128, 1973. www.archivochile.com/Dictadura_militar/doc_jm_gob_pino8/DMdocjm0007.pdf

The Decree Law No. 527, 1974. https://legislacion-oficial.vlex.cl/vid/decreto-ley-aprueba-estatuto-gobierno-470819286

The Decree Law No. 2,191, 1978. https://www.bcn.cl/leychile/navegar?idNorma=6849

Delgado, S. 1980. *Génesis y Vigencia de los Textos Constitucionales Chilenos*. Santiago, Chile: Editorial Jurídica de Chile.

Epp, C. 1998. *The Rights Revolution: Lawyers, Activists, and Supreme Courts in Comparative Perspective*. Chicago: University of Chicago Press.

Evans, R. 2006. "Pinochet in London: Pinochet in Chile: International and Domestic Politics in Human Rights Policy." *Human Rights Quarterly* 207–44.

Fletcher, L. and H. Weinstein. 2015. "Writing Transitional Justice: An Empirical Evaluation of Transitional Justice Scholarship in Academic Journals." *Journal of Human Rights Practice* 7(2), 177–98.

Fuentes, C. 2013. *El fraude*. Santiago: Hueders.

Habermas, J. 1996. *Between Facts and Norms: Contributions to a Discourse Theory of Law and Democracy*. Cambridge, MA: The MIT Press.

Holland, K. ed. 1991. *Judicial Activism in Comparative Perspective*. UK: Palgrave Macmillan.

Huneeus, C. 2006. *The Pinochet Regime.* Boulder, Colorado: Lynne Rienner Publishers.

Huntington, S. 1991. *The Third Wave: Democratization in the Late Twentieth Century.* Oklahoma: University of Oklahoma Press.

Jacob, H., et al. 1996. *Courts, Law, and Politics in Comparative Perspective.* New Haven, CT: Yale University Press.

Kornbluh, P. 1998. "Prisoner Pinochet: The Dictator and the Quest for Justice." *The Nation* 21, 11–21.

Lira, E. and B. Loveman. 1999. "Derechos humanos en la transición 'Modelo': Chile 1988–1999." In *El Modelo Chileno: Democracia y Desarrollo en los Noventa*, edited by P. Drake and I. Jaksic. Santiago, Chile: LOM Ediciones.

Loveman, B. and E. Lira. 2000. *Las Ardientes Cenizas del Olvido: Vía Chilena de Reconciliación Politica, 1932–1994.* Santiago, Chile: LOM Ediciones.

Matus, A. 1999. *El Libro Negro de la Justicia Chilena.* Barcelona: Editorial Planeta.

Moulián, T. 1997. *Chile Actual: Anatomía de un Mito.* Santiago, Chile: LOM Arcis.

Roht Arriaza, N. 2006. *The Pinochet Effect: Transnational Justice in the Age of Human Rights.* University Park, Pennsylvania: Penn State University Press.

Shapiro, M. and A. Stone Sweet. 1994. "The New Constitutional Politics of Europe." *Comparative Political Studies* 26, 397–420.

Skaar, C. 2000. *Judicial Reform and Changes in Human Rights Policies in Chile and Argentina.* Miami: Latin American Studies Association (LASA).

Stone Sweet, A. 2000. *Governing with Judges: Constitutional Politics in Europe.* Oxford, UK: Oxford University Press.

Suprema, Corte. 1991. "Respuesta de la Corte Suprema al Informe de la Comisión Nacional de Verdad y Reconciliación." *Estudios Públicos* 42, 237–50.

Tate, C. and D. Jackson, eds. 1992. *Judicial Review and Public Policy in Comparative Perspective.* New York: Greenwood Press.

Tate, C. and T. Vallinder, eds. 1995. *The Global Expansion of Judicial Power.* New York: New York University Press.

United Nations. 2010. *Guidance Note of the Secretary-General. United Nations Approach to Transitional Justice.* Accessed January 16, 2020. www.un.org/ruleoflaw/files/TJ_Guidance_Note_March_2010FINAL.pdf

6 Coordinated Transition in East-Central Europe and the Role of Constitutional Courts in Transitional Justice

Experiences from Hungary and Moldova

Gábor Attila Tóth

Introduction

After World War II, the East-Central European countries were governed by Soviet-type regimes. The common feature of these states, like those of any other communist country, was their lack of democratic constitutional institutions. The states were characterized by either a single-party system (e.g., Hungary) or a dominant-party system (e.g., Czechoslovakia and Poland) without the possibility of competitive elections. Not only democratic opposition but also various institutions including certain nongovernmental and religious organizations were forced underground by the repressive regimes. Although constitutions formally declared fundamental rights, these were not legally enforceable. The constitutional structures of these states were not based upon the principles of separation of powers and the rule of law. And of course, the Soviet-type regimes did not ensure the independence of the judiciary or the press.

Three decades ago, a new model of constitutional regime change emerged in the East-Central European countries. Constitutional democracies emerged in the region during the political and constitutional transition of 1989 and 1990. Roundtable negotiations between undemocratic power holders and elements of the opposition led to a transition from Soviet-type authoritarian regimes to democracies. Constitutional changes were inseparable from institutional ones. As a crucial element of this transition, the third generation of European constitutional courts started to work in the post-Soviet democracies in the early 1990s. These courts were considered the most important institutional guarantors of constitutionalism, especially in the first, formative years, on account of their decisions favoring human rights, the principles of rule of law, and separation of powers.

Thirty years later, in the light of antidemocratic, authoritarian tendencies, it is far from clear whether the constitutional transformation is a story of success or failure. Today institutional erosion of democracy can be detected in East-Central Europe. After previous waves of democratization spread across the region (Huntington 1991), a new type of constitutional transformation has become the focus

DOI: 10.4324/9780429505089-9

of scholarly attention (Kovács and Scheppele 2018; Sadurski 2019; Tóth 2012, 2019a, 37–61; Tsygankov 2014). The cases ranging from Russia to Hungary and Poland (two EU Member States) and indeed to countries around the world epitomize this phenomenon, where the country in question adopts a process of legal transformation that moves it ever further from, rather than toward, democratic principles. Many countries demonstrate that when a populist authoritarian gains concentrated power, a reshaped constitution may serve antidemocratic aspirations. The emergence of populist authoritarianism is thus a global phenomenon. Even systems with a long pedigree of democratic traditions need not be entirely immune to the outbreak of autocratic political ideas and practices.

In this chapter, I provide an overview of constitutional transition in East-Central Europe, with case studies of Hungary and Moldova. By analyzing cases of transitional justice, I help reassess the emergence and performance of the third generation of European constitutional courts. I first briefly summarize the conceptual framework of the post-communist transition in East-Central Europe with a focus on the models of constitutional regime change and the evolution of constitutional review. Readers will learn about two characteristics of the regional transition: the coordinated nature of the transition and centralized constitutional review. Second, I offer case studies concerning the jurisprudence of two constitutional courts in the region, the Constitutional Court of the Republic of Hungary and the Constitutional Court of the Republic of Moldova, to demonstrate the nature of constitutional disputes related to transitions from an authoritarian past to a democratic present. There is a scholarly consensus that major judicial cases of transitional justice cover such issues as retroactive punishment, open access to political archives, cancellation of party members' pensions, truth and reconciliation processes (including amnesty), prohibitions on autocratic parties, and purges and lustration. In this chapter, the cases of transitional justice are atypical because they concern the death penalty, the status of religions, and official languages. The main reason for the case selection is to demonstrate that the constitutional courts had to deal with questions of transitional justice – or the struggle to overcome the past, as conveyed in the German term *Vergangenheitsbewältigung* – even in cases whose core theme seems unrelated to transitional justice. In this way, I argue that the achievements of the constitutional courts in transforming their respective countries from an autocratic system to constitutional democracies, regardless of their imperfections, cannot be evaluated on the basis simply of legal doctrinal tools. The case studies demonstrate how centuries-old historical circumstances, social environment, and the practices of constitutional courts interact to yield current circumstances.

I offer two conclusions in the chapter. First, the problems of transitional justice, at least in East-Central Europe, are wider and more complex than the core transitional-justice cases. Second, there is no single legal explanation as to why the post-Soviet political and constitutional transition in the region is far from a self-evident success. The problems of transitional justice are deeper and more serious than simple failures of constitutional design or of the constitutional courts. Neither the coordinated transition nor the new constitutional architecture nor yet again the constitutional judiciary is responsible by itself for the unfulfilled project of democratic transformation including transitional justice. The selected judgments of the constitutional courts prove that, beyond institutional shortcomings, such extraconstitutional factors as anomalies in historical narratives, national concepts, and religious roles have had a great influence on the constitutional development of East-Central European democracies.

I. Conceptual Framework

A New Model of Constitutional Regime Change: Coordinated Transition

Modern constitutionalism imposes limits on the power holder's performance of authority. The birth and evolution of modern constitutions are conventionally seen as the emancipation of a country from autocratic government (Arato and Tóth 2018, 73–96; Barendt 1998, 2–3). There are four main models of constitutional regime change that characterize the origins of modern constitutions. The first model is the postcolonial constitutional transformation reflecting lessons learned from a despotic past. An initial example of this kind of constitution was the Articles of Confederation (1777), eventually superseded by the Constitution of the United States of America (1787). As the text of the Declaration of Independence (1777) puts it,

> when a long train of abuses and usurpations . . . evinces a design to reduce [the people] under absolute Despotism, it is their right, it is their duty, to throw off such Government, and to provide new Guards for their future security. Such has been the patient sufferance of these Colonies; and such is now the necessity which constrains them to alter their former Systems of Government. The history of the present King of Great Britain is a history of repeated injuries and usurpations, all having in direct object the establishment of an absolute Tyranny over these States.

Since then, it has become common practice that, on achieving independence and legitimate government, liberated countries adopt their own constitutions, as have, for example, India (1950) and Nigeria (1963).

The second model is revolutionary constitution making. Many constitutions are adopted as a consequence of a revolution, which presupposes the existence of authoritarianism. In other words, revolutions seek to replace an illegitimate regime with a system of constitutionalism. Revolutionary constitutional change is radical transformation in a relatively short timeframe, with a representative body at its center. A classic case of this type is the constitution making of the French Revolution (1791), abolishing absolute monarchial rule. More recently, revolutions have returned in a dramatic manner in the Arabic-speaking world and the Andean republics of Latin America. Extensive empirical evidence from the last three centuries demonstrates, however, the adverse outcomes of revolutionary ruptures: Revolutions often culminate in terror, returning to autocracy, like the Jacobin and the Bolshevik dictatorships (Arato 2016).

In the third model, democratic constitutions represent a fresh start following the defeat of a totalitarian regime. This was the case after the Second World War in Japan (1946), Italy (1947), and Germany (1949). As the Preamble of the Basic Law of Germany puts it, the German people were "inspired by the determination to promote world peace as an equal partner in a united Europe," and for this reason, inviolable human dignity is the foundation of this system of basic rights.

The fourth model of post-authoritarian constitutional change has emerged in several countries. In Spain and Portugal in the 1970s, roundtable negotiations and compromises between reformist incumbents and the opposition led from authoritarian regimes to constitutional democracies. Following these experiences, the peaceful, coordinated, and negotiated constitutional transformations in East-Central Europe, together with the unification of Germany and the disintegration of the Soviet Union, belonged to the new model of regime change (Jaggi 2016). The historical turning point for the transformation from authoritarian regime to democracy in this part of the world was 1989.

The 1989 roundtables were meant to regulate the transition from the old regime to a new one, but they did not actually have a mandate for constitution making. They had neither the formal authorization to make law for the old regime nor the popular authorization to make law for the new regime. The roundtables, therefore, understood their task to be limited to facilitating the run-up to free, competitive elections and were intent on leaving to an elected assembly the task of endowing the new regime with a constitution. The roundtables' decisions, in order for them to come into legal effect, needed to be sent for enactment to the old legislature. Consequently, the roundtables were exceptional bodies having the capacity to start a coordinated process of constitutional change but leaving the completion of the process to an assembly with the democratic mandate they were lacking. Andrew Arato, in this regard, reflects critically on the legitimacy of constitutions in democratic transitions (Arato 1994, 165–94). János Kis characterizes the coordinated transition as an interruption of legitimacy and continuity of legality, and more specifically, he argues that transition consists of two stages: In the first stage, a roundtable agreement determines the ground rules of preparing and holding free elections; the second stage takes place when a body of freely elected representatives adopts, in the sovereign people's name, a new constitution (Kis 1995, 317). This is why we may label the developments in most of the East-Central European countries as "coordinated transition" (Arato 2012, 399–421; Kis 1995, 173–200).

In April 1989, during the aftermath of the Polish Round Table Agreement, the old parliament amended Poland's old constitution. The first democratic parliament then reshaped the relations between the legislative and executive branches of the state (the "Small Constitution"). The reformed constitution was finally replaced in 1997 by a completely new one. In Czechoslovakia in 1989, the old parliament amended the country's constitution, whereas the Charter of Fundamental Rights and Basic Freedoms was established in 1991 by the new parliament. The next year, after the dissolution of the federal state, the Czech Republic and the Slovak Republic each adopted a new constitution. In Bulgaria and Romania, their respective governments took the second step of constitution making in 1991. (Similarly, South Africa replaced its white-supremacist constitution of 1983 with the Interim Constitution of 1994, which in turn led to the Constitution of 1997.)

In Hungary, after four decades of Soviet-type authoritarianism, the turning point for the transition to democracy was the autumn of 1989. At that time, the single-party system collapsed following a series of negotiations between the old regime and the democratic opposition. In formal terms, the resulting 1989 Constitution was a mere modification of the 1949 Constitution. In substantive terms, however, the 1989 political transition breathed new life into the Hungarian Constitution (Tóth 2014, 775–79). Importantly, Hungary was the only post-communist country that omitted the second step of constitution making, as the government did not adopt a formally new constitution between the collapse of the old regime and 2011. The democratically elected government amended the 1989 Constitution several times – for example, to qualify Hungary for membership in the European Convention on Human Rights, NATO, and the European Union. Nevertheless, the country did not accomplish an important symbolic mission: the adoption of a final constitution. Hungary's failure to take this step – one that would have demonstrated the country's completion of its democratic transition – may be surprising insofar as the 1989 Hungarian Constitution was much easier to amend than were the constitutions of other European states. Although the Hungarian government could not change the Constitution by means of ordinary lawmaking procedures based on simple majority rule, the document was regarded as relatively flexible rather than rigid, in the sense that it did not render any provision or principle unamendable and amendments required only the votes of two-thirds of the members of the one-chamber legislative body. Neither a referendum nor any other form of ratification (e.g., approval by the subsequent parliament) was required for the adoption of a new constitution or a constitutional amendment. However, Hungary's increasingly hostile political environment and Hungarians' divergent constitutional views prevented a consensus or even compromises on a formally new constitution (Arato 1996, 31–9).

In Moldova, the story of the peaceful democratic transition also dates back to 1989, when the Moldavian Soviet Socialist Republic, a part of the Soviet Union, took its first step toward independence. For the contemporary Republic of Moldova, 1991 is seen as "year zero," when its independence from the Soviet Union and its own political and legal systems were proclaimed in the Declaration of Independence. In 1994, after adopting initial declarative and interim constitutional measures, the democratically elected parliament approved the final Constitution of the Republic of Moldova. This chain of events, common in the former member states of the Soviet Union, consisted also of two determining stages: In the first stage, the country's independence is declared (e.g., Lithuania and Latvia in 1990, Estonia and Ukraine in 1991); in the second stage, a freely elected parliament adopts a new constitution (e.g., Latvia in 1991, Estonia and Lithuania in 1992, Ukraine in 1996).[1]

Without doubt, the democratic transition in East-Central Europe was a process led not by the common interests of parties but by a clash of values and interests that forced a series of compromises from parties on either end of the political spectrum – communist or democratic. We can say that compromise is one of the underlying characteristics of peaceful transitions. In order to incorporate progressive principles into the new constitutions, the oppositions could not simply exclude the representatives of the old regime from political power and economic advantage. Thus, uneasy compromises with members of the ancien régime were an intrinsic, unavoidable part of the negotiated transition. Moreover, not only pragmatic motives but also principled reasons underlay the absence of mass revenge in East-Central Europe. That is to say, the fundamental legal guarantees of the new constitutional democracies throughout East-Central Europe were extended to everyone, irrespective of which side they had taken, because "everyone" is entitled to human rights.[2]

In sum, we can say that the East-Central European autocratic systems collapsed not because of classical revolutions, but because of peaceful negotiations between the old regimes and democratic opposition. However, the political transitions did result in revolutionary changes in the political and constitutional systems.

The Third Generation of Constitutional Courts

Democratic transformations are inseparable from institutional changes. The four waves, or "generations," of European constitutional courts after the Second World War symbolize how modern institutions of constitutionalism emerged from democratic change (Sólyom 2003, 133–61, 135). First, in the late 1940s and the early 1950s, the Austrian, German, and Italian constitutional courts were (re)established after the fall of totalitarian regimes.[3] Second, in the 1970s, the fall

1 The Socialist Federal Republic of Yugoslavia, by comparison, dissolved into various entities declaring nationhood and adopting new constitutions. Neither Yugoslavia nor its independence-declaring republics satisfactorily addressed ethnic tensions. The result was a series of violent ethnic conflicts and wars at the time of the country's dissolution.

2 Theories of hegemonic preservation, which hold that outgoing elites preserve their interests through constitutional changes and constitutional courts (Hirschl 2007), cannot explain the East-Central European coordinated transition. The new constitutions were written in the language of modern constitutionalism, and the courts were not occupied by representatives of the former elites. Remember that the first freely elected heads of state in Czechoslovakia, Hungary, and Poland – Vaclav Havel, Árpád Göncz, and Lech Wałęsa – had been heroes of the democratic opposition movements.

3 Originally, Favoreu distinguished three waves of constitutional justice, starting with the Austrian and Czechoslovak constitutional courts from the 1920s, then the reestablishment of the Austrian court together with the establishment of the German court, and finally, the Spanish, Portuguese, and East Central European courts (Favoreu 1986; Favoreu and Mastor 2011).

of the regimes of Franco and Salazar made possible the rise of the Spanish and Portuguese constitutional courts. Third, new constitutional courts took shape in the post-Soviet democracies during the early 1990s (Dupré 2003). Finally, in mid-1990s, during the breakup of Yugoslavia, the new independent states reestablished their own constitutional institutions, including constitutional courts.

These transformations stamped the East-Central European countries with the traits of constitutionalism: free and fair elections, representative government, a parliamentary system, an independent judiciary, ombudspersons to guard fundamental rights, and a constitutional court to review the constitutionality of laws. The constitutions were modeled after international human rights instruments and previously drafted democratic constitutions (Czarnota et al. 2005; Garlicki 2005, 263–79; Sadurski 2005; Schwartz 2000; Sólyom and Brunner 2000). Rather than import the presidential architecture of the United States, most of the post-communist democracies followed Western European traditions in establishing an adapted parliamentary system (Garlicki 2005, 264). Either the constitution or judicial interpretations of it clearly established that the prime minister heads the executive and that the government is the supreme body of that branch, responsible to parliament.

Judicial protection of the constitution was also closer to the centralized German model than to the US system of judicial review. This meant that the constitutional courts – or in Poland, the tribunal – were institutionally separated from the ordinary court system and had unique *erga omnes* constitutional interpretative authority.

In Hungary, the 1989 constitutional system bestowed broad competences on the Constitutional Court. The lack of an entirely and formally new constitution increased the responsibilities of the Constitutional Court as the ultimate interpreter of constitutional principles and fundamental rights – it became, in short, the most crucial constitutional check on the powers of parliament. The 1990 starting point for constitutional jurisdiction meant that neither domestic precedents nor a doctrinal framework elaborated by academics guided the court. Chief Justice Sólyom, drawing on his distinguished expertise and striking judicial ambitions, had a chance to dominate the inceptive period of the court's adjudication. In the absence of domestic precedents, the Sólyom Court took many international and foreign standards of judicial review as precedents. The court effectively protected fundamental rights with the help of the proportionality principle, the principle of clear-and-present-danger scrutiny imported from US constitutional adjudication, and the allgemeine Handlungsfreiheit imported from the European Court of Human Rights and the Federal Constitutional Court of Germany. The Sólyom Court placed human dignity at the center of its judicature in an unprecedented way. With only mild exaggeration, we could say that early judicial reading of the Constitution gave rise to theories of justice and dignity in Hungarian constitutional jurisdiction. The substantive protection of fundamental rights went together with the Constitutional Court's consideration of procedural rights based on the rule of law, including supremacy of the law, prohibition of ex post facto law, and arbitrariness.

The Constitutional Court of the Republic of Moldova also belongs to the third generation of centralized, Kelsenian constitutional courts. The Constitution made the court, established in 1995, not only the sole authority in the area of constitutional jurisdiction, rendering the court independent of any other public authority, but also the guarantor of the supremacy of the Constitution. Although the Constitution gives a long list of the court's competences, it contains neither direct individual access to justice nor an *actio popularis.* In contrast with its Hungarian, Polish, and Czech counterparts, Moldova's Constitutional Court, during its first, years played no significant role in constitutional developments. In fact, the court's uncompromising pursuit of constitutional ideas dates back only a few years. Under Chief Justice Alexandru Tănase, who led the court between 2011 and 2017, the court imported many international standards of judicial review. His successor, Chief Justice Mihai Poalelungi, former justice of the European Court of Human Rights, went further and applied the proportionality principle intensively in fundamental-rights protection. His implantation of constitutional ideas and practices in domestic jurisprudence was pioneering work.

In sum, East-Central Europe's establishment of constitutional courts as central institutions of constitutional adjudication can be seen as part of the region's transition from autocracy to constitutional democracy. Characterizing this transition was the public's deep mistrust of the judiciary – that is, of the previous regime's means of judicial oppression. Even though the constitutional adjudication sometimes resulted in bitter failures, the constitutional courts came to be seen as the ultimate guardians of the constitution (Zifcak 1996, 1–56).

II. Cases of Transitional Justice

After the collapse of the Soviet system, the East-Central European countries dealt with similar legal and political questions, applied similar constitutional principles and rules, and operated almost identical procedures. The new constitutional courts faced a seemingly paradoxical two-fold task: They had to explore the legal and moral difference between the old and the new regime and make perfectly clear that their judicial practices were consistent with the rule of law. Each constitutional court aimed to adapt its country's new constitutional system to democratic constitutionalism by introducing standards from the European Court of Human Rights and high-level courts of advanced democracies (Dupré 2003). Although the paths taken varied from one court to the next, the procedures for dealing with autocratic heritages were basically determined by parliaments and constitutional courts reacting to each other's activities. In line with the adopted principles, the constitutional courts confronted not only the Soviet legacy but also the exceptional constitutional issues deriving from democratic transition. Four issues stood out: rehabilitating the victims of Soviet-era regimes' arbitrary punitive measures; compensating victims of such personal and material wrongs as regimes' unjust nationalization of people's material wealth; retroactively prosecuting perpetrators of serious criminal offenses; and assuring freedom of information by the lustration of public figures and the disclosure of previously sealed files, particularly those compiled by state security agencies. In what follows, I shed light on the complexity of transitional justice by citing atypical examples from Hungary and Moldova.

Abolition of the Death Penalty: Responding to Historical Injustice

Capital punishment's long-standing history in East-Central Europe can help us grasp the complexity of the region's transitional justice. After the Second World War, the Nuremberg trials resulted in twelve death sentences. However, as a reaction to the horrors of the war, many Western European countries at this time abolished capital punishment in the name of human dignity (an example being the Basic Law of the Federal Republic of Germany in 1949).

Owing to divergences between abolitionist and retentionist states, the initial international human rights norms did not prohibit the death penalty. The Universal Declaration said nothing about it. The original wording of Article 2(1) of the European Convention on Human Rights (ECHR) stated that courts could impose the sentence of execution on people convicted of crimes for which this penalty was provided by law. In opposition to such sentencing, some human rights norms envisaged a total ban on capital punishment, in the manner of Article 6(6) of the International Covenant on Civil and Political Rights, which declared, "Nothing in this article shall be invoked to delay or to prevent the abolition of capital punishment." European human rights institutions on a supranational level took crucial steps toward achieving this goal. In 1982 the Council of Europe updated the ECHR by passing Protocol 6, the first international legal norm providing for the abolition of the death penalty in peacetime.

Regardless of these wider tendencies, the East-Central European regimes before the 1990s rebuffed pressures to abolish capital punishment. During the countries' coordinated transition, utter disagreement among the constitution makers arose over precisely this issue. At the same time, the Council of Europe made it clear to every new East-Central European democracy that abolishing the death penalty is a precondition for membership. Therefore, some of these countries adopted constitutions prohibiting the death penalty (e.g., Slovakia and the Czech Republic). Likewise, the Constitution of Moldova in 1995 abolished the death penalty almost concurrently with the country's entrance into the Council of Europe.

In other countries, constitutional courts reached a decision about the death penalty. The Constitutional Court of Hungary was the first judicial body on the globe that, in a landmark 1990 judgment, successfully abolished *erga omnes* the death penalty (Hungarian Constitutional Court Judgment no. 23 1990). The Constitutional Court declared capital punishment to be unconstitutional because it violated the right to life and human dignity. In its reasoning, the court emphasized the following points:

> Human dignity, as the unity of personality along with human life, means the essence of man. Dignity is an elevated and absolutely respected quality

> of our human life and values: it is a standard of our human essence. It is an a priori value in the same way as life and expresses the human dimension of life. Being human and human dignity are inseparable from one another. Both are inalienable, imminent, essential properties of man. To be worthy of life means dignity as a human being, and that is why human life and human dignity may not really be handled separately. (Hungarian Constitutional Court Judgment no. 23 1990)

Chief Justice Sólyom explained in obiter dicta democratic transition's relevance to this topic:

> The Constitutional Court has good reasons to rely on our own historical situation when it increases the respect of the right to life through the abolition of capital punishment and drives back the criminal jurisdiction of the State from this area. It is more than a symbolic opposition to a political system that sacrificed human life, without restraint, for its political purposes. . . . The current historical task now is to establish and bind the legislature because as a constitutional order that is interpreted and protected by the Constitutional Court, the State cannot afford to deprive someone of their life. (Hungarian Constitutional Court Judgment no. 23 1990)

The interpretation of human dignity as both a moral value and a constitutional right served as a foundational argument for the abolition of capital punishment in the Ukrainian, Lithuanian, Albanian, and South African Constitutional Courts (Lithuania 1998; Albania 1999; Ukraine 1999; South Africa 1995.). Those courts – by referring to the precedent established by Hungary – also declared capital punishment to be unconstitutional. This change symbolizes constitutional transformation. Indeed, the post-Soviet region (with the exception of Belarus) has been a de facto "capital punishment"–free territory since 1997. In other words, the region shifted from an embrace of politically motivated executions to an unconditional ban on them in the space of a few years. No East-Central European member state of the Council of Europe has carried out an execution in the 21st century.[4]

The judicial abolishment of the death penalty was also a response to historical injustices committed by communist regimes. The constitutional courts announced that states under the rule of law are fundamentally different from their autocratic predecessors. In the courts' judgments, the Hungarian, Ukrainian,

4 On the basis of the new European consensus, the Council of Europe in 2003 adopted Protocol 13 of the ECHR, which abolished the death penalty in all circumstances. Not surprisingly, following this development, the European Union adopted a categorical ban in Article 2(2) of the Charter of Fundamental Rights: "No one shall be condemned to the death penalty, or executed." What is more, Article 19(2) of the Charter adds that "no one may be removed, expelled or extradited to a State where there is a serious risk that he or she would be subjected to the death penalty."

Lithuanian, and Albanian courts demonstrated that both parliaments' power to formulate laws and governments' executive powers are limited by the principles of the rule of law and fundamental rights.

Consider, for example, the case of retroactive punishment in Hungary. Like the courts in other countries in the region, the Hungarian Constitutional Court reviewed the constitutionality of laws calling for the retroactive punishment of people accused of having committed various crimes during the former autocratic regime. In its landmark decision, the Constitutional Court famously stated the following:

> The change of system has been carried out on the basis of legality. The principle of legality imposes on the state governed by the rule of law the requirement that legal regulations regarding the legal system itself should be realized fully. . . . [T]he basic guarantees of the rule of law cannot be set aside by reference to historical situations and the state governed by the rule of law is a requirement of justice. A state governed by the rule of law cannot be created by undermining the rule of law.
>
> The Constitutional Court cannot ignore history since it has to fulfill its task embedded in history. The Constitutional Court is the repository of the paradox of the "revolution under the rule of law": in the process of the peaceful transition, beginning with the new Constitution, the Constitutional Court must, within its competences, in all cases unconditionally guarantee the conformity of the legislative power with the Constitution.
>
> Legal certainty based on formal and objective principles [of the rule of law] is more important than necessarily partial and subjective justice. (Hungarian Constitutional Court Judgment no. 11 1992; Tóth 2007, 281–6)

Acting on these principles, the Constitutional Court invalidated the whole act pertaining to retroactive punishment for political crimes. Specifically, the court dissociated itself from natural law and, with the help of a formalistic concept of the rule of law, positioned itself as strictly positivist. From a comparative perspective, it did not adopt the German Constitutional Court's reception and application of the Radbruch Formula, which was a response to Nazi crimes and East German political crimes and which states, in short, that "legal norms lose their legal validity when they are extremely unjust" (Radbruch 1946, 1957; German Federal Constitutional Court 1968, 23, 28, 1996, 95, 96).

Retributive justice holds that when someone breaks the law, punishment of the perpetrator is a necessary consequence. What the Constitutional Court of Hungary emphasized in its capital punishment and retroactive justice rulings is that the Constitution provides legal protection to individuals who are alleged to have committed political crimes prior to the adoption of the Constitution. Such constitutional guarantees, as the presumption of innocence, the prohibition of ex post facto laws, the right to a defense, and the right of pardon apply in every kind of criminal proceeding regardless of its connection to transitional justice. The court was presumably trying to prevent a political and legal witch hunt. Retributive justice judgment based on the apparently value-neutral, positivist reasoning in ex post facto law represents a substantial value judgment regarding such abstract constitutional ideas as human dignity and the rule of law. In other words, the court aimed at determining transitional justice by expressing the moral and legal preeminence of constitutional democracy even in application to the democracy's most ardent autocratic rivals.

Religion and Churches: Preferential Treatment for Historical Institutions

In contrast to Polish and East German churches, of which the majority played a significant role in the resistance to Soviet-style autocracy, only a few small Hungarian churches or ecclesial communities belonged to the resistance. Nevertheless, churches were undoubtedly victims of Soviet Bloc persecution. While most organized religions were never banned, they were allowed to continue functioning only under oppressive state control. Many religious leaders were imprisoned, believers were harassed, church property was confiscated, and religious faith was publicly ridiculed. After 1989, thus, the constitutional courts of East-Central Europe had to deal with the issues of religious communities and their liberty and property rights. Importantly, the cases of churches and religion were more than a problem of transitional justice, as courts and legislators had to identify the proper place for churches and religious values within a secularized constitutional democracy.

In an early decision, the Hungarian Constitutional Court claimed that "individual freedom of conscience and religion acknowledges that the person's conviction, and, within this, in a given case, religion, is a part of human dignity, so their freedom is a pre-condition for the free development of personality" (Hungarian Constitutional Court Judgment no. 4 1993). In addition to this, the court developed a concept concerning the neutrality of the state originating from the principle of equal liberty of conscience. The requirement that the state adopts religious neutrality simply means that, according to the law, there must be significant separation between church and state. In other words, the state must not be institutionally attached to any religious institution, must not identify itself with the teachings of any religion, must not interfere with the internal workings of any religious institution, and especially must not take a stance in matters of religious declarations. From this, it follows that the state must treat all religious institutions equally (Hungarian Constitutional Court Judgment no. 4 1993).

By applying those principles in cases of transitional justice, the court concluded that separation of church and state does not mean that the state, in its legislative capacity, must disregard either the history or the special characteristics of religious ideas and institutions. "Treating the churches equally does not exclude taking the actual social roles of the individual churches into account" (Hungarian Constitutional Court Judgment no. 4 1993). According to this interpretation, the state may extend preferential treatment to religious institutions that can boast an enduring historical legacy in the area. This outcome is decidedly favorable for religious institutions with deep roots in Hungary. (In its judgments, the court considers the Catholic church and a Calvinist, a Lutheran, and a Jewish church as "historical churches.") In the course of property compensation, the state-run scheme of reprivatization returned only some real estate to some historical churches. All individuals and all the remaining institutions affiliated with religious institutions received only very limited compensation for their previously nationalized real estate. The court declared it constitutional that churches are exempt from the general statutory ban on acquisition of soil (Hungarian Constitutional Court Judgment no. 4 1993; Hungarian Constitutional Court Judgment no. 35 1994). Although the court upheld that obligatory lustration extends beyond state leaders and professional politicians to persons who have carried out "public-opinion-forming tasks," a court decision exempted religious leaders – but curiously enough, not journalists – from lustration (Hungarian Constitutional Court Judgment no. 31 2003). This decision overruled a former one stating that certain religious organizations and their representatives "surely take part in forming the public opinion" (Hungarian Constitutional Court Judgment no. 60 1994). Similarly, the court exempted practicing clergymen from mandatory military service (itself repealed by constitutional amendment in 2005) because these types of "positive discrimination" ensured the believers' free exercise of religion (Hungarian Constitutional Court Judgment no. 46 1994). Thus, for example, the state now had an obligation to practice "positive discrimination" for religious schools but not for secular civil-sector schools operating as nonprofits. As a result, in Hungary today, only religious schools have the right to an auxiliary subsidy, above the normal state allowance (Hungarian Constitutional Court Judgment no. 22 1997).

In a leading judgment on church status, the court explicitly provided preferential treatment for historical churches but not for other churches, religious groups, and communities. Some research has argued that the 1989 Constitution provided for the separation of church and state but that the court undid this separation by adhering to the centuries-old compromises that such countries as Austria and Germany had entered into with Christian institutions (Sajó 1999, 96). Following the ratio decidendi, the court declared constitutional a governmental decree providing for the free military-based exercise of religion and spiritual care only for members of the four historical churches insofar as the privileges of historical religious institutions, far from being unconstitutional, "refer to the real historical role and social significance of such churches" (Hungarian Constitutional Court Judgment no. 970B 1994).

We can see that the judges of Hungary's Constitutional Court applied the concept of preferential treatment to select religious institutions. The court accepted the premises that historical churches were victims of the repressive regime and that they have outstanding social weight playing crucial social and cultural, as well as spiritual, roles. At the same time, with its decisions on transitional justice and beyond, the court influenced communal practices in such a way that some churches were granted exceptionally favorable conditions for their spiritual and other activities.

Official Language: From One National Injustice to Another

In 1989 in Chisinau, the capital of the Moldovan Soviet Socialist Republic, the Moldovan Popular Front, which was a political movement for national awakening, freedom of speech, and revival of Moldovan traditions, staged several mass demonstrations protesting against Soviet Russian oppression. In August 1989, the Popular Front formed the Grand National Assembly, which forced the Moldovan Supreme Soviet to adopt a Language Law proclaiming the country's "Moldo-Romanian linguistic identity" ("identitatea lingvistică moldo-română") and that the country's official language would no longer be Russian: It would henceforth be the Moldovan language written in Latin script. The law granted protective status to four minority languages: Russian, Bulgarian, Gagauz (part of the Turkic language family), and Ukrainian. Seemingly in direct contradiction to Moldova's Language Law of 1989, the 1991 Declaration of Independence states that, in 1989, Romanian (i.e., not Moldovan) became the official state language (White n.d.). Even more puzzling still is the assertion of Article 13(1) of the 1994 Constitution that the official language is "the Moldovan language, based on the Latin alphabet." The Constitution, which goes on to protect use of the Russian language and other languages spoken in Moldova, seems to be a rejection of both the Moldovan Romanian language (the 1989 Language Law) and the Romanian language (the 1991 Declaration of Independence). Because the Moldovan language and the Romanian language are almost identical to each other, with the main differences being pronunciation and vocabulary, several important questions arose: First, does the term "Romanian" in the Declaration of Independence refer also to the Moldovan language? Second and similarly, does the term "Moldovan language" in the 1994 Constitution refer also to the Romanian language? Third, what is the sense in choosing between two nearly identical methods of human communication? And fourth, as though matters weren't already sufficiently confusing, how can the 1989 Language Law praise "Moldo-Romanian linguistic identity" while simultaneously declaring only the Moldovan language the country's official language? As we will see next, the Constitutional Court of Moldova, in addressing these questions almost two decades later, often created more confusion than it resolved.

In 2013, the court faced this issue of official – or "state-sanctioned" – languages. The court was requested to interpret the 1994 Constitution's phrase "Moldovan language, based on the Latin alphabet" and address the apparent contradiction between this constitutional provision and the one in the Declaration of Independence naming the official language "Romanian." Acknowledging the divergence between the two texts, the court decided that the primary constitutional text of the Declaration of Independence prevails. The court implicitly asserted that, in this particular regard, the text of the Constitution was unconstitutional and was superseded by the corresponding text in the declaration. So as to establish a hierarchy of constitutional norms and, at the same time, to resolve this confusing language problem, the court remarkably cited various doctrines of contemporary constitutional jurisprudence, such as basic structure, invisible constitutions, and eternity clauses. This kind of comparative interpretation went hand in hand with the references to history and folklore. As regards the current status of Moldova's constitutional norms, the court in its 2013 judgment emphasized the following points:

> There is no other place where the constitutional understanding of the founding fathers and national belief would be so clearly reflected as in the Declaration of Independence. Therefore, it is the Declaration of Independence, reflecting the fundamental political decisions, that is the national conscience and defines "the constitutional identity" of the Republic of Moldova. Therefore, in the Declaration of Independence there are included elements considered to be essential in defining the constitutional identity of the new state and its population: aspirations for freedom, independence and national unity, linguistic identity, democratization, rule of law, market economy, history, norms of morality and of international law, European geopolitical orientation, assurance of social, economic and cultural rights and political freedoms for all the citizens of the Republic of Moldova, including for people belonging to other national, ethnic, linguistic and religious groups. (Constitutional Court of Moldova 2013, para 86)[5]

The truth, as concluded by the Academy of Science of Moldova and acknowledged by the court, is that the 1994 Constitution's phrase "Moldovan language based on the Latin alphabet" is the semantic equivalent of the Declaration of Independence's phrase "Romanian language." The constitutional difficulty here has its roots in historical circumstances (Ciscel 2007; Prina 2013).

The court's reasoning echoes widely accepted historical narratives, which situate the origins of Moldova as an independent state in the 14th century. For example, in its language judgment, the court emphasized that "the population of ancient Moldova spoke the same language and was of the same origin as the Wallachian and Transylvanian people" (Constitutional Court of Moldova 2013, para 9). These assertions are, however, much simpler than historical facts suggest. The territory that is today Moldova was occupied successively by the Ottoman Empire, the Russian Empire, and the Soviet Union, while between 1918 and 1940, the country was fully a part of Romania. These shifting balances of power triggered political and social conflict, war, and migrations, which in turn resulted in a noticeably multiethnic, multilingual country: Almost 80% of the population are ethnic Moldovans or Romanians, 15% Slavs (Ukrainians, Russians, Bulgarians), and 4% Gagauz, while 30% of the population speak Slavic languages,

5 The court also cited the National Anthem of Moldova, titled "Our Language" (*Limba noastră*) and written by a pro-Romania poet. The emotional eulogy to an unnamed language describes it as being "more than holy," a "burning flame," and a "treasure that surges from deep shadows of the past."

with Russian serving as the language of interethnic communication. Moreover, the difference between Moldovan and Romanian ethnic identities is a matter of controversy. A Norwegian researcher found that less than 2% of Moldovans self-identified exclusively as ethnic Romanians. And regarding the extent to which Moldovan citizens perceive differences between ethnic Moldovans and ethnic Romanians in the country, 26% of self-proclaimed Moldovans described the two demographic groups as "very different," 55% as "somewhat different," and only 5% saw no difference (Kolsto 2002, 34). Although one study found that exclusively Romanian ethnic self-identification was less than 2% among citizens of Moldova, Moldovanism and Romanianism can be seen as two competing visions in Moldova (Iavorschi 2012, 33–7). Adherents to Moldovanism insist that it rests on historical, cultural, religious, and linguistic traits, all of which significantly differ from the corresponding traits in Romanianism. However, adherents to Romanianism insist that all these differences are regional variants of a common Romanian history and pan-Roman culture.

Ethnic identification is often tied up with language. More than one century ago, when nationalism – originally a progressive idea in opposition to outdated empires – was associated with liberalism, the Romanian language and the Latin alphabet were not only a communication tool but also a symbol of regional movements seeking independence from Imperial Russia. In Soviet times, however, the Russian language again became the region's common, official language. Likewise, the Soviet regime simultaneously forced the Cyrillic alphabet on the Moldovan language. In the wake of the Soviet Union's collapse, Moldovans sought to substitute Latin for Cyrillic. This effort, coupled with numerous other tensions, resulted in the separation from Moldova of a narrow strip of land known as Transnistria, which remains a self-proclaimed, pro-Russian republic, where Moscow keeps thousands of "peacekeepers."

Any state is a construction, but the current state borders of the Republic of Moldova are particularly arbitrary. Today, history and identity do not unite but divide the nation. After the democratic transition, the electorate became sharply divided, with almost equal percentages preferring to join the European Union (40 %) and the Russian-led Eurasian Union (43%). Unification with Romania is still the ultimate goal for many people in Moldova. On top of that, the country's considerable popular support for constitutional democracy clashes with widespread nostalgia for Soviet times, encouraged by the current Russian government.

In sum, language influences identity, and a country's official language refers to a collective identity. Disputes over language are thus often the medium through which conflicts, particularly national and political ones, are expressed. The language-related disputes in Moldova are strongly connected to transitional justice. The Constitutional Court's judgment in 2013 is, first and foremost, a judicial response to historical injustices committed during the Soviet era, when Moldovan culture and language suffered at the hands of communist governance. Second, the court's judgment represents Moldova's pursuit of nation building and of "national identity" not only through constitutional principles and institutions but also through historical-cultural references, some more invented than others.[6]

III. Conclusions and Remarks

In the three decades since their democratic transition, many East-Central European countries have grown suspicious of or even hostile toward the ideas of democracy, European transnational cooperation, and universal human rights. Today it is far from evident whether the region's post-Soviet political transitions have been a success or a failure.

My aim in this chapter has been to draw a link between transitional justice in East-Central Europe and constitutional courts' role in creating constitutionalism, which is necessary in any transition from autocracy to constitutional democracy. I have offered atypical examples from case law demonstrating that the courts faced difficulties when handling transitional justice from the perspectives of the criminal-justice system, the legal status of civil-society organizations, and language rights. The examples shed light on the complexity of transitional justice in the sense that the courts dealt with the heritage of the Soviet-type past, from restoration and rehabilitation to retribution and retroactivity, in a range of cases that markedly differed from one another.

Even though we can easily identify bitter failures in the design and activity of East-Central European constitutional courts, the achievements of the courts reveal remarkable progress in European constitutionalism. It would be inaccurate to argue that the founders of the new constitutional systems committed a sin by negotiating regime change; after all, the founders had no reasonable alternative. Under the given historical circumstances, neither revolutionary nor reformatory constitution-making processes were available. Of course, mistakes were made early on. In the Hungarian constitutional design, for example, these mistakes became evident, as the 1989 Constitution, negotiated between the communist party and the opposition, suffered from flaws that were never corrected and that included the two-thirds rule for constitutional amendments. Beset by a disproportionate electoral system and other hazards, the whole constitutional set up in Hungary was fragile from the start. Nevertheless, the 1989 Constitution fulfilled its main purpose: to be an interim constitution regulating Hungary's transition from the old regime to a new one. Hungary's story is, in this regard, the story of many East-Central European countries in transition.

It is true that in some cases, the constitutional courts vindicated even the status of a substitute constitution-making authority, much beyond the role of

6 Similar constitutional difficulties can be detected in other East Central European countries. The language issue is contentious in the Baltic states (Estonia, Latvia, and Lithuania), where Russians (self-identifying ethnic Russians or Russian-speaking people) claim to be victims of language discrimination. A large percentage of Russians in Latvia and Estonia still have noncitizen or alien status. Transitional justice in culture and language often accompany nationalism.

final constitutional arbitrator. The case of capital punishment in Hungary – and subsequently, in Ukraine, Lithuania, and Albania – demonstrates the politicized origins and nature of this controversial issue. In a majority of East-Central European countries, however, courts did not assume control over the constitution making power, as constitutional and statutory amendments on the abolishment of the death penalty show. It would be thus an error to simply treat the East-Central European constitutional courts as representatives of judicial activism or "juristocracy."[7] Perhaps it is better to say that regional and national judicial bodies (i.e., the European Court of Human Rights and the domestic high courts) vertically, as well as legislative and judicial bodies horizontally, have made advances simultaneously.

Compare constitutional adjudication in Hungary with that in Poland. After the collapse of Soviet-style rule, the Sólyom-led Constitutional Court of Hungary was considered to be East-Central Europe's most influential, activist, and liberal guardian of constitutionalism, on account of the court's decisions favoring human rights and the rule of law. By contrast, the Polish Constitutional Tribunal, not to mention the Moldovan Constitutional Court, were much less progressive initially. According to Wojciech Sadurski, in that period, the Polish Tribunal was "the author of surely the most outrageously partisan and illiberal decisions of any constitutional court in the region" (Sadurski 2003, 162). Yet, during East-Central Europe's recent shift in the direction of populist authoritarianism, the previously lauded Hungarian and Polish Constitutional Courts have undergone a decline in power and competences.[8] While there is no empirical evidence that in East-Central Europe, the democratic deliberation resulting from direct

7 The Constitutional Courts received, from the beginning, highly divergent reviews. Bruce Ackerman and Stephen Holmes were doubtful about the courts' initial achievements in promoting democracy (Ackerman 1992, ch. 6; Holmes 1993, 23; Holmes and Sunstein 1995, 300). Recently, considerable new scholarship has emerged, offering intense critiques of constitutional review (Tushnet 1999; Hirschl 2007; Daly 2017).

8 Because it made two fatal mistakes, the Moldovan Constitutional Court does not fit this profile. In 2016, during a deadlock, when the parliament could not elect a new head of state, the court amended the constitution by itself. The court declared a constitutional amendment of 2000 introducing the parliamentary election of the president unconstitutional. Previously, parliament had been able to elect the country's president with a three-fifth majority of MPs; however, following the judgment, Moldovan citizens – not MPs – would directly elect the president. The presidential elections in 2016 resulted in the surprise victory of the populist Igor Dodon (Constitutional Court of Moldova 2016). The court's second fatal mistake took place on June 7, 8, and 9, 2019, when it delivered six rulings ordering the dissolution of the new parliament, declaring all parliamentary acts unconstitutional, invalidating both the nomination of the new prime minister and the appointment of the government, and lastly, removing the Moldovan president from office and replacing him with the former prime minister as interim president. One week later, however, the court announced a new judgment repealing each of its six rulings, and a couple of days later, every justice of the court resigned. In my view, the court adjudicated cases arbitrarily, gave a series of interpretations that were contrary to the text of the constitution, and was unfairly prejudiced in favor of the previous government and against President Dodon (Venice Commission 2019; Tóth 2019b).

participatory forms of democracy, is superior to that resulting from the decision-making of judges, there is plenty of evidence that authoritarian leadership emerges at the expense of not only constitutional judiciaries but also parliamentarianism. The lesson may be that not all problems of transitional justice can be solved with the reasoning of constitutional courts alone, even though none of the problems can be solved without some form of court input.

The problems of transitional justice are deeper than either simple failures of constitutional design or mistakes by constitutional courts. The selected judgments of the Hungarian and Moldovan constitutional courts make the complex legal, historical, and social difficulties tangible.

The Moldovan Constitutional Court attempted to reconcile a fabricated constitutional history with European constitutional ideas. The Moldovan Constitutional Court sometimes replaced judicial interpretation of constitutional history with a mythical account of history. The Moldovan court's approach insists that parts of East-Central Europe suffered at the hands of brutal outsiders (Ottoman, Soviet, and German) but gave rise to homegrown heroes over the centuries. This simplistic account of the region's history fails to acknowledge the tragic failures of nation states and their political leaders. As Adam Michnik argues, people create historical narratives driven by ideological agendas and a sense of victimization (Michnik 2014, 80–6).

The Hungarian Constitutional Court resisted counterfactual historical narratives. For those Hungarians who could not accept the coordinated character of their country's regime change and the legalistic approach represented by the Constitutional Court, 1989 ushered in moral confusion, not revolutionary transformation. For them, the absence of both mass criminal proceedings taking retroactive effect and the total restoration of confiscated material wealth mean nothing less than that the constitutional courts of East-Central Europe failed to satisfactorily pursue justice in the immediate post-Soviet period.

The profoundly influential role of religion – and particularly of Christianity – in East-Central Europe has led to a situation where many of the region's constitutional systems not only reflected the traditional faith of majority populations but indeed openly supported it. Thus, the moral and political foundations of East-Central European constitutionalism overlap extensively with those of Christianity, even though the region's inhabitants are characterized by moral, political, and religious diversity. In its judgments on transitional justice, for example, the Hungarian Constitutional Court acknowledged religious freedom and the separation of church and state but granted exceptionally favorable conditions to certain religious institutions, the "historical churches." The highest court of the land were willing to restore old privileges even if they violated the secular and liberal principles of equality.

Some East-Central European countries have constitutional systems that privilege majority ethnic and religious groups over minority ones. A case in point can be found in the judgments of the Moldovan Constitutional Court, which diverge from European constitutional standards declaring that modern nation states are multiethnic societies where all citizens are equal subjects under the law.

One fact should be perfectly clear: The constitutional courts in East-Central Europe could not bring about a cathartic resolution to past transgressions. One may draw a dark picture of constitutional transition, arguing that the compromised judgments of constitutional courts prevented people from correctly evaluating the moral horrors of the autocratic past and thus the political transitions remain incomplete, if indeed they ever even got underway. In fact, I would argue that it is unreasonable to have expected the courts to provide public satisfaction in the face of such obstacles as dauntingly complex coordinated transitions, markedly diverse social interests, and incompatible views of the region's past. All in all, the constitutional courts' achievements seem a partial success only: The implantation of constitutional ideas and practices into domestic jurisprudence was pioneering work, yet attempts in Hungary to favor certain religious institutions over others mirror attempts in Moldova to favor a single language over the country's various spoken languages.

References

Ackerman, Bruce. 1992. *The Future of the Liberal Revolution*. New Haven: Yale University Press, chapter 6.

Albania. 1999. Case No. 65. Judgment of December 10, 1999.

Arato, Andrew. 1994. "Dilemmas Arising from the Power to Create Constitutions in Eastern Europe." In *Constitutionalism, Difference, Identity, and Legitimacy*, edited by Michael Rosenfeld, 165–94. Durham: Duke University Press.

Arato, Andrew. 1996. "The Constitution-Making Endgame in Hungary." *East European Constitutional Review* 5, no. 4: 31–9.

Arato, Andrew. 2012. "Conventions, Assemblies and Round Tables." *Global Constitutionalism* 1, no. 1: 173–200.

Arato, Andrew. 2016. *Post Sovereign Constitution Making: Learning and Legitimacy*. Oxford: Cambridge University Press.

Arato, Andrew and Gábor A. Tóth. 2018. "The Multifaceted Sovereign: Domestic and International Actors in Constitutional Regime Changes." In *Constitutional Acceleration within the European Union and Beyond*, edited by Paul Blokker, 73–96. London: Routledge.

Barendt, Eric. 1998. *An Introduction to Constitutional Law*. Oxford: Oxford University Press, 2–3.

Ciscel, Matthew. 2007. *The Language of the Moldovans: Romania, Russia, and Identity in an Ex-Soviet Republic*. Lanham: Lexington Books.

Constitutional Court of Moldova. 2013. Judgment no. 36, December 5, 2013, para 9.

Constitutional Court of Moldova. 2013. Judgment no. 36, December 5, 2013, para 86.

Constitutional Court of Moldova. 2016. Judgment no. 7, March 4, 2016.

Czarnota, Adam, Martin Krygier, and Wojciech Sadurski, ed. 2005. *Rethinking the Rule of Law after Communism*. Budapest: Central European University Press.

Daly, Tom. 2017. *The Alchemist: Questioning our Faith in Courts as Democracy-Builders*. Cambridge: Cambridge University Press.

Dupré, Catherine. 2003. *Importing the Law in Post-Communist Transitions: The Hungarian Constitutional Court and the Right to Human Dignity*. Oxford: Hart Publishing.

Favoreu, Louis. 1986. *Les cours constitutionnelles*. Paris: Presses Universitaires de France.

Favoreu, Louis and Wanda Mastor. 2011. *Les cours constitutionnelles: Connaissance du droit*. Paris: Dalloz.

Garlicki, Lech. 2005. "Democracy and International Influences." In *European and U.S. Constitutionalism*, edited by Georg Nolte, 263–79. Chicago: Chicago University Press.

German Federal Constitutional Court. 1968. 14 February 1968, BVerfGE 23, 98.

German Federal Constitutional Court. 1996. BVerfG, 24 October 1996, BVerfGE 95, 96.

Hirschl, Ran. 2007. *Towards Juristocracy: The Origins and Consequences of the New Constitutionalism*. Cambridge: Harvard University Press.

Holmes, Stephen. 1993. "Back to the Drawing Board." *East European Constitutional Review* 2 (winter): 23.

Holmes, Stephen and Cass Sunstein. 1995. "The Politics of Constitutional Revision in Eastern Europe." In *Responding to Imperfection: The Theory and Practice of Constitutional Amendment*, edited by Sanford Levinson, 300. Princeton: Princeton University Press.

Hungarian Constitutional Court. 1990. Judgment no. 23 (31 October).

Hungarian Constitutional Court. 1992. Judgment no. 11 (5 March).

Hungarian Constitutional Court. 1993. Judgment no. 4 (12 February).

Hungarian Constitutional Court. 1994. Judgment no. 35 (24 June).

Hungarian Constitutional Court. 1994. Judgment no. 46 (21 October).

Hungarian Constitutional Court. 1994. Judgment no. 60 (24 December).

Hungarian Constitutional Court. 1994. Judgment no. 970B.

Hungarian Constitutional Court. 1997. Judgment 22 no. (25 April).

Hungarian Constitutional Court. 2003. Judgment 31 no. (4 June).

Huntington, Samuel. 1991. *The Third Wave: Democratization in the Late Twentieth Century*. Norman: University of Oklahoma Press.

Iavorschi, Arina. 2012. "The Problem of National Identity in the Republic of Moldova: Moldovanism and Romanianism." *Oikonomia Journal of Ethics and Social Sciences* 3: 33–7.

Jaggi, Stephan. 2016. *The Forgotten Revolution? The 1989 Revolution in East Germany and Its Impact on Unified Germany's Constitutional Law*. Baden-Baden: Nomos.

Kis, János. 1995. "Between Reform and Revolution: Three Hypotheses about the Nature of Regime Change." *Constellations* 1, no. 3 (January): 317.

Kolsto, Pal. 2002. *The National Integration and Violent Conflict in Post-Soviet Societies: The Cases of Estonia and Moldova*. Lanham: Rowman & Littlefield, 34.

Kovács, Kriszta and Kim L. Scheppele. 2018. "The Fragility of an Independent Judiciary: Lessons from Hungary and Poland – and the European Union." *Communist and Post-Communist Studies* 51, no. 3: 189.

Lithuania. 1998. Case No. 2/98. Judgment of December 9, 1998.

Michnik, Adam. 2014. *The Trouble with History: Morality, Revolution, and Counterrevolution*. New Haven: Yale University Press, 80–6.

Prina, Frederica. 2013. "Linguistic Divisions and the Language Charter: The Case of Moldova." Working Paper no. 64 (March). European Centre for Minority Issues.

Radbruch, Gustav. 1946. "Gesetzliches Unrecht und übergesetzliches Recht." *Süddeutschen Juristenzeitung* 1, no. 5: 105–8.

Radbruch, Gustav. 1957. *Der Mensch in Recht.* Göttingen: Vandenhoeck und Ruprecht.

Sadurski, Wojciech. 2003. "Review of *The Struggle for Constitutional Justice in Post-Communist Europe* by Herman Schwartz." *International Journal of Constitutional Law* 1, no. 1: 162.

Sadurski, Wojciech. 2005. *Rights Before Courts: A Study of Constitutional Courts in Postcommunist States of Central and Eastern Europe.* Dordrecht: Springer.

Sadurski, Wojciech. 2019. *Poland's Constitutional Breakdown.* Oxford: Oxford University Press.

Sajó, András. 1999. "A 'kisegyház' mint alkotmányjogi képtelenség" [The 'Small Church' as Constitutional Nonsense]. *Fundamentum* 3, no. 2: 96.

Schwartz, Herman. 2000. *The Struggle for Constitutional Justice in Post-Communist Europe.* Chicago: University of Chicago Press.

Sólyom, László. 2003. "The Role of Constitutional Courts in the Transition of Democracy: With Special Reference to Hungary." *International Sociology* 18 (March): 133–61, 135.

Sólyom, László and Georg Brunner. 2000. *Constitutional Judiciary in a New Democracy: The Hungarian Constitutional Court.* Ann Arbor: University of Michigan Press.

South Africa. 1995. The State v. T. Makwanyane and M. Mchunu, Case No. 3/94, Judgment of June 6, 1995.

Tóth, Gábor A. 2007. "The Bitter Pills of Political Transition." In *The Transformation of the Hungarian Legal Order 1985–2005*, edited by Andras Jakab, Peter Takács, and Allan Tatham, 281–6. Deventer: Kluwer.

Tóth, Gábor A., ed. 2012. *Constitution for a Disunited Nation: On Hungary's 2011 Fundamental Law.* Budapest: Central European University Press.

Tóth, Gábor A. 2014. "Hungary." In *Constitutional Law of the EU Member States*, edited by Leonard Besselink, Paul Bovend'Eert, Hansko Broeksteeg, Roel de Lange, and Wim Voermans, 775–9. Deventer: Kluwer.

Tóth, Gábor A. 2019a. "Constitutional Markers of Authoritarianism." *Hague Journal on the Rule of Law* 11, no. 1: 37–61.

Tóth, Gábor A. 2019b. "The Most Dangerous Branch: Constitutional Crisis in the Republic of Moldova." *Verfassungsblog*, June 17, 2019. Accessed August 11, 2019. https://verfassungsblog.de/the-most-dangerous-branch/

Tsygankov, Andrei P. 2014. *The Strong State in Russia: Development and Crisis.* Oxford: Oxford University Press.

Tushnet, Mark. 1999. *Taking the Constitution Away from the Courts.* Princeton: Princeton University Press.

Ukraine. 1999. Case No. 11. Judgment of December 29, 1999.

Venice Commission. 2019. *Opinion No. 954.* Accessed August 11, 2019. www.venice.coe.int/webforms/documents/?pdf=CDL-AD(2019)012-e

White, John. n.d. *Planning 'Our Language': Moldova's Language Identity.* Accessed August 10, 2019. www.academia.edu/12579941/Planning_Our_Language_Moldovas_Language_Identity

Zifcak, Spencer. 1996. "Hungary's Remarkable, Radical, Constitutional Court." *Journal of Constitutional Law in Eastern and Central Europe* 1, no. 3: 1–56.

7 The Determinants of the Polish Transformation at the Turn of the 21st Century

In View of the Judgments of the Constitutional Tribunal of Poland

Marek Zubik

Introduction

The year 1989 ushered in the so-called Autumn of Nations, when, over the next several years, communism came to an end in much of Central and Eastern Europe. In particular, the citizens of Poland finally regained control of their country. However, the dark legacy of their communist past has haunted them to this day.

The history of relations among states is in fact the history of wars. This observation applies fully to Central and Eastern Europe. For over 300 years, Poland suffered through incessant conflicts with its neighbors. From the 19th century until the end of World War I (1918), the territory of Poland was divided by Prussia, Austria, and Russia. Poles had no independent country but managed to preserve their cultural identity. The restitution of Poland on the political map of Europe was a prominent settlement in the Treaty of Versailles. The Polish–Soviet War (1919–20), which halted the advance of Bolshevism into Western Europe, left most Poles in the 1920s and 1930s feeling considerable antipathy toward communism. The culmination of these conflicts took place at the end of August 1939, when Nazi Germany and the Soviet Union signed the Ribbentrop–Molotov Pact. This agreement set the stage for the successful invasion of Poland by Nazi Germany and the Soviet Union in September 1939, triggering World War II. The conquerors carved up the vanquished state, which then experienced the horrors of war until the defeat of Germany in 1945. Thereafter, Poland had only the illusion of independence, as occupation by the Red Army put the country firmly in the sphere of Soviet control. The Soviets created a network of Polish communists who would eventually take over the country. The word "created" here is relevant, as the Soviets had killed or imprisoned most of the prewar Polish communist leaders.

Communism always lacked social legitimacy in postwar Poland because outsiders – the Soviets – imposed the ideology on the country. The economic theories of communism were unfamiliar to Poles, who had previously grown accustomed to a free market economy, with its protection of private property and its reliance on supply-and-demand mechanisms. Likewise, the communist

DOI: 10.4324/9780429505089-10

government suppressed one of Poland's cultural pillars – religion – and officially sanctioned atheism. The Cold War–era legal system promoted by Soviet communists had Eastern, Byzantine roots, whereas the system in prewar Poland had reflected Western, Latin culture. Law, rather than protect the people, was a device of repression and of human rights violations. The courts, not excluding the Supreme Court, served the communist state. All in all, the 45 years of imposed communist rule over Poland was disastrous for the country.

After some dramatic failed attempts by Poles to oppose their Eastern Bloc government, a number of factors came into play that strongly supported the anti-communist agenda. In 1978, the Polish cardinal became the head of the Catholic church: Pope John Paul II. A clear sign that Poles were rejecting communism was evident when millions of them attended public masses with John Paul II during his first official visit to Poland in June 1979. The following year, 1980, marked the establishment of the famous trade union Solidarity, led by Lech Walesa. At this time, the Polish people's antigovernment sentiment grew so intense that, in 1981, the communist leadership decided to impose martial law on the country, granting the government unbridled opportunities to arrest and imprison many members of Solidarity. The martial law, which violated provisions of the communist government's own constitution of 1952,[1] was a violently coercive attempt by the crumbling communist regime to suppress a majority of Polish society. Martial law ended in 1983, but its virulent effects, enforced by the military and other oppressive state organs, were to remain in place until the fall of the Polish communist government.

Heightened tensions in the Cold War, coupled with a domestic economic crisis, compelled the Polish communist regime to engage in dialogue with the Solidarity opposition. Nevertheless, Poles increasingly rejected Marxism's dogmatic renunciation of religion, free market principles, and civil liberties. As unrest grew, the national situation became untenable, and in early 1989, negotiations between the government and opposition groups (most notably Solidarity and religious organizations) took place at the Polish Round Table Talks in Warsaw. The communist government counted on the opposition groups making some concessions that would allow it to remain in power or at least to influence state decisions.

The Round Table Agreement, signed on April 4, 1989, was the beginning of Poland's transformation from a communist state into a democratic one. The situation was exceptional, as the agreement required substantive political, economic, legal, and social changes: namely, de-communization and lustration, the establishment of a free market, reprivatization, and the development of civil society.

Internationally, Poland started turning to the West. In November 1991, the country joined the Council of Europe, which required that Polish law be in alignment with the Council's human rights standards. And in 1994, Poland officially

1 In its judgment of 2013 (signature no. K 35/08), the Constitutional Tribunal found that the decree of martial law (December 13, 1981) had in fact violated the 1952 Constitution.

applied for membership in the European Communities (EC). This began a lengthy process of Poland's integration, mostly economic, into the EC. Finally, on May 1, 2004, Poland was granted member status in the European Union (EU; i.e., the EC's legal successor). Milestones along the way include Poland's admittance into NATO.[2] This partnership underlined Poland's willingness to permanently bind itself to transatlantic political and military structures that secured the country's security and sovereignty.

During these years, Poland's legal and economic transformations were generally successful. The country managed to overcome hyperinflation and enormous foreign debt. Today, many economists regard Poland not only as the economic powerhouse of Central and Eastern Europe but also as one of the EU's key developing economies.[3] Indeed, Poland was the only EU member state to have enjoyed positive growth during the 2009 financial crisis. Regrettably, these sweeping reforms have had social costs, the most obvious one being unemployment. The large-scale shift from a command economy to a free market in Poland required privatization and other reforms. Layoffs were inevitable, and when they happened, many Poles found themselves facing poverty.[4] The gap between the rich and the poor deepened. Many Poles emigrated. There was yet another problem, one noticed years later – many of Poland's economic sectors became dependent on foreign capital.

An Overview of Poland's Transition

Obviously, the transition from a communist state to a democracy requires a settling with the past. Some means of transitional justice has to be applied. However, the circumstances in which Central European countries have transitioned are unique. Hence, Central European countries have taken measures quite unlike, for example, Rwanda's and South Africa's. The key to the Central European

2 See: Protocol to the North Atlantic Treaty on the Accession of the Republic of Poland, signed at Brussels on 16 December, 1997. Officially Poland joined NATO 12 March, 1999. Before Poland had been a member of the Warsaw Pact – the communist military alliance created and led by the Soviets in opposition to NATO – to the end of this organization in 1991.

3 For example, in 2020, per capita GDP in Poland was 76% of per capita GDP in other EU countries. In 2010, that figure had been about 63% and, in 2003, less than 48%. Moreover, in 2018, Polish GDP was 10 times as great as it had been in the early 1990s. Poland's GDP has already surpassed Greece's and is right behind Portugal's. Today it is the sixth largest economy in the European Union. Clearly, Poland has made huge advances [available from: https://ec.europa.eu/eurostat/statistics-explained/images/2/2d/GDP_at_current_market_prices%2C_2003–04_and_2012–14_YB15.png, and https://ec.europa.eu/eurostat/databrowser/view/tec00114/default/table?lang=en, viewed at 1 September 2021].

4 For example, the unemployment rate was 16.9% in 1993 and over 20% in 2004. In December 2019, it was 5.2% (available from: https://stat.gov.pl/en/topics/labour-market/registered-unemployment/unemployment-rate-1990-2021,3,1.html, viewed at 1 September 2021).

transformations (except in Romania) has been evolutionary gradualism, not sudden revolution.[5]

Poland and Hungary were the very first countries to abandon the communist system. There was practically no role model, no pattern, that Poland could follow in its transformation[6]. The Spanish and Portuguese experiences were neither congruent with nor applicable to the Polish situation. Their regimes had been "domestic" and "familiar." In these Iberian countries, the main change was one of regime, as they experienced practically no need to make profound changes in property law or related economic areas. Of course, like Portugal (1974) and Spain (1975), Poland has had to face its past. Immediately after the collapse of Polish communism, the new government, which was made up of various anti-communist activists from the previous few years, exhibited deep divisions over the best path forward. These divisions, as well as the intractable nature of truth-and-reconciliation efforts, made it impossible for Poland to agree on a single, widely popular solution to the problems of transition from communism to democracy.

During the early stages of transition, the main focus was on the present and the future: rescue the Polish economy and build a viable state. The general view was that the communist past should be the province of historians, not of lawmakers, judges, and lawyers. And although the new government took steps to prosecute some individuals who were linked to communist-era infractions on human rights, the previous regime's highest-ranking authorities responsible for some of the grossest infractions escaped punishment. This uneven distribution of justice is explainable partly because many of the most notable accused former leaders died at some point during the proceedings, which carried on for years and years.

In contrast to the radical changes that Poland experienced in its economy and political system, the Polish transformation of state organs proceeded step by step and avoided massive and rapid restructuring. On the one hand, the staff and relationships among the military, law enforcement, counterintelligence, the judiciary, and most other public institutions remained largely in place and unchanged after the collapse of the communist government. The main reason for this was the former opposition's lack of satisfactorily trained officials who could assume government positions and restructure state organs. However, not all communist-era government officials retained their positions after 1989, and the lack of overarching structural change should not suggest that all of the pre-1989 institutions escaped targeted, small-scale structural change. Some of the old regime's most infamous institutions were transformed or abolished (e.g., the censorship office, the militia). Also, the new government revamped some of Poland's government

5 During a parliamentary debate, the first Polish non-communist prime minister in 1989 used this phrase: "We split away the history of our recent past with a thick line." The words, originally intended as a reference to Poland's dire economic problems, later was interpreted as a general principle for Polish transitional justice.

6 See very interesting considerations concerning the legal aspects of settling of societies with their own history, Belavusau and Gliszczyńska-Grabias 2017.

leadership and workforce by offering old-regime functionaries the option of early retirement.

Poland's Transition and the Judiciary

Some of the step-by-step changes to the transition-era Polish government concerned the judiciary and the country's constitutional foundations. Obviously, this sphere of transformation could be very sensitive.

The constitutional position of the Tribunal of State in Poland posed very few problems during the country's transition from communism to democracy. The central task of this special organ of the judiciary is to recognize motions against some of the highest officials in the state. Despite the sensitive nature of the Tribunal of State, new parliamentary elections in June 1989 automatically resulted in the replacement of all of its judges, giving this organ a new legitimacy in the post-communist environment.

The Constitutional Tribunal, which considers the constitutionality of various matters, had been established by the communist government in the early and mid-1980s, yet the Polish transformation did not trigger a wholesale dismissal of the Constitutional Tribunal's judges. Somewhat conveniently for the democratization process, the terms of office of half of this body's judges lapsed by 1989. This fact allowed Parliament, whose ranks now included many newly elected opposition members, to appoint to the Constitutional Tribunal a series of judges recommended by democratic organizations. And regarding the remaining communist-era judges on the Constitutional Tribunal, a particular circumstance favored their presence: Their jurisprudence had supported democratic change over the years, and this attitude gave the older judges considerable social standing. For these reasons, the Constitutional Tribunal's previous judgments remained on the books and enforced.

The Supreme Court, by contrast, was not so fortunate. Its main judicial duties are to oversee the decisions of lower courts and to render decisions in particular cases (e.g., the legality of elections). The activities of this court, particularly as they had been executed in the 1980s, did not enjoy a great deal of authority in the public's eyes. Part of the Round Table Agreement replaced all current Supreme Court judges with new ones whose nominations would follow a democratic procedure. This mass judicial shift unfolded according to prescriptions laid out in the old constitution. In 1990, the Supreme Court was headed by a lawyer – a professor of law with the support of the former democratic opposition.

The aforementioned "old constitution" was in force from 1952 until 1997, with some major amendments made in the duration. The new constitution, which parliamentarians struggled to create at the start of Poland's transformation, went into force precisely on October 17, 1997. The drawn-out nature of this process was perhaps due in part to divisions that surfaced within the Solidarity movement following the collapse of the communist regime. These divisions enabled people who had previously held office in the communist state to return to power in the new, democratic state. All in all, however, a tremendous amount of work went into crafting the new constitution. The parliamentary election in 1993 created a new ruling majority, dominated by post-communist parties. Ironically, that composition of deputies prepared the final draft of the constitution, which the nation approved by referendum. In general, the 1997 Constitution is a lengthy text espousing the typical norms of democratic states: free elections, the rule of law, the separation of powers, and the sanctity of human rights. The text also contains provisions regarding Poland's entrance into the EU.

The 1997 Constitution contains three principles for dealing with the communist past and transitional justice. These principles are outlined in the preamble, Article 13, and Article 44, respectively. The preamble clearly characterizes the harm done by Poland's previous communist state, referring to "the bitter experiences of the times when fundamental freedoms and human rights were violated in our Homeland." Article 13 establishes that authoritarianism, be it fascism or communism, is impermissible and cannot benefit from legal protections: "Political parties and other organizations whose programmes are based upon totalitarian methods and the modes of activity of Nazism, fascism and communism, as well as those whose programmes or activities sanction racial or national hatred, the application of violence for the purpose of obtaining power or to influence the State policy, or provide for the secrecy of their own structure or membership, shall be prohibited." As for Article 44, its stipulations clearly serve as the basis for future transitional-justice actions taken by the state against former communist officials: "The statute of limitation regarding actions connected with offences committed by, or by order of, public officials and which have not been prosecuted for political reasons, shall be extended for the period during which such reasons existed." Taken together, these three parts of the 1997 Constitution have helped shape Poland's approach to transitional justice into the present.

Transitional-Justice Cases

The Constitutional Tribunal of the Republic of Poland has dealt with five main types of cases that fall under the category of transitional justice:

(1) de-communization
(2) elimination of privileges for former communist officials
(3) lustration
(4) safeguards ensuring the responsibility of judges and public prosecutors
(5) reprivatization

De-communization

Before 1989, Poland had acquired no experience with democratic transformation and specifically none involving de-communization. This lack of experience, coupled with rifts in the Solidarity movement and the overall complexity of the issue, resulted in severe political conflict concerning how the fledgling democracy ought to deal with former communist officials and collaborators. The post–Round

Table government included many ex-members of the Communist Party, resulting in effective obstacles to total de-communization. No Polish law, for example, has prohibited former communist officials from participating in the political institutions of post-1989 Poland. This situation has resulted in many curiosities. One of them is the fact that the man who served before 1990 as both the leader of the Polish Communist Party and the main organizer of 1981's anti-Solidarity martial law became the newly democratic country's first president.[7] Perhaps just as baffling is the fact that a former communist minister became president in 1995, beating Poland's most well-known democratic activist, Lech Walesa, in elections.[8]

In 2016, the Polish government took incremental steps in erasing Poland's communist legacy. Consider, for example, that year's De-Communization Act, which allowed local authorities to replace communist-themed names of streets, squares, and other public locations. The act resulted in numerous legal and political disputes. In some cases, these disputes had to be settled by administrative courts, often taking the position that it was local-government authorities who should have the last word on any new names of public locations.

Another problematic issue to see the light of day in courts was the post-1989 government's efforts to nationalize property that had belonged to Poland's Communist Party. The Constitutional Tribunal reviewed the Act of November 9, 1990, concerning the Polish government's assumption of control over this property. The Constitutional Tribunal's conclusion was that this type of action does not infringe on the Constitution and that constitutional protections of property are applicable only to lawfully acquired rights free from reasonable moral doubt.[9]

Elimination of Privileges for Former Communist Officials

Not all de-communization efforts, however, have been piecemeal and cosmetic. Among the more substantive governmental actions was the decision to deprive communist-era secret service officials of any awards they might either have received or still receive in relation to Poland's struggle for independence and democracy.[10] Moreover, some former officials were stripped of their pension privileges.

7 General Wojciech Jaruzelski was a Polish military officer who served as Commander-in-Chief of the Army and Ministry of Defence from 1965 to 1983, First Chairman of the Party from 1981 to 1989, Prime Minister from 1981 to 1985, Chairman of the Council of State (the collegial head of state) from 1985 to 1989, and Poland's first president from mid-1989 to late 1990.

8 Aleksander Kwaśniewski, the president of Poland for two terms (1995–2005), had been a minister during the last years of the communist era (1985–1989).

9 Judgment of the Constitutional Tribunal of February 25, 1992, signature no. K 3/91. See also the judgment in the case with signature no. K 6/96, in which the Constitutional Tribunal found that a legislative attempt in 1994 to limit the effects of the former Communist Party's nationalization of property was unconstitutional.

10 See the judgments in two cases, signature nos. K 11/99 and SK 4/02.

According to Polish law, veterans and other officials are entitled to a number of social and economic rights and a special status in official ceremonies and solemn celebrations. In this regard, the newly established government stripped members of the former communist regime's security apparatus of their status as "Veterans of the Struggle for Independence and Democracy." Likewise, the government deprived some of these individuals of their pension privileges.

In 2009, Parliament adopted an act amending the rules that governed pensions for communist-era civil and military officials. After unsuccessfully challenging the act in front of Polish courts, some of the individuals negatively affected by the act took their case before the European Court of Human Rights. The court chose not to hear the complaints because it regarded the act's provisions as legitimate and, indeed, as an acceptable realization of the principle of social justice. It is also worth noting that Article 1 of Protocol No. 1 to the European Convention on Human Rights does not restrict states from passing pension-reduction laws.[11]

Once again, in December 2016, Parliament amended the act concerning pensions for officers who had served in the former state-security apparatus. As amended, the act completely deprived these individuals of any pension money that would have resulted from each year of service during that period. Moreover, the act now stipulated that the pensions of these individuals may not be higher than general pensions. The act even eliminated a disability allowance for these individuals who had suffered a health impairment. This time, and in contrast to the previous legislated reduction in pensions, Polish courts had doubts as to the constitutionality of the disability-allowance provisions. In some cases, the courts began to adjudicate in favor of communist-era state-security functionaries. Related legal questions were also put to the Supreme Court[12] and the Constitutional Tribunal.[13] The Supreme Court ordered the courts to individually consider the situations of former officers of state-security services. Whether or not the old-age pension should be reduced is to be determined by the assessment of all circumstances, including the specific acts of these people, in particular whether they have violated the fundamental rights of other citizens.[14] The final verdict of the Constitutional Tribunal has been issued in June 2021. New provisions of the Act 2016 were found constitutional[15].

Lustration

Similar to the issue of de-communization has been the issue of lustration. Since Poland underwent its transformation, Polish society has grappled with the process of revealing collaborators of the communist regime's security agencies,

11 Judgment of the European Court of Human Rights of May 14, 2013, application no. 15189/10, *Cichopek and 1,627 others v. Poland*.
12 Signature no. III UZP 11/19.
13 Signature no. P 4/18 and no. P 10/20.
14 Judgment of the Supreme Court of September 16, 2020, signature no. III UZP 11/19.
15 Judgment of the Constitutional Tribunal of June 16, 2021, signature no. P 10/20.

particularly if these collaborators were still functionaries in the democratic state. Parliament was unable to reach a consensus necessary for passage of a lustration law. The issue swelled and became a political lightning rod during the collapse of the minority government in the spring of 1992. A deputy submitted to the First Chamber of Parliament a motion requesting that the minister of the interior be obliged to present to parliament a list of secret communist-era collaborators who were still government employees. The minister – despite doubts about the legality of the formulation of the obligation – prepared a list of former security-agency collaborators. The list was initially classified and was unclear about whether the named individuals had been actual or potential collaborators. Made public very quickly, the list named many famous people who had been pro-democracy activists during the communist era. Among the named former activists were the incumbent president and the First Chamber's speaker. The same day as the release of the names, Parliament reacted by passing a vote of no confidence in the Council of Ministers. However, the political life of the list turned out to be more enduring than that of the government. In any case, the question of lustration was now firmly implanted in the mind of the public, and an aura of scandal settled over the political establishment. The Constitutional Tribunal eventually concluded that the resolution of the Chamber of Parliament was unconstitutional.[16]

The parliament elected in 1993 was dominated by parties composed mainly of people from the previous regime. This circumstance was not conducive to the enactment of lustration-related statutes, which did not become a possibility until after the 1997 parliamentary elections, which resulted in a majority of elected officials affiliated with the democratic opposition to the former communist regime. Parliament passed the Lustration Act of 1997, which obliges all officials born before May 11, 1972, to declare whether or not they worked in or collaborated with the communist-era secret police at any time between 1944 and 1989.[17] The act offers no exemptions and, thus, applies to hugely prominent and powerful citizens, including presidents, members of Parliament, and high-ranking judges. Perhaps not surprisingly then, heated debates about the act have taken place on the national political stage.

One reason for the passage of the act was a widespread desire among Poles to create openness and transparency regarding political candidates' past collaboration with the old regime. Rather than bar erstwhile collaborators from political office, the act permits them to stand as candidates in parliamentary elections or in contests for higher public office – but only after they have revealed their past collaboration. If people are untruthful about their past collaboration, the court system may bar them from running for office.

16 Judgment of the Constitutional Tribunal of Poland of June 19, 1992, signature no. U 6/92.

17 The official title of the Lustration Act, as translated into English, is the Act of April 11, 1997, on Revealing Work for or Service in the State's Secret Services or Collaboration with Them between 1944 and 1990.

In autumn 2006, Parliament amended the Lustration Act.[18] The amendment significantly expanded the catalogue of people obliged to submit lustration declarations. It also gave citizens the opportunity to ask a special state body to determine whether communist-era security agencies had ever collected information about them.

The act was appealed to the Constitutional Tribunal, which ruled that some provisions were inconsistent with the Constitution as well as with international law.[19] Among the controversial provisions were the criteria for disclosing information, the "lustration obligation," and the automatically imposed sanctions for failure to comply with the obligation. In particular, the "lustration obligation" was questioned and required scientists, journalists, directors of private schools, bank directors, and other specialists to submit declarations regarding their cooperation with the security services of the communist regime. A 2018 act barred from university work all those individuals who had admitted to cooperating with communist-era security agencies.

The European Court of Human Rights generally held that Poland's lustration procedures violated people's right to a fair trial by not granting them equality of arms.[20] Only the accusing prosecutor had access to all the documents of the special services concerned. Despite the rulings of the Constitutional Tribunal[21] and the European Court of Human Rights, Poland's lustration legislation remains binding as to its general structure.

Interestingly but not surprisingly, lustration influenced the vetting of judges. On April 2, 2015, the Constitutional Tribunal ruled on the importance of protecting judicial immunity in the context of lustration. According to the ruling, if a prosecutor accuses a judge of an untrue lustration declaration prior to commencing lustration proceedings, the relevant court must waive the judge's immunity. However, if investigations reveal that a judge has submitted an untrue lustration declaration, the judge shall be removed from office.[22]

Safeguards Ensuring the Responsibility of Judges and Public Prosecutors

The next type of transitional-justice case considered by the Constitutional Tribunal concerns safeguards that ensure the responsibility of public prosecutors

18 The full title, as translated into English, is the Act of October 18, 2006, on the Disclosure of Information Related to Secret-Service Documents from the Period between 1944 and 1990 and the Content of these Documents.

19 Judgment of the Constitutional Tribunal of May 11, 2007, signature no. K 2/07.

20 See, e.g., the judgment of the European Court of Human Rights of May 31, 2011, application no. 10104/08, *Zabłocki v. Poland* and other judgments cited there.

21 Regarding lustration in the 1990s and early 2000s, see also the judgments and resolutions of the Constitutional Tribunal, signature nos. U 6/92, W 5/93, K 24/98, K 39/97, P 3/00, SK 10/99, SK 28/01, K 7/01, K 11/02, and K 44/02.

22 Judgment of the Constitutional Tribunal of Poland, April 2, 2015, signature no. P 31/12.

and judges. In May 1990, Parliament passed an act that made structural and personal changes to the existing prosecutor's office.[23] The Minister of Justice also became the prosecutor general. The law provided for the reappointment of prosecutors and also permitted existing prosecutors to leave their office independently or to retire. However, regarding public prosecutors previously involved in the communist state, the act provided neither a verification procedure for such involvement nor a general prohibition on communist-linked individuals' continued performance of their prosecutorial duties. Moreover, no legal prohibition prohibited the government's rehiring of these "fired" public prosecutors. In 2007, the government required that prosecutors submit a lustration declaration. However, even prosecutors' admission of collaboration with communist-era security services is not a legal condition for dismissal from office. It was not until 2016 that legislation (specifically, the Act on the Public Prosecutor's Office) prohibited the appointment of an individual to a public-prosecutor position if the individual had collaborated with communist-era secret services.[24]

The consensus at the Round Table was that common-court judges should have the right to implement their own forms of transitional justice in the Polish judiciary without instructions or even guidance from nonjudicial elements of the Polish government. The members of the Round Table justified their advocacy of "judicial self-cleansing" by arguing that judges, because of their lifetime appointments, were more immune from political pressure than other officials. With many Poles arguing that "judicial self-cleansing" is an inadequate system, Parliament passed the Law of December 17, 1997. Regarding judges and prosecutors who had collaborated with the communist-era security apparatus, this act deprived them of their special retirement pension, regardless of (1) whether or not the collaboration had led to the repression of people for their democratic, pro-independence, or human rights stances and (2) whether or not the individuals had issued a true lustration declaration.

The Law of December 17, 1997, constituted a muscular effort to stamp out the vestiges of the communist era in Poland's judiciary. The act specifically did away with Poland's system of "decommissioning." Prior to the act, judges did not retire in Poland: They were "decommissioned" – that is, although they stopped performing all the functions of a judge and started receiving a pension, they continued to occupy some related positions in public service and remained, at least in name, judges for the rest of their lives. These life tenures, which only "for-cause removals" could end, were thought to protect the independence of judges. Thus, the 1997 act eliminated the possibility of "decommissioning" for judges who either had lied on their lustration declaration or had served under a communist

23 Act of March 22, 1990, amending the Act on the Public Prosecutors of the People's Republic of Poland.

24 It is worth mentioning here that, in 2019, a former deputy of the ruling party as well as a prosecutor from the martial law period was elected a Constitutional Tribunal judge by the First Chamber of Parliament.

regime, be it Polish or Soviet, at any point between September 1939 and 1956. Moreover, judges could be removed from office if they had betrayed the principle of judicial independence or had unduly influenced the rulings of other judges. This act, like the previously mentioned 2006 act, was challenged before the Constitutional Tribunal,[25] which, in June 1998, ruled that the provisions regarding the removal of judges were inconsistent not only with the constitution (specifically with the constitution's "removal protection" provision) but also with the general principle *lex retro non agit.* Nevertheless, the Constitutional Tribunal stated that the troubling legacy of Poland's communist regime necessitated a governmental effort to reveal and explain past judicial abuses. With the removal provision taken out, the rest of the 1997 act came into force. On its basis, both the National Council of the Judiciary and various disciplinary courts heard cases pertaining to 48 judges. Of the 48 judges, 42 saw their cases dismissed, 5 saw their cases discontinued, and only 1 was found guilty of having violated the principle of judicial independence: He was removed from judicial service in 2007. It has to be emphasized, though, that the single finding of guilt does not quite reflect the true scale of judges' involvement in the communist regime. First of all, many judges who had served in office during the Stalinist period had died before 1998, and according to Polish criminal law, the state may neither commence nor continue any criminal proceeding against a dead person. Second of all, other judges who had served under the Stalinist communist state had subsequently emigrated from Poland, and it was difficult to bring criminal charges against them. For these very reasons, it will probably never be possible to establish the true scale of the involvement of Polish judges in the crimes of Poland's Stalinist and post-Stalinist communist periods.

There were other occasions when Parliament interfered with the judiciary's handling of transitional-justice matters. In 1991, Parliament passed an act invalidating judicial decisions that, between 1944 and 1989, had targeted anti-communist activists. Parliament recognized that, during the communist period, the government had routinely violated the right to both fair trials and due process in cases involving democratic, pro-independence, and human rights activists. Parliament also recognized that Poland's post-communist court procedures might have been inadequate to the task of resolving unfair communist-era court decisions. Today, in post-transformation Poland, the many years that have passed since allegedly unfair communist-era rulings make them difficult, if not impossible, to properly reconsider. Nevertheless, Parliament's passage of this 1991 act was controversial, as the act granted the legislative branch the power to review judicial judgments. Indeed, the act could have become a dangerous precedent. Thankfully, courts, not the legislature, continued to have the final word regarding whether a concrete judgment was valid or not.

Since its entry into force, the 1991 act has raised a number of ethical and legal concerns. It has been amended several times, with fundamental changes affecting

25 Judgment of the Constitutional Tribunal of Poland, June 24, 1998, signature no. K 3/98.

who is entitled to compensation and redress. The act's main objective was to create a separate, simplified mechanism to compensate people for any damage that Poland's communist-era government had inflicted on people suspected of anti-communist activity. The act's scope was deliberately limited to the negative consequences of invalid judgments terminating criminal proceedings. After the amendment of the law in 2007, all decisions on internment under the Decrees of Martial Law of December 1981 were considered tacitly as such. The aim of the law was not to compensate victims of every nefarious sanction imposed on them by communist authorities. Rather, the aim was to give satisfaction to those who had suffered the most under the communist regime or had contributed the most to its overthrow. The provisions of the 1991 act have been the subject of several judgments of the Constitutional Tribunal.[26]

Reprivatization

Beginning in 1944, the communist government notoriously carried out large-scale expropriations of private property. In their vision of the state, there was very little place for private property. The more widespread the poverty is in a country, the more dependent the citizens are on the government. In turn, the dependence facilitates the government's manipulation of the citizens. This is a general recipe for the long duration of many dictatorships.

Even before World War II, Poland experienced overpopulation in villages and a lack of arable land due to the vast size of privately owned estates. In 1944, communist authorities[27] passed a decree introducing agricultural reform. Although issued by a temporary authority, the reform was considered a normative act with force equal to that of Parliament. The communists transformed all of Poland by parceling and redistributing the lands of private owners. After establishing a system of democratic governance in Poland, ex-owners of land took steps to undo the effects of the communist-era agricultural reform. The central aim of these steps was to nullify the communist decree of 1944. Ex-owners of seized land challenged the decree before the Constitutional Tribunal. In its decision on November 28, 2001, the tribunal stated that the decree on agricultural reform (1) had resulted in irreversible socioeconomic changes to Poland; (2) had been a one-time event; and (3) was no longer in use. The Constitutional Tribunal therefore found that it did not have the power to repeal the decree of 1944.

26 See judgments of the Constitutional Tribunal in the following cases: April 30, 1996, signature no. W 18/95; November 18, 2003, signature no. P 6/03; June 16, 2009, signature no. SK 42/08; March 1, 2011, signature no. P 21/09; and July 26, 2012, signature no. P 8/11.

27 The Polish Committee of National Liberation, a temporary body exercising executive power, was created with the consent of Stalin in Polish territory that the Red Army seized from the German occupiers.

In 1945, the communist authority[28] issued a decree[29] transferring the ownership of all prewar territory in Warsaw to the municipality. Officially, this decree was issued to facilitate the reconstruction of Warsaw, destroyed by the Nazis. Creating a legal structure in which the municipal government could temporarily own real estate, the decree provided for the return of buildings to their former owners at a future date, after the rebuilding of the city. However, this return of property never happened. All the land became the permanent property of the local government of Warsaw. The Constitutional Tribunal dealt with the matter of the 1945 decree several times.[30] However, it was never found to be unconstitutional.

There are no provisions in the Constitution referring to a compensation for loss of property resulting from the communist regime. In general, when considering the legacy of a previous authoritarian regime, democratic legislators should do their best to account for all injustices as soon as possible, because the longer the period of time between an alleged violation of human rights and an investigation into it, the more impediments the investigators are likely to encounter. As an example, the state might have to protect people who, in good faith, received property unfairly seized by the state. The longer the passage of time, the more committed to the property its current owners will be. Additionally, as more and more time passes, future generations who played no role in the late regime's unfair seizure of property will find themselves having to pay for the regime's actions. In such complicated situations, government must apply the principles of equity and social justice to all parties involved.

It is reasonable to assert that Poland has never fairly dealt with property restitution. Therefore, every now and then, a property-restitution case becomes a major issue of public debate. The main point worth bearing in mind is that Poland's post-1989 government has never passed general legislation that would return nationalized property to either the victims of the communist-era seizure of private property or their families. This failure to pass such legislation also applies to real estate specifically in Warsaw. In 2018, the act on establishing real estate ownership[31] asserted that users of property – not former owners of property – would cease to enjoy temporary ownership of the property and would henceforward enjoy full ownership.

The property taken over by the communist regime and returned after 1989 was an exception, as all of this property had belonged to the Catholic Church

28 Domestic National Council, a communist-appointed body, in place of Parliament. It functioned until the first parliamentary elections after WWII in 1947.

29 Decree on the Property and the Perpetual Usufruct in the Capital City of Warsaw, published in the *Journal of Laws of the Republic of Poland*, 1945, no. 50, position no. 279.

30 See also other judgments, decisions, or resolutions of the Constitutional Tribunal of the Republic of Poland in cases with signature nos. W 3/89, W 5/90, W 19/95, P 4/99, SK 31/99, SK 5/01, SK 22/01, and SK 41/09.

31 The full title, translated into English, is the Act of July 20, 2018, on the transformation of the right of perpetual usufruct of land developed for housing purposes into the ownership right to this land, published in the *Journal of Laws of the Republic of Poland*, 2018, position no. 1716, as amended.

and other religious organizations. For this limited return of property, the post-communist government established committees consisting of its own members and of representatives of religious organizations. They set the timetable and compensation rules for the return of the property. Over time, the activities of these committees, particularly insofar as no general compensation mechanism existed in Poland, began to raise doubts among the general citizenry regarding the committees' legal basis, which was challenged before the Constitutional Tribunal.[32] There were also allegations of corruption. The committees, in their decisions, helped shape the legal relationship between the state and religious organizations. Interestingly, the committees operated behind closed doors and were inaccessible to the people and organizations whose rights and obligations were under discussion.

It is also worth noting that, regarding restitution of property, the jurisprudence of Polish courts and then the legislation of parliamentarians opened up the possibility that individual Poles whom communist authorities had deprived of property could pursue related claims. However, even in these cases, these newly opened possibilities covered a somewhat narrow range of matters. For example, Parliament passed legislation that granted citizens the right to seek redress in the court system if they claimed that the communist-era government, by depriving them of private property, had violated Polish law at the time. The lack of a clear, fully encompassing law opened the way to corruption and speculation. Thus, it became necessary for lawmakers to further regulate Poland's fragmented approach to property restitution and compensation – thus, the passage of the Act to Amend the Act on Real Estate, which came into force in September 2016. On July 27, 2016, the Constitutional Tribunal ruled on this act,[33] stating that the municipal government of Warsaw is not obliged to even consider a claim regarding previously seized real estate that presently serves a public purpose. Moreover, according to the Constitutional Tribunal, Poles who received compensation for seized property on the basis of agreements that communist Poland had signed with 14 countries, between 1948 and 1971, have no further claim to additional compensation. These agreements were indemnity treaties according to which the Polish government agreed to financially compensate other countries and entities therein that had suffered losses due to property left behind in Poland. In exchange for the compensation, Poland gained immunity from liability for these land issues. At the same time, these countries undertook not to consider their citizens' claims against Poland regarding this disputed property.

Throughout Poland, social pressure grew for comprehensive property restitution, and Poland's media began to publicize irregularities that, based on dubious ownership titles, characterized Warsaw's handling of real estate. Parliament

32 Judgment of the Constitutional Tribunal in the cases of September 21, 2004, signature no. K 25/10 and of June 8, 2011 r., signature no. K 3/09.

33 Judgment of the Constitutional Tribunal of Poland, of July 27, 2016, signature no. Kp 3/15.

responded to these pressures by once again taking up the matter. In 2017, Parliament passed an act outlining special rules of administrative procedure, applicable to repeal individual decisions on restitution for real estate in Warsaw, issued in violation of the law. The act established a commission to look into the matter. Though initially arousing great public interest, the commission's public appeal has diminished with time, and courts have overruled the special administrative body's decisions. Thus, at present, the legal significance of the commission is difficult to assess.

Conclusion

Transitional-justice proceedings in Poland have been neither innovative nor intense. The Polish government has designed the country's lustration mechanism so that it dovetails nicely with the country's existing legal system and with basic democratic principles. This design, when coupled with relevant legislation and judgments, confirms my assertion that the Polish government has undertaken no profound efforts to redress past wrongs committed by the communist government in Poland. Some thirty years since Poland embraced post-communist democracy, the country still struggles with the legacy of its communist past. The neglectful attitude held by early democratic leaders toward the idea of transitional justice has simply made subsequent efforts to confront the past all the more difficult. Maybe it is too late for Poland to effectively right these past wrongs.

References

Belavusau, U. and A. Gliszczyńska-Grabias (2017) *Law and Memory: Towards Legal Governance of History*. Cambridge: Cambridge University Press.

Cichopek and 1,627 others v. Poland [2013] ECtHR 15189/10.

Judgment of the Constitutional Tribunal of the Republic of Poland [1990] W 3/89.

Judgment of the Constitutional Tribunal of the Republic of Poland [1991] W 5/90.

Judgment of the Constitutional Tribunal of the Republic of Poland [1992] K 3/91.

Judgment of the Constitutional Tribunal of the Republic of Poland [1992] U 6/92.

Judgment of the Constitutional Tribunal of the Republic of Poland [1993] W 5/93.

Judgment of the Constitutional Tribunal of the Republic of Poland [1996] K 6/96.

Judgment of the Constitutional Tribunal of the Republic of Poland [1996] W 18/95.

Judgment of the Constitutional Tribunal of the Republic of Poland [1996] W 19/95.

Judgment of the Constitutional Tribunal of the Republic of Poland [1998] K 3/98.

Judgment of the Constitutional Tribunal of the Republic of Poland [1998] K 24/98.

Judgment of the Constitutional Tribunal of the Republic of Poland [1998] K 39/97.

Judgment of the Constitutional Tribunal of the Republic of Poland [1999] K 11/99.

Judgment of the Constitutional Tribunal of the Republic of Poland [2000] P 3/00.

Judgment of the Constitutional Tribunal of the Republic of Poland [2000] SK 10/99.

Judgment of the Constitutional Tribunal of the Republic of Poland [2000] SK 31/99.

Judgment of the Constitutional Tribunal of the Republic of Poland [2001] P 4/99.

Judgment of the Constitutional Tribunal of the Republic of Poland [2001] SK 5/01.

Judgment of the Constitutional Tribunal of the Republic of Poland [2001] SK 22/01.

Judgment of the Constitutional Tribunal of the Republic of Poland [2002] K 11/02.

Judgment of the Constitutional Tribunal of the Republic of Poland [2002] SK 28/01.
Judgment of the Constitutional Tribunal of the Republic of Poland [2003] K 7/01.
Judgment of the Constitutional Tribunal of the Republic of Poland [2003] K 44/02.
Judgment of the Constitutional Tribunal of the Republic of Poland [2003] P 6/03.
Judgment of the Constitutional Tribunal of the Republic of Poland [2003] SK 4/02.
Judgment of the Constitutional Tribunal of the Republic of Poland [2004] K 25/10.
Judgment of the Constitutional Tribunal of the Republic of Poland [2007] K 2/07.
Judgment of the Constitutional Tribunal of the Republic of Poland [2009] SK 42/08.
Judgment of the Constitutional Tribunal of the Republic of Poland [2011] K 3/09.
Judgment of the Constitutional Tribunal of the Republic of Poland [2011] P 21/09.
Judgment of the Constitutional Tribunal of the Republic of Poland [2011] SK 41/09.
Judgment of the Constitutional Tribunal of the Republic of Poland [2012] P 8/11.
Judgment of the Constitutional Tribunal of the Republic of Poland [2013] K 35/08.
Judgment of the Constitutional Tribunal of the Republic of Poland [2015] P 31/12.
Judgment of the Constitutional Tribunal of the Republic of Poland [2016] Kp 3/15.
Judgment of the Constitutional Tribunal of the Republic of Poland [2021] P 10/20.
Judgment of the Supreme Court of the Republic of Poland [2020] III UZP 11/19.
Zabłocki v. Poland [2011] ECtHR 10104/08.

Part 3

Constitutional Consequences of Transitional Justice

8 Transitional Justice in a 19th-Century Constitution

Cautionary Observations from the United States

Vicki C. Jackson and Harry Larson

Since the late 1980s, the world has witnessed many constitutional regime changes that have raised issues of transitional justice, an idea that has become a celebrated and discussed topic in academic literature (Kritz 1995a, 1995b; Teitel 1997, 2000; for a more recent collection, see Williams et al. 2012). Scholars have debated the roles of narrative and forgiveness; of truth seeking about the past; of criminal prosecution for acts purportedly lawful under a prior regime but in violation of international human rights law, or natural justice principles;[1] of lustration, reparations, and restitution of property. The field of transitional justice studies has grown in both the numbers of scholars engaged and the numbers of countries studied.

This paper focuses on a much older moment of constitutional transition – in the 1860s, as the US Civil War ended with victory by the Northern states over the Southern states' efforts to establish the Confederacy as a new sovereign entity. The principal issue dividing the Northern and Southern states was slavery, which had been abolished in Northern states but continued in the South, with conflict intensifying as more new states sought admission to the Union. In *Dred Scott* v. *Sandford* ([1857] 60 US 393), the Supreme Court exacerbated divisions by treating persons of African descent – even if free – as noncitizens and limiting Congress' power to arrive at political solutions.

Following the Civil War (1861–5), which entailed massive fatalities on both sides, three constitutional amendments were proposed by Congress and were declared ratified by the requisite number of states. The 13th Amendment (1865) abolished slavery. The 14th Amendment (1868) provided for birthright citizenship for all persons born in the United States and subject to its jurisdiction; declared that the states could neither deny any person the equal protection of the law nor deprive a person of life, liberty, or property without due process of law; provided that representation in the House of Representatives should be based on the number of persons within a state and that states would lose representation in proportion to a state's denial of the right to vote to males over 21

1 Concerns about the retroactive application of law echoed earlier debates about the war crimes tribunals that followed World War II.

DOI: 10.4324/9780429505089-12

(except for participation in rebellion or other crime); prohibited certain former government officeholders who supported the Confederacy from holding office; and provided that the public debt of the United States (including debts incurred for pensions and bounties in suppressing rebellion) would be honored but that no payment could be made by either the federal or state governments on Confederate war debts or to compensate for the loss of slaves. The 15th Amendment (1870) directly prohibited denial or abridgment of the right to vote based on race, color, or prior condition of servitude (namely, slavery). Each amendment gave Congress power to enforce its provisions.

Focusing primarily on the 14th Amendment, we suggest, first, that transitional justice provisions are in some sense likely to fail – or achieve at best only incomplete success – as they cannot appear just to all concerned; they may at once be perceived as a form of "victor's justice" and yet, at the same time, fail to provide complete justice to those oppressed by the prior regime.[2] Relatedly, transitional justice provisions are likely to be unstable – because the vanquished seek to resist their force; because interests of the formerly oppressed may shift over time;[3] or because it will be hard to anticipate novel issues and questions of timing, leading to transitional provisions that are either too short or too long. Finally, transitional-justice provisions that do not sunset may assume a role not contemplated at the time of their enactment through interpretation over time.

This is evident from the 14th Amendment's first four sections. As explained below, Section 1 of the 14th Amendment was intended to guarantee citizenship and civil rights to newly freed slaves. But the lack of agreement both within the North and between North and South over just how far the United States would go in guaranteeing formerly enslaved persons equal citizenship meant that Section 1 was little enforced on behalf of its intended beneficiaries for almost a century, even as it took on an unintended role in the late 19th and early 20th century in protecting business interests from economic regulation. Section 2 of the 14th Amendment, meanwhile, was intended to promote voting rights for freed slaves, though ambivalence about that goal – and what it meant for the voting

2 Cf. *Azanian Peoples Organization (AZAPO) and Others v. President of the Republic of South Africa and Others* (1996) ZACC 16 at para. 19 (South Africa), noting that a successful transition requires agreement of not only "those victimized by abuse but also those threatened by the transition to a 'democratic society based on freedom and equality.'" On the "roughness" of transitional justice, see Vermeule (2012); Lanni (2010), at 551, 553 (noting the "inevitably selective nature of transitional justice," praising ancient Athens' "successful reconciliation" after atrocities during a civil war, balancing forgiveness with justice, by providing amnesties for wrongdoers but permitting their victims to raise their bad conduct as "character evidence in unrelated lawsuits"). For recent doubts about the "presumption of perfectability" in achieving the multiple goals of transitional justice, see Meierenrich et al. (forthcoming 2021).

3 On the multiple elements of contemporary transitional-justice approaches and for an argument that these elements should be understood as linked, see De Greiff (2012). The balance among the elements of transitional-justice approaches may shift over time, leading, for example, to greater demands by some for peace as compared to the justice demands of others; Elster (2012) describes how anticipations of justice may act as obstacles to peace.

rights of African Americans in the North – led to an indirect incentive structure whose punitive provisions were never used. The section was, however, relied on a century later to provide a constitutional safe harbor to state laws disenfranchising felons from voting even after service of their sentences. Section 3, which barred most Confederate leaders from holding public office without congressional permission, was intended to lead to a new generation of Southern leadership who would break from the Confederate past. But four years after ratification, Congress passed a General Amnesty removing Section 3's disqualification for state office holders, and over ensuing decades, Southern whites and the southern Democratic Party pushed black and Republican Party leaders from power and erected new forms of racial exclusion. Section 4, which prohibited payments for the emancipation of slaves or for the South's war efforts and prohibited repudiation of the North's war debt, had limited effects at the time it was passed, but seven decades later, it played a role in one of the New Deal–era "gold clause" cases, and it reemerged in contemporary debates over the president's obligations during debt ceiling stand-offs.

I. Background

A. US Constitutional and Historical Background

As originally formulated in the late 18th century, the US Constitution gave the national legislature a structure based on two important compromises: the first, between large and small population states, with representation in the House of Representatives to be based primarily on population, and with each state (regardless of population) receiving two Senators, each having one vote, in the Senate; the second, between slave-holding interests and other interests, by requiring that, for purposes of allocating seats in the House, persons who were not free (i.e., slaves) would count as "three-fifths" of a person (Rakove 1997). This provision, known as the Three-Fifths Compromise, meant that states allowing slavery would generally have more representatives per eligible voter than non-slave states.

The conflicting interests of the North and the South came to a head in 1861. The relatively new Republican political party – dedicated, at that time, to preventing the spread of slavery to Western territories – had succeeded in having its nominee, Abraham Lincoln, elected president (Bordewich 2020, 25). Southern states had uniformly supported the pro-slavery Southern Democratic Party, and following Lincoln's election, several Southern states claimed to have seceded from the Union (an eventual total of eleven states) and to have established a new entity, the Confederate States of America. The US Civil War began when armed forces in one of those states, South Carolina, attacked and captured a national government fort (ibid., 66–8). In the bitter civil war that ensued, massive fighting created casualties higher than combined US casualties in World War I and World War II.

By early 1865, Congress (urged on by President Lincoln) proposed an amendment abolishing slavery, which was sent to the states for ratification about two months before the Civil War's formal end. This Amendment, the 13th, was rapidly approved, including by most of the Southern states, which recognized that the North's victory in the War meant, at the very least, the abolition of slavery. But Lincoln, who had guided the North successfully through the Civil War, died just five days after the surrender of southern troops at Appomattox, in April 1865. His vice president and successor, Andrew Johnson, was from Tennessee, a slave state that was part of the Confederacy.

Within a short time, disagreements arose between the new president and Congress over how far to go in establishing the status of former slaves as free citizens (with some northerners in Congress favoring but President Johnson opposing voting rights) and over the relationship of the rebellious Southern states to the rest of the Union (the president favored readmitting the Southern states to full membership quickly while Congress favored more restrictive readmission conditions to help secure the rights of the freed slaves). After the war's end, some Southern state legislatures enacted "black codes" that, in effect, replicated conditions of slavery by placing onerous limitations on black persons. These developments fed congressional concern and increased support for more aggressive federal intervention. In 1866, Congress, over the president's veto, passed a civil rights act designed to combat the South's new tool of subordinating the recently freed slaves (through the "black codes"). But concern about southern state governments and, for some, doubts about the new law's constitutionality led Congress to propose another amendment, the 14th, designed to more firmly establish the constitutional basis for federal protection of civil rights. The proposed amendment was sent to the states for ratification in mid-1866. Of the states that had seceded, only Tennessee acted promptly in ratifying this amendment, and several others rejected it. In 1867, Congress imposed military reconstruction on the Southern states, requiring them to adopt new constitutions based on universal male suffrage (including suffrage for freed slaves), to hold new elections for legislatures, and to ratify the 14th Amendment before the states' representatives would be permitted to again sit in Congress. The 14th Amendment was finally ratified in 1868.

The 15th Amendment was proposed by Congress in 1869 and ratified by 1870. Although the former Confederate states were already statutorily required to allow black voting as part of Reconstruction, the 15th Amendment was designed to constitutionally secure black voting in border and northern states as well as to prevent backsliding in the South (Foner 2014, Kindle location 8446).

B. The Civil War Amendments as Transitional-Justice Provisions

These three Civil War amendments may be viewed as "transitional justice" provisions. Ruti Teitel explains the context of transitional justice:

> The central question of transitional justice arises within a distinctive context, a shift in political orders. The "transitional" period begins right after the revolution or political change; thus, the problem of transitional justice

> arises within a bounded period, spanning two regimes. . . . [T]here is a close tie between the normative shift in understandings of justice and law's role in the construction of transition. Because transitional justice is justice within defined political parameters, it is limited and partial. . . . Law is caught between the past and the future, between backward-looking and forward-looking, between retrospective and prospective. Transitions imply paradigm shifts in the conception of justice (Teitel 1997, 2013–4).[4]

The Civil War amendments plainly meet these requirements: They arose during a period of transition following an intense civil war, and they marked a divide between two legal regimes, one based on (or tolerant of) slavery (and imposing few restraints on the states to protect individual rights) and one that abolished slavery and committed to at least formal equality without regard to race (and imposed new restraints on the states to protect individual rights). These amendments are at once backward-looking and forward-looking: The 13th Amendment and the first sentence of the 14th Amendment make unconstitutional the system of slavery and the practice of treating free Americans of African descent as noncitizens. They look backward to make unlawful a system of oppression previously protected by law, and they look forward to securing a new status for the formerly enslaved persons and, with the rest of Section 1, to establishing new norms of constitutional justice. The voting provisions of Section 2 of the 14th Amendment were prospective incentives. Section 3 was backward-looking insofar as it denied political office to those who had served the Confederacy and forward-looking insofar as it was designed to enable a new group of officeholders to come to power in the South. Section 4 was backward-looking in that it prohibited the federal and state governments from paying the debt incurred by Southern states in their rebellion or compensation to former slaveholders and forward-looking in that it promised that the federal government's debt "shall not be questioned," thereby protecting the creditors of the victorious Union.[5]

The Civil War Amendments were transitional in a larger sense as well, for their drafters well understood that winning the war did not necessarily mean winning

4 Posner and Vermeuele (2004, 766) likewise describe transitional justice as both backward- and forward-looking. Murphy (2017, 41, 49–75), describes transitional-justice situations as including deep structural inequality, normalized collective wrongdoing, serious existential uncertainty about the state's future, and uncertainty about authority insofar as the state was implicated in prior wrongs, yielding the question of what constitutes a "just pursuit of societal transformation" (ibid. at 34). For a discussion of the Civil War–era and Reconstruction-era amendments in the context of transitional justice, see Teitel (1997, 2074). Primus (2006, 1711) likewise refers to Reconstruction as an extended effort to address transitional-justice problems.

5 Teitel (1997, 2016–2030) also emphasizes the fluid character of the rule of law during periods of transitional justice, arguing that what counts as sufficient notice and rule of law following positive rules is informed by considerations of justice as articulated by those who emerge victorious. The pressure placed on the defeated states to ratify the 14th Amendment perhaps illustrates such fluidity.

the kind of peace that many in the North sought. Scholarly accounts have focused on the anticipated roles of Sections 2, 3, and 4 of the 14th Amendment in preventing a reemergence of the "slave power" in the defeated states. Indeed, Graber (2014) argues that this was the primary concern for several of the 14th Amendment's framers and that the broad value statements in Section 1 of the 14th Amendment (today, the source of nearly all 14th Amendment doctrine)[6] were at the time perceived as less important than – and only achievable through – the concrete steps towards reshaping political power enabled by Sections 2 and 3.[7]

At the end of the Civil War, the pro-Union, anti-slavery Republicans had to contend with two related concerns. First, following the ratification of the 13th Amendment, the impending readmission of Southern states into the United States threatened not just to restore the prewar balance of electoral power but actually to increase the power of Southern whites. Former slaves would now be counted as full (as opposed to three-fifths) persons, which threatened to *increase* Southern representation in the House and the Electoral College[8] relative to the prewar status quo. As calculated by Representative Conkling, Republican of New York, Southern states would have a 28-vote bonus in the House and in the Electoral College – a significant increase over the 18-vote bonus that these states had enjoyed as a result of the Three-Fifths Compromise in 1787 (US Congress 1866, 357; *see also* Nelson 1988, 45–7; Graber 2014, 28).

Second, Republicans worried that the South would use this increased power in the House and in presidential elections to reverse the hard-fought gains of the war. At the time, some Southern states had already begun to enact "black codes," which severely restricted the movement and rights of formerly enslaved persons in ways designed to replicate many of the features of slavery. Representative Thaddeus Stevens, a leader of the Radical Republican wing in Congress most concerned with securing former slaves full citizenship, anticipated that Democrats would "at the very first election take possession of the White House and the halls of Congress," a result that would lead to "ruin" – including "[a]ssumption of the rebel debt or repudiation of the Federal debt" and "oppression of the

6 The drafting history of section 1 of the 14th Amendment has been extensively chronicled and its meaning debated elsewhere (Curtis 1986, 57–91; Nelson 1988, 40–64).

7 More specifically, Graber (2014, 7–8) argues that the framers of the 14th Amendment "sought to construct a constitutional politics that guaranteed to the extent feasible that the persons who remained loyal to the Union during the Civil War, white and black, would control the meaning of the post-Civil War Constitution." He suggests (ibid.) that the focus of much scholarly attention on John Bingham as the 14th Amendment's principal framer, while perhaps true with respect to Section 1, is mistaken when it comes to Sections 2, 3, and 4, in connection with which Thaddeus Stevens and other radicals played a greater role.

8 Under Article II of the US Constitution, the President is selected not by direct popular vote but by the vote of a college of "electors," with each state receiving a number of electors equal to the total number of that state's Representatives and Senators in Congress. Electors, in turn, are chosen in all states based on the popular vote within that state (with most states awarding the popular vote winner all their delegates, although Maine and Nebraska also award electors based on the vote outcome within congressional districts).

freedmen; the reamendment of their State constitutions, and [even] the reestablishment of slavery" (US Congress 1866, 74). Such concerns were widely shared (Graber 2014, 29).[9]

More particularly, while Republicans intended that Section 1 of the 14th Amendment's guarantee of citizenship to all persons born in the United States would reverse *Dred Scott v. Sandford* (1857)'s holding that persons of African descent were not US citizens (Finkelman 2013, 429), they also worried that reversal by amendment, no matter how explicit, would be subject to the same kind of bad-faith judicial interpretation they saw at work in *Dred Scott* itself (Graber 2014, 6). As such, the broad value statements contained in Section 1 would need to be backed up by structural political reforms that would undermine the "Slave Power" and promote Republican power (Graber 2014, 6). Opponents criticized the 14th Amendment on precisely these terms, viewing it as a power grab that would help Republicans and hurt the South; as Representative Fink, Democrat of Ohio, stated, "Stripped of all disguises, this measure is a mere scheme to deny representation to eleven States . . . and perpetuate the power of a sectional and dangerous party" (US Congress 1866, 2461).

Section 2 of the 14th Amendment – with its promise to reduce Southern voting power to the extent the South restricted the voting rights of adult men – was, thus, for some Republicans, "the most important" measure for advancing Republican and limiting Democratic power (US Congress 1866, 2459 [Rep. Stevens]). There was not yet sufficient support in 1866 to explicitly extend the franchise to formerly enslaved persons or overtly reference race, in part because of opposition to voting by African Americans in Northern states (Chin 2004, 268–9; Bickel 1955, 44). The language ultimately proposed and ratified in Section 2 therefore avoided any reference to race, color, or slavery, but for the first (and only) time, it introduced a gender distinction into the US Constitution, contributing to a major rupture between some leaders of the women's suffrage movement and the abolitionist movement (Epps 2006, 214–21).

Although many Republicans may have viewed Section 2 as the most important measure in the 14th Amendment, they also believed something like Section 3 was necessary in order to prevent Confederate leaders from regaining power (Graber 2014, 44; Nelson 1988, 58). Kentucky Representative McKee insisted that Congress must prevent former Confederate leaders "from again seizing the offices of the Federal Government" (US Congress 1866, 2504–5). Massachusetts Representative Boutwell similarly stated, "I see no safety in the present except in some sort of exclusion of those who are its enemies" (US Congress 1866, 2508). As enacted, Section 3 barred certain former office holders from holding

9 For example, Representative Spalding of Ohio declared that "rebel States . . . will repeal many, if not all, of the measures which we have adopted for the welfare and salvation of the country" (US Congress 1866, 2509). Similarly, Representative Ingersol of Illinois predicted that "every man of them will vote to . . . pay for the property that has been destroyed by our armies that marched through the South" (US Congress 1866, 2405).

state or federal office again, unless two-thirds of Congress voted to permit it.[10] The debates surrounding Section 3 focused on both who should be penalized (all who served in the Confederate army and government, or just leaders?) and for how long (until a fixed date or indefinitely?) (Re and Re 2012, 1616–24).

In contrast to the history of Sections 2 and 3, Section 4's history in Congress is less revealing of the reasons the final proposal took the form it did, perhaps because Section 4 was less controversial. An initial version of what became Section 4 referred only to repudiating the Southern debts incurred in the Civil War (Abramowicz 1997, 583 n. 104); another early proposal for language guaranteeing payment of Union debts used narrow language referring only to federal debts from the recent insurrection (ibid., 583 n. 103). The final wording referred in more general language to "[t]he validity of the public debt of the United States," without limitation (ibid., 583–7). However, it is unclear how much these revisions were viewed as expanding the provision's scope, with at least one senator asserting that these changes did not substantially change the provision's meaning (ibid., 584 n.113).

Below, we discuss the first four sections of the 14th Amendment in more detail.[11]

II. 14th Amendment, Section 1

Section 1 of the 14th Amendment provides:

> All persons born or naturalized in the United States and subject to the jurisdiction thereof, are citizens of the United States and of the State wherein they reside. No State shall make or enforce any law which shall abridge the privileges or immunities of citizens of the United States; nor shall any State deprive any person of life, liberty, or property, without due process of law; nor deny to any person within its jurisdiction the equal protection of the laws (US Constitution 1788, amend. XIV).

10 An earlier version proposed by the House would have disenfranchised "all persons who voluntarily adhered to the late insurrection, giving it aid and comfort" from voting in federal elections until 1870 (US Congress 1866, 2545 (Joint Resolution); Re and Re 2012, 1621). Radical Republican Congressman Thadeus Stevens of Pennsylvania praised that version as properly punitive (US Congress 1866, 2544), inquiring of his colleagues, "Gentleman here have said you must not humble these people. Why not? . . . Do not they deserve degradation? If they do not, who does? What criminal . . . deserves it more . . . ?"

11 Given the limited focus of this chapter, we do not discuss Section 5 of the 14th Amendment, which empowered Congress to enforce the Amendment's other provisions and was a central component of even the earliest proposals for what became the 14th Amendment. The story of Section 5's use right after the Civil War, its desuetude for some time thereafter, its reemergence as a powerful tool for racial equality in the 1960s, and its retrenchment by the Supreme Court in recent decades (*e.g.*, *Shelby Co v. Holder* [2013] 570 US 529) is of great importance, but it would require considerable space to address whether Section 5's waxing and waning reflects unique aspects of transition or more general concepts in constitutional law (Murphy 2017; Posner and Vermeuele 2004; Dyzenhaus 2012).

Slavery and the status of black persons were at the core of the issues dividing North and South before and during the Civil War, though public opinion was by no means unanimous or clear on these issues even in the North. Following the abolition of slavery through the 13th Amendment, issues concerning the status of the freed slaves as citizens remained because of *Dred Scott*'s holding that persons of African descent could not be citizens. This holding was overturned by the first sentence of Section 1 of the 14th Amendment, which declares in essence that all people born or naturalized on American soil are citizens of the United States. The second sentence of Section 1 goes on to provide, among other things, that "[n]o State shall" deprive any "person" of life, liberty or property without due process of law nor deny to any person the equal protection of the law. The leading contemporary historian of this period, Eric Foner, concludes that the central purpose of Section 1 was to secure a "national guarantee of equality before the law"; he accounts for this section being less debated in Congress than others because its principles had been so much discussed in the prior years (Foner 2014, Kindle location 5076–89).

In the *Slaughterhouse Cases* ([1873] 83 US 36), decided soon after the 14th Amendment's adoption, the Court rejected efforts by businesses to rely on the 13th Amendment and Section 1 of the 14th Amendment to challenge a state law granting monopoly powers to their competitors. Explaining that the Justices had taken "ample time" for serious deliberation, the Court wrote that "*the one pervading purpose* found in . . . all [three of the Civil War Amendments], lying at the foundation of each, and without which none of them would have been even suggested . . . [was] the freedom of the slave race, the security and firm establishment of that freedom, and the protection of the newly made freeman and citizen from the oppressions of those who had formerly exercised unlimited dominion over him" (ibid., 67, 71–2 [emphasis added]). Yet within a few short years, the 14th Amendment was increasingly invoked by the Court as a basis to review and invalidate state laws challenged by business interests.[12] Not until after World War II did the 14th Amendment come to be used extensively to protect the rights of African Americans.

To be sure, Section 1 had some effect on the status of formerly enslaved persons in the years following the Civil War. For example, the Supreme Court in *Strauder v. West Virginia* ([1880] 100 US 303) and *Ex parte Virginia* ([1880]

12 In *Munn v. Illinois* ([1877] 94 US 113, 125), the Court rejected a challenge to criminal convictions under an Illinois law regulating grain storage warehouses and setting a maximum price for storage and handling services, although it held open the possibility that economic regulations might violate the 14th Amendment's due process clause under certain circumstances. In *Chicago, Milwaukee & St. Paul Railway Company v. Minnesota* ([1890] 134 US 418), the Court held that a particular regulatory rate-setting scheme for railroads violated due process. And in *Lochner v. New York* ([1905] 198 US 45), the Court held that a New York law setting a 60-hour maximum workweek for bakers violated the 14th Amendment Due Process clause. In *Santa Clara Co. v. Southern Pacific* [1886] 118 US 394, the court had also determined, with no reasoning, that corporations were "persons" protected by Section 1 of the Fourteenth Amendment.

100 US 339) found unconstitutional state laws or practices excluding African Americans from serving on juries solely on account of race.[13] However, by the early 1880s, the Court was dramatically curtailing Congress's power to legislate to secure the rights of freed slaves (e.g., *The Civil Rights Cases* [1883] 109 US 3). And in 1896, the Court upheld laws requiring segregation based on race in public facilities, on the fiction that such laws provided for equal, albeit separate, treatment (*Plessy v. Ferguson* [1896] 163 US 537). The Court did not disavow the "separate but equal" doctrine until the 1950s, in *Brown v. Board of Education* [1954] 347 US 483. And only after *Brown* did Section 1 come into wider use as a constitutional basis for securing equality.

III. 14th Amendment, Section 2

Section 2 of the 14th Amendment provides:

> Representatives shall be apportioned among the several States according to their respective numbers, counting the whole number of persons in each State, excluding Indians not taxed. But when the right to vote at any election for the choice of electors for President and Vice President of the United States, Representatives in Congress, the Executive and Judicial officers of a State, or the members of the Legislature thereof, is denied to any of the male inhabitants of such State, being twenty-one years of age, and citizens of the United States, or in any way abridged, except for participation in rebellion, or other crime, the basis of representation therein shall be reduced in the proportion which the number of such male citizens shall bear to the whole number of male citizens twenty-one years of age in such State (US Constitution 1788, amend. XIV).

Prior to the Civil War, representatives were apportioned among states based on the count of all "free persons" and "three fifths of all other persons," namely slaves (US Const Art I, Section 2). The first sentence of Section 2 of the 14th Amendment clarified that, following the abolition of slavery, this apportionment scheme from the original Constitution no longer applied. But even many Northerners were not prepared in early 1866 to fully support African American voting rights, although the more radical among them were. The second sentence of Section 2 of the 14th Amendment embodied the compromise that emerged: On the one hand, the section gave states an incentive to enfranchise African Americans; on the other hand, the section allowed states the freedom to decide whether to do so. Some critics contended that this section of the Amendment did not go far

13 In *Ex parte Yarbrough* ([1884] 110 US 651), the Court also upheld criminal convictions against several Ku Klux Klan members who had attacked a black man to prevent him from voting, reasoning that Congress had power to punish interference with the right to vote in federal elections.

enough in securing rights for freed slaves, while others asserted that it unjustifiably intruded on state sovereignty and went too far toward in promoting racial equality.[14] Section 2 aimed to head off an unintended consequence of the 13th Amendment: an increase in Southern white power because former slaves would count as full, rather than three-fifths, persons in allocating representation in the House and Electoral College. Section 2 aimed to ensure that any increase in the representative power of the Southern states in Congress could only occur if black voters were allowed to vote (Nelson 1988, 45–7; Graber 2014, 28; US Congress 1866, 357 [Rep. Conkling]).

Despite controversy in Congress and some ratifying conventions around Section 2's provisions for reducing states' representation in the House based on states' restriction of the suffrage, those provisions were never invoked. After Southern states initially refused to ratify the Amendment at the same time as they were adopting black codes imposing severe restrictions on freed slaves (including denying them the right to vote), Republicans in Congress moved *by statute* to condition the Southern states' readmission on their ratification of the 14th Amendment and enfranchisement of former slaves. The 1867 Reconstruction Acts required former Confederate states to ratify new state constitutions and to allow near-universal male suffrage in electing delegates to draft new state constitutions; however, these statutes allowed the disenfranchisement of those who had participated in the rebellion from voting to elect delegates to the state constitutional conventions (Rawley 1960, 481, note 7; *Act of Mar. 2, 1867*, 14 Stat. 428–30, c.153, § 5)[15] and also required voters to swear they had not previously held state or federal office and subsequently participated in the rebellion (*Act of Mar. 23, 1867*, ch. 6, § 1, 15 Stat. 2–5, c.6, § 1, 2). The Reconstruction Acts further barred any future amendment of the new state constitutions that would deprive citizens of the right to vote, except as punishment for conviction of felonies at common law (Chin 2004, 271, note 67). While these statutes did not address restrictions on African American voting in border or northern states, the Reconstruction Acts did lead to African American men voting (or even holding office) in considerable numbers in Southern states (Wang 1996, 2208–20).

As the 1867 Reconstruction statutes suggest, even before the 14th Amendment was ratified, public and congressional sentiment on voting by former slaves had begun to shift. Republicans' realization that the party would need votes from African Americans to stay in power led them to favor a federal *constitutional*

14 Bond (1997, 106, 123, 145–147) recounts the opposition of white Southerners at Virginia's and South Carolina's ratifying conventions to Section 2's promise to increase black suffrage, as well as the unhappiness of freed slaves in Alabama that the provision did too little to actually secure their voting rights. Foner (2014, Kindle location 5053) describes how Wendell Philips and others condemned the 14th Amendment as implicitly recognizing the right of states to limit votes on the basis of race.

15 A subsequent act (*Act of Mar. 23, 1867*, 15 Stat. 2–5, c.6) provided for the US Army to register voters in states under reconstruction, which led to the registration of one million black voters (Chin 2004, 271).

requirement for black suffrage (Wang 1996, 2211–20). The enactment of the 15th Amendment, which prohibited denial of the right to vote based on race, rendered Section 2 of the 14th Amendment something of a dead letter, as the disenfranchisement Section 2 aimed to disincentivize was now directly prohibited (Chin 2004, 278–9; Parker, J., dissenting from Hayden v. Pataki ([2006] 449 F.3d 305, 351–52 [2d. Cir.]).

Gabriel Chin argues that the 15th Amendment implicitly repealed Section 2 of the 14th Amendment: because the remedy for an unlawful denial of the right to vote was now to "allow the deprived individuals to vote," Section 2's apportionment remedy, which even if invoked would still leave votes "abridged or denied," could not remain operative (Chin 2004, 293). Others argue that Section 2 was not entirely deprived of potential force: Its lack of explicit reference to race means it might reach facially race-neutral voting rules (such as literacy tests or poll taxes) untouched by the 15th Amendment (e.g., Re and Re 2012, at 1658–60),[16] and the apportionment remedy might simply provide Congress a special tool distinct from its 15th Amendment enforcement powers (ibid., 1657–60). Congress enacted an 1872 Act referring to Section 2 of the 14th Amendment and contemplating future penalties in representation but without specifying any particular enforcement method (Zuckerman 1961, 114–6), and members of Congress continued episodically to consider whether to reduce state apportionment pursuant to Section 2 of the 14th Amendment even after the 15th amendment was adopted, though Congress never did so (Re and Re 2012, 1657; US Congress 1871, 81 [Rep. Shellabarger]). As Professor Chin comments, "Although some members of the Reconstruction Congresses treated Section 2 as potentially applicable, they never persuaded a majority of their colleagues to enforce it" (Chin 2004, 301). To this day, no state has ever lost representation under Section 2.

But that did not stop Section 2 from being deployed in constitutional arguments quite divorced from its primary purpose of incentivizing the enfranchisement of former slaves. In 1874, the Supreme Court relied on Section 2's reference to "male" citizens in rejecting the argument that Section 1's "privileges and immunities" clause entitled all citizens – and in particular, female citizens – to vote (*Minor v. Happersett* [1874] 88 US [21 Wall.] 162, 174). The decision reflected in part the more general contemporaneous understanding that Section 1 did not guarantee voting rights (ibid., 170–5). A century later, the Court cited Section 2 when rejecting a challenge to state felon disfranchisement laws brought under the Equal Protection Clause of Section 1. In *Richardson v. Ramirez* ([1974] 418 US 24), the Court held that Section 2, notwithstanding its more limited language, amounted to an "affirmative sanction" for crime-based

16 But in light of the Supreme Court's interpretation of Section 2 as protecting only "the right to vote . . . as established by the laws and constitutions of the state" (*Lassiter v. Northampton Cty. Bd. of Elections*, [1959] 360 U.S. 45, 51 [quoting *McPherson v. Blacker* (1892) 146 U.S. 1, 29]), it is difficult to imagine precisely which denials for reasons other than race would be implicated (Chin 2004, 288).

suffrage exclusions, meaning such laws need not satisfy heightened standards of scrutiny to survive challenges under Section 1's Equal Protection Clause (ibid., 54). A recent paper lends some support to this view by arguing that members of the Reconstruction Congress viewed equality in voting as linked to moral worth: Former slaves "deserved" the vote, while those guilty of rebellion or serious crimes did not (Re and Re 2012, 1589–93).

However well or poorly such a theory reflects the proposing Congress's original understanding of Section 2, it does not follow that Section 2 insulates felon disenfranchisement from challenge under Section 1's more general principles of equal protection and due process. In his *Ramirez* dissent, Justice Thurgood Marshall argued that there was no reason to construe the "special remedy" for voter exclusions provided by Section 2 as "a limitation on the other sections of the Fourteenth Amendment" (Marshall, dissenting from *Richardson v. Ramirez* [1974] 418 US 24, 74). Second Circuit Court of Appeals Judge Parker has likewise argued that "declining to prohibit something is not the same as protecting it" (Parker, dissenting from *Hayden Pataki* [2006] 449 F. 3d, 349). Indeed, it would have been anomalous to view Section 2 as an implicit exception to Section 1, given prevailing contemporary understandings of Section 1 at the time the 14th Amendment was proposed and ratified as protecting civil but not voting rights.[17] And even if the 14th Amendment's drafters *had* viewed disenfranchisement as an appropriate punishment for serious crimes, that view does not legitimize massive disenfranchisement for dozens of less serious ones.[18] Yet since *Ramirez*, efforts to rely on the Equal Protection Clause to challenge felon disenfranchisement have been unavailing, except where it could be shown that

17 This view has changed over time: *Reynolds v. Sims* ([1964] 377 US 533) held that Section 1's Equal Protection Clause requires districts of roughly equal population size in elections for both chambers of state legislatures; and *Harper v. Virginia Bd. of Elections* ([1966] 383 US 663) held that the Equal Protection Clause forbids conditioning the right to vote on the payment of a poll tax.

18 Re and Re (2012, 1590–1591, 1648–1655) defend *Ramirez*'s reliance on Section 2 but also argue that criminal disenfranchisement should be limited to a subset of serious crimes. In practice, however, staggering numbers of voters have been disenfranchised for broad categories of felony convictions: For example, in the 2020 presidential election, it was estimated that 5.2 million Americans – including, in 11 states, at least one in 10 black voters – were barred from voting due to a felony conviction (Lopez 2020). In 2018, voters in the state of Florida voted to approve a state constitutional amendment that would have restored voting rights to over 1 million individuals with convictions labeled "felonies" who had completed their prison sentences (Lopez 2018). However, the Florida legislature subsequently passed legislation that would prevent individuals from regaining the right to vote until they paid the full balance of any outstanding fines, fees, costs or restitution (*Jones v. Florida* [2020] 975 F.3d, 1025 [11th Cir.])). Though a lower court initially found that this legislation violated the 14th Amendment's Equal Protection Clause as applied to disenfranchised voters who could not afford to pay the requisite amount, the appellate court reversed and allowed the legislation to go into effect, citing *Ramirez*'s analysis of Section 2 of the Fourteenth Amendment (ibid., 1029).

felon-disqualification laws had the purpose (as well as the effect) of discriminating on the basis of race.[19]

What *Ramirez* clearly illustrates is the extent to which very specific transitional-justice provisions, written to serve particular purposes at a particular time – here, to encourage enfranchising African Americans and to prevent defeated slave states from gaining voting power without doing so – may linger past their time, generating uncertainties and risks as they are applied to different contexts.

IV. 14th Amendment, Section 3

Section 3 of the 14th Amendment provides the following:

> No person shall be a Senator or Representative in Congress, or elector of President and Vice President, or hold any office, civil or military, under the United States, or under any State, who, having previously taken an oath, as a member of Congress, or as an officer of the United States, or as a member of any State legislature, or as an executive or judicial officer of any State, to support the Constitution of the United States, shall have engaged in insurrection or rebellion against the same, or given aid or comfort to the enemies thereof. But Congress may by a vote of two-thirds of each House, remove such disability (US Constitution 1788, amend. XIV).

Section 3 of the 14th Amendment occasioned considerable controversy both in the Congress that drafted it and in the state-ratification debates. In its initial form, the proposed amendment that came from the House would have disenfranchised Southern officeholders and ordinary soldiers from voting in federal elections until 1870 (Graber 2014, 78; US Congress 1866, 2545 [Joint Resolution]; US Congress Joint Committee on Reconstruction 1866, xix). Several Republican members of the House argued that even this proposal, in Representative Eckley's words, didn't "go far enough" (US Congress 1866, 2535 [Rep. Eckley]) or was "too lenient" (US Congress 1866, 2460 [Rep. Stevens]; Re and Re 2012, 1621 note 199).

But the Senate scaled back Section 3 to apply its ban only to office holding, not voting, and to target Confederate leaders (insofar as it applied only to those who supported the Confederacy after holding state or federal officeholder prior

19 In *Hunter v. Underwood* [1985] 471 US 222, the Court struck down a felon disenfranchisement provision in Alabama's 1901 state constitution that the Court determined was intended to disenfranchise on the basis of race, reasoning that, in contrast to *Ramirez*, Section 2 of the 14th Amendment was not intended to immunize intentional racial discrimination from challenge under Section 1. But enacting disqualification laws with the knowledge that they will disproportionately affect minority communities may well be insufficient to show the invidious intent needed to establish an equal protection violation (*Personnel Administrator of Massachusetts v. Feeney* [1979] 442 US 256, 278–280).

to the rebellion – a relatively elite group) rather than rank and file.[20] This change reflected both the moral judgment that Confederate soldiers did not deserve as much blame as Confederate leaders, and the practical concern that harsher measures could prevent ratification. As to the first concern, Representative Farnsworth, Republican of Illinois argued that although "some rebels are deserving of a total and lasting disfranchisement, . . . [others] are not near so criminal" (Re and Re 2012, at 1622 & n. 204, quoting US Congress 1866, 2540 [Rep. Farnsworth]). Other voices also supported making distinctions among those connected with the rebellion for purposes of the exclusions of Section 3, as in an 1866 *New York Times* editorial "The Constitutional amendment in the Senate" (NY Times Editorial 1866a, June 2). As to the second concern (for securing ratification), Representative Bingham argued that a proposal for broad disenfranchisement would "furnish demagogues a pretext for raising the howl" that the amendment's purpose was to "control the next presidential election," (US Congress 1866, 2543), while Representative Farnsworth expressed "fears that [the House version] may greatly embarrass, if not defeat, the adoption of the other sections should we pass it through this House" (US Congress 1866, 2543). Another *New York Times* editorial similarly warned that "Southern Legislatures would unquestionably refuse to ratify an amendment of which wholesale disfranchisement is the most prominent feature" (NY Times 1866b, May 25).[21] Some also argued that disenfranchisement would be tantamount to a bill of attainder or ex post facto law, unfairly expanding punishment for actions already taken (Re and Re 2012, 1619–20; US Congress 1866, 2467 (Rep. Boyer);US Congress 1866, 879 [Sen. Hendricks]).

The compromise that emerged did not disenfranchise anyone and targeted only former government officials while, at the same time, having no time limit and barring most of the South's former leadership from both federal *and* state office until such time as Congress lifted the ban (Re and Re 2012, 1622–3). Section 3 as enacted thus narrowed the ban to office holding, not voting; narrowed its sweep (to those who had previously held office and taken an oath to support the Constitution but engaged in insurrection against it); but expanded the elections to which it applied (Foner 2014, Kindle location 5136). In both versions, the purpose of Section 3 was to help create a new political leadership for the Southern states, and, while predictably opposed by former secessionists, the provision enjoyed considerable support from Union supporters in the South as a result (Foner 2014, Kindle location 5317).

20 However, the Senate version went farther than the House version in two ways: First, it regulated both federal *and* state office holding (in contrast to the House version, which would have regulated voting only in federal elections), and second, its restrictions on office holding would continue in force until such time as Congress removed them, whereas the House version's restrictions on voting would have lasted only through 1870 (Re and Re 2012, 1622.)

21 On the strength of the opposition to Section 3 in the Confederate states, see Bond (1997, 123, 145–147) and Foner (2014, Kindle location 514).

Rather than specify a fixed time period for the termination of the ban on office holding by former officials from the South, Section 3 left it to Congress to provide for lifting the ban. And, at least as applied to the Confederate rebels, the ban was necessarily time limited by the life spans of those who had, before the Civil War, taken an oath to uphold the Constitution. It was thus clearly a transitional provision, in all probability not envisioned as having effects beyond the lifetimes of those subject to its ban. In 1872, the disqualification was lifted as to former state officeholders (but not as to most former federal officeholders) who participated in the rebellion (*Act of May 22, 1872*, 17 Stat. 142, c.193). According to Foner (2014), because the ban affected only a small number of people, debates over the 1872 amnesty bill were largely "symbolic" (ibid., Kindle location 9456–69). And in 1898, Congress granted a general amnesty removing all remaining barriers (*Act of June 6, 1898*, 30 Stat. 432, c. 389) as part of a general gesture toward unity during the Spanish–American war (Magliocca forthcoming 2021, 63–64).[22]

But as with Section 2, Section 3 played a role quite different from that presumably contemplated by its congressional proponents in the ultimately aborted treason prosecution of former Confederate President Jefferson Davis. Davis was indicted for treason on May 8, 1866 (Watson 1915, 671), but ultimately was not tried as he fell under President Johnson's general pardon for all acts of treason implicated by secession (US President Johnson 1868). Many Southerners were convinced that Davis' actions could not be treasonous, either because they believed secession itself was legal or because they believed that individuals within states that had seceded could not be held accountable for the state's actions (Connally 2009, 1173). Whether a jury in Richmond would have convicted Davis is unclear (ibid., 1179–80), as is whether the case would even have gone to trial. Davis' lawyers moved to quash the indictment, arguing that Section 3 of the 14th Amendment's disqualification provision – which would have prevented Davis from holding future federal or state office – constituted the exclusive punishment for participation in the rebellion (*Case of Davis* [1867] 7 F. Cas. 63, 90–1 (Cir. Ct. D. Va.)). This argument was suggested to Davis' lawyers ex parte by then Supreme Court Chief Justice Chase, who was one of two judges presiding over the case as part of a lower court bench (Nicoletti 2017, 294–8).[23]

22 In the 1970s Congress, also posthumously removed all disabilities for Robert E. Lee, who commanded Confederate forces during the Civil War, and Jefferson Davis, the president of the Confederacy (Magliocca forthcoming 2021, 64–66). Lee and Davis were former federal officeholders and so would not have been covered by the 1872 amnesty for former *state* officeholders (and Lee died before it in any event), and both men died before the general 1898 amnesty (ibid., 65–66). Similar to the 1898 amnesty, which was motivated in part by a desire for unity during the Spanish American War, the posthumous disability removals for Davis and Lee were motivated at least in part by a desire for unity following debates over extending amnesty to those who evaded military service in the Vietnam War (ibid., 67).

23 Chase's motives have been the subject of speculation, including a possible desire for political support from Democrats for a future run at the presidency (Nicoletti 2017, 293), or an effort to build support for the 14th Amendment among Southerners by using it to save their former leader (ibid., 295–296 & n. 18). Or perhaps Chase wanted to avoid having the Court rule on the legality of secession (Connally 2009, 1199–1120).

The argument seems far-fetched. As the prosecution pointed out, this interpretation of Section 3 would have precluded criminal punishment for senior leaders in the rebellion (who likely served in state or federal office prior to the Rebellion and would therefore have been subject to Section 3 in the first place), while leaving Confederate rank and file (who were unaffected by Section 3) open to punishment. It seems unlikely that most congressional Republicans who advocated for Section 3 would have anticipated its being used as a shield for the Confederacy's erstwhile president. Nevertheless, the argument nearly proved pivotal, as the two-judge bench deadlocked on the motion, causing the question to be certified to the Supreme Court, though never answered (Connally 2009, 1198–9).

While Sections 2 and 3 of the 14th Amendment, in tandem with the Reconstruction Acts, were successful for a brief time in effecting a change in leadership in the South, within a few years gains in black voting and office holding were completely undone in many Southern states, which sank into a more than three-quarters of a century period of white racist domination. The close and disputed 1876 presidential election resulted in a compromise whereby Democrats conceded the presidency to Republican Rutherford B. Hayes in exchange for an end to Reconstruction (Foner 2014, Kindle location 10729–945). Even after the Union Army's withdrawal, African American voting and office holding continued in some areas of the Upper South, Arkansas, and Texas, and the Republican Party remained competitive into the 1890s, while in other areas of the Deep South, the transition was much swifter and often sped along by violence (Foner 2014, Kindle location 10945–994). But throughout the South, African American voting and office holding declined until it ultimately became next to nonexistent (ibid.).

The 14th Amendment, as a whole, arguably failed of its major purpose during this time, as it failed to prevent white "Slave power" from reasserting itself in the South, and the Republican Party shifted its focus to white voters in Western states and stopped fighting for racial equality in the South (Graber 2014, 77–8). But unlike Sections 1 and 2, which, as described above, took on meanings arguably quite disconnected from their original purposes, Section 3 has thus far avoided the problem of transitional provisions drafted without termination dates living on into the future for application (or misapplication) over time. By not specifying a particular time period for the disqualification to be in effect and leaving it to Congress, Section 3 aligned its own probable life span with the duration of the political will underlying Reconstruction.

Following former President Trump's false claims that he won the 2020 presidential election and the resulting January 6, 2021, assault on the US Capitol (while Congress was certifying the electoral results), some commenters have posed the question of whether Section 3 of the 14th Amendment could be applied to bar or expel from office President Trump or other office-holding participants in the attempted insurrection (e.g., Magliocca 2021, *Lawfare*). However, this discussion seems to have given way to more established and conventional modes of punishment; President Trump was impeached by the House for his role in the January 6 assault; although the Senate failed to convict by the requisite two-thirds vote, a conviction in the Senate could have resulted (under Article I of the Constitution) in his disqualification from future office holding (and given that his trial came after his term ended, disqualification was perhaps the goal). Meanwhile, while a large number of those who participated in the insurrection are being criminally prosecuted (Hsu 2021), there does not seem to be any appetite in Congress to revive Section 3 and use it to disqualify participants from possible state or federal office. The possibility of Section 3's revival thus seems fairly remote – but the generality of its language cannot entirely rule this possibility out.

V. 14th Amendment, Section 4

Section 4 of the 14th Amendment provides:

> The validity of the public debt of the United States, authorized by law, including debts incurred for payment of pensions and bounties for services in suppressing insurrection or rebellion, shall not be questioned. But neither the United States nor any State shall assume or pay any debt or obligation incurred in aid of insurrection or rebellion against the United States, or any claim for the loss or emancipation of any slave; but all such debts, obligations and claims shall be held illegal and void (US Constitution 1788, amend. XIV).

Having received reports of Southerners' threats to repudiate the national debt once they regained power and to pay off Southern state war debts (Graber 2014, 25–6; Epps 2006, 80–1), congressional Republicans sought to head off these threats with Section 4 of the 14th Amendment. Although rarely discussed in litigation,[24] in at least one Supreme Court case Section 4 played a role, as it has in recent debates about the debt ceiling.

This case was *Perry v. United States* ([1935] 294 US 330), in which federal bondholders challenged a federal law that allowed repayment in paper money rather than in gold. The Court found that the law, insofar as it overrode a specific term in the bond instruments, conflicted with Congress's power to make binding contracts (ibid., 352–4). But echoing its earlier decision in *Lynch v. United States* ([1934] 292 US 571, 580),[25] the Court distinguished between repudiating the contractual obligations of the bond, which the Constitution prohibits, and withdrawing a judicial remedy for such breach by refusing the government's consent to be sued, which Congress may do under the doctrine of sovereign immunity

24 In a rare example of a court applying Section 4 consistent with its original purpose of disavowing Southern war debt, *Branch v. Haas* ([1883] 16 F. 53 (M. D. Ala.)) relied on Section 4 to decline to enforce a contract providing for the resale of Confederate war bonds.

25 *Lynch* had held that the Government may not simply abrogate its own contracts for the sole purpose of saving money without violating the contractual counterparty's Fifth Amendment rights to due process, though it also reasoned that Congress could withdraw judicial or other remedies (ibid., 579–582), suggesting a distinction between repudiation of debt and actions that may result in nonpayment of debt for a time.

(*Perry*, 352–4).[26] *Perry* then commented on the language of Section 4 of the 14th Amendment providing that "the validity of the public debt of the United States . . . shall not be questioned" (ibid., 354). Although stating that this language was "undoubtedly inspired by the desire to put beyond question the obligations of the government issued during the Civil War," the court argued that it had "a broader connotation . . . *confirmatory of a fundamental principle* which applies as well to the government bonds in question, and to others duly authorized by the Congress" (ibid., 354 (emphasis added)). This language suggests that Section 4 was simply confirming an existing understanding of the Fifth Amendment's Due Process Clause's protection of federal-government contracts. However, the Court also wrote, "The expression 'the validity of the public debt' . . . embrac[es] whatever concerns the integrity of the public obligations" (*Perry*, 354). It is unclear whether this sentence implies that Section 4 expanded protections for United States bondholders beyond the constraints already imposed by the Fifth Amendment's Due Process Clause.

In more recent times, some scholars have argued that Section 4 might require a president to ignore a congressionally set debt ceiling (Buchanan and Dorf 2012, 1188–94; Balkin 2011). In *Perry*, the challenged statute was squarely inconsistent with a term in the bond instrument requiring payment in gold. With respect to the debt-ceiling controversies of recent years, however, it is not clear that the federal debt ceiling statute provides any analogue to a statute specifically directed to impairing a term in a bond instrument. It may be sensible to view the 14th Amendment's language as creating an obligation to not repudiate public debt,[27] without necessarily viewing it as establishing an obligation to pay on time even if there are no funds available or as requiring the violation of other constitutional provisions, such as the Constitution's prohibition on paying money out of the treasury without appropriation by law (US Const. art. I § 9 cl. 7). Yet the question remains uncertain.

The point here is that a specific transitional provision, drafted with three very specific purposes in mind – prohibiting payment for freed slaves, forbidding payment of Confederate war debt, and preventing the repudiation of the Union's war debt – has no clearly intended application to consequential questions arising later on.[28] In a sense, this might be thought no different from many other

26 The court wrote, "The fact that the United States may not be sued without its consent is a matter of procedure which does not affect the legal and binding character of its contracts. While the Congress is under no duty to provide remedies through the courts, the contractual obligation still exists, and . . . remains binding upon the conscience of the sovereign" (*Perry*, 354).

27 Stern (2011) suggests that "threatening default" is different from repudiating debt and that only repudiation would violate Section 4. Epps (2011) agrees that a temporary default or delay in payment may not constitute repudiation but also notes that the language of Section 4 providing that the validity of the debt "shall not be questioned" may extend farther than repudiation.

28 Buchanan and Dorf (2012, 1189–1191) discuss various different "debatable" or "plausible" interpretations of Section 4 as applied to federal debt, emphasizing the absence of definitive application.

constitutional provisions, whose application to future circumstances cannot be foreseen. Provisions adopted during a time of regime change, however, may be particularly susceptible to unforeseen application, unless they had time to percolate and be thoroughly debated during drafting. Most of the provisions of Section 4 are, as a practical matter, time limited – that is, those related to payment for loss of slaves and the Southern debt. This fact and the focus of those involved in the drafting and ratification of the 14th Amendment may contribute to the lack of foreseeability with respect to those aspects of Section 4 that arguably have remained relevant to later controversies.

Conclusion

As shown previously, Section 1, intended as a charter of citizenship and rights to protect the newly freed slaves and other persons from arbitrary or discriminatory government conduct, soon became an unexpected charter of rights for business corporations; its potential for vindicating the equality and other rights of individuals reemerged only slowly in the 20th century. Its success in this regard was long in coming and remains only partial and contested. Perhaps the very breadth and generality of the equal protection and due process clauses of Section 1 helped secure its central role in US constitutional law, by offering a framework for claim making by so many different groups. Section 2 of the 14th Amendment was designed to incentivize states to extend voting rights to freed slaves, but its provisions for reducing a state's seats if voting was denied to a significant part of the male population were never used. This section was, however, relied on more than a century later to deny relief to people challenging disenfranchisement due to felony convictions (a group that is disproportionately African-American [Lopez 2020]), illustrating the unpredictability of transitional justice provisions over time. Section 3 was intended to bar Confederate leaders from public office except as Congress otherwise permitted. But within four years of ratification, Congress passed a General Amnesty removing Section 3's disqualification for state officeholders. Over ensuing decades, once-vanquished white power holders regained power and erected new codes of race-based hierarchy that flew in the face of the underlying purpose of Section 1 of the 14th Amendment. Section 4 of the 14th Amendment, prohibiting payments for the emancipation of slaves or for the South's war efforts and prohibiting repudiation of the North's war debt, had at best unclear effects at the time. Seven decades later, however, it played a role in one of the New Deal–era "gold clause" cases, and it has re-emerged in contemporary debates over the president's obligations during debt ceiling standoffs.

Transitional-justice issues continue to arise about the regime change embodied in the Civil War–era constitutional amendments, including the issue of reparations for slavery (Shifrin 2009; Satz 2012; Vermeule 2012). It is not surprising that such issues remain alive. Transitional provisions are drafted in times of crisis, with the focus being on immediate, rather than long-term, concerns. It is in this light not surprising that they may fail to do full justice: There are plainly limits to the legal imagination of the time, especially in the ability to do full justice to those injured by the prior regime.[29] Many elements of contemporary transitional-justice regimes – including mechanisms for truth telling, formal investigation into past wrongs, and participation by the victims of injustice in framing ways forward – were lacking in this 19th-century moment (Primus 2006, 1711–6). Their presence might have improved the Civil War amendments' prospects for more success as transitional justice measures. And there are tensions between rule of law and justice concerns: Rule of law considerations favored using existing procedures for crafting and enacting amendments which in turn required proposals that could secure ratification. By contrast, considerations of justice would have required far more attention to promoting the equality of the freed slaves, which may have endangered ratification by existing constitutional means.[30]

After amendments are adopted, unforeseen questions may yield unexpected or unstable interpretations. Power may triumph over principle, as it did with respect to the 14th Amendment's demands for civic equality in the late 19th century through the first half of the 20th century, illustrating the limits of law in the face of widely held, pernicious beliefs. These and other limits on the capacity of constitutional amendments to conclusively settle matters may also be viewed as a kind of failure but perhaps also as an inevitable consequence of the need for constitutional law, at least deeply entrenched constitutional law as in the United States, to both settle the rules in the short term yet allow for evolution over the longer term.

At the outset, we suggested (in line with recent doubts expressed about any "presumption of perfectability" in achieving the multiple goals of transitional justice [Meierenrich et al. forthcoming 2021]) that transitional justice provisions are unlikely to fully succeed in appearing just to all concerned. Certainly, it is the case that justice to the former slaves was not achieved by the post–Civil War amendments. Their progeny continue to suffer the continuing effects of slavery and Jim Crow and the discriminatory mindsets these legal and social regimes fostered. We also suggested that transitional justice provisions that remain in force over time are likely to be unstable. Estimating how long they should be in force will be difficult in the transitional moments themselves, and transitional justice provisions that are indefinite in time may assume a role not contemplated, much

29 In 1866 and 1867, free black persons could still not vote in several Northern states despite concerted Republican efforts to seek enfranchisement (Wang 1996, 2197–2198, 2212–2215; Epps 2006, 105).

30 Primus (2006) cites another example of the ways in which rule of law and justice concerns may conflict, arguing that the Senate acted correctly in seating Hiram Revels, a black senator from Mississippi, notwithstanding his opponents' argument that, in light of the *Dred Scott* decision, Revels had not been a citizen of the United States (as is required for senators) for at least nine years. Given the absence of black participation in drafting the 14th Amendment, its legitimacy may depend in part on its substantive results (ibid., 1681, 1712–1714). Dyzenhaus and Diamond (2019) argue that tensions inherent in transitional-justice processes are reflected in special truth procedures and are "best managed by somewhat deflating expectations about what kind of justice a [transitional-justice] process can produce" (4). Likewise, Méndez (2012) discusses inherent tension between rule of law and transitional justice.

less deliberated, by anyone at the time of their enactment.[31] These observations are not meant to cast doubt on the aspirations for transitional justice but rather to suggest that constitutionalizing details of those approaches, perhaps especially in constitutions that are difficult to amend, may have unforeseeable or even, at times, perverse consequences.

References

Abramowicz, M. 1997. "Beyond Balanced Budgets, Fourteenth Amendment Style." *Tulsa Law Review* 33: 561–612.

Act of Mar. 23, 1867, 14 Stat. 428–30, c.153.

Act of Mar. 23, 1867, 15 Stat. 2–5, c.6.

Act of May 22, 1872, 17 Stat. 142, c.193.

Azanian Peoples Organization (AZAPO) and Others v. President of the Republic of South Africa and Others (CCT17/96) [1996] ZACC 16; 1996 (8) BCLR 1015; 1996 (4) SA 672. (South Africa).

Balkin, J. 2011. "Under What Circumstances Can the President Ignore the Debt Ceiling?" *Balkinization.* Accessed April 23, 2020. https://balkin.blogspot.com/2011/07/under-what-circumstances-can-president.html

Bickel, A. 1955. "The Original Understanding and the Segregation Decision." *Harvard Law Review* 69, no. 1: 1–65.

Bond, J.E. 1997. *No Easy Walk to Freedom: Reconstruction and the Ratification of the Fourteenth Amendment.* Westport: Praeger.

Bordewich, Fergus M. 2020. *Congress at War.* New York: Anchor Books. Kindle.

Branch v. Haas [1883] 16 F. 53 (M. D. Ala.).

Brown v. Board of Education [1954] 347 US 483.

Buchanan, N.H. and M. Dorf. 2012. "How to Choose the Least Unconstitutional Option: Lessons for the President (and Others) from the Debt Ceiling Standoff." *Columbia Law Review* 112, no. 6: 1175–243.

Case of Davis [1867] 7 F. Cas. 63 (Cir. Ct D. Va.).

Chin, G.J. 2004. "Reconstruction, Felon Disenfranchisement, and the Right to Vote: Did the Fifteenth Amendment Repeal Section 2 of the Fourteenth Amendment?" *Georgetown Law Journal* 92: 259–316.

Connally, C.E. 2009. "The Use of the Fourteenth Amendment by Salmon P. Chase in the Trial of Jefferson Davis." *Akon Law Review* 42, no. 4: 1165–200.

Curtis, M.K. 1986. *No State Shall Abridge.* Durham: Duke University Press.

Dancy, Geoff and Kathryn Sikkink. forthcoming 2021. "The Data of Transitional Justice." In *The Oxford Handbook of Transitional Justice*, edited by J. Meierhenrich, A. Hinton, and L. Douglas. Oxford: Oxford University Press.

De Greiff, P. 2012. "Theorizing Transitional Justice." In *NOMOS LI: Transitional Justice*, edited by M. Williams, R. Nagy, and J. Elster, 48–102. New York: NYU Press.

Dred Scott v. Sandford [1857] 60 US 393.

31 As leading scholars who have found positive empirical effects from some approaches to transitional justice (such as human rights prosecutions and, under the right conditions, targeted amnesties) acknowledge, "The politics of transitional justice are not deliberative, but agonistic" (Dancy and Sikkink forthcoming 2021, mss 25).

Dyzenhaus, D. 2012. "Leviathan as a Theory of Transitional Justice." In *NOMOS LI: Transitional Justice*, edited by M. Williams, R. Nagy, and J. Elster, 180–217. New York: NYU Press.

Dyzenhaus, D. and A. Diamond. 2019. *The Resilient Constitution*. Unpublished.

Elster, Jon. 2012. "Justice, Truth, Peace." In *NOMOS LI: Transitional Justice*, edited by M. Williams, R. Nagy, and J. Elster, 103–24. New York: NYU Press.

Epps, G. 2006. *Democracy Reborn*. New York: Henry Holt and Co.

Epps, G. 2011. "Our National Debt 'Shall Not Be Questioned', the Constitution Says." *Atlantic*. Accessed April 23, 2020. www.theatlantic.com/politics/archive/2011/05/our-national-debt-shall-not-be-questioned-the-constitution-says/238269/

Ex parte Virginia [1880] 100 US 339.

Ex parte Yarbrough [1884] 110 US 651.

Finkelman, P. 2013. "How the Proslavery Constitution Led to the Civil War." *Rutgers Law Journal* 43: 405.

Foner, E. 2014. *Reconstruction: America's Unfinished Revolution, 1863–1877*. Updated ed. New York: Harper Perennial Modern Classics. Kindle.

Graber, M.A. 2014. "Constructing Constitutional Politics: Thaddeus Stevens, John Bingham, and the Forgotten Fourteenth Amendment." *U of Maryland Legal Studies Research Paper No. 2014–37*. Accessed April 23, 2020. https://ssrn.com/abstract=2483355

Harper v. Virginia Bd. of Elections [1966] 383 US 663.

Hayden v. Pataki [2006] 449 F.3d 305 (en banc) (2d Cir.).

Hsu, S. 2021. "Justice Dept. calls January 6 'Capitol Attack' probe one of largest in U.S. history, expects at least 400 to be charged." *Washington Post*, March 12. Accessed May 7, 2021. www.washingtonpost.com/local/legal-issues/capitol-attack-investigation-largest/2021/03/12/5c07b46c-833d-11eb-9ca6-54e187ee4939_story.html

Hunter v. Underwood [1985] 471 US 222.

Jones v. Florida [2020] 975 F.3d 1016 (11th Cir.).

Kritz, N.J., ed. 1995a. *Transitional Justice: How Emerging Democracies Reckon with Former Regimes, Volume I: General Considerations*. Washington, DC: US Institute for Peace Press.

Kritz, N.J., ed. 1995b. *Transitional Justice: How Emerging Democracies Reckon with Former Regimes, Volume II: Country Studies*. Washington, DC: US Institute for Peace Press.

Lanni, Adriaan. 2010. "Transitional Justice in Ancient Athens: A Case Study." *U. Pa. J. Int'l L.* 32: 551.

Lassiter v. Northampton Cty. Bd. of Elections [1959] 360 US 45.

Lochner v. New York [1905] 198 US 45.

Lopez, G. 2018. "Florida Votes to Restore Ex-Felon Voting Rights with Amendment 4." *Vox*, November 7. Accessed May 8, 2021. www.vox.com/policy-and-politics/2018/11/6/18052374/florida-amendment-4-felon-voting-rights-results

Lopez, G. 2020. "5.2 Million People Can't Vote Due to Their Felony Record, According to a New Report." *Vox*, October 14. Accessed May 6, 2021. www.vox.com/2020/10/14/21515850/voting-rights-sentencing-project-felon-disenfranchisement

Lynch v. United States [1934] 292 US 571.

Magliocca, G. 2021. "The 14th Amendment's Disqualification Provision and the Events of January 6." *Lawfare*, January 19.

Magliocca, G. forthcoming 2021. "Amnesty and Section Three of the Fourteenth Amendment." *Constitutional Commentary* 36.

McPherson v. Blacker [1892] 146 US 1.

Meierenrich, J., A. Hinton, and L. Douglas. forthcoming 2021. "The Critique of Transitional Justice." In *The Oxford Handbook of Transitional Justice*, edited by J. Meierhenrich, A. Hinton, and L. Douglas. Oxford: Oxford University Press.

Méndez, J.E. 2012. "Constitutionalism and Transitional Justice." In *The Oxford Handbook of Comparative Constitutional Law*, edited by M. Rosenfeld and A. Sajó, 1270–86. Oxford: Oxford University Press.

Minnesota Rate Case [1890] 134 US 418.

Minor v. Happersett [1874] 88 US (21 Wall.) 162.

Munn v. Illinois [1877] 94 US 113.

Murphy, C. 2017. *The Conceptual Foundations of Transitional Justice.* Cambridge: Cambridge University Press.

Nelson, W.E. 1988. *The Fourteenth Amendment: From Political Principle to Judicial Doctrine.* Cambridge: Harvard University Press.

Nicoletti, C. 2017. *Secession on Trial: The Treason Prosecution of Jefferson Davis.* Cambridge: Cambridge University Press.

NY Times Editorial. 1866a. "The Constitutional Amendment in the Senate." *New York Times*, June 2.

NY Times Editorial. 1866b. "The Reconstruction Committee's Amendment in the Senate." *New York Times*, May 25.

Perry v. United States [1935] 294 US 330.

Personnel Administrator of Massachusetts v. Feeney [1979] 442 US 256.

Plessy v. Ferguson [1896]163 US 537.

Posner, E.A. and A. Vermeuele. 2004. "Transitional Justice as Ordinary Justice." *Harvard Law Review* 117: 761–825.

Primus, R. 2006. "The Riddle of Hiram Revels." *Harvard Law Review* 119: 1680–734.

Rakove, J.N. 1997. *Original Meanings: Politics and Ideas in the Making of the U.S. Constitution.* New York: Vintage.

Rawley, J.A. 1960. "The General Amnesty Act of 1872: A Note." *Journal of American History* 47, no. 3: 480–4.

Re, R.M. and C.M. Re. 2012. Voting and Vice: Criminal Disenfranchisement and the Reconstruction Amendments, *Yale Law Journal* 121, no. 7: 1584–2031.

Reynolds v. Sims [1964] 377 US 533.

Richardson v. Ramirez [1974] 418 US 24.

Santa Clara Co v. Southern Pacific [1886] 118 US 394.

Satz, D. 2012. "Countering the Wrongs of the Past: The Role of Compensation." In *NOMOS LI: Transitional Justice*, edited by M. Williams, R. Nagy, and J. Elster, 129–50. New York: NYU Press.

Shelby Co v. Holder [2013] 570 US 529.

Shifrin, S. 2009. "Reparations for U.S. Slavery and Justice Over Time." In *Harming Future Persons*, edited by M.A. Roberts and D.T. Wasserman, 333–9. Dordrecht: Springer.

Slaughterhouse Cases [1873] 83 US 36.

Stern, M. 2011. "'Threatening Default': A Response to Professor Balkin." *Point of Order.* Accessed April 23, 2020. www.pointoforder.com/2011/07/01/threatening-default-a-response-to-professor-balkin/

Strauder v. West Virginia [1880] 100 US 303.
Teitel, R.G. 1997. "Transitional Jurisprudence: The Role of Law in Political Transformation." *Yale Law Journal* 106, no. 7: 2009–80.
Teitel, R.G. 2000. *Transitional Justice*. New York: Oxford University Press.
The Civil Rights Cases [1883] 109 US 3.
US Congress, Blair, F.P., J.C. Rives, F. Rives, and G.A. Bailey. 1866. *Congressional Globe*. Vol. 36, 39th Cong., 1st Sess. Washington, DC: Blair & Rives.
US Congress, Blair, F.P., J.C. Rives, F. Rives, and G.A. Bailey. 1871. *Congressional Globe*. Vol. 45, 42nd Cong., 2nd Sess. Washington, DC: Blair & Rives.
US Congress Joint Committee on Reconstruction, Stevens, T., W. Fessenden, and W. Pitt. 1866. *Report of the Joint Committee on Reconstruction*. 39th Cong., 1st Sess. H.R. Rep. No. 30. Washington, DC: Government Print Off.
US Constitution. 1788. National Archives.
US President Johnson, A. 1868. *Granting Full Pardon and Amnesty to All Persons Engaged in the Late Rebellion*. Accessed April 23, 2020. www.loc.gov/item/rbpe.23602600/
Vermeule, A. 2012. "Reparations as Rough Justice." In *Nomos Li: Transitional Justice*, edited by M. Williams, R. Nagy, and J. Elster, 151–65. New York: NYU Press.
Wang, X. 1996. "Black Suffrage and the Redefinition of American Freedom, 1860–1870." *Cardozo Law Review* 17: 2153–223.
Watson, D.K. 1915. "The Trial of Jefferson Davis." *Yale Law Journal* 24, no. 8: 669–76.
Williams, M., R. Nagy, and J. Elster, eds. 2012. *NOMOS LI: Transitional Justice*. New York: New York University Press.
Zuckerman, G.D. 1961. "A Consideration of the History and Present Status of Section 2 of the Fourteenth Amendment." *Fordham Law Review* 30, no. 1: 93–136.

9 "Cadres" in Post-communist Transition

Shifting the Loyalty Standards in Public Service after Regime Change*

Anna Śledzińska-Simon

I. Introduction: Public Service in Post-communist Transitions to Democracy

After the fall of communism in Central and Eastern Europe (hereafter, CEE) in the early 1990s, one of the main challenges of the democratization process was the question of how to ensure the political legitimacy of the new government and generate trust in public authorities (United Nations 2006). New democracies had to accomplish two basic goals: adopt retaliatory measures targeting former communists and eliminate the old patronage networks that had existed under the communist system and that continued to exist in post-communist countries. Therefore, gaining public trust appeared to be the ultimate goal of post-communist transition (Horne 2012, 2017; Nalepa 2010; Teitel 2000). In CEE, this goal inspired a wave of constitutional reforms introducing the rule of law (Czarnota et al. 2005), as well as more specific administrative reforms redefining the public service and loyalty standards of public servants. One result of all this upheaval was at least partial purge in public administration.[1]

The process of dismantling the legacy of the former communist regimes (Council of Europe, Parliamentary Assembly 1996) has had two main functions: (1) a moral function, which has been to administer justice to the victims of the old regime while rebuilding the foundations of public life in the new regime, and (2) a pragmatic function, which has been to create desirable conditions in which the new governments can exercise power (Blankenburg 1995, 223–4). In pursuing these two functions, many post-communist governments introduced criminal measures to punish public servants who had abused their office, committed politically motivated crimes, or violated human rights in the former regime. Many

* "Cadres decide everything" was a famous slogan used by Stalin to characterize the importance of loyal bureaucrats, a new elite, in the making of a communist regime (Fitzpatrick 1979, 377). A Soviet-style bureaucracy in which political loyalty was the main selection criteria and the ground of a permanent purge (Brzeziński 1956) was an inherited feature of all Central and Eastern European countries in the late 1980.

1 The newly accepted rule-of-law standards mandated that a democratic government dealing with the communist past refrain from retroactive punishment, assumption of collective guilt, and unfair (unequal) treatment.

DOI: 10.4324/9780429505089-13

transitioning post-communist countries also found it necessary to adopt administrative measures to verify the integrity and eligibility of public servants on the basis of their past conduct (Mayer-Rieckh and de Greiff 2007; Horne 2002). The verification was contingent on the opening of the former secret-security archives, and together, these two steps formed part of the so-called de-communization and lustration laws.[2]

While both de-communization and lustration contain elements of punishment, their primary role in CEE countries was to clear the public service sector of persons who could not be trusted owing to their past involvement in a communist regime. Further, some verification programs attested to the professional aptitude of public servants in a democratic regime. In CEE countries, the moral and pragmatic rationale of de-communization and lustration programs came in different proportions: Some governments prioritized the sanctioning of public servants for their past conduct, whereas other governments focused on pragmatically assessing both their public servants' individual roles in the former communist regime and the nature of the public servants' duties in the new regime.[3] Moreover, the rationale for verification in the public service sector often changed over time: The zealous disqualification of the most compromised persons in the early period of the post-communist transition later ceded place to a general assessment of moral qualifications deemed necessary for the performance of public service jobs (Elster 2004).

According to the most zealous approach, old party officials and collaborators – because of their participation in the former regime – had to be removed from their offices. This approach assumes that the mere presence of discredited people in public life would undermine the process of building democratic institutions (David 2003, 387). The approach idealizes the individual responsibility of public officials and authorizes a purge in public administration regardless of shortages of qualified personnel.[4] The approach also implies that the retention

2 In a narrow sense, "de-communization" means the "exclusion of certain former communist officials" from running for or occupying "public offices in the new regime," while "lustration" means "the screening of persons seeking (or occupying) certain positions for evidence of involvement with the communist regime (mainly with the secret police apparatus)" (Horne 2009, 9; Los 1995, 121).

3 Cynthia Horne distinguishes four major types of lustration laws in CEE countries: (1) wide and compulsory institutional change based on personnel change and public disclosure (Czech Republic, Latvia, and Estonia); (2) narrow and voluntary institutional change based on public disclosure and voluntary personnel change (Hungary and Poland); (3) symbolic change based on public disclosure and limited or informal vetting (Bulgaria and Romania); and (4) no institutional and no symbolic change (Albania and Russia) (Horne 2014). Until recently, Ukraine fell in the last category, but the Government Cleansing Act of 2014 introduced compulsory removal from the public service sector of people who had served both in the communist regime and under President Viktor Yanukovych.

4 Upon purging the ranks in public offices, a new government is often left with scarce human resources, but this scarcity opens public service positions to people who might be better qualified than the old personnel or who were unfairly barred from public service in the former regime.

of old public servants could expose them to blackmail, with decidedly unhealthy political effects on the new government (see the Czech lustration model). It was therefore expected that a rigid, uncompromising discontinuation of the former regime's personnel would help to legitimize the new government. An alternative approach, and one that is less zealous, consists in either revealing to the public the facts surrounding public servants' active participation in the former communist regime (an approach adopted in Hungary) or mandating the individual confession about one's past to the public (adopted in Hungary or Poland respectively) (Choi and David 2012). Ultimately, the approach adopted in Germany after reunification was based on an individualized assessment of personal aptitude of candidates to the public service (or persons who sought readmission to the public service after reunification), taking into account both their past activities and the ability to guarantee loyalty to a democratic state (Wilke 2007; also Espindola 2015).

In essence, disqualification of the old cadres from participation in the new regime is future oriented but rests on past conduct. Nevertheless, distinguishing the "worst" from the "bad" is no simple undertaking because totalitarian regimes possess power bordering on omnipotence and can involve all citizens in varying degrees of collaboration. Although one could possibly distinguish between voluntary (consciously undertaken) and involuntary acts of collaboration, the legal definition of "collaboration" often raises the problem of over- and underinclusiveness. As a result, some official files are unreliable; in other words, the archives, as a whole, do not tell the whole truth about the past. Therefore, any verification of communist-era public servants, based on secret service archives, requires not only a personalized approach but also a healthy dose of doubt.

Overall, any administrative measures serving to disqualify old public service cadres and collaborators from participation in a new, democratic regime must rest on carefully drafted laws that precisely define the scope of their application and put in place effective remedies against new types of abuse of power. Although equal access to public service jobs is not commonly recognized as a human right, the removal of the old personnel must not violate one's right to a court and a due process or amount to violations of other individual rights like freedom of speech or political association.[5]

II. Changing the Loyalty Standards of Public Servants: From Partisan to Political

In the process of transition from a totalitarian regime to democracy, a new government must bear in mind that some people are willing to change their loyalty

5 See the view of the Venice Commission stressing that "in order to respect human rights, the rule of law, and democracy, lustration must strike a fair balance between defending the democratic society on the one hand and protecting individual rights on the other hand" (Council of Europe, Venice Commission 2015, para. 108).

if necessary. Nevertheless, in some circumstances, loyal service to the previous regime must preclude loyalty to the new regime, especially if a new democracy is not prepared to take the risk of misjudgment.[6] It is clear that in the early years of democratic transition, the new government is more inclined to embrace stricter security measures in a bid to prevent acts of subversion, putsches, and the outright return of the old regime. Yet the question arises: How long should such measures remain in place? Should they wither with time? Or maybe, instead, they should become a permanent element of the constitutional design in a country with a totalitarian past.

In a communist regime, communist loyalty is the duty not only of all state officials but of all citizens as well. Therefore, every candidate applying for public office must show ideological zeal. Such admission criteria mean that only the people openly declaring loyalty to the communist party and its leaders can gain employment in the state apparatus,[7] and the failure of these people to fully accept loyalty is strong grounds for removal from office. Consequently, among the key features of communist regimes in history have been – in addition to ideological propaganda and the instrumental application of the law – total political control over the bureaucracy.

While transitional democracies aim to dismantle the legacy of a past regime, they often seek to align their legislative and policy choices with a model of solutions adopted in established democracies. The Western model of public service assumes that public servants should develop a chameleon-like ability to identify with the democratic regime and faithfully serve any successive government. Although public servants may have their own personal views and political sympathies, their loyalty to the government of the day should take precedence over loyalty to a political party they support as citizens.[8] This understanding marks a departure from the system of political patronage, which functions as an institutional guarantee of effective performance of official duties. Instead, the Western model recognizes that loyalty can be assured by such abstract notions as neutrality and professionalism and not by the fact of belonging to a peer group or political association.

6 After the fall of Nazi Germany, West Germany's newly established Federal Constitutional Court (henceforth, the FCC) affirmed that all public service relations formed in accordance with the principles of National Socialism became extinct with the collapse of Nazi Germany (BVerfG 1953).

7 In the Soviet Union and its Eastern Bloc allies, the term "nomenklatura" referred to the party hierarchy and to key positions in government, industry, agriculture, education, and other spheres of society. These positions required ideological loyalty and entailed client–patron relations. The very nature of the nomenklatura system contravened the principles of neutrality and professionalism.

8 Consider for example the decision of the Canadian Supreme Court in *Frazer v. Public Service Staff Relations Board* 1985, 455, which held that "the public interest in both the actual and apparent impartiality of public service dictates a general requirement of loyalty on the part of the public servant to the Government [of Canada], as opposed to the political party in power."

Yet owing to the specific circumstances of post-communist transition, a typical transitional democracy often takes precautions against the political risk that the old guard might stage a return to power. In this respect, the democracy adopts measures for its defense against internal enemies rooted in the previous, undemocratic state.[9] The specific options available to governments in democratic transition are numerous and varied.[10] The governments may choose to disqualify either only persons proven to be responsible for politically motivated acts of repression or persons who are merely suspected of such acts. Specifically, the vetting programs may target collaborators even though the previous communist regime permitted and indeed encouraged their collaboration. Disqualifications may cover various public-service sectors and may distinguish among various categories of jobs.

Whatever specific vetting choices the fledgling democracy makes, the government needs to justify its measures that bar certain persons from accessing public service jobs as "necessary in a democratic society." In particular, the government should explain how the measures simultaneously protect democracy and honor the principles of democracy, which ideally prohibit purely vengeful acts in contexts of transition (Council of Europe, Parliamentary Assembly 1996).

In light of the previous considerations, it appears that the political legitimacy of public authorities during democratic transition depends on whether or not their adopted measures are commensurate with the actual and potential risks to the functioning of the new government. This means that such measures will be subject to proportionality review in courts. In any case, especially with the passage of time, the proportionality test used to assess these measures may derive from one of several normative models, be it for a state of war, a public emergency, a militant democracy, or business as usual (Sajó 2004, 255).

The following sections of this chapter demonstrate that although the ultimate goal of the democratization process is to become a full-fledged democracy governed by the rule of law, transitional measures often respond to problems posed by the transition rather than to the society's nondemocratic (e.g., communist) past or the society's future prospects. As a result, the transitional measures may become a permanent element of a constitutional system in a country with a totalitarian past. Such measures can signify that, instead of being short-lived, transitional constitutionalism (Sadurski 2016) is a long-lasting project without a distinct end phase. It also appears that the legacy of totalitarian regimes engraves itself in the institutional culture, social practices, and political mindsets of the post-totalitarian state and is likely to reinvent itself in new forms of partisan loyalty.

9 The European Court of Human Rights declared that "every time a State intends to rely on the principle of 'a democracy capable of defending itself' in order to justify interference with individual rights, it must carefully evaluate the scope and consequences of the measure under consideration, to ensure that the . . . balance is achieved" (*Ždanoka v. Latvia* 2006, para. 100).

10 It can be argued that transition to democracy is not a revolution because in revolutions the losers are never allowed any position of power.

III. Lustration Laws in the Czech Republic and Poland

The term "lustration," in the context of this chapter, describes the legal measures that CEE governments have used to handle their countries' communist past (David 2011, ix). The measures range "from identifying and publicly exposing collaborators or officials of the communist regime to barring such persons from employment in positions of public influence" (Boed 1999, 359). The common goal of lustration laws, as noted earlier, is to cleanse public institutions of morally discredited persons and to facilitate personnel change in the public sector. As CEE countries largely differ from one another with regard to their dominant rationale for pursuing lustration, the region presents noticeably distinct types of measures, each with its own characteristics of scope, severity, timing, and duration. Taking just the examples of the Czech and Polish lustration laws, we can note just how striking these differences are.

The communist regime in the former Czech and Slovak Federal Republic (known commonly as Czechoslovakia) fell as a result of massive antigovernment demonstrations in 1989. However, a second "revolution" took place when the new democracy's Parliament passed the country's first lustration law in 1991 (henceforth, the 1991 Act).[11] Its main purpose was not to punish the erstwhile political elite in the toppled communist regime but to prevent their return to power.[12] However, the model of the Czech lustration law was in fact retaliatory. According to experts, the Czech lustration law introduced the harshest, most widespread, and lengthiest vetting program in the post-communist CEE region (Stan 2009; Kaminski and Nalepa 2006). Many experts also agreed that the results of the law were satisfactory (Letki 2002) though not flawless in its implementation.[13]

Although Poland was the first of the Central and Eastern European countries to overthrow communism, it was the last to introduce lustration. The reason for this delayed action was political: The Polish transition was the result of negotiations between representatives of the then communist authorities and the Solidarity opposition in April 1989. Known as the Round Table negotiations, these talks led to the first, partially democratic elections in June 1989. As a consequence of this "pacted" regime change, de-communization was not officially included in the list of the Round Table agreements. It should be noted, however, that the

11 After the dissolution of the federation into two independent states, the Czech Republic and the Slovak Republic, in 1992, the first lustration law remained in use mainly in the Czech Republic. In 1992, an additional piece of lustration law was enacted only for the Czech Republic. In 1995 and 2000, the Czech Parliament extended the validity of the first lustration law, which lost its force in 2016.

12 The Czech lustration law aimed to weaken the networks of former nomenklatura cadres who occupied important positions of power and influence in the society (David 2003, 397).

13 For David Kosař, "the Lustration Acts put the issue of 'dealing with the past' under the carpet since those with a negative lustration certificate are considered 'crystal clear' and those with a positive lustration certificate become so stigmatised that they refrain from speaking out" (Kosař 2009, 484).

lack of lustration in the first years of Polish transformation divided the Solidarity camp and its electorate. As Hanna Suchocka rightly pointed out, "The resultant political rifts have left their imprint on Poland's political life and are reflected by the country's party structure to this day" (Suchocka 2015, 4).

The adoption of the lustration law in Poland in 1997 (henceforth, the 1997 Act) followed a period of "wild" lustration, the informal destruction and unauthorized publication of secret files, two unsuccessful attempts to initiate lustration in 1989 and 1992, a series of political scandals, and the fall of the government in 1992. The Polish lustration model was based on a system of declarations about past involvement in the communist regime by persons holding certain public offices or running for certain public offices. Meanwhile, the Institute of National Remembrance (INR) managed the former archives of the secret security services (henceforth, the INR archives). Until 2006, declarations were verified by both the lustration courts and an independent body, known as the Public Interest Spokesman. Later, a special section of the INR, replacing the office of the Public Interest Spokesman, and criminal divisions of regional courts assumed the responsibility of hearing lustration cases. It is important to emphasize that the Polish model was extremely lenient, as it dealt only with false statements about one's past and with failures to make such declarations. The model did not create a framework for punishing people or "outing" them as former collaborators with the communist regime.

As the implementation of the law remained limited in practice, a more expansive round of lustration began in 2006. The new law (henceforth, the 2006 Act) provided for an extended catalogue of public offices subject to lustration and a new definition of "collaboration." It also granted everyone the right to access files on persons holding certain public offices (2006 Act, Article 22). However, part of the new law was found unconstitutional in 2007 (Polish Constitutional Tribunal 2007). As a result, the lustration process has remained incomplete despite a growing demand for the removal of former collaborators from public offices (CBOS 2007).

According to the Czech lustration law of 1991, all persons who hold, apply for, or stand for senior positions in the civil service, armed and security forces, and police have to undergo the lustration process. The so-called "protected" positions included employees in the offices of the president, government, Parliament, courts, state radio and television, state-owned companies, universities (namely rectors and department heads), state notary institutions, and some security-sensitive concession-based trades (1991 Act, Art. 1). In practice, Czech lustration has rested on two declarations: a certificate issued by the Ministry of the Interior to people concerned about their potentially collaborative involvement with the communist regime[14] and a statement by those people to the effect that they were

14 The truthfulness of the certificate issued by the ministry could be challenged in a civil court, while the content of the certificate could not be revealed to the public without the written consent of the person concerned.

not associated with satellite organizations established by the communist regime (1991 Act, paras. 4[1], 4[3]). The law permanently excluded from certain "protected" positions people who are found to have served in high-ranking positions in the Communist Party or the State Security Police, informed for the State Security Police, belonged to the People's Militia, or attended certain high schools. It is worth noting that lustration applied to senior positions in the civil service (1991 Act, para. 1[2]), but ordinary membership in the Communist Party did not count as a "positive screening" for collaborative involvement. Moreover, the Czech lustration procedure did not apply to candidates in democratic elections.

In contrast, the Polish lustration law of 1997, which was in force until 2006, applied to both senior public officials and candidates in elections.[15] The only "protected" positions under the law were high administrative posts, including the head of the civil service and directors general; the law therefore excluded ordinary civil servants from the lustration process.[16] Subject to the lustration procedure were judges, prosecutors, attorneys, high-ranking academicians, and high-ranking managers in public radio and television (Lustration Act of 1997, Art. 7[1]). Under the 2006 Act, which remains in effect today, all persons in the enlisted categories have the statutory duty to submit their declarations to the relevant appointing authority, while declarations of candidates for elective offices are published in the official gazette[17] and verified by the lustration section in INR. If the declared facts are inconsistent with the information contained in the INR archives, courts resolve the cases. A court's conclusion that a declaration contained an untruthful statement may constitute grounds for removal from public office (2006 Act, Art. 21e(1)), and courts should bar such persons from holding public office for a period between three and ten years (Id., Art. 21a).

The main differences between the Czech and Polish approaches to lustration concern the consequences of individual involvement with the communist regime.[18] In the Czech Republic, a person who was positively lustrated was removed from office, yet this information could in fact remain secret. In Poland, a person who truthfully disclosed the fact of collaboration with the communist regime could not be disqualified from public service. The Polish lustration law attached negative consequences only to two kinds of acts: lying about one's past

15 The backward-looking provisions of the Polish lustration law of 1997 did not include senior party officials who could have actually initiated or supervised human rights violations.

16 However, according to the law regulating the status of civil servants, the periods of employment for the communist party and the organs of the state security services do not count for the calculation of seniority allowances in the civil service (Act of 18 December 1998 on the Civil Service, Art. 90[3]).

17 The publication contains only information concerning the personal data of a lustrated person and a statement regarding past activities (part A of the declaration), whereas part B regarding the description of actual activities remains secret.

18 Note that in some CEE countries, the release of compromising information to the public was the actual sanction that could motivate public servants to resign voluntarily.

or failing to comply with lustration obligations.[19] In this way, Poland actually avoided a complete revamping of the bureaucracy after the regime change.[20]

Another significant difference between the respective models of the Czech Republic and Poland is the handling of lustration cases in courts. In the Czech Republic, the cases were subject to the jurisdiction of civil and administrative courts; in Poland, the cases were heard in criminal courts applying criminal procedure. Czech law explicitly provided for judicial review of positive lustration only in cases concerning people who had been removed from office, not in cases concerning candidates for public office. Nevertheless, in civil courts, many Czechs who have been accused of some form of collaboration have successfully challenged these findings to protect their honor and reputation (Bílková 2015). One additional difference is that Czech lustration did not concern candidates for elected office, while in Poland it has become a permanent element of the election process that, if born before August 1, 1972, candidates for elective office must declare whether or not they were formerly employees of or collaborators with the communist security services. Indeed, such declarations appear alongside the names of people on the electoral register.

In both countries, lustration laws formally applied only to senior positions in public service, excluding rank-and-file members. In this respect, the laws were in line with the standards adopted by the International Labour Organization Committee of Experts on the Application of Conventions and Recommendations (ILO, CEACR 2000a), which called on countries to refrain from applying professional-employment bans to the entire public service or police forces. The Committee further called on state parties to respect Convention No. 111, which asserts that requirements of a political nature should relate to a particular post, function, or task. According to the committee, laws laying down conditions for candidates to positions in the public service should be specific enough to ensure that the laws do not lead to politically discriminatory grounds for employment. The committee also recommended that exclusion from public employment should rest on more than past records – for example, current threats to national

19 Noting this difference, Roman David calls the Czech model "exclusive" and the Polish model "inclusive and reconciliatory." The exclusive model is generally favored by countries in which a revolution topples communism, whereas countries in which democratic transition follows negotiations tend to choose reconciliatory systems (Poland and Hungary) (David 2011, 27).

20 The lustration law had a limited impact on the judiciary because, on request of the INR, a disciplinary court had to waive the immunity of judges who had lied about their past and who could have been not only prosecuted for a "lustration lie" but also subject to a criminal sentence, including deprivation of all public rights, of their status as a retired judge, and of their special pension benefits. In 2015, the Constitutional Tribunal upheld judicial immunity in lustration proceedings as a procedural guarantee of their independence (Polish Constitutional Tribunal 2015). Therefore, there is a grain of truth in the argument that the de-communization process in the judiciary was incomplete because judges were unwilling to harm their peers (Śledzińska-Simon 2018, 1255).

security should be considered.[21] The European Court of Human Rights (henceforth ECHR) followed the same standard in its recent case law (*Polyakh and Others v. Ukraine* 2019).[22]

IV. Germany after Reunification

After the Second World War,[23] West Germany (the Federal Republic of Germany) carried out two mass vetting projects. The first, known as denazification, occurred immediately after the war under the auspices of the victorious Allies and the newly established German authorities. The aim was to screen the entire adult population regarding their wartime conduct. It divided the German population into several categories including major offenders, followers, and nominal Nazi Party members, all according to their level of involvement in the war and loyalty to Nazism. The denazification process failed owing to its scale, lack of political will, and scarcity of qualified personnel. In 1951, the West German government adopted the Reinstatement Act, which authorized reinstatement of previously dismissed or suspended public servants (except for former Gestapo officials). These persons had to provide the employing authority only with a police certificate of good conduct. The consequence of this law was the reintegration of ex-Nazi officials, including judges, into public offices (Teitel 2000, 159–60).

In East Germany (the German Democratic Republic), the Soviet authorities carried out denazification with the aim of replacing Nazism with communist ideology. Although the country's communist party (the German Socialist Unity Party) put a lot of effort into removing former Nazi Party members from public office, those who pledged allegiance to the communist government could remain in their positions (Taylor 2011, 257). As in other countries of the Soviet Bloc, East German labor law regulated public employment, reflecting – at least on paper – a commitment to democratic centralism, socialist rule of law, and

21 Compare with CEARC 2001, para. 6: "The Committee recalls that for measures not to be deemed discriminatory under *Article 4*, they must be measures affecting an individual on account of activities he or she is justifiably suspected or proven to be engaged in which are prejudicial to the security of the State. *Article 4* of the Convention does not exclude from the definition of discrimination measures taken by reason of membership of a particular group or community. The Committee also notes that in cases where persons are deemed to be justifiably suspected of or engaged in activities prejudicial to the security of the State, the individual concerned shall have the right to appeal to a competent body in accordance with national practice."

22 According to the ECHR, the public servant's involvement in the former communist party was not a sufficient reason for removing him from office, given the lack of evidence of his wrongdoing 23 years after Ukraine's transition from totalitarianism to democracy.

23 In 1945, the victorious Allies divided the German territory into four occupation zones, but owing to the sharpening ideological split between the Western authorities (Americans, British, and French) and the Soviet authorities, two German states (commonly known as West Germany and East Germany) were created in 1949 and existed until their reunification in 1990.

comprehensive control by local and regional government and party organs. Politically motivated criteria for employment included active social involvement in party functions and affiliated mass organizations.

By comparison, in West Germany, the Basic Law of 1949 declared that all German citizens should have equal access to public office and that public service was subject to traditional principles of professionalism (Basic Law, Arts. 33[2] and [5]).[24] The constitutional duty of public servants to remain loyal to the constitutional (political) regime reflected the idea of militant democracy (*wehrhafte Demokratie*) – a democracy capable of defending itself against its enemies (Thiel 2003; see also Loewenstein 1937). This concept implied that the state should do everything in its power to prevent both the domestic enemies of a democratic political order from infiltrating its public administration and foreign powers from sabotaging or even overthrowing the government.[25] In West Germany, to this day, the duty of constitutional (political) loyalty constitutes both an eligibility criterion and a service requirement.[26] This means that both a candidate for public office and a civil servant must promise to support the constitution and democracy at all times (BVerfG 1975).[27]

In 1990, the two German states reunited. The process of reunification occurred after the fall of the communist regime in East Germany. Therefore, reunification implicated de-communization and de facto adjustment of the former East German structures and personnel to the legal system of West Germany.[28] The verification process in post-reunification Germany concerned only persons who were employed by the former East German state. In practice, East German public employees had to "retool, retrain, and recertify their constitutional loyalty," while East German judges and prosecutors had to undergo an additional screening of the aptitude to respect the rule of law ("*Rechtsstaat worthiness*" test), which included investigations into their previous decisions (Schwartz et al. 1993).

24 In this chapter, the term "public service" covers all professional groups working in the state: civil servants, judges, members of the armed forces, and other public employees. Within these categories, civil servants are subject to special obligations resulting from the duty of constitutional loyalty.

25 We should bear in mind that "the fall of the Weimar Republic was due among other things to the fact that the State took too little interest in the political views of its civil servants, judges, and soldiers as a result of a misunderstanding of liberal principles" (*Glasenapp v. Germany*, para. 34 of the dissenting opinion of Judge Spielman).

26 The constitutionally enshrined duty of loyalty, though it may conflict with freedom of speech and political association, should be interpreted in practical concordance with the constitutional guarantees of fundamental rights.

27 On May 22, 1975, the Federal Constitutional Court ruled that the duty of loyalty to the free democratic basic order applies to all public servants, regardless of their status and functions. Moreover, membership in a party inimical to the Basic Law should be a relevant factor taken into account in assessing the personal suitability of candidates for a civil service post (BVerfG 1975).

28 Post-reunification Germany differs from other post-communist countries insofar as it eschewed the creation of new democratic institutions in favor of expanding West Germany's existing legal and political system to East Germany.

The Unification Treaty between East Germany and West Germany guaranteed that former East German civil servants could retain their employment if they satisfied the eligibility criteria applicable to West German civil servants (Braunthal 1990, 11). Nevertheless, many former East German state employees were not eligible for public service because they lacked professional qualifications, while all those who had qualifications could be removed from their positions because of their active role in the former East German security services. For these reasons, the reunification process resulted in tens of thousands of East German teachers, judges, and other government employees either losing their jobs or opting for early retirement. In addition, some former state officials faced criminal charges for acts redefined as illegal (Blankenburg 1995, 230).

The Unification Treaty laid out specific grounds for the removal of public servants from their posts. The annex to the treaty provided that public servants who did not meet the requirement of personal aptitude or professional qualifications could be subject to an ordinary dismissal (*ordentliche Kündigung*) (Annex I, chapter XIX, section III, paras. 4 and 5). Ordinary discharge could also apply to dismissals justified on economic grounds (due to the lack of demand for a particular employee or restructuring of the previous place of occupation).[29] The annex provided for extraordinary dismissals (without a termination notice) of employees who had collaborated with the former East German Ministry for State Security (*Ministerium für Staatssicherheit*, Stasi) or the National Security Bureau (*Amt für Nationale Sicherheit*) (Annex I, chapter XIX, section III, para. 4). Extraordinary dismissals also applied to public servants who had violated human rights or the rule of law (Id., para. 5).[30] The Unification Treaty provided that the German government could use personal files in the Stasi archives to examine former East German government workers seeking continued or new appointments in public service (Annex I, chapter II, section II, Arts. 2 b-c; see also *Stasi-Unterlagen-Gesetz* 1991, 2, 272).

In practice, in post-reunification Germany, all persons who had previously been employed by the East German state had to complete a questionnaire addressing whether or not they had either worked for the Ministry for State Security or held a position in East German communist organizations before November 9, 1989. As the Federal Constitutional Court explained, either membership in the Socialist Unity Party of Germany or participation in its affiliated organizations was an important factor to be considered by the employing authority when assessing the personal suitability of candidates for a public service post in reunited Germany but was not grounds for automatic termination of public employment as long

29 See the FCC judgment on provisions of the Unification Treaty regarding termination or suspension of the contracts of employment of public servants (BVerfG 1991).

30 Critics of the "human rights violation" criterion have argued that it lacked clarity, as one could reasonably presume that East Germany's entire legal system violated many international norms. Thus, this provision needed a narrow interpretation providing for extraordinary termination only if the person in question had violated human rights in excess of the violations immanent in East Germany's legal system.

as the person concerned had not been a prominent state or party official (BVerf 1997).[31] Furthermore, even in cases of high-ranking state or party officials, the verification process was based on an assessment not of individual incidents but of overall conduct, including personal development after reunification. In this context, we should note that individual involvement with the East German regime was not in itself a necessarily disqualifying factor for public service employment in reunited Germany, although such involvement might have raised doubts as to a person's eligibility for a post or office in government.

Accordingly, the verification of public servants in post-reunification Germany was not formally based on the principle of retributive justice because former East German employees were dismissed from their positions only if they were found unsuitable for public service. Their past conduct could have been an indication of such unsuitability. In practice, the two rationales of retribution and pragmatism came together when local vetting commissions approached the vetting process as a form of civil sanction for past misconduct (i.e., retribution) while federal authorities preferred a pragmatic approach that focused on an individual appraisal of people's worthiness to become a public servant (i.e., pragmatism). Over time, the latter approach prevailed, affirming the idea that humans can radically shift political loyalties and adapt to new political circumstances. After 1990, newly established labor courts staffed with West German judges were likely to accept that former East German officials either already had or could acquire necessary moral qualities through their public service in the new democratic regime (Wilke 2007, 370).

In sum, the model of vetting adopted in post-reunification Germany followed the West German concept of political loyalty and the jurisprudence of administrative and labor courts (Id., 369).[32] It could thus be argued that the triumphant West German government imposed their model on the newly established authorities in the former East Germany. The implementation of the model, however, was not uniform owing to the decentralization of the vetting process. The vetting commissions set up by diverse appointing authorities within local, territorial, and federal administrations reviewed personal declarations mainly on the basis of Stasi archives and, to a lesser extent on the basis of other sources of information, all

31 The FCC found that the provisions of the Unification Treaty concerning extraordinary dismissals did not violate Art. 33(3)1 of the Basic Law as long as the employing authority evaluated the candidate's eligibility in pursuance of Art. 33(2)

32 Wilke stated, "The 'personal suitability' clause in the unification treaty did not provide factual criteria based on the East German situation, but tacitly imported legal criteria from past disputes about public sector employment. During the early years, the task of establishing and applying the criteria was largely left to the vetting commissions. They established criteria based on their appreciation of facts and the institutional context, but these criteria were not used by the labor courts. The labor courts, newly created in 1992 and initially staffed with judges from the western states, were more competent in legal precedents than in distinguishing among various functions in the SED and different types of Stasi informers" (Wilke 2007, 369).

regarding the past conduct of former East German public servants.[33] As a result, extraordinary dismissals were considered only in cases involving either high-ranking party officials or secret informers for the Ministry of State Security.[34] People who either had been involved in other forms of collaboration with the communist regime or had been responsible for other types of misconduct could escape such consequences (Id., 368).

The dominant feature of the German vetting model involved an individualized assessment of personal suitability, which not only took a balanced view of people's pre-reunification and post-reunification behavior but also took into consideration the specific requirements of a particular position in public administration. It is crucial to note in this context that international bodies, including the European Court of Human Rights, have recognized that the individualized approach (i.e., pragmatism, not retribution) conforms to human rights standards.

V. The European Court of Human Rights on Readmission to Public Service in Post-Communist Contexts

Standards governing the protection of individual rights in the context of public service employment have emerged in cases concerning persons who either were not admitted to or were excluded from public service owing to their involvement in radical political movements (*Glassenaap v. Germany* 1986; *Kosiek v. Germany* 1986; *Vogt v. Germany* 1995). In these cases, the European Court of Human Rights has drawn a line between access to the civil service (and therefore rejection of candidates for public offices in the selection process) and removal from public office. In *Vogt v. Germany*, the court offered the following explanation:

> The right of recruitment to the civil service was deliberately omitted from the Convention. Consequently, the refusal to appoint a person as a civil servant cannot as such provide the basis for a complaint under the Convention. This does not mean, however, that a person who has been appointed as a civil servant cannot complain on being dismissed if that dismissal violates one of his or her rights under the Convention. (*Vogt v. Germany* 1995, para. 43)

Following this view, the court has consistently held inadmissible the actions brought by former East German employees regarding their reappointment in West Germany. Thus, the court concluded that decisions made by appointing authorities regarding individual suitability for public offices concern access to

33 According to German administrative courts, the right of the public employer to obtain true information about prospective employees prevails over their right to informational self-determination.

34 In the *Stasi Collaboration* case, the FCC held that German citizens' right to choose their own occupation prevents the state from passing a law that requires citizens to provide information that would lead to self-incrimination (BVerfG 1997).

the civil service rather than dismissal. In the German post-reunification saga, the court emphasized that a democratic government has a legitimate interest in carrying out "an *ex-post-facto* review of the professional qualifications of persons who had been incorporated into the civil service after reunification and had previously worked in quite different conditions, the aim of such a review being to assure the public of the quality of its officials" (*Petersen v. Germany* 2001). The court also emphasized that the German government enjoys a broad margin of appreciation in such extraordinary circumstances as reunification.

In *Petersen v. Germany* (2001), the ECHR agreed that the German government may reexamine the professional qualifications of university lecturers if they specialize in such socially sensitive areas as history. In *Knauth v. Germany* (2001) and *Bester v. Germany* (2001), the court held that the government could deny public service jobs to persons who had made false declarations about their past collaboration with the Stasi. In both cases, the court confirmed that the government had acted legitimately and that the relevant decisions of the appointing authority had been proportionate. Similarly, in *Volkmer v. Germany* (2001), the court concluded that the decisions of domestic authorities had been justified in finding that the applicant was unsuitable for public service. In particular, the ECHR emphasized that domestic German courts had taken into account both the applicant's function as a party secretary in the Socialist Unity Party of Germany and his actions as a teacher in the past regime. In this context, it should be noted that the Unification Treaty rested on the presumption that a person's former high-ranking position in East Germany's communist party was, in itself, incriminatory (ILO, CEACR 1996, para. 196; ILO, CEACR 2000b, para. 3). However, the way in which domestic courts assessed individual suitability for public service complied with the principle of proportionality.

The proportionality principle, which is the essence of the "necessary in a democratic society" clause, requires individualization of adopted measures (Barak 2012). Such individualization means that domestic authorities must be sensitive to the role of concerned persons in the former regime, taking into account their specific period of service, their individual behavior, their specific tasks, and their potential involvement with the state secret-security services (*Ādamsons v. Latvia* 2008, para. 125; *Žičkus v. Lithuania* 2009, para. 33). In addition, domestic authorities should specify which types of jobs or tasks are off-limits to people who have a compromised past. Finally, when conducting a proportionality review after regime change, domestic authorities should consider when, and for how long, the concerned individual engaged in the questionable act.[35]

The European Court of Human Rights has ruled on the merits of employment bans brought by former public servants against other post-communist countries. In *Sidabras and Džiautas v. Lithuania* (2004), the applicants were former

35 In the court's view, "any threat the former servicemen of the KGB could initially pose to the newly created democracy must have considerably decreased with the passage of time" (*Sõro v. Estonia* 2015, para. 62).

KGB agents who got dismissed from their posts after the entry into force of the Lithuanian KGB Act in January 1999. As a result of this law, the two applicants not only lost their positions as a tax inspector and a prosecutor respectively but also were barred from applying for public sector positions and various private-sector positions from 1999 until 2009. The applicants complained that the ban on employment, which extended to the private sector, amounted to disproportionate interference in their private life. The applicants also alleged that their unemployment was due to the discriminatory treatment of former KGB agents in the private sector. The court upheld their first complaint, finding that such an extensive employment ban served a legitimate purpose but was disproportionate. In this regard, the court found that the Lithuanian government had violated the applicants' right to respect for their private life as well as their right to non-discrimination.[36] However, the court did not find a sufficient link between the prolonged unemployment and the law disqualifying the applicants from public sector jobs. In rendering its judgment, the court relied on such undisputed facts as the applicants' lack of necessary qualifications for private sector jobs and the applicants' failure to even search for new employment opportunities.

In *Naidin v. Romania* (2014), the European Court of Human Rights also ruled on the merits of the case but used a standard laid down in earlier inadmissibility decisions against Germany. The court reaffirmed that a democratic government has a broad margin of appreciation in determining conditions for public service. In the case at hand, the applicant was permanently barred from employment in public service, notwithstanding the incidental nature of his collaboration with the communist regime. Notably, in this case, the Constitutional Court of Romania had earlier found that the public employment ban was justified by the need to guarantee the duty of loyalty of public servants to the democratic regime. In the same vein, the European Court of Human Rights ruled that the Romanian government had not violated the applicant's right to respect for his private life and prohibition of politically motivated discrimination. This decision, although it appears to be in line with previous cases of the Strasbourg Court, raises two intriguing questions: whether or not similar employment bans should be permanent for all relevant former communist officials and collaborators and whether or not these individuals should be subject to a sunset clause, which would draw lines between the past, present, and future, given the low probability that those former communists pose any threat to democratic institutions several decades after the regime change.

VI. Ban on Political Activities of Public Servants in Post-communist Countries

After the fall of communism in CEE countries, some democratic legislators undertook to formally separate politics from public administration and forbade

36 See also *Rainys and Gasparavičius v. Lithuania* 2005.

public servants from joining political parties. As a result, they introduced a very rigid understanding of the principle of neutrality, which translated into a categorical rejection of any involvement by public servants in politics. This approach is different from the way neutrality operates in Western democracies (e.g., France, Germany, the United Kingdom, the United States), where bans on public servants' political activities apply only to certain positions (managerial or sensitive positions) and in specific circumstances (e.g., when individuals are on official premises, on duty, or in uniform) (Śledzińska-Simon 2010). However, it is common practice to apply more stringent rules of political neutrality to members of the police, armed forces, and security services.

The political party ban for members of the police has become a point of controversy in *Rekvényi v. Hungary* (1999). The 1993 amendment to the Hungarian Constitution of 1949 prohibited members of the police, armed forces, and security services from joining a political party and engaging in political activities other than voting (Law No. 107 1993). Mr. Rekvényi, who was a police officer, had submitted an application to the European Commission of Human Rights, arguing that the term "political activities" used in the previously mentioned constitutional amendment was not sufficiently precise. He thus alleged that the amendment constituted an unjustified interference in his freedom of speech and association. The case was referred to the Grand Chamber, which held that the impugned legislation met the standard of interference "provided by law." In this regard, the court explained that the challenged amendment, when considered together with other domestic provisions, enabled police officers to regulate their conduct according to the law in place (*Rekvényi*, para. 37). Moreover, in the court's view, the law passed the "legitimate aim" test and was justified as "necessary in the democratic society."

The Court noted that depoliticization of the police, including a ban on their political party membership, served to protect national security, public safety, and public order. Further, the court emphasized that domestic authorities enjoy a broad margin of appreciation for regulating the duties of public servants in a context of regime change. Taking into account the totalitarian past, in which police were politically subordinated to the ruling party, the court agreed that there was a pressing social need for far-reaching separation between the police and party politics in a democratic regime.

Clearly, in *Rekvényi*, the transitional context played an important role in the court's assessment of the proportionality of the adopted measures.[37] The court found that the ban on political activities was not absolute, as police officers retained the right to "expound election programmes, promote and nominate candidates, organise election campaign meetings, vote in and stand for elections

37 We should distinguish the political party ban for members of the police in *Rekvényi v. Hungary* from *Ahmed and Others v. the United Kingdom*, which involved a more limited set of restrictions imposed only on senior local government officials regarding only certain types of political activities.

to Parliament, local authorities and the office of mayor, participate in referenda, join trade unions, associations and other organisations, participate in peaceful assemblies, make statements to the press, participate in radio or television programmes or publish works on politics" (Id., para. 49). Hence, the police officers' status as citizens was not totally devoid of content.

A similar problem regarding the scope of prohibited political activities has emerged in Poland, as a number of laws have prohibited prosecutors, members of the armed forces, members of the police, security officers, customs officers, border guards, prison guards, firefighters, civil servants, and other specific categories of government officials from joining political parties. The Ombudsman challenged these laws before the Constitutional Tribunal in 2001, arguing that they were contrary to the guarantees of freedom of expression and association contained in the Polish Constitution and the international human rights treaties. Importantly, the Ombudsman pleaded that there is a terminological difference between the duty of neutrality understood as the duty to be "apolitical" and the principle of "nonpartisanship." In his view, a person can remain neutral even as a formal member of a political party. Therefore, the Ombudsman argued that bans on political party membership for certain public-service posts were excessive, as the purpose of the restriction, i.e. ensuring political neutrality and impartiality, could be achieved through a less restrictive measure, namely the ban on public manifestation of political views and the prohibition on following one's own political beliefs in the performance of official duties.

However, the Constitutional Tribunal upheld the impugned laws as consistent with the Polish Constitution, as well as with Article 22 of the ICCPR and Article 11 of the ECHR. It reiterated that political neutrality and impartiality in the public service requires distancing oneself from political party structures. It also explained that public officials must remain politically neutral at all times, both on and off duty. The tribunal emphasized that the prohibition of party membership did not affect public servants' right to associate in associations or other non-political national and international organizations. It confirmed that the legislator has a wide margin of discretion in shaping restrictions on the individual rights and freedoms arising from the exercise of public authority by certain public officials. In the case at hand, the tribunal found that these restrictions contained safeguards against abuses of power which proved to be necessary in the given political context. It admitted however that the restrictions imposed on public servants may be lifted if the legislator deems them unnecessary (Polish Constitutional Tribunal 2002).

In conclusion, these two judicial decisions concerning Hungary and Poland demonstrate that governments in transitional democracies take specific precautions against the politicization of public service in order to ensure a safe distance between administrations and politics (Wilson 1887, 197; Goodnow 1900). However, all successive governments in these countries understood that the post-communist transition requires a complete ban on political activity in the public service. The experiences of Hungary and Poland also suggest that in post-communist countries restrictions on the freedom of speech and association of public officials must be greater than in full-fledged (Western) democracies. Yet, this position implies that such severe restrictions should be only temporary in nature because transitional democracies, not democracies in general, face the challenge of responding to an existential threat of political and social distrust.

Both the case-law of the constitutional courts in post-communist countries and that of the European Court of Human Rights show that preventive measures interfering with political rights of public servants must be evaluated in the light of "a pressing social need," which – by definition – refers to the material time of a concrete case. Still, based on the prior examples, it is difficult to determine whether or not any time limits should apply to restrictions on public servants' rights and who, if such time limits exist, should estimate the duration of the restrictions: National legislators? The ruling government? National courts? International courts? Perhaps non-governmental expert bodies?

Whatever the answer may be, three decades after the collapse of communism, both Hungary and Poland officially defend the position that the requirement of neutrality demands nonpartisanship, yet the current governments in these countries deploy subtle measures to staff key public-service posts with supporters of the ruling party and require unconditional loyalty to its political agenda. With the benefit of hindsight, one can therefore question the wisdom of transitional measures, since both countries have reverted to the same public service practices that were in place during the communist era.

VII. Conclusions: The Risk of Unfinished Transition and the Return to Undemocratic Practices

The democratization that took place in Central and Eastern Europe after the fall of communist regimes revealed a dynamic relationship between the national imperative to protect democracy from a resurgence of Soviet-inspired authoritarianism and the creation of a new public service based on the criteria of neutrality and professionalism. Although there was an urgent social need (and public demand) to screen and disqualify public servants who had been involved in the communist regime, the adopted measures were not always narrowly tailored to serve the legitimate aim of democratic transition. Rather, democratic transition served to exonerate the sweeping nature of personnel change.

In the context of post-communist transition, making public offices available to all who are "fit" for public service is part of regime change. More precisely, public offices are seen as a public good to which access must be guaranteed on equal terms. Equal access to public offices ensures that citizens can exercise power directly and also influence how power is exercised. While democratization requires that the principles of neutrality and professionalism apply in the public service, replacing standards of partisan loyalty with the new standards of political loyalty to the democratic regime is not a simple undertaking. The biggest challenge is certainly to introduce rules that will create a new legal culture and eradicate inherited habits of political corruption, nepotism and appointments in the public service according to merit for the ruling political party.

In general, there are two types of risks inherently related to decommunization: First, by its very nature, de-communization carries an enormous risk "of being misused" by members of the new government who seek "to win political battles or settle old scores, producing witch-hunts against left-leaning or other political opponents of the current government" (Council of Europe, Committee on Legal Affairs and Human Rights 1996). One should therefore be aware that even a benign use of vetting procedures may once again politicize public administration and encourage new elites to introduce a new partisan loyalty standard. In sum, any political purge brings with it the risk of discrimination based on political association. Second, democratization can fail in the long run if purging of a public sector is insufficient. In fact, in many CEE countries, the reconstitution of a rational-moral political community proved impossible because members of the former communist elite retained influential positions in the post-communist state and economy. In this regard, one can speak only of "partial justice," as a just and complete reckoning with the past regime remains unfinished (Safjan 2007).

Paradoxically, the problem of incomplete decommunization can resurface decades after the fall of communism. As the cases of Hungary and Poland show, the shortcomings of the transformation process, and in particular the incomplete decommunization, have been used by populist governments in these countries as a pretext to initiate new political purges in public administration and courts (CJEU 2019). Although the new administrative and judicial purges are part of a populist strategy to win public support by attacking the current elites, they have proved effective because of growing public dissatisfaction with liberal democracy. It would seem that the principle of neutrality and professionalism in public service will foster public trust in government, a return to the principle of partisan loyalty – albeit not based on membership of the ruling political party, but adherence to its values and support for its actions has become a reality in these countries. It is true, however, that the victory of populist governments in Hungary and Poland released the desire for people who had not made a career in a system based on meritocratic principles to get into office (Applebaum 2020). The question that arises here is to what extent the democratic standard of political loyalty can be implemented on a permanent basis in a post-communist country, where the politicization of public administration was the accepted social norm for several decades.

References

Applebaum, A. 2020. *Twilight of Democracy: The Seductive Lure of Authoritarianism.* New York: Doubleday Publishing House.

Barak, A. 2012. *Proportionality: Constitutional Rights and Their Limitations.* New York: Cambridge University Press.

Bílková, V. 2015. *Lustration: The Experience of Czechoslovakia/ the Czech Republic.* Accessed June 1, 2020. www.venice.coe.int/webforms/documents/default.aspx?pdffile=CDL-PI(2015)028-e

Blankenburg, E. 1995. "The Purge of Lawyers after the Breakdown of the East German Communist Regime." *Law & Social Inquiry* 20(1), 223–4.

Boed, R. 1999. "An Evaluation of the Legality and Efficacy of Lustration as a Tool of Transitional Justice." *Columbia Journal of Transitional Law* 37, 357–402.

Braunthal, G. 1990. *Political Loyalty and Public Service in West Germany: The 1972 Decree Against Radicals and Its Consequences*. Amherst: University of Massachusetts Press.

Brzeziński, Z. 1956. *The Permanent Purge. Politics in Soviet Totalitarianism*. Cambridge: Harvard University Press.

BVerfG. 1953. Judgment of the Federal Constitutional Court of December 17, 1953, 1 BvR 147/52, BVerfGE 3, 58.

BVerfG. 1975. Judgment of the Federal Constitutional Court of May 22, 1975, 2 BvL 13/73, BVerfGE 34, 339.

BVerfG. 1991. Judgment of the Federal Constitutional Court of April 24, 1991, 1 BvR 1341/90, BVerfGE 1, 101.

BVerfG. 1997. Judgment of July 8, 1997, 1 BvR 2111/94, BVerfGE 96, 171.

CBOS. 2007. "O lustracji i sposobie ujawniania informacji przez IPN." *Survey Report, BS 102/2007*. Accessed June 1, 2020. www.cbos.pl/SPISKOM.POL/2007/K_102_07.PDF

Choi, S. and David, R. 2012. "Lustration Systems and Trust: Evidence from Survey Experiments in the Czech Republic, Hungary, and Poland." *American Journal of Sociology* 117(4), 1172–201.

Council of Europe, Committee on Legal Affairs and Human Rights. 1996. "Measures to Dismantle the Heritage of Former Communist Totalitarian Systems." *Report, Doc. 7568*. Accessed June 1, 2020. http://assembly.coe.int/nw/xml/XRef/X2H-Xref-ViewHTML.asp?FileID=7506&lang=EN

Council of Europe, Parliamentary Assembly. 1996. "Measures to Dismantle the Heritage of Former Communist Totalitarian Systems." *Resolution 1096*. Accessed June 1, 2020. http://assembly.coe.int/Documents/AdoptedText/ta96/ERES1096.HTM.

Council of Europe, Venice Commission. 2015. "Final Opinion on the Law on Government Cleansing (Lustration Law) of Ukraine." CDL-AD(2015)012-e.

Court of Justice of the European Union. 2019. Judgment of June 24, 2019, Case C-619/18, ECLI:EU:C:2019:531.

Czarnota, A., Krygier, M., and Sadurski, W. 2005. *Rethinking the Rule of Law after Communism*, Budapest: Central European University.

Czech and Slovak Federal Republic: Act No. 451/1991 (October 4, 1991) on Standards Required for Holding Specific Positions in the State Administrations of the Czech and Slovak Federal Republic, Czech Republic and Slovak Republic.

David, R. 2003. "Lustration Laws in Action: The Motives and Evaluation of Lustration Policy in the Czech Republic and Poland (1989–2001)." *Law & Social Inquiry* 28(2), 387–439.

David, R. 2011. *Lustration and Transitional Justice: Personnel Systems in the Czech Republic, Hungary, and Poland*. Philadelphia: University of Pennsylvania Press.

ECHR: *Ādamsons v. Latvia*. 2008. Judgment of June 24, 2008, Appl. No. 3669/03.

ECHR: *Bester v. Germany*. 2001. Decision of November 22, 2001. Appl. No. 42358/98.

ECHR: *Glasenapp v. Germany*. 1986. Judgment of August 28, 1986. Appl. No. 9228/80.

ECHR: *Knauth v. Germany*. 2001. Decision of November 22, 2001. Appl. No. 41111/98.

ECHR: *Kosiek v. Germany*. 1986. Judgment of August 28, 1986. Appl. No. 9704/82.
ECHR: *Naidin v. Romania*. 2014. Judgment of October 21, 2014. Appl. No. 38162/07.
ECHR: *Polyakh and Others v. Ukraine*. 2019. Judgment of October 17, 2019. Appl. Nos. 58812/15, 53217/16, 59099/16, 23231/18 and 47749/18.
ECHR: *Petersen v. Germany*. 2001. Decision of November 22, 2001. Appl. No. 39793/98.
ECHR: *Rainys and Gasparavičius v. Lithuania*. 2005. Judgment of April 7, 2005. Appl. Nos. 70665/01 and 74345/01.
ECHR: *Rekvényi v. Hungary*. 1999. Judgment of May 20, 1999. Appl. No. 25390/94.
ECHR: *Sidabras and Džiautas v. Lithuania*. 2004. Judgment of July 27, 2004. Appl. Nos. 55480/00 and 59330/00.
ECHR: *Sõro v. Estonia*. 2015. Judgment of September 3, 2015. Appl. No. 22588/08.
ECHR: *Vogt v. Germany*. 1995. Judgment of September 26, 1995. Appl. No. 17851/91.
ECHR: *Volkmer v. Germany*. 2001. Decision of November 22, 2001. Appl. No. 39799/98.
ECHR: *Ždanoka v. Latvia*. 2006. Grand Chamber judgment of March 16, 2006, Appl. No. 58278/00.
ECHR: *Žičkus v. Lithuania*. 2009. Judgment of April 7, 2009, Appl. No. 26652/02.
Elster, J. 2004. *Closing the Books: Transitional Justice in Historical Perspective*. New York: Cambridge University Press.
Espindola, J. 2015. *Transitional Justice after German Reunification*. New York: Cambridge University Press.
Fitzpatrick, S. 1979. "Stalin and the Making of a New Elite. 1928–1939." *Slavic Review* 38(3), 377–402.
Germany: Gesetz über die Unterlagen des Staatssicherheitsdienstes der ehemaligen Deutschen Demokratischen Republik. 1991. *Stasi-Unterlagen- Gesetz, StUG*.
Goodnow, F. 1900. *Politics and Administration*. New York: Russell and Russell.
Horne, C. 2002. "Vetting and Lustration." In *Research Handbook on Transitional Justice*, edited by C. Lawther, L. Moffett, and D. Jacobs, 242–444. United Kingdom: Edward Elgar Publishing.
Horne, C. 2009. "International Legal Rulings on Lustration Policies in Central and Eastern Europe: Rule of Law in Historical Context." *Law & Social Inquiry* 34(3), 713–44.
Horne, C. 2012. "Assessing the Impact of Lustration on Trust in Public Institutions and National Government in Central and Eastern Europe." *Comparative Political Studies* 45(4), 412–46.
Horne, C. 2014. "Lustration, Transitional Justice and Social Trust in Post-Communist Countries: Repairing and Wresting the Ties That Bind?" *Europe-Asia Studies* 66(2), 225–54.
Horne, C. 2017. *Building Trust and Democracy: Transitional Justice in Post-Communist Countries*. Oxford: Oxford University Press.
Hungary: *Law No. 107*. 1993. (December 24, 1993) on Certain Amendments to the Constitution (*az Alkotmány módosításáról szóló 1993. évi CVII. törvény*).
ILO, Committee of Experts on the Application of Conventions and Recommendations (CEACR). 1996. General Survey, Discrimination (Employment and Occupation) Convention No. 111 (with regard to Germany).

ILO, Committee of Experts on the Application of Conventions and Recommendations (CEACR). 2000a. Report of the Committee of Experts on the Application of Conventions and Recommendations.

ILO, Committee of Experts on the Application of Conventions and Recommendations (CEACR). 2000b. Observation with Regard to Application of the Discrimination (Employment and Occupation) Convention No. 111 in Germany.

Kaminski, M. and Nalepa, M. 2006. "Judging Transitional Justice: A New Criterion for Evaluating Truth Revelation Procedures." *Journal of Conflict Resolution* 50(3), 383–408.

Kosař, D. 2008. "Lustration and Lapse of Time: 'Dealing with the Past' in the Czech Republic." *European Constitutional Law Review* 4, 460–87.

Letki, N. 2002. "Lustration and Democratisation in East-Central Europe." *Europe – Asia Studies* 54(4), 529–55.

Loewenstein, K. 1937. "Militant Democracy and Fundamental Rights." *American Political Science Review* 31(3), 417–32.

Los, M. 1995. "Lustration and Truth Claims: Unfinished Revolutions in Central Europe." *Law & Social Inquiry* 20(1), 117–61.

Mayer-Rieckh, A. and De Greiff, P. 2007. *Justice as Prevention: Vetting Public Employees in Transitional Societies.* New York: Social Science Research Council.

Nalepa, M. 2010. *Skeletons in the Closet: Transitional Justice in Post-Communist Europe.* New York: Cambridge University Press.

Poland: Act (April 11, 1997) on the Disclosure by Persons Holding Public Offices of Work, Service or Co-operation with State Security Services during the Years 1944–90.

Poland: Act (December 18, 1998) on the Civil Service.

Poland: Act (December 18, 1998) on the Institute of National Remembrance – the Commission for Prosecution of Crimes against the Polish Nation.

Poland: Act (October 18, 2006) on the Disclosure of Information on State Security Documents from 1944 to 1990 and the Content of Those Documents or Information.

Polish Constitutional Tribunal. 1998. Judgment of November 10, 1998, Case No. K 39/97.

Polish Constitutional Tribunal. 2002. Judgment of April 10, 2002, Case No. K 26/00.

Polish Constitutional Tribunal. 2007. Judgment of May 11, 2007, Case No. K 2/07.

Polish Constitutional Tribunal. 2015. Judgment of April 2, 2015, Case No. P 31/12.

Sadurski, W. 2016. "Transitional Constitutionalism versus the Rule of Law." Sydney Law School, Legal Studies Research Series Paper No. 16/56.

Safjan, M. 2007. "Transitional Justice: The Polish Example, the Case of Lustration." *European Journal of Legal Studies* 1(2), 8–9.

Sajó, A. 2004. "Militant Democracy and Transition Towards Democracy." In *Militant Democracy*, edited by A. Sajó, 209–30. Utrecht: Eleven International Publishing.

Schwartz, H., Wilburn, W.K., and Galuška, V. 1993. "Penalties for Prior Political Association." *Proceedings of the Annual Meeting (American Society of International Law)* 87, Challenges to International Governance (March 31 – April 3, 1993), 174–89.

Śledzińska-Simon, A. 2010, *Prawa polityczne urzędników publicznych.* Warszawa: Wydawnictwo Sejmowe.

Śledzińska-Simon, A. 2018. "The Rise and Fall of Judicial Self-Government in Poland: On Judicial Reform Reversing Democratic Transition." *German Law Journal* 19(7), 1251–81.

Stan, L. 2009. *Transitional Justice in Eastern Europe and the Former Soviet Union: Reckoning with the Communist Past.* New York: Routledge.

Suchocka, H. 2015. *Lustration: The Experience of Poland.* Accessed June 1, 2020. www.venice.coe.int/webforms/documents/default.aspx?pdffile=CDL-PI(2015)029-e

Supreme Court of Canada. 1985. *Frazer v. Public Service Staff Relations Board.* 2.S.C.R. 455.

Taylor, F. 2011. *Exorcising Hitler: The Occupation and Denazification of Germany.* London, New York: Bloomsbury Press.

Teitel, R.T. 2000. *Transitional Justice.* New York: Oxford University Press.

Thiel, M. 2003. *Wehrhafte Demokratie: Beiträge über die Regelungen zum Schutze der freiheitlichen demokratischen Grundordnung.* Heidelberg: Mohr Siebeck.

United Nations. 2006. *Rule-of-Law Tools for Post-Conflict States – Vetting: An Operational Framework.* UN Document HR/PUB/06/5. Commission on Human Rights, New York, United Nations.

Wilke, C. 2007. "The Shield, the Sword, and the Party: Vetting the East German Public Sector." In *Justice as Prevention: Vetting Public Employees in Transitional Societies*, edited by A. Mayer-Rieckh and P. De Greiff, 348–400. New York: Social Science Research Council.

Wilson, W. 1887. "The Study of Administration." *Political Science Quarterly* 2, 197–222.

10 Between Blaming and Naming

Constitutional Review of Bans on Communist Parties in Post-Soviet States

Alexei Trochev

During the last quarter century, transitional justice in fifteen post-Soviet states has ranged from a preoccupation with blaming to an exercise in naming when the issue of Soviet and post-Soviet human rights abuses has arisen. All post-Soviet regimes have officially blamed Stalinist regimes in general, while only six – Estonia, Latvia, Lithuania, Georgia, Moldova, and Ukraine – have also blamed post-Stalinist systems, going so far as to name specific perpetrators of abuses and to attempt lustration of government officials in ancien régimes. Most post-Soviet states have kept their Soviet-era secret-police archives a secret. These states permit court-ordered rehabilitation, compensation, and memorialization of victims of Stalin's purges without naming concrete perpetrators of the purges. This is an inheritance from the last years of the USSR. Most of these post-Soviet states glorify the memory of the victims and promote repatriation of the victims' ancestors, as in Kazakhstan. The identities of the offending officials and their collaborators remain unannounced.

Continued rule by Soviet-era leadership in the wake of the break-up of the USSR accounts for this decision to disallow broad truth-seeking, property restitution, and lustration – all measures that have been used in the former communist countries of Eastern Europe (Stan 2009; Horne 2017; Horne and Stan 2019; Smith 1996). Post-Soviet states in the mid-1990s witnessed a rise in rigid nationality policies, violent ethnic conflicts, and mass exoduses of ethnic Russians to Russia – events that functioned as spontaneous forms of lustration. In other words, the departure of ethnic Russians from prestigious positions in post-Soviet non-Russian states back to Russia substituted for government actions that would have held systems and people formally responsible for historical injustices. The general public, unaware of the actual scale of Soviet atrocities and pre-occupied with survival in the context of the severe economic crisis of the early 1990s, did not demand full-blown transitional justice.

By contrast, in Estonia, Latvia, Lithuania, Georgia, and Ukraine, where Soviet-era elites were removed, with varying speed, from political and law enforcement leadership positions, vocal anti-Soviet presidents opened Communist Party archives and KGB archives to the public, launched museums devoted to Soviet-era crimes, prosecuted former Soviet officials, and attempted to conduct

DOI: 10.4324/9780429505089-14

lustration of post-Soviet members of the ancien régime. The European Court of Human Rights reviewed parts of these states' transitional-justice policies, including Georgia's rehabilitation of victims and Latvia's sentencing of former Soviet collaborators to prison (Fijalkowski 2018).

According to many scholars, whichever transitional-justice policy a given post-Soviet state adopted, the choice depended largely on the degree to which the ruling governmental powers controlled the policy (Grodsky 2008; Horne and Stan 2019). And ruling powers carefully timed their adoption or cessation of these policies to gain the most advantage over resources at home or abroad (e.g., international funding). Often these attempts at transitional justice have been elite-driven, half-hearted, quickly abandoned, and thus symbolic projects, neither requiring nor accepting substantial input or demands from civil society. As a result, constitutions and courts have remained largely symbolic instruments useful for blaming "the past" without involving a serious reckoning with the past. The few cases of constitutional litigation over bans on communist parties and symbols in former Soviet states also show that constitutional courts have not always invalidated bans, constrained the executive, and championed the freedoms of speech and of association. Because of their pragmatic and formalistic decision-making approaches, constitutions and their guarding tribunals have lacked the capacity to prevent a return of non-democratic regimes. Witness Putin's Russia, Yanukovych's Ukraine, and Lukashenko's Belarus – all of which had functioning constitutional and supreme courts famous for anti-presidential rulings yet too weak to prevent non-democratic tendencies because of the weak societal demand for accountability of rulers.

In this chapter, I explore the varying roles and the limits of post-Soviet constitutions and courts in transitional justice by first developing an argument about the three waves of elite-driven transitional-justice policies in which key decisions of ruling elites rather than those of courts determined bans on communist parties and symbols, prosecutions of former communist leaders and their subordinates, and rehabilitation of the victims of Soviet-era atrocities. Then, I analyze how post-Soviet constitutional courts legalized these high-stakes political compromises regarding bans on various communist parties and their attendant symbols in Russia, Ukraine, and Moldova. I conclude by discussing how state – society relations must change substantially if constitutions and courts are to play meaningful roles in these countries' efforts to reckon seriously with the past.

The Third Wave of Elite-Driven Transitional Justice in Post-Soviet States

Post-Soviet transitional justice is the third attempt by the region to deal with its Stalinist past, whose mass atrocities took place under the façade of various human rights declarations in the 1936 Constitution of the USSR. Thus, the large gap between the constitutional text and state practice has been an inescapable facet of both the Soviet and post-Soviet periods. The first attempt at de-Stalinization began a month after Stalin's death, in March 1953, when the Central Committee of the Communist Party of the Soviet Union (CPSU) condemned the "unlawful activities of the state security agency" for the fabrication of criminal cases against doctors who had allegedly conspired to murder Stalin. This condemnation was in large part a result of power struggles inside the Kremlin – a condemnation that unleashed hundreds of thousands of complaints to the CPSU leadership about other victims of falsified criminal charges and extrajudicial repression. Nikita Khrushchev, the first secretary of the Communist Party of Ukraine (CPU(SU)) from 1938 to 1949, won the internal power struggle and became Stalin's successor in September 1953. In 1956, Khrushchev famously denounced Stalin's repressions in a secret speech at the Twentieth Congress of the CPSU. He focused on a particular segment of Stalin's crimes, those perpetrated solely against party functionaries between 1935 and 1940. In the 1950s and early 1960s, Khrushchev struggled to subordinate the state-security apparatus to the rule of the CPSU by (1) separating the Soviet Union's main security agency, the KGB, from the rest of the country's law enforcement apparatus; (2) authorizing numerous government commissions to uncover even more illegalities committed by Stalin's political police; (3) creating rehabilitation commissions made up of regional Communist Party functionaries and procurators in each of the fifteen Soviet Republics; (4) rehabilitating hundreds of thousands of convicted and executed persons; and (5) releasing thousands of people from exile and labor camps. The Soviet government, however, identified only a few "denouncers" and "prosecutors" who had perpetrated purges. For example, in 1957, the government demoted and stripped of his awards a former NKVD (pre-KGB security agency) investigator for having framed and tortured the famous Kazakh literary figure Saken Seifullin (Trochev 2018). Khrushchev reminded party members in his speech at the Twenty-Second Congress of the CPSU in 1961 that Stalin's purges had touched all Soviet citizens, not communists alone. Nevertheless, Khrushchev stopped short of rehabilitating deported ethnic groups, such as Crimean Tatars, Volga Germans, Meskhetian Turks, Chechens and Ingush, and Koreans. The CPSU's ouster of Khrushchev from office in 1964 put an end to rehabilitation and de-Stalinization, yet the two policies of selective and controlled transitional justice shaped future state-led attempts to deal with the Stalinist past.

The second transitional-justice attempt in the USSR began in November 1987, when Mikhail Gorbachev, the last Soviet president, denounced Stalin's reign in an effort to reform the CPSU and to build socialism "with a human face." His policy of *glasnost* (openness) allowed Soviet citizens to learn about the communist past, including Stalinist repression, and permitted activists to demand thorough investigations into atrocities committed not only during Stalin's rule but throughout the Soviet period, as well. These activists quickly mobilized in various NGOs, such as Memorial (which had branches in the capitals of several Soviet Republics), the All-Ukrainian Society of Political Prisoners and Repressed People, the Kazakh Adilet Society, the Belarus Martirolog Society, Latvia's Riga Club of the Repressed, and the Lithuanian Union of Political Prisoners and Deportees (Smith 1996). Gorbachev repeatedly demanded that his subordinates increase the number of rehabilitated victims of Stalin's purges – the assumption being that all this anti-Stalinist rhetoric would reform the Communist Party and, in turn, rejuvenate the Soviet Union. As a result of Gorbachev's policy, many political prisoners were indeed pardoned, released from prisons, and allowed to run for political office.

Because of these events, the leaders of the Soviet Republics faced reformist pressure from above and below, yet they only grudgingly supported truth-telling efforts. After all, revelations about this history served chiefly to undermine the foundations of Soviet rule, the socialist system as a whole, and its cornerstone, the CPSU, which was always flanked by its secret police. In some cases, the unwillingness of officials to uncover the past slowed the pace at which society recognized Stalin's crimes. For example, the lowest numbers of rehabilitated persons were recorded in western Ukraine, which had the largest share of filed rehabilitation claims and the strongest anti-Soviet sentiment. The Supreme Court of the Ukrainian Soviet Socialist Republic repeatedly refused to handle rehabilitation claims of deportees and claims against sentences issued by Stalin's military tribunals (Trochev 2013). Moreover, the leaders of the Soviet Republics during this tumultuous period desperately tried to solidify their power base by pursuing concessions from the Kremlin and by manipulating the rehabilitation movement led, ironically, by the Kremlin and human rights activists. For example, Kazakh authorities approved only a few of Gorbachev's de-Stalinization proposals even though, starting in early 1988, intelligentsia in the Kazakh Republic had been using Gorbachev's *glasnost* to criticize his appointees, to frame the December 1986 Alma-Ata riots as a failure of the Soviet nationalities policy, and to demand rehabilitation of formerly purged Kazakh writers and scholars, including the Alash Orda leaders (Smith 1996, 20–2). Nevertheless, by mid-1991, Latvia, Lithuania, Russia, and Ukraine had laid the legislative foundations for rehabilitation of the victims of political purges.

The third attempt at transitional justice began in late August 1991 – in the wake of the failed coup d'état against Gorbachev. At this time, practically all of the Communist Party leadership in the Soviet Republics realized that the Kremlin no longer maintained an invincible grip over them. Shortly after the failed coup, most of these rulers quit the Communist Party and either dissolved or suspended it in their republics, as Table 10.1 shows. Some of the rulers banned the party outright, transferred its enormous and lucrative property holdings to the state, and chose to spearhead declarations of independence from the Soviet Union, with all of the declarations occurring in the fall of 1991. Several leaders of the former Soviet Republics became presidents of the newly independent states and chose to build new polities in which the presidency constituted a "meta-branch of government" (Newton 2017, 149), elevated above the other branches of government and the other key political actors. These presidents treated constitution-drafting as their pet project, maintaining tight control over it. They personally and repeatedly edited constitutional drafts, which eventually enshrined presidential supremacy, prior to sending them out for stamps of approval from parliaments or referendums. With varying degrees of success, post-Soviet rulers tried to tightly control key policy areas, including transitional justice. The importance of centralized rule had been made perfectly clear to these rulers by three events, in particular: the failure of Mikhail Gorbachev's Union Treaty to contain the spread of centripetal forces, Boris Yeltsin's suspension of the Soviet-era Constitution during his bloody rivalry with the Russian Parliament in 1993, and other countries' experiences with transitional-justice policies.

Table 10.1 Fates of the Communist Parties in the Post-Soviet States

	Date of Self-Dissolution	*Date of Suspension*	*Date of Ban*	*Removal of Ban*	*Reconstitution of the Communist Party*
Armenia	Sept. 7, 1991				
Azerbaijan	Sept. 14, 1991				
Belarus		Aug. 24, 1991		Feb. 3, 1993	Dec. 7, 1991
Estonia		Aug. 22, 1991			
Georgia		Aug. 26, 1991			
Kazakhstan	Sept. 7, 1991				Oct. 1991[1]
Kyrgyzstan		Aug. 31, 1991			June 22, 1992
Latvia			Sept. 10, 1991		
Lithuania			Aug. 23, 1991		
Moldova			Aug. 24, 1991	Sept. 7, 1993	
Russia		Aug. 23, 1991	Nov. 6, 1991		March 13, 1993
Tajikistan		Oct. 2, 1991	Sept. 21, 1991	Sept. 23, 1991 Dec. 25, 1991	Dec. 26, 1991
Turkmenistan	Aug. 26, 1991				
Ukraine		Aug. 26, 1991	Aug. 30, 1991		June 19, 1993
Uzbekistan	Nov. 1, 1991		Nov. 1, 1991		

1 The exact day of the 19th Congress of the Communist Party of Kazakhstan, at which this party was reconstituted, is not known. The Justice Ministry registered this party on February 28, 1994.

Indeed, by breaking with the Stalinist past, many post-Soviet constitutions, which were products of elite bargaining and not of broad public deliberation, prioritized human rights and made the state fully liable for its abuse of these rights (article 68 of the Azerbaijani constitution, article 59 of the Belarusian constitution, article 42 of the Georgian constitution, article 39 of the Kyrgyzstani constitution, article 53 of the Moldovan constitution, article 53 of the Russian constitution, article 32 of the Tajikistani constitution, article 61 of the Turkmenistani constitution, article 56 of the Ukrainian constitution). At the same time, these states' compensation of victims for physical and moral harm done by Soviet-era states has typically been symbolic and determined exclusively by executive branches, which are subordinate to presidents. For example, Ukraine's Cabinet of Ministers limited compensation to a maximum of 15 minimal monthly salaries in 1991, and since then, this figure has not changed. In Kazakhstan, the total compensation may not exceed 10 minimum monthly salaries, and payments have been repeatedly suspended by presidential orders (Trochev 2018). The Georgian government offered only a one-time payment and unimpressive social-protection measures as compensation to the oppressed supporters of the first post-Soviet president, Zviad Gamsakhurdia, who had been ousted in a coup in early 1992 before being acquitted in 2004 (Machavarashvili 2007).

In former Republics, post-Soviet rulers timed their adoption or cessation of such transitional-justice policies to maximize domestic and international benefits, which often took the form of investments and other revenue sources. For example, the late Uzbek President Islam Karimov launched, in 1999, the Commission for the Promotion of the Memory of Victims, a truth-seeking body with two central and somewhat conflictual responsibilities: (1) analyze political repression from the entire Soviet period but (2) avoid naming the perpetrators. As Grodsky (2008) convincingly argues, the timing and the mandate of this commission and the lack of public attention paid to its work all suggest that this transitional-justice instrument was a symbolic concession to Western actors engaged in Karimov's authoritarian regime. Georgia's President Eduard Shevardnadze finally gave in to international pressure (and secured a massive World Bank loan) when, in 2000, he rehabilitated the supporters of his predecessor, the first post-Soviet president of Georgia, Zviad Gamsakhurdia, who had been ousted in a violent coup in early 1992 (Machavarashvili 2007). Mikheil Saakashvili, who compelled Shevardnadze to abandon the presidency in the peaceful 2003 coup known as the Rose Revolution, described the 1992 anti-Gamsakhurdia coup as the "communist nomenklatura's revenge" yet did not seek to legally punish the conspirators. Instead, he engaged in a wholesale purge of Shevardnadze's appointees in order to build his power base as well as his international support. At about the same time, in 2002, Belarusian authorities announced that they had completed the rehabilitation process for over 220,000 victims of Stalin's terror (Babii et al. 2005, 25). A mere four years later, Belarusian President Alyaksandr Lukashenko hailed Stalin and Lenin as symbols of the Belarusian people. In May 2020, a year after his election, President Tokayev of Kazakhstan, a protégé of his predecessor, sought to boost his personal popularity by setting up a 49-member state commission for the rehabilitation of victims of political repression,. One of his aides was quick to point out that the commission would rehabilitate some 6,000 persons, including participants in uprisings that had occurred before Soviet rule over Kazakhstan (*Kazakhstanskaia Pravda*, 30 May 2020).

Decisions to ban or suspend the communist parties in post-Soviet states reflect fairly obvious compromises and half-hearted attempts at transitional justice. Except in Georgia, where its communist party was quickly discredited in the wake of the bloody confrontation between anti-Soviet protesters and Soviet troops on April 9, 1988, adherents to communism remained a powerful political force in most non-Baltic former Soviet republics. There, Communist Party leaders who had deeply resented Gorbachev and incumbent presidents for their perceived betrayal of "the Party" and of the socialist state actively mobilized to achieve the three following goals: (1) overturn suspensions or bans targeting the given communist party, (2) prevent personal criminal prosecution, and (3) regain control over the given communist party's assets. The first two goals were accomplished in Belarus (February 1993), Moldova (September 1993), and Tajikistan (September and December 1991) through direct bargaining with parliamentary and executive leaders (see Table 10.1). These communist leaders in most non-Baltic former Soviet republics had a strong legal case because they had not directly participated in the August 1991 coup d'état against Gorbachev and because, according to the heavily amended Soviet-era constitutions that were in place in these Soviet republics, only courts could ban political parties. But what mattered most to the rulers of all Soviet republics was their own newly gained control over expropriated assets of the CPSU and its subordinate branches.

For example, in Belarus, many parliamentary leaders were former political prisoners of the Soviet Union who understandably expressed hostility to communist parliamentarians' successful effort, in 1991, to prevent the Belarusian government from banning the Communist Party of Belarus. Nevertheless, the parliamentary leaders who opposed the communists engaged in "complicated political maneuvering" (Feduta et al. 2003, 35) that secured the transfer of Communist Party assets to the Belarusian state. According to March (2006, 351), in the Moldovan case, which I will explore separately next, the lifting of the ban on the Soviet-era Communist Party of Moldova "appeared to be made for very short-term reasons." Likewise, Niesen (2012) argued that the motives of post-communist rulers in outlawing communist parties and then in allowing their "symbolic re-entry without restituting their property" seemed "to lie neither in the merits of militant democracy nor in the symbolic 'working through' of the past, but in prosaic material redistribution, a redistribution without which" the ensuing political playing field would not be level (p. 553).

Prevailing political expediency in dealing with the communist parties of the former Soviet republics made the involvement of courts in this process of transitional justice unlikely, as new political leaders claimed credit for banning or suspending a country's communist party when such an action promised to be popular with the country's newly established electorate. These leaders would quickly transfer the key assets of the parties to state coffers. Throughout the complex processes underlying these activities, the politically sensitive leaders of the new republics tended to distrust judicial chiefs, and for good reason: Many of the leaders had held senior posts in the Soviet-era Communist Party and, after the collapse of the Soviet Union, had become clients of presidents-former Communist Party leaders. For these reasons, the current leaders of the republics did not want any judicial investigation that might reveal skeletons in their closets. Nevertheless, the leaders delegated to courts various tasks so long as they were politically safe: One such task was that of transitional justice – rehabilitating the victims of Stalin's terror.

Only a few constitutional cases dealt directly with the liability of former Communist Party leaders for Soviet-era misdeeds. One case took place in the Kazakhstani Constitutional Court and pertained to the brutal Soviet repression of participants in the December 1986 Alma-Ata riots against Gorbachev's appointment of a non-Kazakh CPSU functionary to a leadership position in the Kazakh Communist Party. The three ensuing days of rioting involved some 55,000 Soviet troops, claimed the lives of nearly two hundreds of individuals and left hundreds more wounded and many others punished for having taken part in the riots (Lillis 2019, 159–71). This case in the Constitutional Court of Kazakhstan arose from constitutional complaints lodged by prosecuted participants in the rioting, all of whom had been non-members of the ruling elite (*Zheltoqsan-86* 2006). In October 1992, the 10-month-old Constitutional Court of Kazakhstan agreed to hear the litigators' constitutional complaints targeting the actions and decisions by which Soviet-era Kazakh leaders quelled the December 1986 riots. In December 1992, two opposition political parties joined these complainants and demanded that the current Kazakh government bring to justice the former Kazakh Communist Party leaders who had ordered a violent crackdown against protesters. In January 1993, the Constitutional Court, with some reluctance, held its first public hearing in this case. Throughout the year, the complainants assembled twelve volumes of documents from the Soviet government and the CPSU's Kazakh branch related to the 1986 riots. Meanwhile, the Constitutional Court judges, in pairs, heard witness testimonies from the participants in the riots. In parallel, the court held public hearings, which initially aroused considerable interest in the national media. Yet, after almost two years, in December 1994, the court refused to formally hear the complaint on the grounds that the court lacked jurisdiction to do so (Constitutional Court of the Republic of Kazakhstan ruling of December 19, 1994). The complainants accused the court of fulfilling the wishes of the incumbents, most of whom had held senior posts in the Kazakh Communist and in Soviet law enforcement and security services. One complainant alleged that a Constitutional Court judge had told him that the court had nixed the case on orders from above, that the presidential administration had been constantly monitoring developments in the case, and that the case could threaten President Nazarbayev, who had held a key position in the leadership of the Kazakh Communist Party in 1986 (Ryskozha 2008). The closure of this case did not trigger a public outcry, however, because ordinary people in the struggling former republic were preoccupied simply with day-to-day survival during the massive economic crisis that followed the collapse of the Soviet Union and because the supporters of the victims of the 1986 riots had not been well organized. In short, the abrupt end to the two years of constitutional litigation in this case offers additional evidence supporting my central claim that in the absence of strong social demand for public accountability for past crimes, the ruling elites controlled transitional-justice policies: When the elite rulership benefited politically from the policies, they were implemented and praised; and when the elite rulership sensed that it was at personal risk from the policies, they were denounced and ended.

These attempts at post-Soviet transitional justice were elite-driven projects, often half-heartedly undertaken and quickly abandoned. They were short-term and symbolic, with little input from civil society. Scholars agree that post-Soviet rulers used these transitional-justice policies in order to gain political capital: Nations were presented as victims of Soviet (and Russian) rule, but little thought was given to seeking cold, hard truths and improving accountability (Grodsky 2008; Stan 2009; Horne and Stan 2019). As I will show next regarding Russia, Ukraine, and Moldova, in cases in which Constitutional Courts decided the constitutionality of bans on communist parties, these symbolic transitional-justice policies – as enforced by courts – imposed a minimal risk, at most, on the leaders of the concerned states and did not invite a serious reckoning with the states' totalitarian past.

The Constitutional Court and the Communist Party Ban in Russia

A month prior to the failed August 1991 coup d'état against Gorbachev, Russian President Boris Yeltsin banned CPSU cells in Russia's state agencies, enterprises, and organizations. The "de-partyization" of these institutions was needed so that control of them could be stripped from Soviet authorities, at which point the state-owned institutions could begin to undergo privatization. However, in line with my argument about symbolic and half-hearted transitional-justice attempts, Yeltsin's aides were quick to soothingly assure the pro-communist elements in government that this ban would remain enforced for the rest of the year (Volgin 2014, 115). By that time, both the CPSU and its Russian successor, the Communist Party of the Russian Soviet Federative Socialist Republic (CPRSFSR, est. June 1990), had party cells in all state agencies, enterprises, and organizations, and the leaders of these party cells most often held leadership posts in these agencies, enterprises, and organizations. Many of the individuals defied the nation-wide ban, while the Soviet president Mikhail Gorbachev refrained from overruling the ban because he needed Yeltsin's support in renegotiating the Soviet Union treaty with the leaders of fifteen Soviet Republics. Viewing Gorbachev's inaction as an act of supreme betrayal, CPSU and CPRSFSR lawyers argued that Yeltsin's ban on their party violated both international human rights law and the constitutionally protected freedom of association. The lawyers further argued that Yeltsin's ban exceeded his presidential prerogatives and encroached on the Soviet Union's jurisdiction over the regulation of public associations. Indeed, the 1991 Law "On the RSFSR President" did not mention, in its list of presidential powers, the power to regulate the activities of political parties.

Immediately following the attempted coup, on August 23, 1991, Yeltsin took two significant steps: He completely suspended the activities of both the CPSU and the CPRSFSR until a judicial determination could be made regarding the two organizations' constitutionality, and he ordered law enforcement agencies both to investigate the suspended parties' alleged unconstitutional activities and to send the investigative findings to Russia's courts. On August 25, 1991, Yeltsin expropriated both the property of the CPSU and that of the CPRSFSR. On November 6, 1991, a month before the dissolution of the USSR, Yeltsin banned both parties the outright yet declared that membership in either party alone would not serve as grounds for criminal prosecution. Thirty-seven communist members of parliament (MPs) protested the suspension, expropriation, and ban, and petitioned the newly created Russian Constitutional Court (RCC) to declare Yeltsin's decrees unconstitutional. Once the RCC had accepted the MPs' petition, in May 1992, a group of over seventy MPs – supporters of Yeltsin – asked the RCC to examine the constitutionality of both communist parties and to declare the ban constitutional. These petitioners had "consulted" with RCC Chairman Valery Zorkin prior to filing their petition. The openly communist justice Viktor Luchin publicly complained that Zorkin had overstepped his authority by discussing the matter with the politicians in advance, while Zorkin justified his action by saying that he had simply been trying to strengthen Russia's nascent constitutional order (Steele 1995, 348–9). The RCC eventually declined to rule on the constitutionality of the CPSU and the CPRSFSR, in effect, leaving it a legal political party, much to the displeasure of Boris Yeltsin.

Why did it take the RCC six months to issue a decision in this case (Barry 1996, 255–62; Henderson 2007; Sharlet 1993; Smith 2002, 11–29)? The process was lengthy because judges could not reach a quick compromise, had to design procedures from scratch, faced defiance from Gorbachev, who had refused to appear at the hearing, and had to fend off attempts by both the old guard and the reformers to transform the public hearing into a censure of either Yeltsin or the Soviet regime. Throughout the six-month trial, judges slammed the opposing sides for bringing politics into the courtroom. The RCC's skillfully crafted 10–3 majority opinion (Russian Constitutional Court decision 9-P of November 30, 1992) was a result of political compromise rather than of legal reasoning, according to both Chief Justice Zorkin and Justice Gadzhiev (Vishnevskii 2011). The RCC upheld the most important clause of Yeltsin's ban on the CPSU: the ban on the top CPSU bodies, which governed the Soviet Union through violence (but not of local CPSU cells). The RCC ruled that the CPSU had the right to ask courts for the return of its expropriated property but that, because the RCC had found Yeltsin's ban on CPSU governing bodies to be constitutional, nobody had a legal standing to ask for the return of the Party's property. This tricky legal reasoning, in effect, meant that the transfer of lucrative CPSU property to the Russian state could not be undone (Trochev 2008, 192). A majority of the RCC found that the president, as the "highest official of the republic and the head of its executive power," could ban political parties in order to safeguard the state and public security and to protect Russia's sovereignty in the aftermath of the August 1991 coup d'état, even though the Russian constitution did not enumerate this power.

Dissenting Justices Ebzeev and Luchin objected to this expansion of presidential powers as an infringement upon the separation-of-powers principle. Dissenting Justice Kononov who served as a co-reporter in this case criticized the RCC for its refusal to examine the constitutionality of the CPSU and CPRSFSR. Speaking in May 2017, Kononov revealed that he had wanted the RCC to establish two guarantees of non-repetition with respect to totalitarianism in Russia: first, a ban on the successors of the CPSU; second, a ban on any and all parties pursuing communist ideology or using the word "communist" in their name (Bobrinskii 2018). He had also wanted the RCC to list the CPSU's constitutional violations and crimes against humanity. He claimed that Chief Justice Zorkin had refused to include evidence of these crimes in the case materials (Bobrinskii 2017). Indeed, it was alleged that Zorkin had repeatedly defended his choice not to declare the CPSU a criminal organization. Otherwise, lustration of Communists would throw Russia in the abyss of the civil war, according to Zorkin. Interestingly, the RCC lacked the power to implement a system of lustration, and moreover, Kononov's opinion never mentioned lustration. According to him, however, the RCC's decision prevented a system of lustration from taking shape and targeting communists, thus worsening tensions that led to the coup d'état (Bobrinskii 2017). Making similar comments to the media, Justice Gadzhiev admitted in 2011 that most of his colleagues in the early 1990s had wanted to avoid being blamed for a potential breakdown of post-Soviet society were they to declare the entire CPSU a criminal entity (Vishnevskii 2011).

These and other insights into the thinking of the RCC help explain the majority opinion that the court announced on of November 30, 1992. Ultimately, these judges justified their refusal to outlaw the CPSU and the CPRSFSR on the basis of three central arguments: (1) the CPSU had ceased to exist in the wake of the failed August 1991 coup d'état, (2) the ban targeting the governing bodies of the CPSU and the CPRSFSR was constitutional, and (3) the CPRSFSR was a branch of the CPSU rather than a full-fledged political party. In fact, the RCC's refusal to declare the CPSU and CPRSFSR unconstitutional was interpreted by Yeltsin's circle as a sign of a pro-communist bias permeating a majority of the tribunal. Justice Gadzhiev admitted that this RCC decision produced the bench's first serious schism (Vishnevskii 2011), which only worsened with time. President Yeltsin used this schism as a pretext for suspending the RCC's operations in the fall of 1993 (Trochev 2008, 75).

Indeed, communists appeared to be the key beneficiaries of the trial: The CPRSFSR remained legal, and they presented themselves as "victims" of government repression, as ardent proponents of the freedom of association, as skillful litigators, and as the framers of a debate over the meaning of patriotism in the new Russia (Smith 2002, 29). Gennady Zyuganov, one of the CPRSFSR's representatives during the RCC's hearings, later became a leader of the Communist Party of the Russian Federation (CPRF), a successor to the CPRSFSR, which held its founding congress in February 1993 and soon boasted half-a-million members. To be sure, the federal and the regional governments benefited from the RCC's judgment: They quickly expropriated the property of the CPSU, and the Justice Ministry refused to register any successor to the CPSU in order to prevent legal challenges to the expropriation. But Russia's law enforcement agencies allowed the CPRSFSR to continue its uninterrupted functioning despite criticism from some RCC justices (Trochev 2008, 192). Why was this allowance granted? The reason, in part, concerns the fact that both the RCC and the Kremlin were too weak to compel law enforcement officials to enforce the judgment. All the RCC could do was to slap a symbolic fine on the perpetrators. Meanwhile, Yeltsin's administration faced not only formal communist opposition in parliamentary bodies (be they federal or regional) but also informal communist opposition in the ranks of the law enforcement community, which harbored communist sympathizers. Crucially, in his fight against the legislature, Yeltsin needed the support of regional leaders, many of whom were still loyal communists. The ensuing inability of the rulers to compel compliance or, to use Lucan Way's phrase, "pluralism by default," impeded the enforcement of the RCC's ruling (Way 2005, 231–61).

Yeltsin reportedly contemplated banning the CPRF prior to the 1996 presidential elections, in which Yeltsin faced off against the CPRF leader Zyuganov. Interestingly, Yeltsin's Minister of Internal Affairs told him that police would not be able to arrest CPRF officials (Chernykh 2011). Following his resignation from the presidency at the end of 1999, Yeltsin admitted that he had delayed banning the CPRF in order to maintain a degree of calm in Russian society. This reasoning is similar to the reasoning that guided many of the RCC judges in 1992, when they had refused to declare the CPSU and the CPRSFSR unconstitutional. Yeltsin also wrote that he should have banned the CPRF rather than leave the decision to his successor. In any case, in December 2002, President Putin issued a decree that entitled former CPSU and CPRSFSR functionaries – members of those communist party institutions with respect to which Yeltsin's ban had been declared constitutional by the RCC – to relatively generous state pensions. Therefore, the Russian government's only partial implementation of the RCC's most famous decision bolstered the CPRF as the main opposition party, and thus indirectly promoted pluralism and some degree of accountability in Russian politics in the 1990s.

The Constitutional Court and the Communist Party Bans in Ukraine

On August 24, 1991, Ukraine's parliament, led by Leonid Kravchuk, who would soon become Ukraine's first president, declared Ukraine's independence. The parliamentary leaders, most of whom promptly quit the Communist Party of

Ukraine, a branch of the Soviet Union's Communist Party, (CPU(SU)), blamed it for complicity in the failed coup against Soviet President Gorbachev, a complicity that had threatened Ukraine's independence. On August 26, 1991, the parliament's presidium suspended the activities of the three-million-member CPU(SU), froze CPU(SU) bank accounts, and ordered police to seal and guard CPU(SU) property until the completion of a parliamentary inquiry into the party's role in the coup. Four days later, the presidium completed the inquiry and banned the CPU(SU) for its support of the anti-Gorbachev coup and for facilitating this coup on the territory of Ukraine. According to the presidium, these actions amounted to a forcible, though failed, change of the constitutional order. The CPU(SU) ban dealt a serious symbolic blow to pro-Soviet sentiments in Ukraine and involved the transfer of the party's enormous financial resources and infrastructure to the rulers of independent Ukraine.

However, in May 1993, the Presidium of the Ukrainian Parliament declared that the law enforcement agencies failed to establish the guilt of the CPU(SU) leadership in the 1991 coup, that the CPU(SU) members could not be restricted in their rights outside the court procedure, and that the citizens who shared Communist ideas had the right to create parties. Shortly after this decision, which stopped short of lifting the CPU(SU) ban, in June 1993, a new Ukrainian communist party was formed in Donetsk, the industrial center of Donbas region in East Ukraine. Named after its predecessor, the Communist Party of Ukraine (CPU) took full advantage of the heavily amended Soviet-era Ukrainian constitution, which guaranteed a multi-party system. Communists remained a potent force in Ukrainian politics in the 1990s, effectively blocking any attempts by the Ukrainian parliament to acknowledge the crimes of the communist regime. Communists actively campaigned for a repeal of the CPU(SU) ban with an eye to claiming the valuable property of the CPSU located on the territory of Ukraine. However, the Ukrainian government would not countenance such claims. Parliament refused to repeal the ban. In 1997, in the wake of the adoption of the 1996 Constitution of Ukraine and the creation of the Constitutional Court in the fall of the same year, 139 communist legislators asked the Constitutional Court to lift the CPU(SU) ban. They argued that the ban was unconstitutional for two central reasons: First, the presidium of the parliament had exceeded its authority and impinged on the judiciary, which, alone, could ban political parties under both the 1978 and the 1996 Ukrainian constitutions; second, the ban violated the constitutionally protected principle of freedom of association and unjustifiably punished millions of party members for their political views.

The 18-member Constitutional Court accepted this petition of communists and waded into what would quickly prove to be a tumultuous case. It took the court three years to complete oral hearings with numerous testimonies from witnesses and experts. And it took another year for justices to reach a final decision, which a minimum of ten justices had to support. On December 27, 2001, one day before the official start of the parliamentary election campaign, the Constitutional Court, in an 11–5 vote (two justices recused themselves), declared the

CPU(SU) ban unconstitutional.[2] The thin majority of the Constitutional Court justices agreed with the petitioners that the ban had violated the freedom of association of the party members, and that the presidium had usurped powers of the judiciary. Only courts, according to the Constitutional Court, had the power to ban political parties under both the Soviet-era constitution and the 1996 constitution. Both constitutions had direct applicability, and, according to the Constitutional Court, the presidium had to ask courts to ban the CPU(SU). The court held that CPU(SU) policies complied with both the Soviet-era constitution and the 1996 constitution because the CPU(SU)'s charter aspired to "follow the laws and the Constitution," and because the CPU(SU), as registered in July 1991, was a regular political party, not a branch of the CPSU, which had ceased to exist after the failed August 1991 coup. The court did not recognize the CPSU as a regular political party because it had retained its Soviet-era leadership. Therefore, the court reasoned, the CPU(SU), as a new party, was not a "legal successor to the CPSU." The court then concluded that the CPU(SU) could lay claim only to the property that it had acquired during its five weeks of existence in 1991. The court's ruling meant that the Ukrainian government, which was housed in the former CPSU buildings, did not have to return any CPSU property to the CPU(SU) (Trochev 2003).

Similar to the Russian Constitutional Court case analyzed previously, this case of the Constitutional Court of Ukraine produced dissenting opinions from five justices, including Chief Justice Skomorokha. He claimed that the CPU(SU) was a subordinate branch in the state-like hierarchy of the CPSU, and not an ordinary political party; therefore, banning it did not require a court decision. According to him, the Presidium could not ask courts to ban CPU(SU) because Ukraine at that time did not have a legal procedure of petitioning courts about banning political parties. All dissenters put forth the following three arguments in support of their view that the Constitutional Court had exceeded its authority in this case: (1) the 1996 Constitution authorized the court to review the acts of rule-making only, while the CPU(SU) ban was an act of one-time application of a law to a specific entity, not an act of rule-making; (2) the 1996 Constitution did not directly mention the power of the court to review the constitutionality of the acts of the presidium of the parliament; and (3) the court lacked the discretionary powers necessary for it to expand its own jurisdiction beyond the one mentioned in the 1996 Constitution. As had occurred in Russia nine years earlier, all the dissenting justices publicly accused the court of exceeding its own powers, while the court's judge rapporteur staunchly defended the majority opinion in front of journalists. Former President Kravchuk, who, as the presidium's chair in 1991, had signed the bans of the CPU(SU), declared that a majority of the court was essentially the "Communist Politburo," meddling in the politics of a struggling democracy.

2 All materials of this case are available at the official website of the Constitutional Court of Ukraine, at https://ccu.gov.ua/docs/443.

Serving as Ukraine's president between 1994 and 2005, Leonid Kuchma was in office when the Constitutional Court issued its decision of December 27, 2001. President Kuchma had previously urged the court to drop the CPU(SU)-ban case, an action that the former and then sitting Chief Justices had insisted on. However, Kuchma made no public comments about the court's 2001 decision.

As a result of this Constitutional Court decision, the CPU(SU) returned to legal existence in Ukraine, much to the cheer of the CPU leaders who framed this legal victory as reinforcement against Kuchma's regime. The CPU leaders invited the remaining leaders of the CPU(SU) to a "reunification" congress of the party in May 2002 and declared that this congress reconstituted Communist Party of Ukraine as the legal successor to the CPU(SU) yet with the CPU leadership remaining in charge. This meant that the CPU(SU) no longer legally existed. President Kuchma's government did not ban this CPU congress, much as Yeltsin's government had refrained from barring an important meeting attended by old and new Russian communist parties in February 1993 (March 2006). In contrast with the Communists in Yeltsin's Russia, the CPU had been losing its importance in Ukrainian politics, as evidenced by its weakening performance in elections since 2002.

In April 2015, the Ukrainian parliament adopted a de-communization law that criminalized both Nazism and communism as totalitarian criminal ideologies and prohibited both the dissemination of related propaganda and the use of related symbols in the country. In addition to establishing criminal punishment – up to five years in prison – for the violation of these prohibitions, the law authorized the central executive authority (i.e., the Justice Ministry) to exclude political parties from the electoral process if their activities, name, or symbols were not in compliance with the de-communization law. In contrast to the 1991 ban on the CPU(SU), the de-communization law did not call for the expropriation of the CPU's property. Instead, the law was part of a set of de-communization laws that were passed in the wake of two critical events: One was Ukraine's Euromaidan protests (2013–4), which opposed closer ties with Russia; and the other was the emergence of widespread suspicion that Ukrainian communists had colluded with Russian authorities in both Russia's annexation of Crimea in 2014 and Russia's use of force in East Ukraine (2014–present). Proving the latter suspicion turned out to be very difficult, and the Justice Ministry's attempts to ban the CPU on the grounds of criminal collusion went nowhere, as courts delayed considering cases filed by the Justice Ministry (Guz 2019). The Justice Ministry then chose to ask courts to ban the CPU on the basis of the parliamentary ban on communist ideology. In December 2015, the Justice Ministry cited the findings of its own De-Communization Commission and asked the Kyiv City Administrative Court to ban the CPU. The court did just that. Amnesty International and the Council of Europe's Venice Commission slammed the ban as a blow to the freedoms of speech and association in Ukraine (Guz 2019). The CPU, which had steadily been losing popularity since 2002, immediately complained to the European Court of Human Rights and appealed the ban in the Kyiv appellate court. This appeal prevented the implementation of the CPU's ban. Meanwhile, in May 2017, forty-six communist legislators, led by former Constitutional Court Justice Nimchenko, who had been elected to Parliament in 2014, challenged the constitutionality of the de-communization laws in the Constitutional Court. Petitioners relied on the conclusions of the Venice Commission and argued that these laws infringed on societal pluralism and on freedom of expression, which were guaranteed under both the 1996 Constitution and international human rights obligations pertaining to Ukraine. In the meantime, the administrative courts delayed handling the CPU-ban case until the ruling of the Constitutional Court on the constitutionality of de-communization laws. This delay meant that the CPU could continue functioning.

It took the Constitutional Court two years to decide this case.[3] On July 16, 2019, two months after the ouster of Chief Justice Shevchuk from the bench, the court declared the entire law that banned Nazi and communist ideologies constitutional (Constitutional Court of Ukraine decision 9-R of July 16, 2019). In his concurring opinion, justice Pervomaysky wrote that the delay had been caused by political maneuvering and by the already-divided bench's difficulties in reaching a last-minute compromise. While the vote on the bench is not known, in total four justices, including the judge-rapporteur Kolisnyk, wrote separate opinions. The majority opinion of the court focused on the legitimacy of the aims of the de-communization law, evaluated the causes and consequences of the Soviet regime in Ukraine, and concluded that the natures of the Soviet and Nazi regimes were, in essence, similar to each other. The court found that both of the regimes had occupied Ukrainian lands, "implemented repressive state policies," and caused devastation and huge loss of human life. The majority opinion upheld the ban on communist (Soviet) symbols because they had been – and were still being – used to delegitimize Ukrainian statehood during the ongoing Russian aggression (e.g., Russia's 2014 seizure of the Crimean Peninsula and Russia's support of the War in Donbas, beginning that same year). Likewise, the court argued that the symbols were tied to "negative and destructive ideas" that had not only deprived Ukrainians of an independent nation-state between 1917 and 1991 but also confined Ukraine to "the outskirts of civilizational processes."

Both Russia's ongoing occupation of Ukrainian territory and the existential threat that Russia posed to Ukraine's statehood justified, according to a majority of the justices on the court, its decision to support bans on communist (Soviet) symbols and on communist parties. Justice Pervomaysky in his separate opinion similarly justified the bans as an important form of protection against powerful communist agitators who were threatening the independent statehood and national security of Ukraine. According to Pervomaysky, the court's decision that authorized the executive branch to ban the CPU, in the context of overt Russian aggression, legitimately served the aim of protecting Ukraine's independence. In his separate opinion, the judge-rapporteur Kolisnyk also concurred with

3 All materials of this case are available at the official website of the Constitutional Court of Ukraine, at https://ccu.gov.ua/docs/2802, accessed April 4, 2021.

the reasoning of the majority about the harm done to Ukraine by the Soviet regime. However, he argued that the court should have declared unconstitutional the provision of the de-communization law that allowed the Justice Ministry to ban political parties. Kolisnyk reasoned that such a declaration was justified because the provision contradicted both the constitutional requirement granting only the judiciary the right to perform such bans and the 2001 Constitutional Court decision. Dissenting Chief Justice Shaptala accused the majority of making unwarranted political and historical claims and of focusing too closely on the de-communization law's alleged goals. She argued that the court should have devoted much more time to the constitutionality of the law's means and mechanisms. Despite her criticism, she offered no prescription as to how the court should have conducted such an examination.[4]

As expected, the CPU leaders slammed this Constitutional Court decision and complained to the media that the decision itself threatened Ukrainian statehood. Meanwhile, the Justice Ministry asked an appellate court to resume the proceedings in the CPU-ban case – something that, as of this writing, has yet to happen. Despite these setbacks, including the Central Election Commission's refusal to register CPU candidates in elections, the CPU continued to function. In 2019, incumbent President Zelenskyy made no public comments about the Constitutional Court decision.

In sum, both the 2001 and 2019 decisions of the Constitutional Court of Ukraine did not seem to advance the country's transitional-justice policies. Both of the decisions were reached after lengthy delays and were products of political compromises among justices. In 2001, the court focused on the irreversibility of the expropriation of Soviet Communist Party assets. In 2019, rather than conduct a thorough proportionality analysis of the Ukraine state's bans on communist parties and communist (Soviet) symbols, the Constitutional Court presented a highly stylized version of the country's communist past and never either embarked on a meaningful debate about or undertook a serious reckoning with this past (Nekoliak 2019; Neviadomskii 2020). As in Russia, the two Constitutional Court decisions produced several dissenting opinions, yet the dissenting justices did not take the majority to task for their failure to pursue a serious debate. Neither the 2001 decision nor the 2019 decision improved the legitimacy of the court in the eyes of the public or in the eyes of the ruling elite. If anything, both decisions split the bench even further, making it easier for Ukraine's rulers in the other branches of government to manipulate the court. Indeed, in October 2020, President Zelensky sent a bill to Parliament that would have sacked the entire Court (Nekoliak 2020). Nothing came of the bill, but the issue of decommunization in Ukraine is going to intensify, especially in light of the ongoing Russia's war in Ukraine.

4 The fourth dissenting justice, Litvinov, argued that to decide the constitutionality of the decommunization law as a whole, the court had to examine the constitutionality of the procedure through which the law had been adopted, something that the court did not do.

The Constitutional Court and the Ban on Communist Symbols in Moldova

The case of Moldova is a fascinating one, as the country is the only post-Soviet state in which an unreformed communist party held a majority in government. Following the failed coup against Gorbachev on August 23, 1991, the presidium of Moldova's parliament banned the Communist Party of Moldova (CPM). At the time, 53% of the MPs were members of the party. The following day, Moldova's prime minister ordered a governmental expropriation of the banned party's property. A year later, in August 1992, former communists began mobilizing to lift the ban and to restore the party. If these two aims could be achieved, the resurrected party might be able to reacquire the expropriated property. The communists succeeded in their first aim but not in their second one – following a pattern very similar to what happened in Russia in 1992 and in Ukraine in 2001. In September 1993, the presidium of Moldova's parliament effectively abolished the ban, agreeing with the communists that only courts, not the presidium, had the power to ban political parties, and that there was no legally obtained, valid, and reliable evidence of communists' participation in the coup against Gorbachev (Moshniaga 2002, 44). The presidium declared (1) that only courts through regular criminal proceedings could prosecute former Moldovan communists for having supported the 1991 coup and for having belonged to the CPM, and (2) that Moldovan citizens had a right to join communist organizations, whose legal status would be equal to that of other political parties, in line with Moldovan laws on parties. Nevertheless, reasoning that it had no jurisdiction over property relations, the presidium refused to return the property of the former CPM to any newly established communist party in the country. According to one observer, the presidium's decision amounted to both a declaration that the ban on communist parties was unconstitutional and a demonstration that all political organizations merited equal treatment under the law (Moshniaga 2002, 23–83). Yet, as March (2006, 351) persuasively argued, the lifting of the ban on the CPM "appeared to be made for very short-term reasons that underestimated the party's future potential": Moldova's rulers wanted to look democratic and hoped that the nation's communist sympathizers would split the left-leaning electorate. Note that the lifting of the CPM ban in Moldova occurred in a context similar to the one characterizing Ukraine after 2014. The presidium lifted the ban after a stalemate had established itself in the armed conflict between Moldova's "vehemently anti-communist regime" and the breakaway region of Transnistria, where Russian troops had been stationed and where the state emblem had featured the Soviet hammer and sickle (Kolstø and Malgin 1998). Still, in the years following these decisions, Moldovan courts consistently refused to suspend – much less ban – political parties, including those challenging Moldova's statehood (Moshniaga 2002, 46).

Having succeeded in lifting the ban, a small group of former communist activists announced in October 1993 the creation of the Party of Communists of the Republic of Moldova (PCRM). Curiously, the PCRM succeeded in holding its founding congress only in December 1994, half a year after the Moldovan Constitution had been adopted. The Justice Ministry delayed the registration of the PCRM for about a year in order both to prevent – through courts – the PCRM from claiming any title to the Soviet-era CPM's property and to prevent the PCRM from competing as a fully operational party in the 1994 parliamentary elections, which were supposed to produce a parliament responsible for adopting a new constitution. This executive maneuvering supports my argument that the rulers controlled transitional-justice policies, including control over the expropriation of lucrative property of the CPSU in Russia and of subordinate branches of the CPSU outside Russia. Despite these delays and threats of criminal prosecutions of its leaders, the PCRM quickly gained popularity, captured a parliamentary majority and the presidency, and effectively ruled the country through 2009 (March 2006; Tudoroiu 2011). The PCRM even declared itself, in 2008, a legal successor and heir to the ideas and traditions of the CPSU.

However, as soon as the PCRM lost its ruling status, in January 2010, the acting president, Mihai Ghimpu, whose brother had been an imprisoned political dissident in the USSR, created the Commission for the Study and Evaluation of the Communist Totalitarian Regime in the Republic of Moldova. This 30-member commission, consisting of historians, lawyers, and social scientists, and modeled after Romania's Tismaneanu Commission, was supposed to provide the president of the country a comprehensive report that would, in essence, condemn communism as experienced by Moldovan people. At the end of May 2010, the commission produced a 1,000-page report based on secret KGB and Soviet-police archival materials. The commission recommended that the totalitarian communist regime be condemned for having committed crimes against humanity and that the parliament enact lustration laws as well as laws forbidding political parties and other organizations from using communist symbols and even the very term "communism." In effect, the commission's recommendations, if implemented, amounted to a ban on the PCRM, as one of the critics of the commission argued (Tulbure 2016, 380).

Acting President Mihai Ghimpu, over objections of other members of the ruling coalition, decreed June 28 the Day of Soviet Occupation, ordered local governments to commemorate the day in public spaces and in schools, and ordered Russia to remove its troops from Moldova's territory. Eighteen PCRM members of parliament immediately appealed to the Constitutional Court to declare Ghimpu's decree unconstitutional. They argued that Ghimpu had exceeded his authority on several counts: engaging in the unconstitutional act of imposing on the Moldovan people an official ideology; usurping the parliament's authority over establishing holidays; usurping the cabinet's authority over external affairs; violating the autonomy of local governments; and generating divisions within society. In contrast to the Russian and Ukrainian courts, the Moldovan Constitutional Court did not delay. After three weeks of deliberations, the court declared Ghimpu's decree unconstitutional, having largely agreed with the PCRM's argument that the president had overstepped his constitutional bounds. Yet the court explicitly refused to define the legal status of the 1940–91 period by relying on the political-question doctrine (the Constitutional Court of the Republic of Moldova Decision No. 17 of July 12, 2010). Justice Pushkash in his concurring opinion criticized the majority for this refusal, insisted that the Constitutional Court had a right to use political arguments in its reasoning and to evaluate the Soviet regime, and blamed President Ghimpu for acting unilaterally and provoking the public controversy. The day following the court's decision, communists praised it while Ghimpu slammed it. He succeeded in forcing Chief Justice Pulbere to resign from the post in September 2011 for making political statements.

Having his decree overruled, Ghimpu continued his anti-communist agenda in the newly elected parliament with little public support. At the time, according to Socor (2012), condemnation of "Communism, repudiation of the Soviet system, and even non-political commemoration of the victims, were never popular issues with the majority of Moldova's voters from the early 1990s onward. Moldovan governments and parliaments never faced any serious political pressure to address those issues." In July 2012, exactly two years after the Constitutional Court decision explored previously, Ghimpu managed to convince the ruling coalition to use the 2010 commission's recommendations as justification for condemning the Soviet-era communist regime's crimes against humanity. As a result, the parliament adopted, with 53 votes out of 101, two documents: a resolution and a law. The resolution, which was a symbolic act with no legal force, condemned totalitarian communism and banned the use of communist symbols in political and propaganda activities (Decree of the Parliament of the Republic of Moldova No. 191 of July 12, 2012). Regarding the symbols, Articles 1 and 3 of the law banned "the use by political parties of symbols of the totalitarian communist regime (sickle and hammer, any carrier with such symbols), as well as propaganda of totalitarian ideologies" (Law of the Republic of Moldova No. 192 of July 12, 2012). Article 2 of the law imposed fines up to US$1,300 for one-time violations of the ban and called for automatically terminating all activities undertaken by any political party found to have repeatedly violated the ban.

Twenty-nine PCRM members of parliament, whose party's official symbols were a hammer, sickle, and open book, and who were fined by the government for using them, contested the ban in the Constitutional Court of Moldova in September 2012, arguing that the ban violated their freedom of speech and freedom of association. The petitioners requested that the Constitutional Court invalidate both the resolution and the law. In response, the court promptly nixed the petition against the parliamentary resolution on the grounds that the resolution had no legally binding force, that the resolution was a political and historical statement, and that the court did not have the power to rule on it. The court reiterated its explicit refusal to offer historical and political evaluation of the Soviet period (the Constitutional Court of the Republic of Moldova Ruling No. 30a of October 4, 2012). While examining the constitutionality of the 2012 law, the court consulted with both the Venice Commission, which belongs to the Council of Europe, and the Office for Democratic Institutions and Human Rights, which belongs to the Organization for Security and Cooperation in Europe. Specifically, the court was seeking expert opinions regarding the compatibility of the ban with international human rights standards. In March 2013, the two organizations issued a joint opinion (Venice Commission Joint *Amicus Curiae* Brief No. 697 2012), in which they argued that the ban could serve legitimate aims. However, according to the joint opinion, the Moldovan government had to show a pressing social need for the adoption of such a ban in the absence of a potential threat of a communist dictatorship in Moldova. Moreover, the joint opinion stated that the ban on displaying the hammer and sickle and the automatic ban on political parties that repeatedly violate the law were incompatible with the freedoms of expression and association, while the ban on propaganda expressing totalitarian ideologies was too vague to be compatible with the freedom of expression. In June 2013, the four-member Moldovan Constitutional Court in a 3–1 vote declared the entire law containing this ban to be unconstitutional (the Constitutional Court of the Republic of Moldova Decision No. 12 of June 4, 2013). The court applied the European Court of Human Rights' interference-with-freedoms test to the legislated ban. The results of this proportionality test, which lay out criteria for determining whether or not a law constitutes a legitimate legislative response to "a pressing social need," convinced the court that the ban served no "pressing social need," was unacceptably vague, and was thus unconstitutional. The Constitutional Court's Chief Justice Tanase dissented from this conclusion and argued three main points: (1) the ban served a legitimate aim in the specific historical context of Moldova's suffering under the Soviet regime, (2) the hammer and sickle constituted a specific and clearly perceived Soviet symbol, and (3) the hammer-and-sickle symbol was used by the PCRM and by authorities in the breakaway Transnistria region, indicating that the symbol, as well as its users, threatened the territorial integrity of Moldova. Chief Justice Tanase's arguments were similar to those put forward in the aforementioned 2019 decision of the Ukrainian Constitutional Court, which rested on the idea that such a ban could be proportional to a specific historical context. Both Chief Justice Tanase's dissenting opinion and the majority opinion scolded the governing coalition, which has been seeking to bring Moldova closer to Europe, for their failure to amend the ban in ways that would have brought it in compliance with the recommendations of the Venice Commission. The PCRM applauded the Constitutional Court's decision while the pro-European ruling coalition vowed to adopt another ban, this time, taking into account European human rights standards. However, the parliament has been unable to adopt a ban despite several attempts and despite the massive drop in the PCRM's popularity – the party failed to gain a single seat in the 2019 parliamentary elections (Nescutu 2020).

In contrast to Russia and Ukraine, where constitutional courts struck down post-Soviet governments' bans on communist parties while upholding these same governments' expropriation of communist-party property, the presidium of the Moldovan parliament repealed its ban on the CPM but refused to return the party's property. In contrast to the delayed decision-making of the Russian and Ukrainian constitutional courts handling these cases, the Moldovan Constitutional Court promptly decided the cases concerning bans on communist symbols, consistently declared the bans to be unconstitutional, and even applied proportionality tests to the bans, with additional input from European human rights theory and practice. Similarities among the three countries did exist, however: The decisions of the constitutional courts in Russia, Ukraine, and Moldova similarly resulted in dissenting opinions (by chief justices in Moldova and Ukraine) yet sparked no nationwide discussion about the Soviet regime's legacies in Moldova and Russia.

Conclusion: The Limits of Post-Soviet Constitutional Reviews of Bans on Communist Parties and Symbols

As I have shown in this chapter, the ruling elites in Russia, Moldova, and Ukraine have encountered significant controversy regarding whether or not communist parties and symbols should be banned. One concrete legal consequence of such bans would be the prosecution of both former communist officials for their past deeds and those officials and organizations who display communist symbols today. Constitutional courts in Russia, Ukraine, and Moldova chose not to deal with the issue of prosecutions, but did deal, though in different ways, with twin issues: the existence of communist parties and the use of communist symbols (see Table 10.2). The Russian Constitutional Court upheld the constitutionality of President Yeltsin's ban on the CPSU's Communist party's governing bodies, made Yeltsin's order to transfer the CPSU's assets to the Russian state irreversible, and overruled Yeltsin's ban on local Communist Party organizations and on the party as a whole. The Constitutional Court of Ukraine declared the government's 10-year-old ban on the CPU(SU) unconstitutional yet upheld the constitutionality of the government's expropriation of CPU(SU) assets. The decisions of these two constitutional courts were results of judicial pragmatism, in which the key question of the expropriated property of a communist party was resolved to the satisfaction of the incumbent heads of state. Still, Boris Yeltsin and Leonid Kuchma viewed these judgments as unfavorable. So too did the 2010–13 governing coalition in Moldova, when the Moldovan Constitutional Court twice overruled de-communization policies and declared bans on communist symbols unconstitutional, as well. The previously mentioned courts in Russia and Moldova did not extensively examine the legacies of their respective nation's Soviet-era communist regimes. By contrast, the Constitutional Court of Ukraine in July 2019, much to the satisfaction of Ukrainian rulers, evaluated the former Soviet regime as a foreign occupier of Ukraine and upheld the constitutionality of de-communization policies, including the Ukrainian government's ban on communist symbols and communist parties. All these constitutional-court decisions were products of constitutional challenges brought by communist-party officials and by pro-communist MPs. Each court decision produced dissenting opinions on the bench, and each court decision was a product of political compromises on the bench. True, the dialogue among justices about the nature of the Soviet regime may have helped these courts to mature and may have contributed to deliberative democracy in their respective countries. Yet in these three countries, this intra-bench dialogue led neither to the people's stronger respect for their

Table 10.2 Constitutional Court Decisions Regarding Bans on Communist Parties and Communist Symbols in Moldova, Ukraine, and Russia, 1992–2019

	Constitutional Court Decisions about Bans on Communist Parties	*Constitutional Court Decisions about Bans on Communist Symbols*	*Time Taken by the Constitutional Courts to Decide the Cases*	*The Results of the Constitutional Court Decisions*	*Dissenting Opinions in These Cases?*	*Reaction of the Ruling Governments*
Moldova		July 12, 2010; Oct. 4, 2012; June 4, 2013	3 weeks in 2010. 9 months in 2012 & 2013	Ban struck down	Yes, including the dissenting chief justice	Public criticism; resignation of the chief justice in September 2011
Russia	Nov. 30, 1992		6 months	Ban struck down in part	Yes	Public criticism; suspension of the court in October 1993
Ukraine	Dec. 27, 2001	July 16, 2019	4.5 years (1997–2001); 2 years (2017–9)	Ban struck down in 2001; ban upheld in 2019	Yes, including the dissenting chief justice	Criticism in 2001; support in 2019; draft on the removal of all justices in October 2020

respective country's court nor to heightened public interest in achieving a serious reckoning with the past.

These cases of constitutional litigation over bans on communist parties and communist symbols in Russia, Ukraine, and Moldova clearly show the challenges that previously authoritarian states must face when trying to pursue both a serious reckoning with their totalitarian past and a genuine embrace of their newfound liberal democratic freedoms of speech and of association. In all but one case (i.e., the 2019 decision of the Ukrainian Constitutional Court), the three constitutional courts dared to hold bans on communist parties and symbols unconstitutional. Those bans had been imposed by incumbent legislatures and executives. Nevertheless, in each case, the constitutional court's decisions represented a mixture of serious political compromise and substantive legal reasoning. Both Russian and Ukrainian constitutional courts approved the expropriation of lucrative communist-party property respectively in 1992 and in 2001. The expropriation was what the newly elected leaders wanted most, as they were struggling with building their economic base. Finally, in all but one case (the 2019 decision of the Ukrainian Constitutional Court), the courts concluded that these governmental actions exceeded the constitutional powers granted to the governments.

Undoubtedly, the strenuous effort involved in formulating, defending, and rebutting legal and political arguments about an explosive topic – the legacy and nature of the Soviet regime – constituted a remarkable learning experience for state leaders, regardless of their political affiliations. Whether in Russia, Ukraine, or Moldova, perhaps the most important lesson learned is that, before these states can effectively address the topic, there must be broader compromises regarding how people collectively understand it. Ultimately, transitional-justice policies, such as bans on the relics, remnants, and attempted restorations of ancien régimes, are political; in this context, courts seeking to caution political leaders against overreaching their constitutionally granted powers may have to decide between procedural responses and substantive rulings. But the courts can do so only if there is strong societal demand for the accountability of rulers and judges.

References

Babii, A., V. Kirillov, G. Kuzovkin, and V. Khvostenko. (2005) "Vozvrashchennye imena": Programma i problem ee realizatsii. *Voprosy Istorii*, 1, pp. 24–40.

Barry, D. (1996) The trial of the CPSU and the principles of Nuremberg. *Review of Central and East European Law*, 22(3), pp. 255–62.

Bobrinskii, N. (2017) Anatolii Kononov o dele KPSS. *Zakon.Ru*, May 20. https://zakon.ru/blog/2017/05/20/anatolij_kononov_o_dele_kpss. Accessed April 23, 2022.

Bobrinskii, N. (2018) Postsovetskoe perekhodnoe pravosudie v Rossii: dostizheniia i upushchennye vozmozhnosti. *Sravnitel'noe konstitutsionnoe obozrenie*, No. 1. https://academia.ilpp.ru/wp-content/uploads/2019/08/SKO-1-122-2018-142–168-%D0%91%D0%BE%D0%B1%D1%80%D0%B8%D0%BD%D1%81%D0%BA%D0%B8%D0%B9.pdf. Accessed April 23, 2022.

Chernykh, Y. (2011) Yeltsin gotovil tainyi perevorot i zapret Kompartii. *Komsomolskaia Pravda*, March 17. www.kp.ru/daily/25653.3/815947/. Accessed April 23, 2022.

Constitutional Court of the Republic of Kazakhstan Ruling of December 19, 1994. (2006) *Zheloqsan-86*. Volume 10. Alma-Ata: Altynbek Sarsenbaiuly, 266.

Constitutional Court of the Republic of Moldova Decision No. 12 of June 4, 2013. (2013) *Monitorul Oficial*, no. 167–72, item 22. http://lex.justice.md/md/349032. Accessed April 23, 2022.

Constitutional Court of the Republic of Moldova Decision No. 17 of July 12, 2010. (2010) *Monitorul Oficial*, no. 126–8, item 17. http://lex.justice.md/ru/335354. Accessed April 23, 2021.

Constitutional Court of the Republic of Moldova Ruling No. 30a of October 4, 2012. (2012) *Monitorul Oficial*, no. 228, item 19. http://lex.justice.md/ru/345204. Accessed April 4, 2021.

Constitutional Court of Ukraine Decision 9-R of July 16, 2019. (2019) *The Official Bulletin of Ukraine*, no. 62, p. 96, item 2163. https://ccu.gov.ua/sites/default/files/docs/9_p_2019.pdf. Accessed April 4, 2021.

Decree of the Parliament of the Republic of Moldova No. 191 of July 12, 2012. (2012) *Monitorul Oficial*, no. 181–184, item 610. http://lex.justice.md/ru/344634. Accessed April 4, 2021.

Feduta, A., O. Bogutskii, and V. Martinovich. (2003) *Politicheskie partii Belarusi – neobkhodimaia chast' grazhdanskogo obshchestva*. Minsk: Friedrich Ebert Foundation.

Fijalkowski, A. (2018) Historical politics and court redress in the Baltic states. In: C. Horne and L. Stan eds. *Transitional Justice and the Former Soviet Union*. New York: Cambridge University Press, pp. 216–39.

Grodsky, B. (2008) Justice without transition: Truth commissions in the context of repressive rule. *Human Rights Review*, 9(3), pp. 281–97.

Guz, S. (2019) Ukraine's communists were banned, or so we thought. *OpenDemocracy.Net*, February 28. www.opendemocracy.net/en/odr/ukraines-communists-were-banned-or-so-we-thought/. Accessed April 23, 2022.

Henderson, J. (2007) The Russian constitutional court and the Communist Party case: Watershed or whitewash? *Communist and Post-Communist Studies*, 40(1), pp. 1–16.

Horne, C.M. (2017) *Building Trust and Democracy: Transitional Justice in Post-Communist Countries*. Oxford: Oxford University Press.

Horne, C.M. and L. Stan eds. (2019) *Transitional Justice and the Former Soviet Union*. New York: Cambridge University Press.

Kazakhstanskaia Pravda. (2020) Establishment of state commission is a step towards restoration of historical justice – *Abaev*, May 30. www.kazpravda.kz/en/news/politics/establishment-of-state-commission-is-a-step-towards-restoration-of-historical-justice – abaev. Accessed April 23, 2022.

Kolstø, P. and A. Malgin. (1998) The Transnistrian Republic: A case of politicized regionalism. *Nationalities Papers*, 26(1), pp. 103–27.

Law of the Republic of Moldova No. 192 of July 12, 2012. (2012) *Monitorul oficial*, no. 190–2, item 646. http://lex.justice.md/viewdoc.php?action=view&view=doc&id=344744&lang=1. Accessed April 23, 2022.

Lillis, J. (2019) *Dark Shadows: Inside the Secret World of Kazakhstan*. London: I. B. Tauris.

Machavarashvili, N. (2007) Is Georgia following international experience of national reconciliation by rejecting the retributive model? *The Caucasus & Globalization*, 1(4), pp. 12–27.

March, L. (2006) Power and opposition in the former Soviet Union: The communist parties of Moldova and Russia. *Party Politics*, 12(3), pp. 341–65.

Moshniaga, V. (2002) Partiino-politicheskoe razvitie Moldovy za desiat' let nezavisimosti: politologicheskii analiz. *MOLDOSCOPIE*, 2, pp. 23–84.

Nekoliak, A. (2019) Ukraine's Constitutional Court, historical narrative-making, and the law. *MELA Project Blog*, October 15. http://melaproject.org/blog/601. Accessed April 23, 2022.

Nekoliak, A. (2020) A Damaged Court Causing a Constitutional Crisis. *VerfBlog*, December 5. https://verfassungsblog.de/a-damaged-court-causing-a-constitutional-crisis/. Accessed April 23, 2022.

Nescutu, M. (2020) Thirty years on, Moldova still debating Soviet symbols. *Balkan Insight*, July 13. https://balkaninsight.com/2020/07/13/thirty-years-on-moldova-still-debating-soviet-symbols/. Accessed April 23, 2022.

Neviadomskii, D. (2020) Zakon o dekommunizatsii: Sootvetstvuiut li sredstva presleduemoi tseli? *Zakon i biznes*, January 30. https://zib.com.ua/ua/print/141170-zakon_o_dekommunizacii_sootvetstvuyut_li_sredstva_presleduem.html. Accessed April 23, 2022.

Newton, S. (2017) *The Constitutional Systems of the Independent Central Asian States: A Contextual Analysis.* London: Bloomsbury Publishing.

Niesen, P. (2012) Banning the former ruling party. *Constellations*, 19(4), pp. 540–61.

Russian Constitutional Court Decision 9-P of November 30, 1992. (1994) *Statutes and Decisions*, 30(4), pp. 8–43.

Ryskozha, B. (2008) Zhasaral Kuanyshalin: Dokumenty po Zheltoksanu sistematicheski unichtozhaiutsia. *Radio Azattyq*, November 28. https://rus.azattyq.org/a/1354069.html. Accessed April 23, 2022.

Sharlet, R. (1993) The Russian Constitutional Court: First term. *Post-Soviet Affairs*, 9(1), pp. 1–39.

Smith, K.E. (1996) *Remembering Stalin's Victims: Popular Memory and the End of the USSR*. Ithaca, New York: Cornell University Press.

Smith, K.E. (2002) *Mythmaking in the New Russia: Politics and Memory during the Yeltsin Era*. Ithaca, New York: Cornell University Press.

Socor, V. (2012) Moldova's Communist Party haunted by its past and its present. *Eurasia Daily Monitor*, 9(135). https://jamestown.org/program/moldovas-communist-party-haunted-by-its-past-and-its-present. Accessed April 23, 2022.

Stan, L. ed. (2009) *Transitional Justice in Eastern Europe and the former Soviet Union: Reckoning with the Communist Past.* Abingdon on Thames: Routledge.

Steele, J. (1995) *Eternal Russia: Yeltsin, Gorbachev, and the Mirage of Democracy.* Cambridge, MA: Harvard University Press.

Trochev, A. (2003) Ukraine: Constitutional court invalidates ban on Communist Party. *International Journal of Constitutional Law*, 1(3), pp. 534–540.

Trochev, A. (2008) *Judging Russia: Constitutional Court in Russian Politics, 1990–2006.* New York: Cambridge University Press.

Trochev, A. (2013) Ukraine. In: L. Stan and N. Nedelsky eds. *Encyclopedia of Transitional Justice.* New York: Cambridge University Press, pp. 490–7.

Trochev, A. (2018) Transitional justice attempts in Kazakhstan. In: C. Horne and L. Stan eds. *Transitional Justice and the Former Soviet Union.* New York: Cambridge University Press, pp. 88–108.

Tudoroiu, T. (2011) Communism for the Twenty-first century: the Moldovan experiment. *Journal of Communist Studies and Transition Politics*, 27(2), pp. 291–321.

Tulbure, A. (2016) Zhertvy politicheskikh repressii v Moldavii: zakonodatel'stvo i ego realizatsiia. In: I. Rachinskii ed. *Reabilitatsiia i pamiat': Otnoshenie k zhertvam sovetskikh politicheskikh repressii v stranakh byvshego SSSR*. Moscow: Memorial – Zven'ia, pp. 339–94.

Venice Commission Joint *Amicus Curiae* Brief No. 697. (2012) Joint *Amicus Curiae* brief for the Constitutional Court of Moldova on the compatibility with European standards of law no. 192 of 12 July 2012. European Commission for Democracy through Law (Venice Commission) and the OSCE Office for Democratic Institutions and Human Rights (OSCE ODIHR). www.venice.coe.int/webforms/documents/default.aspx?pdffile=CDL(2013)006-e. Accessed April 23, 2022.

Vishnevskii, B. (2011) Sudia Gadis Gadzhiev: 'My sobralis' vecherom, deistvitel'no, bez mantii'. *Novaia Gazeta*, June 16. www.novayagazeta.ru/articles/2011/06/16/45133-sudya-gadis-gadzhiev-my-sobralis-vecherom-deystvitelno-bez-mantiy. Accessed April 23, 2022.

Volgin, E. (2014) Problema departizatsii v Rossii v nachale 90-kh gg: Vestnik Moskovskogo universiteta. *Seriia 8. Istoriia*, 4, pp. 102–23. https://cyberleninka.ru/article/n/problema-departizatsii-v-rossii-v-nachale-1990-h-gg. Accessed April 23, 2022.

Way, L.A. (2005) Authoritarian state building and the sources of regime competitiveness in the Fourth Wave: The cases of Belarus, Moldova, Russia, and Ukraine. *World Politics*, 57(2), 231–61.

Index

228 Incident 71, 74–6
228 Memorial Foundation 75
228 Peace Memorial Park 75
518 Movement *see* Gwangju Incident (May 18th Movement)
1936 Constitution of the Soviet Union 223

aboriginal populations 34
Ackerman, Bruce 2n1
African National Congress (ANC) 23, 24, 25, 27, 28
Albania 140–1, 148
Allende, Salvador 120
alternative justice-system reforms 100–1
amnesty 5, 7, 21, 22, 27–8, 30, 35, 101, 121, 175
Andrássy, Gyula 49
Angola 28
April Revolution 61
Arato, Andrew 134
Arbour, Louise 33
Argentina 118
Arrow Cross Party 43, 49
Articles of Confederation 133
Australia 34
Austria 136, 136n3
Autumn of Nations 153
Aylwin, Patricio 4, 28–9, 32, 122–4
Azanian Peoples Organization (AZAPO) and Others v. President of the Republic of South Africa and Others ([1996] ZACC 16) 7, 30, 174n2

Barros, Robert 120
Basic Law of the Federal Republic of Germany, 1949 4, 139, 208
Bauer, Carl 121
Belarus 227, 228
Berlin, Isaiah 48
Bester v. Germany (2001) 212
birthright citizenship 173, 177, 180–2
Biszku, Béla 52
Bosnia and Herzegovina 33
Boutwell, George S. 179
Brown v. Board of Education ([1954] 347 US 483) 182
Bulgaria 135

Canada 34
capital punishment 139
case law 41
Central and Eastern Europe (CEE): abolition of capital punishment 139–42, 148; ban on political activities of public servants 213–17; coordinated transition 131–6; dismantling the legacy of former communist regimes 198–200; ECHR on readmission to public service in post-communist contexts 211–13; erosion of democracy 131–2; loyalty 200–2; lustration law 138, 199, 199n3, 203–7; official status of language 144–7; preferential treatment for historical institutions 142–3; rule of law 131, 138, 198, 198n1, 202; third generation of constitutional courts 131, 136–8, 147–50; *see also* Hungary; Moldova
Centro Democratico party 110
change-through-interpretation 118
Chang Myon 61
Chase, Salmon P. 188
Cheng Jian-tsai 79
Chen Shui-bian 76
Chen Yi 74

Chiang Ching-kuo 73–4
Chiang Kai-shek 72
Chiang Kai-shek Memorial Hall 76
Chile: Amnesty Law of 1978 5, 121, 125–7; arrest of Pinochet 29, 125–7; Constitution of the Republic of Chile, 1925 120; Constitution of the Republic of Chile, 1980 121–2, 124; democratic transition 122–5; legacy of authoritarianism. 127–9; military coup 120–1; National Commission for Truth and Reconciliation (Rettig Commission) 5–6, 11, 28–9, 122, 128; Pinochet dictatorship 5, 11, 28–9, 120–8; Rettig Report 5, 11, 122–3, 127; rule of law 120, 123, 126; Supreme Court 5, 11, 119–25, 127, 128
China 71–2, 73–4, 78, 79–80, 87
Chin, Gabriel 184
Christianity 149
Chun Doo-hwan 57, 59, 62–3, 65, 68, 69, 70
churches 142–3, 149
Churchill, Winston 21
Civil Rights Cases ([1883] 109 US 3) 182
Cold War 57, 154
Colombia: alternative justice-system reforms 100–1; amnesty 101; *Centro Democratico* party 105, 110; Constitutional Court of Colombia 97–9, 101–8, 110–11; constitutional reforms 3, 102–4, 105; Constitution of the Republic of Colombia 3, 11–12, 97–9, 101, 102–3, 103n7, 105, 105n8, 107–10, 108n10, 108n11, 111; *Corriente de Renovacion Socialista* 98; ELN (National Liberation Army) 98–9; EPL (Popular Liberation Army) 98; FARC-EP (Revolutionary Armed Forces of Colombia – People's Army) 11–12, 98–100, 104–10; fast-track mechanism 107–9; JEP 109–10; Law 975 of 2005 (Justice and Peace Law) 11–12, 100–1, 110; Legal Framework for Peace 3, 12, 102–4, 111; M-19 98; Movement of the "Seventh Ballot" 98; *Movimiento Revolucionario Quintin Lame* 98; pardons 101; peace agreement 104–12; peace negotiations 99–100, 102, 106–7; referendum 106–7; Special Jurisdiction for Peace 109; United Self-Defense Forces of Colombia (*Autodefensas Unidas de Colombia*, AUC) 99n2, 100
Commission for the Promotion of the Memory of Victims 227
Commission for the Study and Evaluation of the Communist Totalitarian Regime in the Republic of Moldova 240
Communist Party of Belarus 228
Communist Party of Moldova (CPM) 228, 239, 242
Communist Party of the Russian Federation (CPRF) 233
Communist Party of the Russian Soviet Federative Socialist Republic (CPRSFSR) 230–3
Communist Party of the Soviet Union (CPSU) 223–5, 228, 230–3, 235, 240, 243
Communist Party of Ukraine (CPU(SU)) 224, 234–5, 243
Communist Party/symbols ban: limits 243–5; in Moldova 228, 239–45; in post-Soviet states 15–16, 223–30; in Russia 230–3, 243–5; in Ukraine 222, 233–8, 243–5
Conkling, Roscoe 178
Constitutional Court: Austria 136; Colombia 97–9, 101–8, 110–11; Germany 25, 136, 137, 141, 209; Hungary 4, 8, 10, 39–41, 44, 119, 137, 142–3, 148–9; Italy 136; Kazakhstan 229–30; Moldova 15–16, 138, 146–7, 148–9, 148n8, 241–5; Poland 119; roles 118–19; Russia 5, 15, 230–3, 235, 238, 242–5; South Africa 3, 25–6, 30, 35; South Korea 4, 65, 66–71, 85–9; Taiwan 4, 9, 58, 77–89; third generation of 131, 136–8, 147–50; Ukraine 15–16, 234–6
constitutionalizing transitional justice: definition 2–3; models 3–6
constitutional regime change models 133–4
Constitution of Hungary, 1949 40, 135, 214
Constitution of Hungary, 1989 4, 40–1, 47, 49, 53, 135, 147
Constitution of Moldova 139, 144–5
Constitution of South Africa 26

Constitution of South Korea 3–4, 68, 69, 70
Constitution of the Republic of Chile, 1925 120
Constitution of the Republic of Chile, 1980 121–2, 124
Constitution of the Republic of China (Taiwan) 71, 83
Constitution of the Republic of Colombia: amending 103n7; Article 66 3, 11–12, 102–4, 105; doctrine of substitution 105n8; Legal Framework for Peace 3, 12, 102–4, 111; as peace pact 97–9, 101, 107–10, 108n11, 111
Constitution of the Republic of Poland: Article 13 3, 158; Article 44 3, 158; ban on political activities of public servants 215
Constitution of the United States: 13th Amendment 12, 173, 177, 181; 14th Amendment 3, 12–13, 174–92; 14th Amendment, Section 1 12, 174, 177, 179, 180–2; 14th Amendment, Section 2 12–13, 174–5, 177–80, 182–6, 192; 14th Amendment, Section 3 12–13, 175, 177–80, 186–90; 14th Amendment, Section 4 13, 175, 178, 180, 190–2; 14th Amendment, Section 5 180n11; 15th Amendment 12, 174; Equal Protection Clause 184–5, 185n17; First Amendment 83; historical background 175–6; writing of 133
Convention on the Non-Applicability of Statutory Limitation to War Crimes and Crimes against Humanity 65
Convention on the Prevention and Punishment of the Crime of Genocide 64
coordinated transition 133–6
Correa, Jorge 124
Corriente de Renovacion Socialista 98
Council of Europe 139, 154
court-enforced constitutionalism 4–6
crimes of international concern 22n3
Czechoslovakia 134–5, 136n2, 136n3
Czech Republic: constitutional reforms 135; lustration law 43, 45, 203–7

Davis,Jefferson 188
Declaration of Independence 133
de-communization 5, 14, 15, 39, 154, 158–9, 160, 199, 199n2, 203, 206n20, 208, 217, 236–8, 243
de Klerk, F.W. 7, 24, 27
democratic backlash/democratic breakdown 17
Democratic Progressive Party (DPP) 57, 76, 77, 86
denazification 207
de-Stalinization 223–9
domestic human rights infringement 22n3
Dred Scott v. *Sandford* ([1857] 60 US 393) 173, 179
Dyzenhaus, David 2n1

East-Central Europe 131–50
East Germany 14, 43–6, 207–10
Eckley, Ephraim R. 186
Elkins, Zachary 2
ELN (National Liberation Army) 11, 98–9
Elster, Jon 2, 2n1
embedded mandate 6
EPL (Popular Liberation Army) 98
Estonia 222
ethnic identification 145–7, 149
European Commission of Human Rights 214
European Communities (EC) 155
European Convention on Human Rights (ECHR) 135, 139
European Court of Human Rights 10, 14, 42, 137–8, 148, 160, 162, 202n9, 207, 211–13, 216, 223, 236, 242
European Union 135
European Union (EU) 46, 52, 155, 158
Ex parte Virginia ([1880] 100 US 339) 181–2

FARC-EP (Revolutionary Armed Forces of Colombia – People's Army) 11–12, 98–100, 104–10
February 28 Incident ("228 Incident") 71, 74–6
Finck, William E. 179
Formosa Incident (Kaohsiung Incident) 73–4, 76
Franco, Francisco 137
freedom of academic research 69
freedom of assembly 71
freedom of association 15, 83, 200, 208n26, 214, 215, 230, 232, 234, 234–5, 235, 241
freedom of conscience 69, 142

freedom of demonstration 71
freedom of expression 16, 73, 78, 215, 237, 242
freedom of information 45, 138
freedom of occupation 70
freedom of religion 142
freedom of speech 69, 82, 83, 84, 144, 200, 208n26, 214, 241
freedom of the press 69
freedom of thought 82
French Revolution 133

Gabriel, Archangel 49
Gamsakhurdia, Zviad 227
García Villegas, Mauricio 109
general amnesty 22
Geneva Conventions 42
Geochang Incident 61, 64
Georgia 14, 222–3, 227–8
Germany: Basic Law of the Federal Republic of Germany, 1949 4, 139, 208; Constitutional Court of Germany 25, 136, 137, 141; coordinated transition 136n3; denazification 207; duty of constitutional (political) loyalty 208–11; ECHR on readmission to public service in post-communist contexts 211–12; Federal Constitutional Court 209; grounds for removal of public servants from posts 209–10; lustration law 207–12; Nuremberg trials 21–2; occupation of Hungary 48–9; 'personal suitability' clause 210n32; Reinstatement Act 207; reunification 134, 207–11; Ribbentrop–Molotov Pact 153; rule of law 207, 208, 209; secret service files 44, 45; Unification Treaty 14, 209, 212; vetting model 210–11
Ghimpu,Mihai 5, 15, 240–1
Ginsburg, Tom 2, 57–8
Göncz, Árpád 136n2
Gorbachev, Mikhail 224–5, 228, 230, 239
Graham, Katherine 74
"Guidance Note of the Secretary-General: United Nations Approach to Transitional Justice" (United Nations) 115–16
Gwangju Incident (May 18th Movement) 57, 62, 65, 67, 73, 86
Gyurcsány, Ferenc 46–7

Harper, Stephen 34
Havel, Václav 2, 136n2
Hayes, Rutherford B. 189
history 47–50
Hitler, Adolf 48
Hobbes, Thomas 2n1
Holocaust 22, 48, 49
Horthy, Miklós 49, 50
House of Habsburg 49, 50
human dignity 10, 26, 134, 137, 139–42
Hungary: 1956 Revolution. 8, 41, 42, 47, 49, 51; abolition of death penalty 10–11, 139–40; Christian Democratic Party 47; churches 142–3, 149; Committee of National Memory 50; communist pension allowances 51; constitutional adjudication 148; Constitutional Court of Hungary 4, 8, 10, 39–41, 44, 119, 137, 142–3, 148–9; constitutional reforms 135; Constitution of Hungary, 1949 40, 135, 214; Constitution of Hungary, 1989 4, 40–1, 47, 49, 53, 135, 147; coordinated transition 136n2; Decision No. 11/1992 8, 41; Decision No. 15/1991 44; Decision No. 20/1990 44; Decision No. 23/1999 44; Decision No. 37/2005 45; Decision No. 53/1993 8, 42; Decision No. 60/1994 43–4; Fidesz party 46, 47; foreign occupation 48–9; freedom fights 49–50; Fundamental Law 39, 46–53; Fundamental Law, Fourth Amendment, Article U 4, 8, 50–2; House of Terror 48; Jews 48–9; Kossuth Square 49; Law CCX of 2011 on the Punishability and the Exclusion of the Statute of Limitations of Crimes against Humanity and the Prosecution of Certain Crimes Committed During the Communist Dictatorship 51–2; Law CCXVI of 2013 50; Law CXII of 2012 51; Law III of 2003 on the Disclosure of the Secret Service Activities of the Communist Regime and on the Establishment of the Historical Archive of the Hungarian State Security 45; Law LXVII of 1996 on Amending the Lustration

Law 44; Law XXIII of 1994 on Controlling Certain Persons in Important Positions (Lustration Law) 43–4; legal certainty 8; lustration 43–6, 53; lustration law 143; martial law 42; Memorial of National Unity 49; National Avowal 47; political party ban for members of police 214–16, 217; privacy rights 43–6; reappropriation of past 47–50, 53; religion 142–3, 149; retroactive punishment 141–2; rule of law 4, 5, 8, 10, 35, 40–3, 47, 51, 53, 137, 140–2, 148; Socialist Workers' Party 50–1
Hunter v. Underwood ([1985] 471 US 222) 186n19

India 133
Indian Residential Schools 34
inferred mandate 6
Institute of National Remembrance (INR) 204, 205
institutional reforms 119
Inter-American Court of Human Rights 12, 100, 101
International Covenant on Civil and Political Rights (ICCPR) 139, 215
international crimes 22n3
International Human Rights Day 78
International Human Rights Law 119, 128
International Labour Organization Committee of Experts on the Application of Conventions and Recommendations (ILO CEACR) 206
International Military Tribunal for the Far East (Tokyo War Crimes Tribunal) 22n3
Italy 136

Japan 21–2, 59, 71
Jaruzelski, Wojciech 159n7
Jeju 4.3 Incident 59–60, 63–4
John Paul II, Pope 154
Johnson, Andrew 188
József, Attila 49
judges 162–5
June Democratic Struggle 57

Karimov, Islam 227
Károlyi, Mihály 49
Kazakh Communist Party 229–30
Kazakhstan 14, 222, 227–8, 229–30
Kenya: Truth and Reconciliation Act 34; Truth, Justice and Reconciliation Commission of Kenya 34–5
KGB agents 213
Khrushchev, Nikita 223
Kim Dae-jung 63
Kim Il Sung 59
Kim Jae-gyu 62
Kim Young-sam 57, 58, 63, 64, 65, 85
Kis, János 134
Knauth v. Germany (2001) 212
Korbely, János 42
Korean War 60–1, 64–5, 72
Kravchuk, Leonid 233, 235
Kuchma, Leonid 236
Kukje Group 70
Kuomintang (KMT, Chinese Nationalist Party) 9, 57, 71–88
Kwasniewski, Aleksander 159n8

language 11, 144–7
Latvia 222–3
Law and Justice party (PiS) 10
Lee Teng-hui 58, 74, 75
legal certainty 8, 41–2
legal formalism 4, 5
Lithuania 140–1, 148, 212–13, 222
loyalty 200–2
Lukashenko, Alexander 223, 227
lustration law: Central and Eastern Europe 138, 199, 199n3, 203–7; Czech Republic 13–14, 43, 203–7; Estonia 222; European Court of Human Rights 14; Germany 207–12; goal of 13; Hungary 43–6, 53; Latvia 222; Lithuania 222; Poland 13–14, 160–2, 203–7
Lynch v. United States ([1934] 292 US 571, 580) 190–1

M-19 98
Malan, Magnus 32
Mandela, Nelson 23, 24, 25, 27–9, 32, 33
martial law: Hungary 42; lifting of 2; Poland 154, 159, 165; South Korea 59, 61, 62; Taiwan 9, 57, 72, 74, 75, 78–82, 84
Ma Ying-jeou 76
McKee, Samuel 179
Medgyessy, Péter 44–5
Melton, James 2

Michnik, Adam 149
Moldova: ban on Communist Party and symbols 15–16, 228, 239–45; Commission for the Study and Evaluation of the Communist Totalitarian Regime in the Republic of Moldova 240; Communist Party of Moldova 228; Communist Party of Moldova (CPM) 239, 242; Constitutional Court of the Republic of Moldova 15–16, 138, 146, 148–9, 148n8, 241–5; constitutional reforms 135–6; Constitution of Moldova 139, 144–5; Day of Soviet Occupation 15; Declaration of Independence 135; de-communization 5, 14; ethnic identification 145–7; lustration law 222; official status of language 11, 144–7; Party of Communists of the Republic of Moldova 15; Party of Communists of the Republic of Moldova (PCRM) 239–42; rule of law 145
Moldovan Popular Front 144
Motsuenyane, S.M. 28
Movement of the "Seventh Ballot" 98
Movimiento Revolucionario Quintin Lame 98

Nagy, Imre 46–7, 49
Naidin v. Romania (2014) 213
National Commission for Truth and Reconciliation (Rettig Commission) 5–6, 11, 28–9
national consultations 116n1, 119
National Guidance Alliance 60
national identity 11
NATO 135, 155
Nazarbayev, Nursultan 229
New Power Party 86
Nigeria 133
No Gun Ri Massacre 61
"nomenklatura" 201n7
North Korea 60–1
nulla poena sine lege 2, 69
Nuremberg-style trials 21–2, 28
Nuremberg trials 22, 22n3

Office for Democratic Institutions and Human Rights 16
office holding 175
Orban, Viktor 4, 48–9
Ottoman empire 50

Pacific War 59
Pan-Africanist Congress 23
Park Chung-hee 59, 61–2, 70–1
Party of Communists of the Republic of Moldova (PCRM) 15, 239–42
party-state 77, 78, 84, 87, 88
Perry v. United States ([1935] 294 US 330) 190–1
Petersen v. Germany (2001) 212
Pharmaceutical Manufacturers Association of South Africa and Another: In re Ex Parte President of the Republic of South Africa and Others (2000 ZACC 1) 26
Pinochet, Augusto 5, 11, 28–9, 120–8
Plessy v. Ferguson ([1896] 163 US 537) 182
Poalelungi, Mihai 138
Poland: act invalidating judicial decisions that, 164–5; ban on political activities of public servants 215–16, 217; conflicts 153; constitutional adjudication 148; Constitutional Court of Poland 119, 148; constitutional reforms 134; Constitutional Tribunal 10, 148, 157–67, 215; Constitution of the Republic of Poland 3, 158, 215; coordinated transition 136n2; de-communization 158–9; elimination of privileges for former communist officials 159–60; "judicial self-cleansing" 163; Law and Justice party (PiS) 10; lustration law 154, 160–2, 203–7; martial law 154, 159, 165; occupation by USSR 153–4; Polish Committee of National Liberation 165n27; Polish Round Table Agreement 134; reprivatization 165–8; responsibility of public prosecutors 162–3; Round Table Agreement 154, 157, 163, 203–4; rule of law 158; statute of limitations 158; Supreme Court 154, 157, 160; system of "decommissioning" judges 163–4
politicization of public administration 14, 217
populist authoritarianism 132
Portugal 134, 156
positive discrimination 154
postcolonial constitutional transformation 133

post-communist transition 198–200
Preventive Detention Case 69
privacy rights 43–6
property rights 51, 142, 165–8
proportionality 16, 41, 70, 81, 100, 137, 138, 202, 212, 214, 238, 242, 243
prosecution initiatives 116n1, 119, 162–5
public debt 174, 180, 190–2
public participation 116–17n1
Putin, Vladimir 223

Radbruch Formula 141
Reconstruction 5, 177n4, 183–5, 189
Red Army 46, 48, 153, 165n27
Rekvenyi v. Hungary (1999) 214
religion 142–3, 149
reparations 27, 31–2, 39, 76, 97, 101, 102, 115, 116n1, 119, 122, 128, 173, 192
reprivatization 165–8
Republic of China 4
restitution 173
retributive justice 141–2
retroactive punishment 141–2
retroactivity 42, 147
Rettig, Raúl 28
Rettig Report 5, 11, 122–3, 127
Rév, István 47
revolutionary constitution making 133–4
Ribbentrop–Molotov Pact 153
Richardson v. Ramirez ([1974] 418 US 24) 184–5, 185n18
right to informational self-determination 44
right to vote 174, 179, 182–6
Roh Moo-hyun 64
Roh Tae-woo 57, 58, 63, 65, 68, 69, 85
Romania 135, 146, 213
Rome Statute of the International Criminal Court 65, 100
Roosevelt, Franklin 21
Rose Revolution 227
roundtable negotiations 131, 134, 154
Rudd, Kevin 34
rule of law: Central and Eastern Europe 131, 138, 198, 198n1, 202; Chile 120, 123, 126; Germany 207, 208, 209; Hungary 4, 5, 8, 10, 35, 40–3, 47, 51, 53, 137, 140–2, 148; Moldova 145; *nulla poena sine lege*, 2; Poland 158; roles 116; South Africa 26, 35; South Korea 70, 88; Taiwan 75, 88; United States 177n5, 193, 193n30
Russia: annexation of Crimea 236–7; ban on Communist Party and symbols 14–15, 230–3, 243–5; Communist Party of the Russian Soviet Federative Socialist Republic (CPRSFSR) 230–3; Constitutional Court of the Russian Federation 5, 15, 230–3, 235, 238, 242–5; de-communization 5, 14; division of Poland 153; non-democratic regime 223; occupation of Ukrainian territory 237, 238; official status of language in Moldova 144, 146; troops in Moldova 239–40; *see also* USSR (Union of Soviet Socialist Republics)
Rwanda 22, 155

Saakashvili, Mikheil 227
Sadurski, Wojciech 148
Salazar, António de Oliveira 137
Sanchez, Nelson Camilo 11–12
Santa Fe de Ralito Accord 100
separate but equal doctrine 182
Shevardnadze, Eduard 227
Shi Xi-en 79
show trials 21–2
Sidabras and Džiautas v. Lithuania (2004) 212–13
Sierra Leone 23
Slaughterhouse Cases ([1873] 83 US 36), 181
slavery 173, 177, 181
Slovak Federal Republic 135, 203
Solidarity 154, 157, 158
Sólyom, László 10, 137, 140, 148
South Africa: abolition of capital punishment 140; amnesty 7, 27–8, 30, 35; Constitutional Court of South Africa 3, 25–6, 30, 35; Constitution of South Africa 26; founding values 26; Interim Constitution 3, 7, 24–6, 30; Promotion of National Unity and Reconciliation Act 3, 7, 27, 29; rule of law 26, 35; Standing Commission of Inquiry Regarding the Prevention of Public Violence and Intimidation, 7–8; violence 7, 23–4
South African Communist Party 23
South African Defence Force 24

South African Police 24
South African Truth and Reconciliation Commission: amnesty applications 7, 30; Amnesty Committee 30; considerations 27–9; establishment 29–30; Human Rights Violations Committee. 29–30; international consequences 32–5; Reparation and Rehabilitation Committee 29–30, 31; successes/failures 31–2
South Korea: Act for Restoring Honor for Victims of Geochang and Other Massacres 64; Act for Restoring the Honor of Participants in the Democratization Movement and for Providing Compensation to Them 65; Act on the Special Measures for the Punishment of Persons Involved in Anti-State Activities (SPAA) 69; Anti-Communist Act 61; Basic Press Act 62; Constitutional Court of South Korea 4, 65, 66–71, 85–9; Constitution of South Korea 3–4, 68, 69, 70; Emergency Decree No. 1 62, 71; Emergency Decree No. 2 62, 71; Emergency Decree No. 9 62, 71; emergency orders 62, 71; Framework Act on Clearing Up Past Incidents for Truth and Reconciliation 64, 66; Geochang Incident 61, 64; Gwangju Incident (May 18th Movement) 57, 62, 65, 67, 73, 86; human rights violations 58–63, 65–6; Jeju 4.3 Incident 59–60, 63–4; Korean Central Intelligence Agency 62; Korean War 60–1, 64–5, 72; Law Concerning Registration of Social Organizations 61; Law on Punishment of Specified Crimes 61; Law on the National Movement for National Reconstruction 61; legacy of authoritarianism. 57–8, 61–3; martial law 59, 61, 62; National Commission for the Investigation of the Truth about the Jeju 4.3 Incident 63; National Security Act 69–70; nationwide systematic killing of civilians 60–1; Political Climate Renovation Law 62; Presidential Truth Commission on Suspicious Deaths 65; Private School Act 70; Review Committee for Restoring Honor for Victims of Geochang and Other Massacres 64; Review Committee for Restoring the Honor of Participants in the Democratization Movement and for Providing Compensation to Them 65; rule of law 70, 88; Social Protection Act 62, 69; Social Safety Law 61; Special Act on the May 18th Democratic Movement Etc. 9, 65, 68, 85; Special Act to Find the Truth on Suspicious Deaths 65; Special Committee for National Security Measures, 62; Special Law for the Investigation of the Jeju 4.3 Incident and Recovering the Honor of Victims 63–4; statute of limitations 68; Supreme Council for National Reconstruction 61–2; Transitional Justice Law for Truth and Reconciliation 66; Truth and Reconciliation Commission of South Korea 60, 63, 64, 65–6; Yushin Constitution 62, 70–1
Soviet Union *see* USSR (Union of Soviet Socialist Republics)
Spain 134, 156
Spalding, Rufus P. 179n9
Special Act on the May 18th Democratic Movement Etc. 65
stability 58, 66–8, 77–8
Stalin, Joseph 22, 165n27, 223–4
Standing Commission of Inquiry Regarding the Prevention of Public Violence and Intimidation, 7–8
statute of limitations 42, 68, 158
Stevens, Thaddeus 178
Strauder v. West Virginia ([1880] 100 US 303) 181
substitution 105n8, 117, 118
Suchocka, Hanna 204
Sunflower Movement 78, 86
Sunstein, Cass 88
Supreme Court: Canada 201n8; Chile 5, 11, 119–25, 127, 128; Poland 154, 157, 160; South Africa 24; South Korea 65, 66, 68, 87; Taiwan 79; Ukrainian Soviet Socialist Republic 225; United States 83, 173, 180n11, 181–2, 184–6, 188–90
S v. Makwanyane and Another [1995] 26
Syngman Rhee 59, 60, 63–4

Taiwan: 228 Incident 71, 74–6; 228 Incident Disposition and Compensation Act (228

Compensation Act) 75; Act Governing the Recovery of Damage of Individual Rights During the Period of Martial Law (Restitution Act) 75, 81; Act Governing the Settlement of Ill-Gotten Properties by Political Parties and Their Affiliate Organizations (Ill-Gotten Party Assets Act) 76–7, 84; Act of Compensation for Wrongful Detentions and Executions 81–2; Act of Martial Law 74, 78; Act on Promoting Transitional Justice (Transitional Justice Act) 76–7; Assembly and Parade Act 83; Civil Association Act 83; Compensation Act for Improper Trials on Charges of Sedition and Espionage During the Martial Law Period (White Terror Compensation Act) 75; Constitutional Court of Taiwan 4, 9, 58, 77–89; court-enforced constitutionalism 4; Court-Martial Act 78, 81; Disciplinary Measures Governing the Prevention of Recidivism by Communist Espionage Criminals during the Period of National Mobilization for the Suppression of Communist Rebellion (Recidivism Prevention Measures) 82; emergency orders 78; Formosa Incident (Kaohsiung Incident) 73–4, 76; Interpretation No. 272 78–81, 87; Interpretation No. 328 80; Interpretation No. 381 82; Interpretation No. 445 83; Interpretation No. 477 81; Interpretation No. 499 82; Interpretation No. 567 82, 83; Interpretation No. 624 81; Interpretation No. 793 77, 78, 85; Kuomintang (KMT, Chinese Nationalist Party) 71–88; legacy of authoritarianism. 57–8; legality of authoritarian-era laws 81–3; legislation/policies after democratization 74–7; legitimacy of authoritarian rule 83–5; martial law 9, 57, 72, 74, 75, 78–82, 84; mistreatment of aboriginal populations 34; National Security Act during the Period of National Mobilization for Suppression of the Communist Rebellion (National Security Act) 9, 74, 77, 78, 83; political oppression after World War II 71–4; rule of law 75, 88; stabilizing legacy of authoritarian rule 78–80; Temporary Provisions of the Republic of China Constitution 74; Wild Lily student movement 74
Tajikistan 228
Tanase, Alexandru 138, 242
Tangwai ("outside the party") 73
Tanzania 28
Teitel, Ruti 1
third way of democratization 115
Tisza, István 49
Tokayev, Kassym-Jomart 227
Tokyo trials 21–2, 22n3
Treaty of Trianon 48, 49
Treaty of Versailles 153
Trump, Donald 189–90
truth-and-reconciliation commissions: National Commission for Truth and Reconciliation (Rettig Commission) 5–6, 11, 28–9, 122, 128; South African Truth and Reconciliation Commission 27–35; Truth and Reconciliation Commission of South Korea 60, 63, 64, 65–6; Truth, Justice and Reconciliation Commission of Kenya 34–5; use 22–3
truth initiatives 119
Tsai Ing-wen 76
Tutu, Desmond 31, 32, 33

Ukraine: abolition of capital punishment 140–1, 148; ban on Communist Party and symbols 15–16, 222, 233–8, 243–5; Communist Party of Ukraine (CPU(SU)) 224, 243; compensation of victims 277; Constitutional Court of Ukraine 15–16, 234–6, 242–5; Constitution of Ukraine 234; de-communization 5, 14; lustration law 222; non-democratic regime 223; unilateral executive decisions 5
unilateral executive decisions 4–5
United Nations 101, 115–16
United Nations International Criminal Tribunal for the former Yugoslavia (ICTY) 8
United Self-Defense Forces of Colombia (*Autodefensas Unidas de Colombia*, AUC) 99n2, 100

United States: abolishment of slavery 173, 177, 179; Articles of Confederation 133; birthright citizenship 173–4, 177, 180–2; "black codes" 178; Civil War 173; Constitution of the United States 3, 12–13, 133, 173–92; Declaration of Independence 133; *Dred Scott* v. *Sandford* 173; General Amnesty 175; Korean War 59; office holding 186–90; public debt 174, 180; relations with Taiwan 74; right to vote 174, 179, 182–6; rule of law 177n5, 193, 193n30; separate but equal doctrine 182; Three-Fifths Compromise 178
Uribe, Álvaro 99
Uruguay 117
US Air Force 61
US Army Military Government in Korea (hereinafter USAMGIK) 59
USSR (Union of Soviet Socialist Republics): 1936 Constitution of the Soviet Union 223; Communist Party of the Soviet Union (CPSU) 223–5, 228, 229, 230–3, 235, 240, 243; de-Stalinization 223–9; disintegration of 134, 146, 222, 225, 229; "nomenklatura" 201n7; occupation of Hungary 50; occupation of Moldova 135, 145; occupation of Poland 153–4; political prisoners 228; Ribbentrop–Molotov Pact 153; support in North Korea 59, 60; Union Treaty 225
Uzbekistan 14, 227

Venice Commission 16, 50, 52, 200n5
vetting model 210–11
Vogt v. Germany (1995) 211
Volkmer v. Germany (2001) 212

Walesa, Lech 136n2, 154
West Germany 14, 208–10
White Terror 72, 75, 76
Wild Lily student movement 74
World War I 48, 49
World War II 21, 59, 71, 139

Yang Jih-jan 79
Yanukovych, Viktor 223
Yeltsin, Boris 5, 15, 225, 230
Yugoslavia 22, 137
Yun Bo-seon 61

Zalaquett, José 29
Zambia 28
Zubik, Marek 3
Zyuganov, Gennady 233

For Product Safety Concerns and Information please contact our EU representative GPSR@taylorandfrancis.com
Taylor & Francis Verlag GmbH, Kaufingerstraße 24, 80331 München, Germany

www.ingramcontent.com/pod-product-compliance
Ingram Content Group UK Ltd.
Pitfield, Milton Keynes, MK11 3LW, UK
UKHW020149200926
475702UK00016B/2618
9781032369440